IMDG
CODE

2008 Edition

INTERNATIONAL MARITIME DANGEROUS GOODS CODE

SUPPLEMENT

D1295851

INTERNATIONAL
MARITIME
ORGANIZATION

London, 2008

Published in 2008
by the INTERNATIONAL MARITIME ORGANIZATION
4 Albert Embankment, London SE1 7SR

Printed by Polestar Wheatons Ltd, Exeter

2   4   6   8   10   9   7   5   3   1

ISBN: 978-92-801-4242-6

IMO PUBLICATION
Sales number: IG210E

Foreword

The International Maritime Dangerous Goods Code relates to the safe carriage of dangerous goods by sea, but does not include all details of procedures for packing of dangerous goods or actions to take in the event of an emergency or accident involving personnel who handle goods at sea. These aspects are covered by the publications that are associated with the IMDG Code, which are included in this Supplement.

Within a continuing process of revision of publications that are relevant to the IMDG Code, *The EmS Guide: Emergency Response Procedures for Ships Carrying Dangerous Goods* has been further amended at the eighty-fourth session of MSC in May 2008 and the details have been described in MSC.1/Circ.1262. The International Code for the Safe Carriage of Packaged Irradiated Nuclear Fuel, Plutonium and High-Level Radioactive Wastes on board Ships has also been amended by resolution MSC.241(83).

The Supplement also includes texts of the *Medical First Aid Guide*, descriptions of the reporting procedures for incidents involving dangerous goods, harmful substances and/or marine pollutants, the IMO/ILO/UNECE Guidelines for Packing of Cargo Transport Units, the Recommendations on the Safe Use of Pesticides in Ships and other appropriate Assembly resolutions, resolutions and Circulars of the Maritime Safety Committee and Circulars of the Facilitation Committee and of the Sub-Committee on Dangerous Goods, Solid Cargoes and Containers.

Note: The IMO/ILO/UN ECE Guidelines for Packing of Cargo Transport Units are currently under review by the IMO Sub-Committee on Dangerous Goods, Solid Cargoes and Containers and have not yet been updated to reflect, where necessary, the changes in Amendment 34-08 of the IMDG Code. Users of the Guidelines should refer to chapters 5.2 and 5.3 of the IMDG Code for the correct labels, placards, marks and signs.

Contents

THE EMS GUIDE

EMERGENCY RESPONSE PROCEDURES FOR SHIPS

CARRYING DANGEROUS GOODS

EmS

Foreword

This *EmS Guide* contains guidance on *Emergency Response Procedures for Ships Carrying Dangerous Goods* including the *Emergency Schedules* (EmS) to be followed in case of incidents involving dangerous substances, materials or articles, or harmful substances (marine pollutants), regulated under the *International Maritime Dangerous Goods Code* (IMDG Code).

This edition takes into account the 30th, 31st, 32nd, 33rd and 34th amendments to the IMDG Code (2008 Edition). The *EmS Guide* will be further amended as and when necessary to reflect amendments made to the IMDG Code.

Contents

Preamble

The purpose of this Guide is to provide guidance for dealing with fires and spillages (leakages) on board ships involving the dangerous goods listed in the International Maritime Dangerous Goods Code (IMDG Code).

In accordance with the International Safety Management (ISM) Code, all ships, and the companies responsible for their operation, are required to maintain a *Safety Management System* (SMS). Within the SMS, procedures for responding to potential shipboard emergencies are required. This Guide is intended to assist shipowners, ship operators and other parties concerned with developing such emergency response procedures, which should be integrated into the ship's contingency plan.

In November 1997, the IMO Assembly adopted resolution A.852(20) on Guidelines for a structure of an integrated system of contingency planning for shipboard emergencies. This Guide should be integrated into Module IV on Response actions, as contained in paragraph 3.2.4.6 of the aforementioned resolution, for cargo-related incidents.

In the event of a fire or spillage incident, initial actions should be carried out in accordance with the shipboard emergency plan. Where dangerous goods are involved, the responses in the emergency plan should be based on this Guide for specific dangerous goods having regard to, *inter alia*, the type of ship, the quantity and type of packaging of the dangerous goods and whether the goods are stowed on or under deck.

How to use this Guide

1   The guidance contained in this Guide is intended for fire and/or spillage (leakage) emergencies on board a ship involving packaged dangerous goods transported in accordance with the provisions of the IMDG Code. The Guide should not be used for emergencies involving bulk cargoes or any other fire and/or spillage on board a ship which does not involve packaged dangerous goods as cargo.

2   This guidance is for shipboard use where master and crew have to respond to a fire or a spillage without external assistance. The recommendations are based on the fire safety provisions contained in chapter II-2 of the 1974 Safety of Life at Sea Convention (SOLAS), as amended, and the provisions of the IMDG Code. The guidance should be integrated into the contingency plan for shipboard emergencies, which should be specific to the individual ship and should take into account the equipment on board.

3   There are international and national requirements for ships to contact or report to the nearest coastal State when an incident takes place involving the loss or likely loss of packaged dangerous goods (see Reporting Procedures). Contacting shore-based experts at an early stage irrespective of how insignificant the incident may seem to be is recommended. However, it should be noted that shore-based personnel or rescue/coastguard experts may use different techniques to fight a fire or to deal with spillage on board a ship.

4   In this Guide, there is separate advice for fire and spillage emergencies which should be consulted accordingly.

5   This Guide should be used as follows:

    .1   for fire and spillage, read and incorporate into the ship's training regime the **INTRODUCTIONS to the emergency schedules**, before any emergency occurs;

    .2   in the event of an emergency involving packaged dangerous goods, consult the **GENERAL GUIDELINES** as a first step; and

    .3   obtain detailed advice for the specific cargo(es) involved by reading the relevant **EMERGENCY SCHEDULE (S)** (EmS) for the cargo(es).

Fire

Introduction to the Emergency Schedules for FIRE

1   Be prepared

1.1   Preventing a fire from occurring is the most important part of a shipboard safety programme. However, once a fire has started, a well trained crew is the best defence for bringing the fire under control. Given the complexity of extinguishing a fire involving dangerous goods, it is essential that the advice in this Guide be incorporated into the ship's training regime so that the crew will be able to respond to a fire casualty in a timely and effective manner.

1.2   This Guide should be integrated into a *Safety Management System (SMS)*. Procedures contained in the shipboard emergency plan should be tailored to the individual ship.

1.3   The fire-fighting procedures within the EmS SCHEDULES are different for "on deck" and "under deck" stowage. For specific ship types (e.g., hatchless container ships) or cargo holds (e.g., open vehicle decks of ferries), these two procedures have to be assigned specifically to the individual ship.

1.4   Given the toxic nature of some of the dangerous goods involved, accommodation spaces should be protected from fire and smoke as far as possible (e.g., water spray). Therefore, the ventilation systems for working and living spaces should be shut off, closed and secured to reduce the possibility of vapours, dusts and gases penetrating these spaces. In some instances, it may be necessary to turn the ship's accommodation spaces upwind, if possible.

1.5   The safety of fire-fighting personnel is most important. Use of appropriate protective clothing (i.e., a firefighter's outfit when dealing with a fire) and self-contained breathing apparatus, to protect skin and lungs from toxic and/ or corrosive liquids, vapours, dusts and gases, is essential. This equipment should be suitable for each individual member of the fire-fighting team, as working with such equipment requires a high level of fitness and training. It should be kept in mind that even a weak acute illness may interfere with a crew member's fitness. In addition, pregnant crew members should not be exposed to dangerous vapours.

1.6   It is also essential to ensure that there is always an escape route for fire-fighting personnel despite the limitations due to narrow exit paths and the danger of falling overboard.

2   Identification of the dangerous good(s) involved

2.1   It is essential to identify the dangerous good(s) involved in the fire in order that the specific EmS FIRE SCHEDULE (S) for the cargo(es) may be consulted and appropriate action taken. This is important because some dangerous goods are incompatible with some fire-fighting media and could exacerbate the situation (e.g., use of a water-based extinguishing medium on water-reactive cargoes).

2.2   An identification number with four digits preceded by the letters "UN" is assigned to all dangerous goods. From the UN Number, it is possible to find the appropriate EmS FIRE SCHEDULE. The Dangerous Goods List in part 3, chapter 3.2, of the IMDG Code contains the names and the UN Numbers, as well as the EmS SCHEDULE NUMBERS. The special Dangerous Goods Manifest and the detailed Stowage Plan required by SOLAS regulation VII/5 will also contain the Proper Shipping Name and UN Number of the dangerous good(s) concerned. Packages will usually be labelled as well.

2.3   Specific information as to properties of dangerous goods may also be found in the Dangerous Goods List in the IMDG Code. Dangerous goods are classified and labelled according to their hazards. Labels and marks on packages provide a warning of the general risks to be encountered. Personnel should understand the labelling system.

2.4 Emergency preparedness should form part of the ship's Safety Management System as required by the ISM Code. Prepared information can reduce errors during a fire emergency. Therefore, it is recommended that the EmS SCHEDULE(S) be identified and included on the Dangerous Goods Manifest and Stowage Plan recording the stowage position of the cargo. That will enable key members of the crew to know in advance which emergency procedures could be necessary. In the event of a fire, the allocation of a specific EmS FIRE SCHEDULE via identification of cargo via the UN Number takes time and is open to error, especially in mixed cargoes in one container. Furthermore, some fire-fighting procedures may require specific media and operations could be affected by the stowage location of such media. The advice given in the EmS FIRE SCHEDULE should be directly usable based on the stowage information, without time-consuming identification and location of the cargo involved.

3 Cool and suffocate

3.1 In general, fires require heat (energy) and oxygen to start burning. Only a limited number of chemicals do not need oxygen from the air. Therefore, the aim of fire fighting is to exclude oxygen and to cool the cargo(es). On board ship, this is generally carried out by using water spray or gas extinguishing systems.

3.2 Some burning cargoes will need special fire-fighting media (like dry inert material) to suffocate the fire. In such circumstances, normal fire-fighting procedures are often impracticable, and concentrating on cooling nearby cargo and ship structures is recommended in such cases.

3.3 Firefighters should be made aware of the hazards of opening doors of an over-heated space or freight container which is suspected of containing cargo on fire. There may be a lack of oxygen inside and fresh air from outside the space may instantly start a fire, and cause a flashback that could injure the firefighters. Cool down the container first!

4 Seek advice

4.1 Expert advice should be sought irrespective of how insignificant the fire may seem to be when dealing with dangerous goods fires. Such advice could be given by:

.1 ship operating companies (e.g., designated persons);

.2 emergency information centres (such as CHEMTREC in the USA);

.3 specialized agencies;

.4 professional responders;

.5 port State authorities;

.6 coastguard;

.7 fire brigades; and

.8 manufacturers of the products.

5 Evacuation

Within some EmS FIRE SCHEDULES the phrase "Sudden or short-term events (e.g., explosions) may endanger the safety of the ship" has been introduced. Depending on the type of ship and on the volume of dangerous goods allocated to this specific FIRE SCHEDULE, it may be necessary to consider abandoning the ship at an early stage. In this case, the master should be aware of the hazard and should decide whether the *ship requires assistance*.

6 Fire-fighting media

6.1 Water

6.1.1 Water is the obvious fire-fighting medium at sea and is recommended for most fires involving dangerous goods. However, it should be noted that shore-based firefighters may use a different medium.

6.1.2 When water is applied to a burning cargo, the temperature is reduced and the fire will be extinguished when the temperature drops below the ignition point. However, water is not suitable to extinguish all fires involving dangerous goods. Different fire-fighting media should be used if so indicated on the specific EmS FIRE SCHEDULE.

6.1.3 If the fire is under deck, consideration should be given to the stability of the ship when flooding the hold with water.

6.1.4 Some dangerous goods will react chemically with water, producing flammable and/or toxic gases. The most effective way to extinguish a fire involving these dangerous goods is to smother them with a dry inert powdered material. However, the availability of suitable inert material on board is limited. It may also be dangerous to approach the fire in order to use inert material properly. Consequently, the most appropriate method of extinguishing the fire may be to use copious quantities of water. This would have an overall cooling effect on the fire even though the water may react with the dangerous goods involved.

6.1.5 Ships are equipped with a number of dual-purpose spray/jet nozzles as required by SOLAS. Most EmS FIRE SCHEDULES recommend that the nozzles be set to spray when used to fight fires. Water spray may also be achieved by using water jets from some distance. This method of producing water spray is generally recommended. However, it is dangerous to direct a water jet onto the fire at close range because this could result in the spread of burning material.

6.1.6 The term "copious quantities of water" used within the EmS FIRE SCHEDULES refers to the minimum total quantities of water provided for optimal fire fighting using four jets of water, as required by SOLAS regulation II-2/4. The master and crew should know the practical limitations that may be encountered at specific stowage locations in this respect.

6.1.7 Following the advice "use copious quantities of water" or "water spray from as many hoses as possible" may interfere with the safety of the ship with regard to the ship's stability. Stress forces on the hull due to increased quantities of water in the ship should be considered.

6.2 Fixed gas fire-extinguishing systems

6.2.1 If a fixed gas fire-extinguishing system is used for incidents under deck, all hatches and vent dampers should be closed and ventilation shut off before the system is activated. If smoke is seen coming from around the hatches, the leaks should be sealed with any suitable material available.

6.2.2 The majority of the fixed gas fire-extinguishing systems use carbon dioxide (CO_2), but some use nitrogen (N_2) as the extinguishing medium. The instructions on board should be followed. The fire control plan will sometimes specify a given volume of gas to be applied to a given space. No advantage will be gained by exceeding this volume of gas where burning dangerous goods are involved.

6.2.3 It is important to realise that it will take an appreciable time for the space to cool after the fire has been extinguished. Therefore it would be extremely dangerous to reopen the hatches since the extinguishing gas would escape and air would enter the space again, thus allowing the fire to re-ignite. The ship's on-board instructions for such cases should be followed.

6.2.4 Fixed gas fire-extinguishing systems are not effective against all fires. EmS FIRE SCHEDULES may contain specific information in this regard.

6.3 Fixed pressure water spraying systems

6.3.1 In some ships (e.g., ro–ro ships and car ferries), some cargo spaces may be fitted with a water drencher or spray system instead of a fixed gas fire-extinguishing system. There will be instructions on board which should be followed.

6.3.2 A closed cargo space should be ventilated to clear it of smoke and toxic gases after the fire has been extinguished and the space has cooled. The ventilation equipment should be of a certified safe type for smoke removal. Evidence that the space is cooling down can be obtained by monitoring adjacent bulkheads and decks. Thereafter, a fire-fighting team should look for any small remaining fires and inspect the surrounding cargo. After the fire has been extinguished, the cargo should be kept under surveillance until its normal temperature is reached.

6.4 Foam

In general, foam is an effective fire-fighting medium for fires involving flammable liquids. The foam forms a layer on the liquid thereby excluding oxygen and reducing heat. However, it is less effective on solid substances on fire. Most foams contain water and should not be used on fires where the use of water is restricted because of adverse chemical reaction.

6.5 Dry chemicals

Dry chemicals may be an effective extinguishing medium for fires involving water-reactive substances and metals. The dry chemical should not react with the dangerous goods involved in the fire. Some dangerous goods require a specific dry chemical to extinguish a fire.

7 Dangerous goods exposed to fire

7.1 Rupture and cooling

7.1.1 Where possible, packages should be removed from the vicinity of the fire. In general, heated material will expand, thus needing more volume and creating pressure in the package. This will affect the integrity of the package which could lead to rupture and dispersal of the contents. Effective cooling can lower the possibility of rupture.

7.1.2 Where there is a danger that heat will have already started to cause a chemical or physical change to the dangerous substance, packages should not be moved. Care should always be exercised, for example, with those substances liable to polymerize, as this reaction may continue for a long time after the removal of the heat source. Provided no discharge or pumping overboard problem arises, cooling should continue for many hours after the fire has been extinguished. After heat evolution has ceased, cooling with water may be stopped. A careful watch should be kept on the stability of the ship.

7.1.3 The EmS FIRE SCHEDULES advise that a number of dangerous goods should be removed or jettisoned if there is a likelihood of their involvement in a fire. However, where full or nearly full cargo transport units are involved, such guidance may be impractical. In that case, the advice should be taken to indicate that the goods are particularly dangerous. Personnel on board should fight the fire and cool nearby cargo as far as possible. It should be borne in mind that some heated dangerous goods may have already damaged the packaging or may explode during handling. Consequently, moving or jettisoning burning cargo should only be attempted with utmost caution.

7.2 Spillage

7.2.1 It should be remembered that leakage of dangerous goods can be very dangerous for the crew and for the ship. Fire and explosion can rupture nearby packages or tanks, creating a spillage.

7.2.2 If a leak is discovered, the hazards associated with that leak should be ascertained immediately. In cases involving leaks of flammable liquids or flammable gases (class 3 and class 2.1 labels respectively), the crew should withdraw to a well protected position. Air–vapour and air–gas mixtures are liable to explode and such an explosion may injure crew members and damage the ship.

7.2.3 Many toxic gases are odourless and colourless. A number of liquids will produce toxic vapours if exposed to heat. In an emergency, the ship should be manoeuvred to keep the bridge, living quarters and crew upwind as far as possible.

7.2.4 The EmS SPILLAGE SCHEDULES should be consulted when dealing with a leakage.

8 Personal protection

8.1 Ship's personnel

8.1.1 Many vapours and gases of dangerous goods produced by a fire are hazardous to health. In the case of fire, the use of a firefighter's outfit and self-contained breathing apparatus is essential. Only trained personnel should use this equipment, which should be well maintained. Particular attention should be given to ensuring that toxic vapours or fumes do not penetrate occupied areas of the ship (e.g., bridge, living quarters, machinery spaces, working areas, etc.).

8.1.2 According to the ship's fire emergency plan, ventilation systems to living and working spaces should be shut off, closed and secured to reduce the possibility of vapours, dusts, and gases from penetrating these areas.

8.2 Fire-fighting team

8.2.1 Chapter II-2 of SOLAS requires firefighter's outfits, full chemical protective suits and self-contained breathing apparatus to be readily available on board. Masters are reminded that personnel will need regular training in the use of self-contained breathing apparatus and that special attention should be given to ensure that face masks fit satisfactorily at all times.

8.2.2 Self-contained breathing apparatus is essential for fire fighting because dangerous goods on fire produce various substances hazardous to health. Handling water jets from some distance or cooling of heated cargo may not require the use of self-contained breathing apparatus. However, decisions not to use self-contained breathing apparatus should be undertaken carefully and on a case-by-case basis.

8.2.3 Fire-fighting outfits offer only limited protection from dangerous goods. Fire-fighting outfits are not chemical suits. Chemical protective clothing is designed to protect against specific properties of chemicals. In general, there will be no such thing as a single type chemical protective suit on board. Therefore, contact with dangerous goods should be avoided. Chemical protective clothing is not resistant to fire or heat.

9 First aid and actions after termination of fire fighting

9.1 Any contamination with hazardous material should be immediately removed from the skin and then washed, for example with copious quantities of water. Information on medical first aid is provided in the IMO/WHO/ILO *Medical First Aid Guide for Use in Accidents Involving Dangerous Goods (MFAG)* published by IMO. **Be prepared to use the *MFAG*!**

9.2 Cargo may re-ignite after a fire has been extinguished. An efficient patrol should be maintained in the spaces in which the fire occurred and in any adjoining spaces to ensure that any new ignition or leakages are dealt with promptly. Fire-extinguishing systems should remain on stand-by. Post a fire watch.

9.3 After extinguishing the fire, all emergency team personnel should ensure that all contamination of equipment and protective clothing is removed and washed immediately. Equipment should to be restored and re-stowed for use.

9.4 There are reporting procedures under SOLAS and MARPOL which have to be followed (see Reporting Procedures).

10 Special notes on classes of dangerous goods

10.1 Explosives – class 1

10.1.1 In the event of a fire, everything should be done to prevent the spread of the fire to containers which contain class 1 goods. If it is not possible to prevent the spread of the fire, all personnel should immediately withdraw from the area.

10.1.2 Many explosives will burn to the point of an explosion. The master's main concern will be whether or not there is likely to be a mass explosion. Such an explosion could damage the ship. If goods of division 1.1 or division 1.5 are involved, this likelihood will exist. The time between fire reaching the explosives and the subsequent mass explosion will be of the order of a few seconds to minutes. The master should ascertain how large a quantity of such explosives is involved. A few kilograms are unlikely to sink the ship, but above this a clear risk to the safety of the crew and the stability of the ship should be considered. Sudden or short-term events may endanger the safety of the ship.

10.1.3 Explosives of divisions 1.2, 1.3, 1.4, and 1.6 are unlikely to explode *en masse*. Irrespective of the division of the explosives, any fire fighting should take place from behind substantial cover. If the risk to firefighters is too high, hoses could be lashed to the rail or other suitable fixtures and left unmanned.

10.1.4 Neither exclusion of air nor the use of smothering material is likely to be effective against a fire involving explosives. The use of the largest possible quantity of water in the shortest possible time is the only means of attempting to prevent a rise in temperature that could affect the chemical stability of the explosives.

10.1.5 Some dangerous goods of this class have been wetted or immersed in water. As they dry, they become unstable. The master should seek advice (see section 4 above).

10.2 Gases – class 2

10.2.1 Gases are substances usually transported in cylinders, flasks, portable tanks, aerosol dispensers and bottles under varying degrees of pressure. The gases may be flammable, toxic or corrosive and may be compressed, liquefied or refrigerated.

10.2.2 Gases will not start burning at the valve, unless there has been an ignition source nearby (e.g., fire or heat). The location of the burning gas needs to be identified because it may be the heart of the fire. The heating of the receptacle is the most serious danger because of the possibility of rupture, rocketing or explosion. In the event of a fire, receptacles containing gas should be liberally sprayed with water to keep them as cool as possible.

10.2.3 Non-burning leakages from receptacles of flammable gases may give rise to explosive mixtures in air. If a fire caused by the ignition of leaking gas is extinguished within a cargo space before the leak is stopped, accumulation of gas will occur. This will result in an explosive mixture or a toxic or suffocating atmosphere. The EmS SPILLAGE SCHEDULES should be consulted.

10.2.4 Extremely low temperatures around leakages of some liquefied gases are an additional hazard (other than flammability and toxicity). Emergency teams should avoid contact with such leakages and the immediate vicinity.

10.3   Flammable liquids – class 3

10.3.1 It is dangerous to direct a jet of water onto a fire involving flammable liquids. Many flammable liquids float on water and the water jet would spread the liquid, thus creating a greater danger. Closed containers exposed to fire will become pressurized and a rupture will occur.

10.3.2 Heated flammable liquid will release vapours that may start burning instantly with explosive effect. Consequently, fire-fighting personnel should stay in a well protected position and use water spray on the area of the fire. This will cool down the temperature of the liquid and the air–vapour mixture.

10.4   Flammable solids – class 4.1

10.4.1 This class of substances includes flammable solids, water-wetted explosives (i.e., desensitized explosives) and self-reactive substances.

10.4.2 Flammable solids will easily ignite, and the appropriate EmS FIRE SCHEDULE should be consulted. In the event of a fire, water-wetted explosives (i.e., desensitized explosives) will effectively have the properties of a class 1 product. The special notes on class 1 explosives (see 10.1) and the relevant EmS FIRE SCHEDULES should be consulted.

10.4.3 Self-reactive substances are sometimes transported under temperature controlled conditions where the control temperature will depend upon the specific properties of the substance being transported. If the control temperature is exceeded, the refrigeration unit has to be inspected. If the temperature control cannot be restored, the manufacturer should be consulted as soon as possible. The manufacturer should be similarly consulted if smoke is observed. The cargo should then be kept under surveillance.

10.5   Spontaneously combustible substances – class 4.2

10.5.1 This class of substances includes pyrophoric substances, which will instantly burn on contact with air, and self-heating substances, which lead to spontaneous combustion.

10.5.2 Although the use of dry inert powdered material to smother the fire would be the preferred option, in most circumstances such a procedure may not be possible. Two methods of dealing with such a fire are possible:

    .1   Controlled burning: Stay in a well protected position. Let the product burn as long as no other cargo is in danger from the ensuing fire. The fire in the product should be left to burn out completely. Nearby cargo should be cooled down with water spray from as many hoses as possible.

    .2   Fight the fire from a safe distance: Refer to the relevant EmS FIRE SCHEDULE since it is possible for the product to explode.

10.6   Substances dangerous when wet – class 4.3

10.6.1 This class of substances reacts violently with water, evolving flammable gases. The heat of the reaction is sometimes sufficient to initiate a fire.

10.6.2 Although the use of dry inert powdered material to smother the fire would be the preferred option, in most circumstances such a procedure may not be possible. Two methods of dealing with such a fire are possible:

    .1   Controlled burning: Stay in a well protected position. Let the product burn as long as no other cargo is in danger from the ensuing fire. The fire in the product should be left to burn out completely. Nearby cargo should be cooled down with water spray from as many hoses as possible.

    .2   Fight the fire from a safe distance: Refer to the relevant EmS FIRE SCHEDULE since it is possible for the product to explode.

10.7   Oxidizing substances – class 5.1

10.7.1 This class of substances is liable to evolve oxygen and therefore to accelerate a fire. These substances, while in themselves not necessarily combustible, may cause the combustion of other material (e.g., sawdust or paper) or contribute to the fire, leading to an explosion.

10.7.2   Fires in which these substances are present are difficult to extinguish, because the ship's fire-fighting installation may not be effective. Everything possible should be done to prevent the spread of fire to containers containing these dangerous goods. However, if fire reaches the cargo, personnel should be withdrawn immediately to a well protected position.

10.8   **Organic peroxides – class 5.2**

10.8.1   This class of substances is liable to burn vigorously. Some substances have a low decomposition temperature and are transported under temperature controlled conditions, where the control temperature will depend upon the specific properties of the substance being transported.

10.8.2   If the temperature control cannot be restored, the manufacturer should be consulted as soon as possible even if evolution of smoke has ceased. The cargo should then be kept under surveillance. The surrounding area should be kept isolated because liquid may be ejected from relief arrangements.

10.9   **Toxic substances – class 6.1**

Substances of this class are poisonous by contact or inhalation, and the use of self-contained breathing apparatus and firefighters' outfits is therefore essential.

10.10   **Infectious substances – class 6.2**

These are substances which are known or reasonably expected to contain pathogens, (i.e., micro-organisms that are known or reasonably expected to cause infectious disease in humans or animals). Pathogens may survive the fire and self-contained breathing apparatus should therefore be used.

10.11   **Radioactive material – class 7**

10.11.1   Many radioactive materials are transported in packages designed to retain their containment and shielding in accidents. However, under extreme fire conditions, failure of containment or loss of shielding or criticality safety could result in significant hazard to personnel. Long-term exposure of any class 7 package to extreme heat should be avoided and in emergencies they should be kept as cool as possible using copious quantities of water. If a packaging of radioactive material has been exposed to any significant fire, expert advice should be sought. Suspected contamination of safety and fire-fighting equipment should be removed as quickly as possible.

10.11.2   Some packages may have a class 7 label and other hazard labels. Such additional hazards may be greater than the radiation hazard. In that case, actions as specified in the applicable EmS FIRE SCHEDULE should be followed.

10.11.3   Although radiation monitors are not required by regulation on board ships, applicable relevant provisions on segregation, separation or radiation protection programmes (e.g., paragraphs 1.1.3.2 and 7.2.9.7 of the IMDG Code) or the INF Code may require monitors on board. For ships carrying radiation monitoring equipment, monitoring of radiation levels is recommended.

10.12   **Corrosive substances – class 8**

These substances are extremely dangerous to humans, and many may cause destruction of safety equipment. Burning cargo of this class will produce highly corrosive vapours. Consequently, wearing self-contained breathing apparatus is essential.

10.13   **Miscellaneous dangerous substances and articles – class 9**

This class includes those substances, materials and articles which are deemed to possess some danger, but which are not classified within the criteria of classes 1 to 8. No general guidelines are applicable to these goods. They have been allocated to the relevant EmS FIRE SCHEDULE according to their hazards in the event of a fire.

10.14   **Marine pollutants**

10.14.1   A number of substances within all of the above classes have also been designated as marine pollutants. Packages containing these substances will bear a Marine Pollutant mark.

10.14.2   In the case of leakage resulting from burning cargo, it is important to be aware that any spillage of a marine pollutant which is washed overboard will pollute the sea. It is, however, more important to fight a fire on board a ship rather than to prevent pollution of the sea.

General guidelines for FIRE

- Think safety first!
- Avoid any contact with dangerous substances.
- Keep away from fire, smoke, fumes and vapours.
- Sound the fire alarm and start fire-fighting procedures.
- Keep the bridge and living quarters upwind if possible.
- Locate stowage position of cargo that is burning or evolving smoke.
- Identify cargo.
- Obtain UN Numbers and the EmS FIRE SCHEDULE of the dangerous goods involved.
- Consider which measures of the EmS FIRE SCHEDULE are applicable and should be followed.
- Check if other dangerous goods may potentially be involved in the fire and identify the relevant EmS FIRE SCHEDULE.
- Wear suitable protective clothing and self-contained breathing apparatus.
- Be prepared to use the *Medical First Aid Guide (MFAG)*.
- Contact the designated person of the company responsible for the operation of the ship or a rescue co-ordination centre to obtain expert advice on dangerous goods emergency response measures.

Precaution: Contamination of the skin with dangerous goods should be removed and washed immediately.

Emergency Schedules for FIRE

FIRE SCHEDULE Alfa

F–A
GENERAL FIRE SCHEDULE

General comments		In a fire, exposed cargoes may explode or their containment may rupture. Fight fire from a protected position from as far away as possible.
Cargo on fire on deck	Packages	Create water spray from as many hoses as possible.
	Cargo Transport Units	
Cargo on fire under deck		Stop ventilation and close hatches. Use cargo space fixed fire-extinguishing system. If this is not available, create water spray using copious quantities of water.
Cargo exposed to fire		If practicable, remove or jettison packages which are likely to be involved in fire. Otherwise, keep cool using water.
Special cases: UN 1381, UN 2447		After extinguishing the fire, treat immediately as for spillage (see relevant EmS SPILLAGE SCHEDULE).

FIRE SCHEDULE Bravo

F–B
EXPLOSIVE SUBSTANCES AND ARTICLES

General comments		In a fire, exposed cargoes may explode or their containment may rupture. Fight fire from a protected position from as far away as possible. All crew members should be made aware of the explosion hazard and instructed to take appropriate action. SUDDEN OR SHORT-TERM EVENTS (E.G., EXPLOSIONS) MAY ENDANGER THE SAFETY OF THE SHIP.
Cargo on fire on deck	**Packages**	Use copious quantities of water from as many hoses as possible. Cargo will explode or burn fiercely. Extinguishing may not be possible.
	Cargo Transport Units	
Cargo on fire under deck		Cargo will explode or burn fiercely. Extinguishing will not be possible. Stop ventilation and close hatches. Use cargo space fixed fire-extinguishing system. If this is not available, create water spray using copious quantities of water.
Cargo exposed to fire		Do not move packages that have been exposed to heat. If practicable, remove or jettison packages which are likely to be involved in the fire. If the packages are not directly involved in the fire, efforts should be concentrated on preventing the fire from reaching the cargo. This is done by keeping the packages wet by using water jets from as far away as practicable to drive the fire away. If the fire reaches the cargo, the firefighters should withdraw to a safe area and continue to fight the fire. Where practicable, articles having been exposed to the fire should be kept separated from unexposed articles. They should be kept wet and monitored from a safe distance.
Special cases: **UN 0018, UN 0019, UN 0020, UN 0021, UN 0301**		Ammunition producing tear or toxic gas. The crew should be aware of the hazard. After explosion, only self-contained breathing apparatus will protect efficiently. Consult SPILLAGE SCHEDULE S-Z.
UN 0248, UN 0249		These water-activated devices will become more liable to explosion on contact with water.
UN 3268		AIR BAG INFLATORS/MODULES PYROTECHNIC could be subject to self-sustaining decomposition if heated. The temperature could reach 500°C, producing gas. This process may lead to an explosion of the cargo even after the exposure to heat has ended.

FIRE SCHEDULE Charlie

F–C
NON-FLAMMABLE GASES

General comments		Gases in closed tanks exposed to heat may explode suddenly in or after a fire situation by a *Boiling Liquid – Expanding Vapour Explosion* (BLEVE). Heated or ruptured cylinders may rocket. Gases listed under this schedule are non-flammable. However, some gases will support combustion though not flammable itself. Fire may produce leakages. Most gases allocated to this schedule are hazardous to health. Some are corrosive. Create water spray. Identify the source of the fire and take appropriate action.
Cargo on fire on deck	Packages	Use copious quantities of water from as many hoses as possible.
	Cargo Transport Units	
Cargo on fire under deck		Use fixed fire-extinguishing system.
Cargo exposed to fire		If practicable, remove or jettison packages which are likely to be involved in the fire. Otherwise, cool for several hours using water. Heated or ruptured cylinders may rocket.
Special cases: UN 1003, UN 1070, UN 1072, UN 1073, UN 2201, UN 3156, UN 3157		Although these cargoes are non-flammable, they will intensify the fire.

FIRE SCHEDULE Delta

F–D
FLAMMABLE GASES

General comments		Gases in closed tanks exposed to heat may explode suddenly in or after a fire situation by a *Boiling Liquid – Expanding Vapour Explosion* (BLEVE). Crew members should be aware of the explosion hazard and take appropriate action. Keep tanks cool with copious quantities of water. Fight fire from a protected position from as far away as possible. Extinguishing a burning gas leak may lead to the formation of an explosive atmosphere. Flames may be invisible.
Cargo on fire on deck	**Packages**	Create water spray from as many hoses as possible. Do not try to extinguish a gas flame.
	Cargo Transport Units	Cool burning transport units and nearby cargo exposed to the fire with copious quantities of water. Do not try to extinguish a gas flame.
Cargo on fire under deck		Stop ventilation and close hatches. Use cargo space fixed fire-extinguishing system. If this is not available, create water spray using copious quantities of water.
Cargo exposed to fire		If practicable, remove or jettison packages which are likely to be involved in the fire. Otherwise, keep cool for several hours using water.
Special cases: **UN 1038, UN 1075,** **UN 1965, UN 1966,** **UN 1972, UN 3138,** **UN 3160, UN 3309,** **UN 3312**		SUDDEN OR SHORT-TERM EVENTS (E.G., EXPLOSIONS) MAY ENDANGER THE SAFETY OF THE SHIP.
UN 1001, UN 3374		*Acetylene* is a gas which is particularly dangerous due to its potential to explode. Rough handling or local heating may lead to delayed explosion. Keep cool for several hours using water. Do not move receptacles. All cylinders that have been subjected to rough handling or to local heating should be jettisoned.

FIRE SCHEDULE Echo

F–E
NON-WATER-REACTIVE FLAMMABLE LIQUIDS

General comments		Cargoes in tanks exposed to heat may explode suddenly in or after a fire situation by a *Boiling Liquid – Expanding Vapour Explosion* (BLEVE). Keep tanks cool with copious quantities of water. Fight fire from a protected position from as far away as possible. Stop leakage or close open valve if practicable. Flames may be invisible.
Cargo on fire on deck	Packages	Create water spray from as many hoses as possible.
	Cargo Transport Units	Cool burning transport units and nearby cargo exposed to the fire with copious quantities of water.
Cargo on fire under deck		Stop ventilation and close hatches. Use cargo space fixed fire-extinguishing system. If this is not available, create water spray using copious quantities of water.
Cargo exposed to fire		If practicable, remove or jettison packages which are likely to be involved in the fire. Otherwise, keep cool for several hours using water.
Special cases: UN 1162, UN 1250, UN 1298, UN 1717, UN 2985		Cargoes will create hydrochloric acid in contact with water: stay away from effluent.

F–F
TEMPERATURE-CONTROLLED SELF-REACTIVES AND ORGANIC PEROXIDES

General comments		Exposed cargoes may decompose violently. Crew members should be aware of the explosion hazard and take appropriate action. Fight fire from a protected position from as far away as possible. Switch off electrical power supplies only during fire fighting. Check temperature readings if possible. Measures have to be taken to alert the crew when the temperature of the cargo increases. In case of a temperature increase or smoke evolution, follow the relevant instructions. Contact the manufacturer (consignor) of the cargo as soon as possible.
Cargo on fire on deck	**Packages**	Not applicable.
	Cargo Transport Units	Cool burning transport units and nearby cargo exposed to the fire with copious quantities of water. After the fire has been extinguished, do not open the unit until well after smoke evolution has ceased. If possible, restore cooling. Keep under surveillance.
Cargo on fire under deck		Not applicable. According to the IMDG Code, under deck stowage is not allowed. Radio for expert ADVICE.
Cargo exposed to fire	**Cargo Transport Units with IBCs, Packages**	Cool units exposed to fire with water. After the fire has been extinguished, check and restore cooling. Keep under surveillance. Check temperature frequently. In case of temperature increase or smoke evolution, follow the relevant instructions.
	Tanks	Keep personnel away from tanks as liquid may be ejected from relief arrangements. Cool units exposed to fire with copious quantities of water. After the fire has been extinguished, check and restore cooling. Keep under surveillance. After the fire has been extinguished, water spray should be continued to cool down the outer parts of the tanks. Check refrigeration unit, keep tanks under surveillance. Check temperature frequently.
Temperature increase	**Cargo Transport Units with IBCs, Packages**	If the *control temperature* is exceeded, the refrigeration unit has to be inspected (consult manual) and repaired. If not possible and/or temperature control cannot be restored, contact the manufacturer of the cargo. If the *emergency temperature* is reached but the refrigeration unit is operating correctly, contact the manufacturer of the cargo and consider disposal of packagings. Keep fire-fighting team on stand-by. If the *emergency temperature* is reached due to cooling unit failure, contact the manufacturer of the cargo. When emergency temperature is reached, 12 hours are left for repairing the cooling unit and/or disposal of packaging. After that time, keep a safe distance and prepare for fire fighting.
	Tanks	If the *control temperature* is exceeded, the refrigeration unit has to be inspected (consult manual) and repaired. If not possible and/or temperature control cannot be restored, contact manufacturer of the cargo. If the *emergency temperature* is reached but the refrigeration unit is operating correctly, contact the manufacturer of the cargo. Keep at a safe distance and consider emptying of tank overboard via bottom outlet using a flexible hose. If the *emergency temperature* is reached due to failure of the cooling unit, repairs may be undertaken as long as the temperature has not exceeded the emergency temperature by more than 5°C. After that, consider emptying the tank using a flexible hose attached to the bottom opening of the tank if provided.

F–F
TEMPERATURE-CONTROLLED SELF-REACTIVES AND ORGANIC PEROXIDES

Smoke evolution	Cargo Transport Units with IBCs, Packages	Keep fire-fighting team on stand-by. The freight container should not be approached. When smoke evolution increases, keep safe distance and prepare for fire fighting. After smoke has ceased, check refrigeration system. Follow guidelines for temperature increase. Keep under surveillance, as new smoke evolution might take place.
	Tanks	Keep personnel away from the tank, as liquid may be ejected from relief arrangements. Cool unit exposed to fire with water. Use water spray from a protected position. In case smoke or pressure-relief venting is moderate and temperature is below the emergency temperature, consider emptying the tank overboard via bottom outlet, using a flexible hose. Even when smoke evolution or pressure-relief venting has ceased, water spray should be continued for some hours and the tank should be kept under surveillance, as new smoke evolution might take place.
Special cases: None.		

FIRE SCHEDULE Golf

F–G
WATER-REACTIVE SUBSTANCES

General comments		In a fire, exposed cargoes may explode or their containment may rupture. Fight fire from a protected position from as far away as possible. Use of copious quantities of water at once is recommended to cool down the heat radiation of the fire and to cool down heated cargo nearby. Only as a secondary effect, water will start or intensify burning of that material. Do not use small quantities of water – this will react strongly.
Cargo on fire on deck	Packages	DO NOT use water or foam; smother with dry inert powdered material or let fire burn. If not practicable, cool nearby cargo with copious quantities of water, although burning of cargo could intensify for a short period of time. Do not spray small quantities of water onto the fire. Use copious quantities of water only.
	Cargo Transport Units	If the fire is not igniting nearby cargoes, let the fire burn. Otherwise, cool the burning transport unit with copious quantities of water. Try to avoid getting water into the container.
Cargo on fire under deck		Stop ventilation and close hatches. The fixed gas fire-extinguishing system should be used. If this is not available: *Do not* use water onto the material in enclosed spaces under deck. With open hatches, cool nearby cargo with copious quantities of water, although the fire could intensify for a short period of time. Do not spray small quantities of water onto the fire, use copious quantities of water.
Cargo exposed to fire		If practicable, remove or jettison packages which are likely to be involved in the fire. Otherwise, cool using water.
Special cases: UN 1415, UN 1418		*LITHIUM, non-pyrophoric* and *MAGNESIUM POWDER* require the use of dry lithium chloride or dry sodium chloride or graphite powder to extinguish the fire. Do NOT use water or foam.

FIRE SCHEDULE Hotel

F-H
OXIDIZING SUBSTANCES WITH EXPLOSIVE POTENTIAL

General comments		In a fire, exposed cargoes may explode or their containment may rupture. Crew members should be aware of the explosion hazard and take appropriate action. Fight fire from a protected position from as far away as possible. SUDDEN OR SHORT-TERM EVENTS (E.G., EXPLOSIONS) MAY ENDANGER THE SAFETY OF THE SHIP.
Cargo on fire on deck	Packages	Create water spray from as many hoses as possible.
	Cargo Transport Units	
Cargo on fire under deck		OPEN HATCHES to provide maximum ventilation. Fixed gas fire-extinguishing systems may not be effective on these fires. Create water spray from as many hoses as possible.
Cargo exposed to fire		Do not move packages that have been exposed to heat. If practicable, remove or jettison packages which are likely to be involved in the fire. If the packages are not directly involved in the fire, efforts should be concentrated on preventing the fire from reaching the cargo. This is done by keeping the packages wet by using water jets from as far away as practicable to drive the fire away. If the fire reaches the cargo, the firefighters should withdraw to a safe area and continue to fight the fire from a safe position. Where practicable, articles having been exposed to the fire should be kept separated from unexposed articles. They should be kept wet and monitored from a safe distance.
Special cases: None.		

FIRE SCHEDULE India

F-I
RADIOACTIVE MATERIAL

General comments		Evacuate compartment or downwind area of non-essential personnel. Do not touch damaged packages. In cases of suspected radioactive contamination, limit entry of firefighters for the shortest time possible. For ships carrying radiation monitoring equipment, measure radiation levels. Radio for expert ADVICE. After the fire has been extinguished, clean ship's surfaces with copious quantities of water. Decontaminate firefighters before protective clothing is removed. Isolate potentially contaminated clothing and equipment. If exposure of personnel is suspected, clean body and hair with warm water and soap; discharge resultant washings directly overboard. Record the names of potentially exposed persons. Ensure medical examination of these persons after reaching any medical staff. For ships carrying radiation monitoring equipment, continue monitoring of radiation levels after fire is extinguished.
Cargo on fire on deck	Packages	Create water spray from as many hoses as possible.
	Cargo Transport Units	Create water spray from as many hoses as possible. Cool burning transport units and nearby cargo exposed to the fire with copious quantities of water.
Cargo on fire under deck		Stop ventilation and close hatches. Use cargo space fixed fire-extinguishing system. If this is not available, create water spray using copious quantities of water.
Cargo exposed to fire		If practicable, remove or jettison packages which are likely to be involved in the fire. Otherwise, cool for several hours using copious quantities of water.
Special cases:		
UN 2977, UN 2978		Chemical hazard greatly exceeds radiation hazard. Material reacts with moisture to form toxic and corrosive gas. The run-off may be corrosive. Keep clear. Exposed cargoes may explode in a fire. Create water spray. Leak may be evident by visible and irritating vapours. Released vapours may also react violently with hydrocarbons (fuel).
UN 3332, UN 3333		If the source capsule is identified as being out of its packaging, do not touch. Stay away, minimize exposure to radiation by limiting time near material and by maximizing distance. Radio for expert ADVICE.
Subsidiary label class 4.2 or class 4.3		All radioactive material with subsidiary risk label 4.2 or 4.3 affixed (e.g., pyrophoric uranium or thorium metal): Radio for expert ADVICE. *On deck:* Do not use water onto the material. Cool nearby cargo with copious quantities of water, although the fire could intensify for a short period. Do not spray small quantities of water onto the fire, use copious quantities of water. *Under deck:* Stop ventilation and close hatches. The fixed gas fire-extinguishing system should be used. If this is not available, do not use water onto the material in enclosed spaces under deck. With open hatches, cool nearby cargo with copious quantities, although the fire could intensify for a short period. Do not spray small quantities of water onto the fire, use copious quantities of water only.

FIRE SCHEDULE Juliet

F–J
NON-TEMPERATURE-CONTROLLED SELF-REACTIVES AND ORGANIC PEROXIDES

General comments		Exposed cargoes may decompose violently. Crew members should be aware of the explosion hazard and take appropriate action. Fight fire from a protected position from as far away as possible. Exposed cargoes may decompose violently in a fire.
Cargo on fire on deck	**Packages**	Not applicable.
	Cargo Transport Units	Cool burning transport units and nearby cargo exposed to the fire with copious quantities of water. After the fire has been extinguished, carry on water spraying of the container for several hours. Do not open container until well after smoke evolution has ceased. After this, cool down packages or IBCs if practicable for at least one hour with water. Otherwise, check contents on regular intervals. In case smoke is evolved again, apply further water cooling. Dispose of residues overboard. Clean the area thoroughly. After the fire has been extinguished, keep cargo transport unit under surveillance.
Cargo on fire under deck		Not applicable – According to the IMDG Code, under deck stowage is not allowed. Radio for expert ADVICE.
Cargo exposed to fire	**Cargo Transport Units with IBCs, Packages**	Cool unit exposed to the fire with water. After the fire has been extinguished, keep transport unit under surveillance. In case of smoke evolution, follow the relevant instructions.
	Tanks	Keep personnel away from tank, as fluid ejection from relief arrangements might take place. Cool unit exposed to the fire with water. Contact the manufacturer (consignor) of the cargo. Cooling the tank should be continued until the temperature is below 50°C. Check temperature frequently. If temperature increases again, cool unit with water. Consider emptying the tank overboard via bottom outlet, using a flexible hose.
Smoke evolution	**Cargo Transport Units with IBCs, Packages**	Cool unit with water. Use water spray from a protected position. Do not open the unit until well after smoke evolution has ceased. After this, cool down packages or IBCs if practicable for at least one hour with water. Otherwise, check contents on regular intervals. In case smoke is evolved again, apply further water cooling. Dispose of residues overboard. Clean the area thoroughly.
	Tanks	Keep personnel away from the tank, as fluid ejection from relief arrangements might take place. Cool unit exposed to fire with water. Use water spray from a protected position. Even when smoke evolution or pressure-relief venting has ceased, cooling the tank should be continued until the temperature is below 50°C. Check temperature frequently. If temperature increases again, cool unit with water. Consider emptying tank overboard via bottom outlet, using a flexible hose.
Special cases: None.		

Spillage

Introduction to the Emergency Schedules for SPILLAGE

1   Be prepared

1.1   Incidents involving dangerous goods may result in spillages from such goods, and the magnitude of the effects of an incident depends upon the type and amount of product released, together with the type of any other product involved and whether the spillage is on deck or in enclosed spaces.

1.2   Spillages could create additional hazards to those indicated by classification and labelling of the dangerous goods (e.g., the spillage of a flammable liquid may create an explosive atmosphere). Of particular concern are leakages of reactive chemicals, which in contact with other materials or further spillages will produce additional or other chemicals (e.g., toxic gases).

1.3   When dealing with a spillage on board a ship, the value of crew training and of familiarity with the general contingency plan will become evident. Drills and exercises specific to the cargoes on board at the time should be a part of shipboard routine.

1.4   This Guide should be integrated into the ship's *Safety Management System*. Procedures contained within the shipboard emergency plan have to be tailored to the individual ship. Spillage response procedures within the EmS SPILLAGE SCHEDULES are differentiated for "on deck" and "under deck" stowage. For specific ship types (e.g., hatchless container ships) or cargo spaces (e.g., open vehicle decks of ferries) these two procedural categories have to be assigned specifically to the individual ship (e.g., run-off considerations concerning bilges and drains).

2   Personal protection

2.1   The safety of the emergency personnel is of paramount importance.

2.2   The likelihood of the development of an explosive, flammable or toxic atmosphere should be considered.

2.3   Full protective clothing resistant to the effects of the specific dangerous substance involved should be worn. The protective clothing should cover all skin so that no part of the body is unprotected. Wearing self-contained breathing apparatus is essential to protect against inhalation of toxic or corrosive dusts, vapours or gases.

2.4   Emergency teams should avoid direct contact with any dangerous goods regardless of the protective clothing being used. If direct contact takes place when dealing with a spillage, the contact time should be kept to a minimum.

2.5   It is a requirement of SOLAS that four sets of full protective clothing resistant to chemical attack should be provided in addition to firefighters' outfits.

2.6   Firefighters' outfits are not designed to protect against chemical hazards and chemical-resistant clothing is not designed to protect against fire. Masters are reminded that personnel should have regular training in the use of self-contained breathing apparatus, and that special attention should be paid to ensuring that face masks fit satisfactorily at all times.

2.7   Responders should also ensure that any chemical protective clothing is used with other suitable protection against the specific hazards involved.

3   General response

3.1   The safety of the emergency personnel is most important.

3.2   Working spaces and living quarters should be protected by water spray wherever possible. Ventilation systems for living quarters and working spaces should be shut off, closed and secured to reduce the possibility of smoke, dust, fumes and gases from entering these areas. Particular care should be given to ventilation inlets (e.g., machinery and accommodation spaces). It may be necessary to turn the ship to ensure that the accommodation spaces are upwind.

3.3   Before entering cargo holds or compartments, the emergency personnel should determine the oxygen content of the space's atmosphere and should test for the presence of dangerous vapours. If a confined space entry is attempted, the use of self-contained breathing apparatus is essential. Only trained personnel should use this equipment, which should be well maintained.

3.4   It is essential to ensure that there is always an escape route for emergency personnel despite the limited means of escape due to narrow exit paths and the danger of falling overboard.

3.5   Decontamination and medical first aid also need to be considered. Arrange for a decontamination station to be set up at a suitable safe location.

3.6   The general response to spillage involving dangerous goods can be subdivided into the following tactical objectives:

 .1   Identification;

 .2   Rescue;

 .3   Isolation; and

 .4   Response.

Experience from previous incidents has shown that these objectives can normally be achieved in this order.

4   Identification of the dangerous goods involved

4.1   It is essential to identify the dangerous good(s) involved in the spillage in order that the specific EmS SPILLAGE SCHEDULE(S) for the cargo(es) may be consulted and appropriate action taken. This is important because some dangerous goods are incompatible with some media available for dealing with a spillage.

4.2   An identification number with four digits preceded by the letters "UN" is assigned to each dangerous good. From the UN Number, it is possible to find the appropriate EmS SPILLAGE SCHEDULE. The Dangerous Goods List in part 3 of chapter 3.2 of the IMDG Code contains the names and the UN Numbers, as well as the EmS SCHEDULE numbers. The Dangerous Goods Manifest and the Stowage Plan required by SOLAS regulation VII/5 will also contain the Proper Shipping Name and UN Number of the dangerous good(s) concerned. Packages will usually be labelled as well.

4.3   Specific information as to properties of dangerous goods may also be found in the Dangerous Goods List in the IMDG Code. Dangerous goods are classified and labelled according to their hazards. Labels and marks on packages provide a warning of the general risks to be encountered. Personnel should understand the labelling system. It will also be beneficial to consult other sources of information. A safety data sheet provided by the manufacturer may be one such source of additional information. Seek expert advice from manufacturers, specialized agencies or professional responders.

4.4   Emergency preparedness should form part of the ship's Safety Management System as required by the ISM Code. Prepared information can reduce errors during a spillage emergency. Therefore, it is recommended that the EmS SCHEDULE(S) be identified and included within the Dangerous Goods Manifest and Stowage Plan, so directly connected to the stowage position of the cargo. This will enable key members of the crew to know in advance which emergency procedures would be necessary. In the event of a spillage, the allocation of a specific EmS SPILLAGE SCHEDULE via identification of the cargo via the UN Number takes time and is open to error, especially in mixed cargoes in one container. Furthermore, some spillage response procedures may require specific use of material which could be hampered by an inaccessible stowage location. After locating the spillage area, the advice given in the EmS SPILLAGE SCHEDULE should be directly available from the Dangerous Goods Manifest and Stowage Plan.

5 Rescue

5.1 The safety of personnel should be the highest priority. One of the first concerns after evaluating the situation of the incident is finding and rescuing victims. This includes searching for and evacuating persons who may be exposed or who are disoriented or disabled by the release. It might be necessary to rescue persons from elevated places or confined spaces or those who are pinned under wreckage.

5.2 Appropriate equipment will need to be available, and prior training is essential for such circumstances.

6 Isolation

6.1 The objective of isolation is to limit the number of personnel exposed to the spilled material. This may be achieved by simply roping or taping off dangerous areas. Consider sealing off ventilation, air conditioning and other openings to living and working spaces.

6.2 At sea, the master has the capability and discretion to alter course and speed to ensure that dangerous gases or vapours are kept away from personnel, living quarters or ventilation inlets.

6.3 Consider the evacuation of passengers and members of the crew.

7 Response

7.1 At sea, human and other resources are limited. So in most cases involving spillage of dangerous goods, the most effective response will probably be to wash the substance overboard or jettison it. Attempts to repack dangerous goods may expose personnel to unreasonable risks.

7.2 The response to the spillage should be in accordance with the appropriate EmS SPILLAGE SCHEDULE(S) for the dangerous good(s) involved in the incident. The emergency team should take all reasonable precautions when dealing with the spillage and remember that the safety of personnel is most important.

8 Seek advice

8.1 Always seek expert ADVICE when dealing with dangerous goods spills. Such ADVICE could be given by:

.1 ship operating companies (e.g., designated persons);

.2 emergency information centres (such as CHEMTREC in the USA);

.3 specialized agencies;

.4 professional responders;

.5 port State authorities;

.6 coastguard;

.7 fire brigades; and

.8 manufacturers of the products.

9 Materials to be used

9.1 Water is the obvious medium to be used when dealing with a spillage on board a ship. It is recommended in the majority of cases to be used in copious quantities to wash the spillage overboard. However, certain dangerous goods react violently with water, producing flammable and toxic vapours. Others, for example marine pollutants, will produce pollution if washed overboard.

9.2 The term "copious quantities of water" used within the SPILLAGE SCHEDULES refers to the minimum total quantities of water provided for optimal fire fighting with four jets as defined by SOLAS chapter II-2 regulation 4 – Construction requirements. Master and crew should consider practical limitations at specific stowage locations in this respect.

9.3 Inert material should be used for spillages where it would be dangerous to use water. The inert material should be dry.

9.4 Sawdust should not be used as it is liable to be ignited by ignition sources or in contact with a number of substances. Cement may be used as an inert material for barricading.

9.5 An electric discharge may ignite some materials (e.g., explosives). Therefore, the use of non-certified safe type equipment within spillage areas may be dangerous. For some materials, "non-sparking footwear" is recommended (e.g., rubber boots without metal parts).

10 Action after spillage has been dealt with

10.1 Decontamination of personnel, clothing and ship's structures

10.1.1 After the spillage has been dealt with, the emergency team personnel should ensure that all contamination of equipment and protective clothing is removed and washed immediately. All equipment should be restored and re-stowed for further use.

10.1.2 Areas not affected initially may have been contaminated during response procedures. Crew members coming in contact with improperly decontaminated areas may become contaminated. Clean the site thoroughly before any unprotected personnel are allowed to enter.

10.1.3 Contaminated material should be properly disposed of or be cleaned.

11 First aid

11.1 Information on medical first aid is provided in the IMO/WHO/ILO *Medical First Aid Guide for Use in Accidents Involving Dangerous Goods (MFAG)*. **Be prepared to use the *MFAG*!**

11.2 Any contamination of the skin with a dangerous substance should be immediately removed and then washed, for example with water. Radio for expert advice if personnel have been exposed to dangerous goods.

12 Special notes on specific dangerous goods classes

12.1 Based on the specific properties of the individual dangerous goods listed under one UN Number, experts have allocated the substances, articles and materials to EmS SPILLAGE SCHEDULES. The allocation has not been based on the classification and labelling of the substances only. However, to help the mariner who is used to the handling and labelling of packaged dangerous goods to understand the advice given in the EmS SPILLAGE SCHEDULES, this introduction based on classification properties of substances is given.

12.2 Explosives – class 1

12.2.1 Properly packaged explosives are unlikely to detonate unless exposed to a fire or source of ignition. Within the divisions of this class, there are differences in explosive power. From a mariner's standpoint, the volumes of explosives concerned are of primary importance for the safety of the ship. However, even small volumes of spilled material may ignite and injure individual crew members. In general, spilled explosive substances are less hazardous when kept wet (see SPILLAGE SCHEDULE S-X).

12.2.2 Some explosive mixtures are stabilized in such a way that water will separate explosives from the stabilizer, thus creating a higher risk. The explosive component becomes very sensitive to shock and heat. The explosive should be kept mixed under water and washed overboard. Wetted articles should be jettisoned (see SPILLAGE SCHEDULE S-Y).

12.2.3 Some ammunition types contain a toxic material or a tear-gas substance. In addition to the explosive hazard, the toxicity hazard has to be realized. Use of self-contained breathing apparatus is essential (see SPILLAGE SCHEDULE S-Z).

12.3 Gases – class 2

12.3.1 A release of a flammable gas (class 2.1) is the preliminary step leading to a potential *Vapour Cloud Explosion* (VCE). For a blast to take place, the substance has to mix with air in a quantity that will allow the mixture to form a cloud. As soon as a friction (electrostatic potential) lies within the explosive range and encounters an ignition source, a flash fire, a deflagration or, sometimes, even a detonation may occur, with devastating consequences. In dealing with gas leakages, let the gas evaporate and drift away. Keep away all sources of ignition. Water spray could reduce the ignition potential of the cloud (see SPILLAGE SCHEDULE S-U).

12.3.2 Non-toxic, non-flammable gases (class 2.2) may displace oxygen, creating a suffocation hazard. Ventilation of all areas concerned is important (see SPILLAGE SCHEDULE S-V).

12.3.3   Toxic gases (class 2.3) when released may fill an area of the ship or a compartment with a toxic atmosphere. Therefore, it is important to shut off, close and secure all ventilation supplying the accommodation, machinery spaces and bridge to protect against such gases. Self-contained breathing apparatus is essential for the emergency team (see SPILLAGE SCHEDULE S-U).

12.3.4   Liquefied gases can cause the additional hazard of very low temperatures around the point of leakage. Such a leakage will be particularly dangerous when the leakage is in the liquid phase from a container where very low temperatures will be experienced. The emergency team should avoid contact with liquefied gases if at all possible.

12.3.5   Oxidizing gases can react violently with a number of organic materials. These reactions can generate heat, produce flammable gases and are liable to ignite combustible materials.

12.4   Flammable liquids – class 3

12.4.1   The release of a vaporized flammable liquid is the preliminary step leading to a potential *Vapour Cloud Explosion* (VCE). For a blast to take place, the vapour has to mix with air in a quantity that will allow the mixture to form a cloud. As soon as a friction (electrostatic potential) lies within the explosive range and encounters an ignition source, a flash fire, a deflagration or, sometimes, even a detonation may occur, with devastating consequences. Water spray will reduce the vaporization and the ignition potential of the cloud. Keep away all sources of ignition (see SPILLAGE SCHEDULE S-D).

12.4.2   At high concentrations, many flammable liquids exhibit a narcotic effect (which is not labelled accordingly), a short-term potentially lethal effect (which is identified by a class 6.1 label) or a long-term toxic effect (not labelled). In all cases, the use of self-contained breathing apparatus is therefore recommended (see SPILLAGE SCHEDULE S-D).

12.4.3   Some flammable liquids are corrosive to human skin, the ship's hull or normal personal protection equipment. Their vapours are toxic by inhalation. Therefore, washing of spillages and forcing vapours overboard with water spray is the method of choice. It is important to close all ventilation to protect the accommodation and machinery spaces and the bridge from the vapours. Crew members should stay away from any effluent (see SPILLAGE SCHEDULE S-C).

12.4.4   Many flammable liquids are not soluble in water and will float on the water (e.g., mineral oil, gas oil, petroleum). In general, high concentrations of these substances are not lethal but exhibit a narcotic effect. The crew should be aware of that and stay away from highly concentrated vapours. Mineral oil is considered to be a marine pollutant although not classified nor labelled as such. Depending on the quantities, oil spilt into the sea may cause problems and is usually given a high profile by the media. In case of spillage on board, the dominating hazard is flammability. Keep away all sources of ignition (see SPILLAGE SCHEDULE S-E).

12.5   Flammable solids – class 4

12.5.1   This class contains many different substances and varying hazards within its three sub-classes. Many are not solids. Some of these materials require special agents to be used for cleaning/absorbing as they react unfavourably with water, sand or other inert material. The procedures and materials to be used in case of a spillage are identified in ten different schedules.

12.5.2   Spilled flammable solids may create an explosive atmosphere that could be ignited easily. Whereas some solids (e.g., articles) can be repacked (see SPILLAGE SCHEDULE S-I), others will contaminate ships' surfaces, which have to be cleaned thoroughly by washing the substances overboard (see SPILLAGE SCHEDULE S-G).

12.5.3   A few flammable substances are transported in a molten state. To clean contaminated areas, the use of inert materials is possible to enable the emergency team to shovel up the spillage and dispose of it overboard (see SPILLAGE SCHEDULE S-H).

12.5.4   Flammable solids that exhibit explosive properties when spilt from a package should be kept wet and disposed of overboard. Drying material being ignited (e.g., by heat or friction) would lead to a detonation (see SPILLAGE SCHEDULE S-J).

12.5.5   Temperature-controlled self-reactive substances are also classified as flammable solids under class 4.1. Spillage is often connected to a failure of temperature control, leading to chemical reaction and creating a fire hazard. If not disposed of overboard, the relevant FIRE SCHEDULE should be consulted (see SPILLAGE SCHEDULE S-K).

12.5.6   Some spontaneously combustible substances could react with water (see SPILLAGE SCHEDULE S-L). Smothering with dry inert material and the immediate disposal overboard could limit the ignition hazard. Others will ignite within minutes (see SPILLAGE SCHEDULE S-M) and fire fighting will be necessary (see FIRE SCHEDULE F-G).

12.5.7 Depending on the chemical properties, substances which are dangerous when wet (class 4.3) could be collected and disposed of overboard (see SPILLAGE SCHEDULE S-P), or could be kept dry and disposed of overboard or could be washed overboard with copious quantities of water even though a reaction with water will occur (see SPILLAGE SCHEDULES S-N and S-O). The use of water spray is recommended in case of the development of flammable gases (see SPILLAGE SCHEDULE S-O).

12.5.8 Many flammable solids, substances liable to spontaneous combustion and most substances that are dangerous when wet are hazardous to health by skin contact or by inhalation of dust. The use of self-contained breathing apparatus and appropriate chemical protection (e.g., chemical suit) is therefore recommended in all cases.

12.6 Oxidizing substances and organic peroxides – class 5

12.6.1 Dangerous goods of class 5 contain oxygen, and some will ignite combustible material on contact. In general, contact with substances of class 5 will be harmful to the skin, eyes and mucous membranes. The use of self-contained breathing apparatus and appropriate chemical protection (e.g., chemical suit) is therefore recommended.

12.6.2 Spilled oxidizing substances (class 5.1) could ignite combustible material or destroy materials (e.g., personal protection) by their chemical reactivity. Such spillages should be washed overboard. All crew members should stay away from effluent (see SPILLAGE SCHEDULE S-Q).

12.6.3 Organic peroxides (class 5.2) are highly reactive and some may explode when ignited. Class 5.2 liquids are flammable liquids which should be kept away from all sources of ignition. These substances will instantly destroy eyes. Some substances are transported under temperature control which is necessary to prevent reaction (mostly noticed as smoke evolution) and development of heat which may lead to fire (see SPILLAGE SCHEDULE S-R).

12.7 Toxic and infectious substances – class 6

12.7.1 The effects of toxic substances (class 6.1) may appear at once during exposure to them or may be delayed until after exposure. Inhalation is the major route for vapours, gases, mists and dusts. Skin and eye contact is of concern for the emergency team. The use of self-contained breathing apparatus and appropriate chemical protection (e.g., chemical suit) is recommended in all cases. Vapours of toxic liquids may fill an area of the ship or a space with a toxic atmosphere. Therefore, in case of vapour development, it is important to shut off, close and seal off all ventilation leading to accommodation and machinery spaces and the bridge (See SPILLAGE SCHEDULE S-A).

12.7.2 Some toxic substances are also flammable. In this case, the safety advice for both flammable and toxic liquids should be followed (see SPILLAGE SCHEDULE S-D).

12.7.3 In case of spillage of toxic substances, be prepared to use the *MFAG*.

12.7.4 The substances of class 6.2 are infectious, biological products, diagnostic specimens, clinical waste, etc. In case of spillage of such substances, different types of a biohazard may develop. Some spilled goods of class 6.2 could create illness of crew members after skin contact or inhalation. Whereas washing overboard is advised for on-deck spillage, waiting for expert ADVICE is recommended for under-deck spillages. Any skin contact or inhalation of mists or dusts should be avoided. Expert ADVICE is particularly important in respect of exposure risk, decontamination methods and reporting procedures (see SPILLAGE SCHEDULE S-T).

12.7.5 Most toxic substances and many infectious substances are also toxic to marine animals. Consult safety data sheets or experts for individual properties if needed.

12.8 Radioactive material – class 7

12.8.1 Many radioactive materials are transported in packages designed to retain their containment and shielding under accident conditions. Failure of the containment resulting in spillage that could be a significant hazard to personnel would only be expected under very severe conditions. Damp surfaces on undamaged or slightly damaged packages are seldom an indication of packaging failure. If a packaging of radioactive material appears to have leaked its accidental contents, expert ADVICE should be sought.

12.8.2 Some packages may have both a class 7 label and other hazard labels. Such additional hazards may be greater than the radiation hazard. In that case, actions as specified in the applicable SPILLAGE SCHEDULES should be followed.

12.8.3 Although radiation monitors are not required by regulation on board ships, applicable relevant provisions on segregation, separation or radiation protection programme (e.g., paragraphs 1.1.3.2 and 7.2.9.7 of the IMDG Code) or the INF Code may require monitors on board. For ships carrying radiation monitoring equipment, monitoring the extent of contamination is possible.

12.8.4 Spillage may constitute a release of any solid, liquid or gaseous radioactive material from its packaging. Personal protection material and equipment on board cannot generally provide protection against the health effects of penetrating ionizing radiation. Therefore, to protect personnel from the potential effects of radiation from spilled cargo (which may include the release from the packaging of special form radioactive material), two parameters are important when responding to spillages of these materials: TIME and DISTANCE. Entry of personnel into the area involving the spill of radioactive material should be limited to the shortest time possible, and the distance between the spillage and any personnel should be maximized. In addition, radiation contamination of personnel by inhalation, ingestion or skin contact should be of concern, and appropriate protective actions should be taken (protective clothing and self-contained breathing apparatus is recommended in all cases) (see SPILLAGE SCHEDULE S-S).

12.9 **Corrosive substances – class 8**

12.9.1 Corrosive solids and liquids can permanently damage human tissue. Some substances may corrode steel and destroy other materials (e.g., personal protection equipment). Corrosive vapours are highly toxic, often lethal by destroying lung tissue. All corrosive chemicals will be dangerous to human health (toxic). Avoid direct contact with the skin, protect against inhalation of vapours or mists. The use of self-contained breathing apparatus and appropriate chemical protection (e.g., chemical suit) is recommended in all cases. Washing spillages and forcing vapours overboard with water spray is the method in all cases. It is important to shut off, close and secure all ventilation leading into the accommodation of choice, machinery spaces and the bridge. All personnel should stay away from effluent (see SPILLAGE SCHEDULE S-B).

12.9.2 Some corrosive substances are also flammable. In these cases, the safety advice for both flammable and corrosive substances should be followed. Use of copious quantities of water and water spray is recommended. In general, the flammability hazard is more important than the corrosive properties for the safety of the ship and the crew (see e.g., SPILLAGE SCHEDULES S-C and S-G).

12.10 **Miscellaneous dangerous substances and articles – class 9**

This class contains miscellaneous dangerous substances that do not fit easily under the criteria for other hazard classes. Nonetheless, these substances represent hazards. There are no common properties that apply to all goods of this class. They have been allocated to the relevant EmS SPILLAGE SCHEDULE according to their hazards in the event of a spillage.

12.11 **Marine pollutants**

12.11.1 A number of substances within all classes have also been designated as marine pollutants because they are hazardous to marine life. Packages containing these substances will bear a Marine Pollutant mark.

12.11.2 In the case of spillage, it is important to be aware that any marine pollutant which is washed overboard will pollute the sea and must therefore be reported in accordance with the Reporting Procedures by the fastest tele-communication channel available with the highest possible priority to the nearest coastal State (see Reporting Procedures).

12.11.3 It is, however, more important to ensure the safety of the crew and the integrity of the laden ship, rather than to prevent pollution of the sea by marine pollutants.

General guidelines for SPILLAGE

- Think of safety first!
- Avoid any contact with dangerous substances. Do not walk through spilled liquids or dust (solids).
- Keep away from vapours or gases.
- Sound alarm.
- Keep the bridge and living quarters upwind if possible.
- Wear full protective clothing resistant to chemical attack and self-contained breathing apparatus.
- Locate stowage position of leaking cargo.
- Identify cargo.
- Obtain UN Numbers and the EmS SPILLAGE SCHEDULE of dangerous goods involved.
- Consider which measures of the EmS SPILLAGE SCHEDULE are applicable and should be followed.
- Be prepared to use the *Medical First Aid Guide (MFAG).*
- Contact the designated person of the company responsible for the operation of the ship to obtain expert advice on dangerous goods emergency response measures.

Precaution: Contamination of the skin with any dangerous goods should be removed and washed immediately.

Emergency Schedules for SPILLAGE

SPILLAGE SCHEDULE Alfa

S–A
TOXIC SUBSTANCES

General comments		Wear suitable protective clothing and self-contained breathing apparatus. Avoid contact, even when wearing protective clothing. Stop leak if practicable. Contaminated clothing should be washed off with water and then removed.
Spillage on deck	Packages (small spillage)	Wash overboard with copious quantities of water. Do not direct water jet straight onto the spillage. Keep clear of effluent. Clean the area thoroughly.
	Cargo Transport Units (large spillage)	Keep bridge and living quarters upwind. Wash overboard with copious quantities of water. Do not direct water jet straight onto the spillage. Keep clear of effluent. Clean the area thoroughly.
Spillage under deck	Packages (small spillage)	Do not enter space without self-contained breathing apparatus. Check atmosphere before entering (toxicity and explosion hazard). If atmosphere cannot be checked, do not enter. Let vapours evaporate. Keep clear. *Liquids:* Provide good ventilation of the space. Restrict flow of liquid to an enclosed area (e.g., by barricading with inert material or cement if available). *Solids:* Collect spillage. Dispose of overboard. Otherwise, keep clear. Radio for expert ADVICE.
	Cargo Transport Units (large spillage)	Keep clear. Radio for expert ADVICE. After hazard evaluation by experts, you may proceed. Provide adequate ventilation. Do not enter space without self-contained breathing apparatus. Check atmosphere before entering (toxicity and explosion hazard). If atmosphere cannot be checked, do not enter. Let vapour evaporate, keep clear. Where the ventilation system is used, particular attention should be taken to prevent toxic vapours or fumes entering occupied areas of the ship, e.g., living quarters, machinery spaces, working areas. *Liquids:* Provide good ventilation of the space. Wash down to the bottom of the hold. Pump overboard. *Solids:* Collect spillage. Keep spilt solids dry and cover with plastic sheet. Dispose of overboard. Otherwise, close hatches. Wait until the ship arrives in port.
Special cases: Marine Pollutant Mark		Keep disposal overboard as low as possible. Dilute with copious quantities of water. Report incident according to MARPOL reporting requirements.

SPILLAGE SCHEDULE Bravo

S–B
CORROSIVE SUBSTANCES

General comments		Wear suitable protective clothing and self-contained breathing apparatus. Avoid contact, even when wearing protective clothing. Keep clear of effluent. Keep clear of evolving vapours. Even short-time inhalation of small quantities of vapour can cause breathing difficulties. Use of water on the substance may cause a violent reaction and produce toxic vapours. Substance may damage ship's construction materials. Contaminated clothing should be washed off with water and then removed.
Spillage on deck	**Packages (small spillage)**	Wash overboard with copious quantities of water. Do not direct water jet straight onto the spillage. Keep clear of effluent. Clean the area thoroughly.
	Cargo Transport Units (large spillage)	Keep bridge and living quarters upwind. Protect crew and living quarters against corrosive or toxic vapours by using water spray to drive vapours away. Wash overboard with copious quantities of water. Do not direct water jet straight onto the spillage. Keep clear of effluent. Clean the area thoroughly.
Spillage under deck	**Packages (small spillage)**	Provide adequate ventilation. Do not enter space without self-contained breathing apparatus. Check atmosphere before entering (toxicity and explosion hazard). If atmosphere cannot be checked, do not enter. Let vapour evaporate. Keep clear. *Liquids:* Provide good ventilation of the space. Wash down to the bottom of the hold. Use copious quantities of water. Pump overboard. *Solids:* Collect spillage. Dispose overboard. Wash residues down to the bottom of the hold. Use copious quantities of water. Pump overboard.
	Cargo Transport Units (large spillage)	Keep bridge and living quarters upwind. Protect crew and living quarters against corrosive or toxic vapours by using water spray to drive vapours away. Do not enter space. Keep clear. Radio for expert ADVICE. After hazard evaluation by experts, you may proceed. Provide adequate ventilation. Do not enter space without self-contained breathing apparatus. Check atmosphere before entering (toxicity and explosion hazard). If atmosphere cannot be checked, do not enter. Let vapours evaporate, keep clear. Where a ventilation system is used, particular attention should be taken in order to prevent toxic vapours or fumes entering occupied areas of the ship, e.g., living quarters, machinery spaces, working areas. *Liquids:* Provide good ventilation of the space. Wash down to the bottom of the hold. Use copious quantities of water. Pump overboard. *Solids:* Collect spillage. Dispose overboard. Wash residues down to the bottom of the hold. Use copious quantities of water. Pump overboard.
Special cases: **Marine Pollutant Mark** **UN 2802, UN 2809**		Report incident according to MARPOL reporting requirements. No reaction with water. Not highly corrosive to protective clothing. Collect spillages if practicable. Try to avoid disposal overboard. Radio for expert ADVICE.

SPILLAGE SCHEDULE Charlie

S-C
FLAMMABLE, CORROSIVE LIQUIDS

General comments		Wear suitable protective clothing and self-contained breathing apparatus. Avoid contact, even when wearing protective clothing. Keep clear of effluent. Keep clear of evolving vapours. Even short-time inhalation of small quantities of vapour can cause breathing difficulties. Use of water on the substance may cause violent reaction and produce toxic vapours. Substance may damage the ship's construction materials. Spillage or reaction with water may evolve flammable vapours. Avoid all sources of ignition (e.g., naked lights, unprotected light bulbs, electric handtools, friction). Contaminated clothing must be washed off with water and then removed.
Spillage on deck	Packages (small spillage)	Wash overboard with copious quantities of water. Do not direct water jets straight onto the spillage. Keep clear of effluent. Clean the area thoroughly.
	Cargo Transport Units (large spillage)	Keep bridge and living quarters upwind. Protect crew and living quarters against corrosive or toxic vapours by using water spray to drive vapours away. Wash overboard with copious quantities of water. Do not direct water jets straight onto the spillage. Keep clear of effluent. Clean the area thoroughly.
Spillage under deck	Packages (small spillage)	Provide adequate ventilation. Do not enter deck without self-contained breathing apparatus. Check atmosphere before entering (toxicity and explosion hazard). If atmosphere cannot be checked, do not enter. Let vapours evaporate, keep clear. *Liquids:* Provide good ventilation of the space. Use water spray on effluent in hold to avoid ignition of flammable vapours. Wash down to the bottom of the hold. Use copious quantities of water. Pump overboard. *Solids:* Collect spillage. Dispose overboard. Wash residues down to the bottom of the hold. Use copious quantities of water. Pump overboard.
	Cargo Transport Units (large spillage)	Keep bridge and living quarters upwind. Protect crew and living quarters against corrosive or toxic vapours by using water spray to drive vapours away. Do not enter space. Keep clear. Radio for expert ADVICE. After hazard evaluation by experts, you may proceed. Provide adequate ventilation. Do not enter space without self-contained breathing apparatus. Check atmosphere before entering (toxicity and explosion hazard). If atmosphere cannot be checked, do not enter. Let vapours evaporate, keep clear. Where a ventilation system is used, particular attention should be taken in order to prevent toxic vapours or fumes entering occupied areas of the ship, e.g., living quarters, machinery spaces, working areas. *Liquids:* Provide good ventilation of the space. Use water spray on effluent to avoid ignition of flammable vapours. Wash down to the bottom of the hold. Use copious quantities of water. Pump overboard. *Solids:* Collect spillage. Dispose overboard. Wash residues down to the bottom of the hold. Use copious quantities of water. Pump overboard.
Special cases:		
Marine Pollutant Mark		Report incident according to MARPOL reporting requirements.
UN 2029, 2030 (if flammable)		Self-ignition of spilt material is possible.

SPILLAGE SCHEDULE Delta

S–D
FLAMMABLE LIQUIDS

General comments		Wear suitable protective clothing and self-contained breathing apparatus. Avoid all sources of ignition (e.g., naked lights, unprotected light bulbs, electric handtools, friction). Stop leak if practicable. Avoid contact, even when wearing protective clothing. Spillage may evolve flammable vapours. Contaminated clothing must be washed off with water and then removed.
Spillage on deck	Packages (small spillage)	Wash overboard with copious quantities of water. Do not direct water jet straight onto the spillage. Keep clear of effluent. Clean the area thoroughly.
	Cargo Transport Units (large spillage)	Keep bridge and living quarters upwind. Wash overboard with copious quantities of water. Do not direct water jet straight onto the spillage. Keep clear of effluent. Clean the area thoroughly.
Spillage under deck	Packages (small spillage)	Shut off all possible sources of ignition in the space. Provide adequate ventilation. Do not enter space without self-contained breathing apparatus. Check atmosphere before entering (toxicity and explosion hazard). If the atmosphere cannot be checked, do not enter. Let vapours evaporate, keep clear. Provide good ventilation of the space. Use water spray on effluent in hold to avoid ignition of flammable vapours. Wash down to the bottom of the hold. Pump overboard.
	Cargo Transport Units (large spillage)	Keep bridge and living quarters upwind. Protect crew and living quarters against corrosive or toxic vapours by using water spray to drive vapours away. Do not enter space. Keep clear. Radio for expert ADVICE. After hazard evaluation by experts, you may proceed. Provide adequate ventilation. Do not enter space without self-contained breathing apparatus. Check atmosphere before entering (toxicity and explosion hazard). If atmosphere cannot be checked, do not enter. Let vapour evaporate, keep clear. Where a ventilation system is used, particular attention should be taken in order to prevent toxic vapours or fumes entering occupied areas of the vessel, e.g., living quarters, machinery spaces, working areas. Provide good ventilation of the space. Use water spray on effluent in the space to avoid ignition of flammable vapours. Wash down to the bottom of the hold. Use copious quantities of water. Pump overboard.
Special cases:		
Marine Pollutant Mark		Report incident according to MARPOL reporting requirements.
UN 2749		Self-ignition of spilt material is possible.
UN 3359		This is a cargo transport unit under fumigation. When opened, it will be ventilated. However, experience has shown that toxic fumigants will stay within packaging material and in non-ventilated areas. Obtain information about the fumigation agent.

SPILLAGE SCHEDULE Echo

S-E
FLAMMABLE LIQUIDS, FLOATING ON WATER

General comments		Avoid sources of ignition (e.g., naked lights, unprotected light bulbs, electric handtools). Liquid is flammable and spillage may evolve flammable vapours. Wear suitable protective clothing and self-contained breathing apparatus. Stop leak if practicable. In general, substances covered under this schedule will have fuel-oil-like properties. They are immiscible with water and are liable to float on the surface of water. The use of inert absorbent material, as used in machinery spaces, is appropriate in all cases. For sticky liquids, shovels may be used, preferably shovels made of non-sparking or non-ferrous material. You may use light oil or soap-like products (surfactants) to clean small areas. Clean the area thoroughly because of the flammability hazard. Any pumping of spilled liquid overboard will create an oil spill on the sea surface. In this case, contact coastal authorities. Report discharge overboard according to MARPOL reporting requirements.
Spillage on deck	Packages (small spillage)	Collect spillage in oil drums, metal boxes or salvage packagings. You may use inert absorbent material.
	Cargo Transport Units (large spillage)	Restrict flow of leakage to an enclosed area (e.g., by diking with inert material or cement). Collect spillage in oil drums, metal boxes or salvage packagings. You may use inert absorbent material. Otherwise, wash overboard with copious quantities of water.
Spillage under deck	Packages (small spillage)	Shut off possible sources of ignition in the space. Provide adequate ventilation. Do not enter space without self-contained breathing apparatus. Check atmosphere before entering (toxicity and explosion hazard). If atmosphere cannot be checked, do not enter. Let vapours evaporate. Collect spillage in oil drums, metal boxes or salvage packagings. You may use inert absorbent material. Keep collected spillages in well ventilated areas or on deck only.
	Cargo Transport Units (large spillage)	Shut off possible sources of ignition in the space. Provide adequate ventilation. Do not enter deck without self-contained breathing apparatus. Check atmosphere before entering (toxicity and explosion hazard). If atmosphere cannot be checked, do not enter. Let vapours evaporate. Where a ventilation system is used, particular attention should be taken in order to prevent toxic vapours or fumes entering occupied areas of the ship, e.g., living quarters, machinery spaces, working areas. Provide good ventilation of the space. Use water spray on effluent in the space to avoid ignition of flammable vapours. Wash down to the bottom of the hold. Use copious quantities of water. Treat effluent according to Shipboard Oil Pollution Emergency Plan. Otherwise, radio for expert ADVICE.
Special cases: UN 1136, UN 1993		These substances may be miscible with water and hence not float on the surface. In this case, SPILLAGE SCHEDULE S–D will be appropriate.
UN 1139, UN 1263, UN 1866		No thorough cleaning of spillage site necessary. Residues will dry out and coat surfaces.

SPILLAGE SCHEDULE Foxtrot

S–F
WATER-SOLUBLE MARINE POLLUTANTS

General comments		Wear suitable protective clothing and self-contained breathing apparatus. Stop leak if practicable. Substances covered under this schedule will present a hazard to the marine environment. Try to avoid disposal overboard. The use of inert absorbent material, as used in machinery spaces, is appropriate in all cases. For sticky liquids, shovels may be used. Discharge of spilled substance overboard will damage the marine environment, including living resources of the sea. In this case, contact coastal authorities. Report discharge overboard according to MARPOL reporting requirements.
Spillage on deck	Packages (small spillage)	*Liquid:* Smother spillage with inert absorbent material. Collect spillage in oil drums, metal boxes or salvage packagings. *Solid:* Collect material.
	Cargo Transport Units (large spillage)	Restrict flow of leakage to an enclosed area (e.g., by barricading with inert material or cement if available). *Liquid:* Collect spillage in empty tanks, oil drums, metal boxes or salvage packagings. You may use inert absorbent material. *Solid:* Collect spillage in oil drums or metal boxes.
Spillage under deck	Packages (small spillage)	*Liquid:* Smother spillage with inert absorbent material. Collect spillage in oil drums, metal boxes or salvage packagings. *Solid:* Collect material.
	Cargo Transport Units (large spillage)	Restrict flow of leakage to an enclosed area (e.g., by barricading with inert material or cement if available). *Liquid:* Collect spillage in empty tanks, oil drums, metal boxes or salvage packagings. You may use inert absorbent material. *Solid:* Collect spillage in oil drums or metal boxes. Otherwise, wash down to the bottom of the hold. Use copious quantities of water. Treat effluent according to Shipboard Oil Pollution Emergency Plan.
Special cases: None.		

SPILLAGE SCHEDULE Golf

S–G
FLAMMABLE SOLIDS AND SELF-REACTIVE SUBSTANCES

General comments		Wear suitable protective clothing and self-contained breathing apparatus. Avoid all sources of ignition (e.g., naked lights, unprotected light bulbs, electric handtools, friction). Wear non-sparking footwear. Stop leak if practicable.
Spillage on deck	Packages (small spillage)	Wash overboard with copious quantities of water. Keep clear of effluent.
	Cargo Transport Units (large spillage)	
Spillage under deck	Packages (small spillage)	Do not enter space without self-contained breathing apparatus. Check atmosphere before entering (toxicity and explosion hazard). Collect and contain spillage if practicable. Dispose overboard. Collect spillage using soft brushes and plastic trays.
	Cargo Transport Units (large spillage)	Provide adequate ventilation. Do not enter space without self-contained breathing apparatus. Check atmosphere before entering (toxicity and explosion hazard). Collect and contain spillage if practicable. Dispose overboard. Collect spillage using soft brushes and plastic trays.
Special cases: None.		

SPILLAGE SCHEDULE Hotel

S–H
FLAMMABLE SOLIDS (MOLTEN MATERIAL)

General comments		Wear suitable protective clothing and self-contained breathing apparatus. Avoid all sources of ignition (e.g., naked lights, unprotected light bulbs, electric handtools, friction). Wear non-sparking footwear. Stop leak if practicable. Do not touch or walk on spilled material.
Spillage on deck	Packages (small spillage)	Smother with dry inert material. Dispose overboard.
	Cargo Transport Units (large spillage)	
Spillage under deck	Packages (small spillage)	
	Cargo Transport Units (large spillage)	
Special cases: None.		

IMDG CODE SUPPLEMENT *(Amdt. 34-08)*

SPILLAGE SCHEDULE India

S-I
FLAMMABLE SOLIDS (REPACKING POSSIBLE)

General comments		Wear suitable protective clothing and self-contained breathing apparatus. Avoid all sources of ignition (e.g., naked lights, unprotected light bulbs, electric handtools, friction). Wear non-sparking footwear. Stop leak if practicable.
Spillage on deck	Packages (small spillage)	Collect spillage and repack if practicable. Otherwise, wash overboard with copious quantities of water. Keep clear of effluent.
	Cargo Transport Units (large spillage)	
Spillage under deck	Packages (small spillage)	Collect spillage and repack if practicable.
	Cargo Transport Units (large spillage)	
Special cases: None.		

SPILLAGE SCHEDULE Juliet

S–J
WETTED EXPLOSIVES AND CERTAIN SELF-HEATING SUBSTANCES

General comments		Wear suitable protective clothing and self-contained breathing apparatus. Avoid all sources of ignition (e.g., naked lights, unprotected light bulbs, electric handtools, friction). Wear non-sparking footwear. Stop leak if practicable. Dried out material may explode if exposed to heat, flame, friction, or shock.
Spillage on deck	Packages (small spillage)	Keep spillage wet. Dispose of solid material overboard. Wash overboard with copious quantities of water. Keep clear of effluent.
	Cargo Transport Units (large spillage)	
Spillage under deck	Packages (small spillage)	Keep spillage wet. Collect and contain spillage if practicable. Dispose of overboard. Collect spillage using soft brushes and plastic trays.
	Cargo Transport Units (large spillage)	
Special cases: None.		

SPILLAGE SCHEDULE Kilo

S-K
TEMPERATURE-CONTROLLED SELF-REACTIVE SUBSTANCES

General comments		If smoke is observed, see FIRE SCHEDULE F-F. Check temperature reading if possible. If temperature is increasing: see FIRE SCHEDULE F-F. Wear suitable protective clothing and self-contained breathing apparatus. Avoid all sources of ignition (e.g., naked lights, unprotected light bulbs, electric handtools, friction). Wear non-sparking footwear.
Spillage on deck	Packages (small spillage)	Wash overboard with copious quantities of water. Keep clear of effluent.
	Cargo Transport Units (large spillage)	Wash overboard with copious quantities of water. Keep clear of effluent. Leave units closed.
Spillage under deck	Packages (small spillage)	Not applicable. According to the IMDG Code, under deck stowage not allowed. Radio for expert ADVICE.
	Cargo Transport Units (large spillage)	
Special cases: None.		

SPILLAGE SCHEDULE Lima

S–L
SPONTANEOUSLY COMBUSTIBLE, WATER-REACTIVE SUBSTANCES

General comments		Wear suitable protective clothing and self-contained breathing apparatus. Avoid all sources of ignition (e.g., naked lights, unprotected light bulbs, electric handtools, friction). Wear non-sparking footwear. DO NOT USE WATER.
Spillage on deck	Packages (small spillage)	Avoid getting water on spilled substances or inside cargo transport units. Smother with dry inert material. Dispose overboard immediately.
	Cargo Transport Units (large spillage)	
Spillage under deck	Packages (small spillage)	Not applicable. According to the IMDG Code, under deck stowage not allowed. Radio for expert ADVICE.
	Cargo Transport Units (large spillage)	
Special cases: UN 2210, UN 2968		These substances are allowed to be carried under deck. Take action as given for on deck stowage.

SPILLAGE SCHEDULE Mike

S–M
HAZARD OF SPONTANEOUS IGNITION

General comments		Substances covered by this schedule may ignite within five (5) minutes after contact with air. See fire-fighting guidance: FIRE SCHEDULE F–G.
Spillage on deck	Packages (small spillage)	
	Cargo Transport Units (large spillage)	
Spillage under deck	Packages (small spillage)	
	Cargo Transport Units (large spillage)	
Special cases: None.		

SPILLAGE SCHEDULE November

S–N
SUBSTANCES REACTING VIGOROUSLY WITH WATER

General comments		Wear suitable protective clothing and self-contained breathing apparatus. Avoid all sources of ignition (e.g., naked lights, unprotected light bulbs, electric handtools, friction). Wear non-sparking footwear. Stop leak if practicable.
Spillage on deck	Packages (small spillage)	If dry, contain and collect spillage if practicable. Dispose of overboard. Avoid contact with water except to wash residues overboard with copious quantities of water. Keep clear of effluent.
	Cargo Transport Units (large spillage)	
Spillage under deck	Packages (small spillage)	Provide adequate ventilation. Check atmosphere before entering space (toxicity and explosion hazards). If atmosphere cannot be checked, do not enter. Do not enter space without self-contained breathing apparatus. Keep dry. Collect spillages using soft brushes and plastic trays. *If dry*, collect and contain spillage if practicable. Dispose overboard. *If wet*, use inert absorbent material. Do not use combustible material. Dispose of overboard.
	Cargo Transport Units (large spillage)	
Special cases: None.		

SPILLAGE SCHEDULE Oscar

S–O
SUBSTANCES DANGEROUS WHEN WET (NON-COLLECTABLE ARTICLES)

General comments		Wear suitable protective clothing and self-contained breathing apparatus. Avoid all sources of ignition (e.g., naked lights, unprotected light bulbs, electric handtools, friction). Wear non-sparking footwear. Stop leak if practicable.
Spillage on deck	**Packages (small spillage)**	Wash overboard with copious quantities of water. Keep clear of effluent.
	Cargo Transport Units (large spillage)	
Spillage under deck	**Packages (small spillage)**	Do not enter space without self-contained breathing apparatus. *If dry*, collect and contain spillage if practicable. Keep dry. Dispose of overboard. Avoid contact with water except to wash residues with copious quantities of water. Keep clear of effluent. *If wet*, wash down to the bottom of the hold. Use copious quantities of water. Pump overboard. If gas is developing, provide good ventilation of the hold. Use water spray on effluent in hold to avoid ignition of flammable vapours.
	Cargo Transport Units (large spillage)	Do not enter space without self-contained breathing apparatus. *If dry*, collect and contain spillage if practicable. Keep dry. Dispose of overboard. Avoid contact with water except to wash residues with copious quantities of water. Keep clear of effluent. *If wet*, wash down to the bottom of the hold. Use copious quantities of water. Pump overboard. If gas is developing, provide good ventilation of the hold. Use water spray on effluent in hold to avoid ignition of flammable vapours. Where a ventilation system is used, particular attention should be taken in order to prevent toxic vapours or fumes entering occupied spaces of the ship, e.g., living quarters, machinery spaces, working areas.
Special cases:		
UN 1295		Beware of a highly flammable atmosphere.

SPILLAGE SCHEDULE Papa

S-P
SUBSTANCES DANGEROUS WHEN WET (COLLECTABLE ARTICLES)

General comments		Wear suitable protective clothing and self-contained breathing apparatus.
Spillage on deck	Packages (small spillage)	Contain and collect spillage if practicable. Dispose of overboard.
	Cargo Transport Units (large spillage)	
Spillage under deck	Packages (small spillage)	Provide adequate ventilation. Do not enter space without self-contained breathing apparatus. Contain and collect spillages if practicable. Dispose of overboard.
	Cargo Transport Units (large spillage)	
Special cases:		
UN 3257, UN 3258		Hot substance. No hazard when cool.
UN 3316		If FIRST AID KIT, collect articles and repack.
UN 3363		If DANGEROUS GOODS IN MACHINERY, collect articles and repack. Take care of hazardous properties according to transport documents or radio for expert ADVICE.

SPILLAGE SCHEDULE Quebec

S–Q
OXIDIZING SUBSTANCES

General comments		Wear suitable protective clothing and self-contained breathing apparatus. Avoid all sources of ignition (e.g., naked lights, unprotected light bulbs, electric handtools, friction). Wear non-sparking footwear. May ignite combustible material (e.g., wood, paper, clothing). Stop leak if practicable.
Spillage on deck	Packages (small spillage)	Wash overboard with copious quantities of water. Keep clear of effluent.
	Cargo Transport Units (large spillage)	
Spillage under deck	Packages (small spillage)	Do not enter space without self-contained breathing apparatus. *If dry*, contain and collect spillage if practicable. Dispose of overboard. *If wet*, use inert absorbent material. Do not use combustible material. *If liquid*, wash down to the bottom of the hold, using copious quantities of water. Pump overboard. Dispose of overboard.
	Cargo Transport Units (large spillage)	Provide adequate ventilation. Do not enter space without self-contained breathing apparatus. *If dry*, contain and collect spillage if practicable. Dispose of overboard. *If wet*, use inert absorbent material. Do not use combustible material. *If liquid*, wash down to the bottom of the hold, using copious quantities of water. Pump overboard. Dispose of overboard.
Special cases: None.		

SPILLAGE SCHEDULE Romeo

S-R
ORGANIC PEROXIDES

General comments		Wear suitable protective clothing and self-contained breathing apparatus. Contact of substance (or vapour) with eyes may cause blindness within minutes. Avoid all sources of ignition (e.g., naked lights, unprotected light bulbs, electric handtools, friction). Wear non-sparking footwear. Stop leak if practicable. Substances covered by this schedule are liable to explode by exposure to heat or ignition. In case of *smoke evolution*, see appropriate FIRE SCHEDULE. Radio for expert ADVICE or contact manufacturer.
Spillage on deck	Packages (small spillage)	Wash overboard with copious quantities of water. Keep clear of effluent. Collect damaged or leaking receptacles and dispose of overboard. Handle with care.
	Cargo Transport Units (large spillage)	
Spillage under deck	Packages (small spillage)	Not applicable. According to the IMDG Code, under deck stowage not allowed. Radio for expert ADVICE.
	Cargo Transport Units (large spillage)	
Special cases: None.		

S–S
RADIOACTIVE MATERIAL

General comments		Evacuate compartment or downwind area of non-essential personnel. Provide respiratory protection to personnel in downwind area. For ships carrying radiation monitoring equipment, measure radiation levels. In this case, assess the extent of contamination and resultant radiation level of the package, the adjacent areas and, if necessary, all other material which has been carried in the conveyance. Define a zone for restricted entry. Personnel should not enter this zone without suitable protective clothing and self-contained breathing apparatus. Limit entry of personnel to the restricted zone for the shortest time possible. Cover liquid spill with inert absorbent materials, if available. Cover powder spills with plastic sheet or tarpaulin to minimize spread. If exposure of personnel is suspected, clean body and hair with warm water and soap; discharge resultant washings directly overboard. Record the names of potentially exposed persons. Ensure medical examination of these persons after reaching any medical staff. Emergency procedures, if established for the ship or the specific cargo by relevant authorities or the shipper, should be followed. For ships carrying radiation monitoring equipment, continue monitoring the radiation levels. Radio for expert ADVICE.
Spillage on deck	Packages (small spillage)	Wash spillages overboard with copious quantities of water. Keep clear of effluent. Packages damaged or leaking radioactive contents may be removed to an acceptable restricted access interim location. Isolate and sheet over. Do not remove packages from restricted access zone until approved by the competent authority.
	Cargo Transport Units (large spillage)	Let released gas escape. Keep clear. Use water spray to protect bridge, living quarters and personnel from precipitation of vapours (water curtain). Absorb liquid spillage, where practicable, using absorbent material. Isolate and sheet over. Packages damaged or leaking radioactive contents may be removed to an acceptable restricted access interim location. Isolate and sheet over. Do not remove packages from restricted access zone until approved by the competent authority. Wash residues of liquids or solids overboard with copious quantities of water (use spray nozzles). Do not allow water to enter receptacles.
Spillage under deck	Packages (small spillage)	Provide adequate ventilation. Let released gas escape, keep clear. Where a ventilation system is used, particular attention should be taken in order to prevent radioactive vapours or fumes entering occupied areas of the ship, e.g., living quarters, machinery spaces, working areas. Keep solids dry. Absorb liquid spillage, where practicable, using inert absorbent material. Isolate and sheet over. Packages damaged or leaking radioactive contents may be removed to an acceptable restricted access interim location. Isolate and sheet over. Do not remove packages from restricted access zone until approved by the competent authority. Keep working period of emergency team in space as short as possible.
	Cargo Transport Units (large spillage)	Do not enter space. Radio for expert ADVICE. *If liquid, or vapour is developing:* Where a ventilation system is used, particular attention should be taken in order to prevent radioactive vapours entering occupied areas of the ship, e.g., living quarters, machinery spaces, working areas. Use water spray to protect bridge, living quarters and personnel from precipitation of vapours evolving from the hold (water curtain).

S-S
RADIOACTIVE MATERIAL

Special cases:	
UN 2977, UN 2978	Avoid contact, even when wearing protective clothing. Keep clear of evolving vapours. Even short-time inhalation of small quantities of vapour can cause breathing difficulties. Bear in mind that gases are heavier than air. Measures should be taken to prevent leaking gases from penetrating into any other part of the ship. Keep bridge and living quarters upwind. Protect crew and living quarters against corrosive and toxic vapours by using water spray to drive vapours away. Do not enter space without protective equipment. Keep clear. Radio for expert ADVICE.
UN 2919, UN 3331	For radioactive material, *transported under special arrangement*, use special precautions, operational controls or emergency procedures as specifically designated by the competent authorities in their approval certificates and declared by the shipper in its transport documents.
Subsidiary labels class 4.2 or class 4.3	These are pyrophoric substances, water will ignite the material. DO NOT USE WATER. Radio for expert ADVICE.
Restowing of packages **UN 2977, UN 3324,** **UN 3325, UN 3326,** **UN 3327, UN 3328,** **UN 3329, UN 3330,** **UN 3331**	Check package labels and transport documents to determine whether packages contain fissile material. Prior to any restowing of these packages, radio for expert ADVICE.

SPILLAGE SCHEDULE Tango

S-T
DANGEROUS GOODS WITH BIOHAZARD

General comments		Wear suitable protective clothing and self-contained breathing apparatus. Avoid handling leaking or damaged packages or keep handling to a minimum. Inform the public health, veterinary or other competent authority if persons or the marine environment might have been exposed. A competent authority to which actual or suspected leakage is reported should notify the authorities of any countries in which the goods may have been handled, including countries of transit. Radio for expert ADVICE. Notify consignor/consignee.
Spillage on deck	Packages (small spillage)	Stop leak if practicable. Collect potentially contaminated packages or equipment. Isolate and sheet over. Wash spillage or residues overboard with copious quantities of water. Keep clear of effluent. Clean contaminated area thoroughly using bleach-like products (like sodium hypochlorite 1–6% solution or Javel water). Keep clear of effluent.
	Cargo Transport Units (large spillage)	
Spillage under deck	Packages (small spillage)	Do not enter space.
	Cargo Transport Units (large spillage)	
Special cases: None.		

SPILLAGE SCHEDULE Uniform

S–U
GASES (FLAMMABLE, TOXIC OR CORROSIVE)

General comments		Spaces and areas where leakages or spillages have occurred should be evacuated downwind immediately. Take care: Flames may be invisible. Leaking gas may be extremely cold. Measures should be taken to prevent leaking gases from penetrating into any other part of the ship. Bear in mind that some gases are heavier than air or may otherwise accumulate in lower or non-ventilated parts of the ship. Ensure that there is no smoking or any other open fire on board unless the leak has been closed and all spaces have been ventilated. Particular attention should be taken in order to prevent gases drifting into occupied areas of the ship, e.g., living quarters, machinery spaces, working areas. Wear protective clothing suitable for gas protection and self-contained breathing apparatus. Avoid all sources of ignition (e.g., naked lights, unprotected light bulbs, electric handtools, friction). Wear non-sparking footwear. Even short inhalation of small quantities of gas can cause breathing difficulties. Keep clear of evolving gases. Avoid all skin contact. Let *spilt liquefied gas* evaporate. When in contact with cold liquefied gases, most materials become brittle and are likely to break without warning. Avoid all contact, even when wearing protective clothing. If practicable, protect ship's superstructure with copious quantities of water. Do not direct water jet onto the spill.
Spillage on deck	Packages (small spillage)	Let gas dissipate. Keep clear.
	Cargo Transport Units (large spillage)	Let gas dissipate. Keep bridge and living quarters upwind. Otherwise, protect crew and living quarters against flammable or toxic gases by using water spray to drive gases away (water curtain). **Spilt liquefied gas:** Use water jets from as far as practicable to accelerate evaporation, not directing them straight onto the spill.
Spillage under deck	Packages (small spillage)	Do not enter space. Provide adequate ventilation. Where a ventilation system is used, particular attention should be taken in order to prevent gases penetrating into other areas of the ship. Let gas evaporate. Keep clear. Radio for expert ADVICE. Check atmosphere before entering (toxicity and explosion hazard). Do not enter space without self-contained breathing apparatus.
	Cargo Transport Units (large spillage)	Do not enter space. Provide adequate ventilation. Where a ventilation system is used, particular attention should be taken in order to prevent gases drifting into other areas of the ship. Keep bridge and living quarters upwind. Otherwise, protect crew and living quarters against flammable or toxic gases by using water spray to drive gases away (water curtain). If practicable, use water spray to avoid ignition of flammable gases in the space. Radio for expert ADVICE. Check atmosphere before entering (toxicity and explosion hazard). Do not enter deck without self-contained breathing apparatus.
Special cases: UN 1001, UN 3374		Heated or roughly handled receptacles may explode even after several hours of being removed from external sources of heat. Cool for several hours by using water.
UN 1614		The gas is absorbed in a porous inert material, but will evaporate if the receptacle is damaged.

SPILLAGE SCHEDULE Victor

S–V
GASES (NON-FLAMMABLE, NON-TOXIC)

General comments		Measures should be taken to prevent leaking gases from penetrating into any other part of the ship. Bear in mind that some gases are heavier than air or may otherwise accumulate in lower or non-ventilated parts of the ship. Particular attention should be taken in order to prevent gases drifting into occupied areas of the ship, e.g., living quarters, machinery spaces, working areas. Leaking gas may be extremely cold. Wear suitable protective clothing and self-contained breathing apparatus (suffocation hazard). Let *spilt liquefied gas* evaporate. When in contact with cold liquefied gases, most materials become brittle and are likely to break without warning. Avoid all contact, even when wearing protective clothing. If practicable, protect ship's superstructure with copious quantities of water. Do not direct water jet onto the spill.
Spillage on deck	**Packages (small spillage)**	Let gas dissipate. Keep clear.
	Cargo Transport Units (large spillage)	Let gas dissipate. ***Spilt liquefied gas:*** Use water jets from as far as practicable to accelerate evaporation, not directing them straight onto the spill. Keep clear of evolving gases.
Spillage under deck	**Packages (small spillage)**	Provide adequate ventilation. Stop leak if practicable. Otherwise, let gas evaporate. Keep clear. Check atmosphere before entering space (suffocation hazard). Do not enter space without self-contained breathing apparatus.
	Cargo Transport Units (large spillage)	Provide adequate ventilation. Stop leak if practicable. Otherwise, let gas evaporate. Keep clear. ***Spilt liquefied gas:*** Use water jets from as far as practicable to accelerate evaporation, not directing them straight onto the spill. Check atmosphere before entering space (suffocation hazard). Do not enter space without self-contained breathing apparatus.
Special cases: UN 2990, UN 3072		No suffocation hazard. Collect articles and repack.

SPILLAGE SCHEDULE Whisky

S–W
OXIDIZING GASES

General comments		Areas containing leakages or spillages should be evacuated downwind immediately. These gases may ignite combustible material and enhance fire. Take care: Flames may be invisible. Leaking gas may be extremely cold. Measures should be taken to prevent leaking gases from penetrating into any other part of the ship. Ensure that there is no smoking or any other open fire on board unless the leak has been closed and all spaces have been ventilated. Particular attention should be taken in order to prevent gases drifting into occupied areas of the vessel, e.g., living quarters, machinery spaces, working areas. Wear suitable protective clothing and self-contained breathing apparatus. Avoid all sources of ignition (e.g., naked lights, unprotected light bulbs, electric handtools, friction). Wear non-sparking footwear. Even short inhalation of small quantities of gas can cause breathing difficulties. Keep clear of evolving gases. Avoid all skin contact. Let *spilt liquefied gas* evaporate. When in contact with cold liquefied gases, most materials become brittle and are likely to break without warning. Avoid all contact, even when wearing protective clothing. If practicable, protect ship's superstructure with copious quantities of water. Do not direct water jet onto the spill.
Spillage on deck	Packages (small spillage)	Let gas evaporate. Keep clear.
	Cargo Transport Units (large spillage)	Let gas evaporate. Keep bridge and living quarters upwind. Otherwise, protect crew and living quarters against flammable or toxic gases by using water spray to drive gases away (water curtain). **Spilt liquefied gas:** Use water jets from as far as practicable to accelerate evaporation, not directing them straight onto the spill.
Spillage under deck	Packages (small spillage)	Do not enter space. Provide adequate ventilation. Where a ventilation system is used, particular attention should be observed in order to prevent gases penetrating into other areas of the ship. Let gas evaporate. Keep clear. Radio for expert ADVICE. Check atmosphere before entering space (toxicity and explosion hazard). Do not enter space without self-contained breathing apparatus.
	Cargo Transport Units (large spillage)	Do not enter space. Provide adequate ventilation. Where a ventilation system is used, particular attention should be observed in order to prevent gases drifting into other areas of the ship. Keep bridge and living quarters upwind. Otherwise, protect crew and living quarters against gases by using water spray to drive gases away (water curtain). If practicable, use water spray to avoid ignition of gases in the space. Radio for expert ADVICE.
Special cases:		
UN 1003		This is compressed air. No inhalation or ignition hazard.
UN 1014, UN 1072, UN 1073		This is concentrated oxygen. No inhalation hazard in some distance from a leak. No skin irritation hazard.

IMDG CODE SUPPLEMENT *(Amdt. 34-08)*

S–X
EXPLOSIVE ITEMS AND ARTICLES

General comments		Avoid all sources of ignition (e.g., naked lights, unprotected light bulbs, electric handtools). **Electrostatic hazard:** Electric charge may ignite ammunition. Keep spilled material away from generators of static electricity (e.g., mobile phones, friction of synthetic polymers like PVC gloves). Wear non-sparking footwear.
Spillage on deck	Packages (small spillage)	**Articles:** Sweep or pick up articles. If the articles remain intact but appear damaged, separate out and radio for expert ADVICE. **Spilled substance:** Keep wet. Wash spillage overboard with copious quantities of water.
	Cargo Transport Units (large spillage)	
Spillage under deck	Packages (small spillage)	**Articles:** Sweep or pick up articles. If the articles remain intact but appear damaged, separate and radio for expert ADVICE. **Spilled substance:** Keep wet. Collect spillage where practicable. Dispose of overboard.
	Cargo Transport Units (large spillage)	
Special cases: None.		

EmS

SPILLAGE SCHEDULE Yankee

S–Y
EXPLOSIVE CHEMICALS

General comments		Avoid all sources of ignition (e.g., naked lights, unprotected light bulbs, electric handtools). Stop leak if practicable. *Electrostatic hazard:* Electric charge may ignite ammunition. Keep spilled material away from generators of static electricity (e.g., mobile phones, friction of synthetic polymers like PVC gloves). Wear non-sparking footwear. Some explosive mixtures are stabilized in such a way that water will separate explosives from the stabilizer, thus creating a higher risk. The explosive component becomes very sensitive to shock and heat. Radio for expert ADVICE.
Spillage on deck	Packages (small spillage)	*Articles:* Sweep or pick up articles. If the articles remain intact but appear damaged, separate out and ask for expert ADVICE. Wetted articles should be jettisoned. *Spilled substance:* Keep it under water. Wash spillages overboard with copious quantities of water.
	Cargo Transport Units (large spillage)	
Spillage under deck	Packages (small spillage)	*Articles:* Sweep or pick up articles. If the articles remain intact but appear damaged, separate out and radio for expert ADVICE. Wetted articles should be jettisoned. *Spilled substance:* Keep it under water. Collect spillages where practicable. Dispose of overboard.
	Cargo Transport Units (large spillage)	
Special cases: None.		

SPILLAGE SCHEDULE Zulu

S-Z
TOXIC EXPLOSIVES

<table>
<tr>
<td colspan="2">General comments</td>
<td>Wear suitable protective clothing and self-contained breathing apparatus.
Even short inhalation of small quantities of gas can cause breathing difficulties or lead to severe poisoning.
Avoid all sources of ignition (e.g., naked lights, unprotected light bulbs, electric handtools).
Electrostatic hazard: Electric charge may ignite ammunition. Keep spilled material away from generators of static electricity (e.g., mobile phones, friction of synthetic polymers like PVC gloves). Wear non-sparking footwear.
Particular attention should be taken in order to prevent developing gases drifting into occupied areas of the ship, e.g., living quarters, machinery, working areas.
Keep bridge and living quarters upwind. Otherwise, protect crew and living quarters against gases by using water spray to drive gases away (water curtain).
Radio for expert ADVICE.</td>
</tr>
<tr>
<td rowspan="2">Spillage on deck</td>
<td>Packages (small spillage)</td>
<td rowspan="2">Let vapours dissipate, keep clear.
Articles: Sweep or pick up articles. If the articles remain intact but appear damaged, separate out and ask for expert ADVICE.
Spilled substance: Keep wet. Wash spillage overboard with copious quantities of water. Keep clear of effluent.</td>
</tr>
<tr>
<td>Cargo Transport Units (large spillage)</td>
</tr>
<tr>
<td rowspan="2">Spillage under deck</td>
<td>Packages (small spillage)</td>
<td rowspan="2">Do not enter space without self-containing breathing apparatus. Check atmosphere before entering. Let vapours dissipate, keep clear.
Articles: Sweep or pick up articles. If the articles remain intact but appear damaged, separate out and ask for expert ADVICE.
Spilled substance: Keep wet. Collect spillages where practicable. Dispose of overboard.</td>
</tr>
<tr>
<td>Cargo Transport Units (large spillage)</td>
</tr>
<tr>
<td colspan="3">Special cases: None.</td>
</tr>
</table>

The EmS Guide – Index

Each current UN substance identification number (UN Number) is allocated to EmS Fire and Spillage Schedules as shown below. Underlined EmS codes (special cases) indicate a substance, material or article for which additional advice is given in the emergency response procedures.

UN No.	EmS Fire	EmS Spill		UN No.	EmS Fire	EmS Spill		UN No.	EmS Fire	EmS Spill
0004	F-B	S-Y		0078	F-B	S-Y		0167	F-B	S-X
0005	F-B	S-X		0079	F-B	S-Y		0168	F-B	S-X
0006	F-B	S-X		0081	F-B	S-Y		0169	F-B	S-X
0007	F-B	S-X		0082	F-B	S-Y		0171	F-B	S-X
0009	F-B	S-X		0083	F-B	S-Y		0173	F-B	S-X
0010	F-B	S-X		0084	F-B	S-Y		0174	F-B	S-X
0012	F-B	S-X		0092	F-B	S-X		0180	F-B	S-X
0014	F-B	S-X		0093	F-B	S-X		0181	F-B	S-X
0015	F-B	S-X		0094	F-B	S-Y		0182	F-B	S-X
0016	F-B	S-X		0099	F-B	S-X		0183	F-B	S-X
0018	F-B	S-Z		0101	F-B	S-X		0186	F-B	S-X
0019	F-B	S-Z		0102	F-B	S-X		0190	F-B	S-X
0020	F-B	S-Z		0103	F-B	S-X		0191	F-B	S-X
0021	F-B	S-Z		0104	F-B	S-X		0192	F-B	S-X
0027	F-B	S-Y		0105	F-B	S-X		0193	F-B	S-X
0028	F-B	S-Y		0106	F-B	S-X		0194	F-B	S-X
0029	F-B	S-X		0107	F-B	S-X		0195	F-B	S-X
0030	F-B	S-X		0110	F-B	S-X		0196	F-B	S-X
0033	F-B	S-X		0113	F-B	S-Y		0197	F-B	S-X
0034	F-B	S-X		0114	F-B	S-Y		0204	F-B	S-X
0035	F-B	S-X		0118	F-B	S-Y		0207	F-B	S-Y
0037	F-B	S-X		0121	F-B	S-X		0208	F-B	S-Y
0038	F-B	S-X		0124	F-B	S-X		0209	F-B	S-Y
0039	F-B	S-X		0129	F-B	S-Y		0212	F-B	S-X
0042	F-B	S-X		0130	F-B	S-Y		0213	F-B	S-Y
0043	F-B	S-X		0131	F-B	S-X		0214	F-B	S-Y
0044	F-B	S-X		0132	F-B	S-Y		0215	F-B	S-Y
0048	F-B	S-X		0133	F-B	S-Y		0216	F-B	S-Y
0049	F-B	S-X		0135	F-B	S-Y		0217	F-B	S-Y
0050	F-B	S-X		0136	F-B	S-X		0218	F-B	S-Y
0054	F-B	S-X		0137	F-B	S-X		0219	F-B	S-Y
0055	F-B	S-X		0138	F-B	S-X		0220	F-B	S-Y
0056	F-B	S-X		0143	F-B	S-Z		0221	F-B	S-X
0059	F-B	S-X		0144	F-B	S-Y		0222	F-B	S-Y
0060	F-B	S-X		0146	F-B	S-Y		0224	F-B	S-Z
0065	F-B	S-X		0147	F-B	S-Y		0225	F-B	S-X
0066	F-B	S-X		0150	F-B	S-Y		0226	F-B	S-Y
0070	F-B	S-X		0151	F-B	S-Y		0234	F-B	S-Z
0072	F-B	S-Y		0153	F-B	S-Y		0235	F-B	S-Y
0073	F-B	S-X		0154	F-B	S-Y		0236	F-B	S-Y
0074	F-B	S-Y		0155	F-B	S-Y		0237	F-B	S-X
0075	F-B	S-Y		0159	F-B	S-Y		0238	F-B	S-X
0076	F-B	S-Z		0160	F-B	S-Y		0240	F-B	S-X
0077	F-B	S-Z		0161	F-B	S-Y		0241	F-B	S-X

UN No.	EmS Fire	EmS Spill		UN No.	EmS Fire	EmS Spill		UN No.	EmS Fire	EmS Spill
0242	F-B	S-X		0315	F-B	S-X		0364	F-B	S-X
0243	F-B	S-X		0316	F-B	S-X		0365	F-B	S-X
0244	F-B	S-X		0317	F-B	S-X		0366	F-B	S-X
0245	F-B	S-X		0318	F-B	S-X		0367	F-B	S-X
0246	F-B	S-X		0319	F-B	S-X		0368	F-B	S-X
0247	F-B	S-X		0320	F-B	S-X		0369	F-B	S-X
0248	<u>F-B</u>	S-Y		0321	F-B	S-X		0370	F-B	S-X
0249	<u>F-B</u>	S-Y		0322	F-B	S-X		0371	F-B	S-X
0250	F-B	S-X		0323	F-B	S-X		0372	F-B	S-X
0254	F-B	S-X		0324	F-B	S-X		0373	F-B	S-X
0255	F-B	S-X		0325	F-B	S-X		0374	F-B	S-X
0257	F-B	S-X		0326	F-B	S-X		0375	F-B	S-X
0266	F-B	S-Y		0327	F-B	S-X		0376	F-B	S-X
0267	F-B	S-X		0328	F-B	S-X		0377	F-B	S-X
0268	F-B	S-X		0329	F-B	S-X		0378	F-B	S-X
0271	F-B	S-X		0330	F-B	S-X		0379	F-B	S-X
0272	F-B	S-X		0331	F-B	S-Y		0380	F-B	S-X
0275	F-B	S-X		0332	F-B	S-Y		0381	F-B	S-X
0276	F-B	S-X		0333	F-B	S-X		0382	F-B	S-X
0277	F-B	S-X		0334	F-B	S-X		0383	F-B	S-X
0278	F-B	S-X		0335	F-B	S-X		0384	F-B	S-X
0279	F-B	S-X		0336	F-B	S-X		0385	F-B	S-Y
0280	F-B	S-X		0337	F-B	S-X		0386	F-B	S-Y
0281	F-B	S-X		0338	F-B	S-X		0387	F-B	S-Y
0282	F-B	S-Y		0339	F-B	S-X		0388	F-B	S-Y
0283	F-B	S-X		0340	F-B	S-Y		0389	F-B	S-Y
0284	F-B	S-X		0341	F-B	S-Y		0390	F-B	S-Y
0285	F-B	S-X		0342	F-B	S-Y		0391	F-B	S-Y
0286	F-B	S-X		0343	F-B	S-Y		0392	F-B	S-Y
0287	F-B	S-X		0344	F-B	S-X		0393	F-B	S-Y
0288	F-B	S-X		0345	F-B	S-X		0394	F-B	S-Y
0289	F-B	S-X		0346	F-B	S-X		0395	F-B	S-X
0290	F-B	S-X		0347	F-B	S-X		0396	F-B	S-X
0291	F-B	S-X		0348	F-B	S-X		0397	F-B	S-X
0292	F-B	S-X		0349	F-B	S-X		0398	F-B	S-X
0293	F-B	S-X		0350	F-B	S-X		0399	F-B	S-X
0294	F-B	S-X		0351	F-B	S-X		0400	F-B	S-X
0295	F-B	S-X		0352	F-B	S-X		0401	F-B	S-Y
0296	F-B	S-X		0353	F-B	S-X		0402	F-B	S-Y
0297	F-B	S-X		0354	F-B	S-X		0403	F-B	S-X
0299	F-B	S-X		0355	F-B	S-X		0404	F-B	S-X
0300	F-B	S-X		0356	F-B	S-X		0405	F-B	S-X
0301	<u>F-B</u>	S-Z		0357	F-B	S-Y		0406	F-B	S-Y
0303	F-B	S-X		0358	F-B	S-Y		0407	F-B	S-Y
0305	F-B	S-Y		0359	F-B	S-Y		0408	F-B	S-X
0306	F-B	S-X		0360	F-B	S-X		0409	F-B	S-X
0312	F-B	S-X		0361	F-B	S-X		0410	F-B	S-X
0313	F-B	S-X		0362	F-B	S-X		0411	F-B	S-Y
0314	F-B	S-X		0363	F-B	S-X		0412	F-B	S-X

UN No.	EmS Fire	EmS Spill		UN No.	EmS Fire	EmS Spill		UN No.	EmS Fire	EmS Spill
0413	F-B	S-X		0465	F-B	S-X		1008	F-C	S-U
0414	F-B	S-X		0466	F-B	S-X		1009	F-C	S-V
0415	F-B	S-X		0467	F-B	S-X		1010	F-D	S-U
0417	F-B	S-X		0468	F-B	S-X		1011	F-D	S-U
0418	F-B	S-X		0469	F-B	S-X		1012	F-D	S-U
0419	F-B	S-X		0470	F-B	S-X		1013	F-C	S-V
0420	F-B	S-X		0471	F-B	S-X		1016	F-D	S-U
0421	F-B	S-X		0472	F-B	S-X		1017	F-C	S-U
0424	F-B	S-X		0473	F-B	S-Y		1018	F-C	S-V
0425	F-B	S-X		0474	F-B	S-Y		1020	F-C	S-V
0426	F-B	S-X		0475	F-B	S-Y		1021	F-C	S-V
0427	F-B	S-X		0476	F-B	S-Y		1022	F-C	S-V
0428	F-B	S-X		0477	F-B	S-Y		1023	F-D	S-U
0429	F-B	S-X		0478	F-B	S-Y		1026	F-D	S-U
0430	F-B	S-X		0479	F-B	S-Y		1027	F-D	S-U
0431	F-B	S-X		0480	F-B	S-Y		1028	F-C	S-V
0432	F-B	S-X		0481	F-B	S-Y		1029	F-C	S-V
0433	F-B	S-Y		0482	F-B	S-Y		1030	F-D	S-U
0434	F-B	S-X		0483	F-B	S-Y		1032	F-D	S-U
0435	F-B	S-X		0484	F-B	S-Y		1033	F-D	S-U
0436	F-B	S-X		0485	F-B	S-Y		1035	F-D	S-U
0437	F-B	S-X		0486	F-B	S-X		1036	F-D	S-U
0438	F-B	S-X		0487	F-B	S-X		1037	F-D	S-U
0439	F-B	S-X		0488	F-B	S-X		1038	<u>F-D</u>	S-U
0440	F-B	S-X		0489	F-B	S-Y		1039	F-D	S-U
0441	F-B	S-X		0490	F-B	S-Y		1040	F-D	S-U
0442	F-B	S-X		0491	F-B	S-X		1041	F-D	S-U
0443	F-B	S-X		0492	F-B	S-X		1043	F-C	S-V
0444	F-B	S-X		0493	F-B	S-X		1044	F-C	S-V
0445	F-B	S-X		0494	F-B	S-X		1045	F-C	S-W
0446	F-B	S-X		0495	F-B	S-Y		1046	F-C	S-V
0447	F-B	S-X		0496	F-B	S-Y		1048	F-C	S-U
0448	F-B	S-Y		0497	F-B	S-Y		1049	F-D	S-U
0449	F-B	S-X		0498	F-B	S-Y		1050	F-C	S-U
0450	F-B	S-X		0499	F-B	S-Y		1051	F-E	S-D
0451	F-B	S-X		0500	F-B	S-X		1052	F-C	S-U
0452	F-B	S-X		0501	F-B	S-X		1053	F-D	S-U
0453	F-B	S-X		0502	F-B	S-X		1055	F-D	S-U
0454	F-B	S-X		0503	F-B	S-X		1056	F-C	S-V
0455	F-B	S-X		0504	F-B	S-Y		1057	F-D	S-U
0456	F-B	S-X		0505	F-B	S-X		1058	F-C	S-V
0457	F-B	S-X		0506	F-B	S-X		1060	F-D	S-U
0458	F-B	S-X		0507	F-B	S-X		1061	F-D	S-U
0459	F-B	S-X		0508	F-B	S-Y		1062	F-C	S-U
0460	F-B	S-X		1001	<u>F-D</u>	<u>S-U</u>		1063	F-D	S-U
0461	F-B	S-X		1002	F-C	S-V		1064	F-D	S-U
0462	F-B	S-X		1003	<u>F-C</u>	S-W		1065	F-C	S-V
0463	F-B	S-X		1005	F-C	S-U		1066	F-C	S-V
0464	F-B	S-X		1006	F-C	S-V		1067	F-C	S-W

The EmS Guide

UN No.	EmS Fire	EmS Spill		UN No.	EmS Fire	EmS Spill		UN No.	EmS Fire	EmS Spill
1069	F-C	S-U		1136	F-E	S-E		1195	F-E	S-D
1070	F-C	S-W		1139	F-E	S-E		1196	F-E	S-C
1071	F-D	S-U		1143	F-E	S-D		1197	F-E	S-D
1072	F-C	S-W		1144	F-E	S-D		1198	F-E	S-C
1073	F-C	S-W		1145	F-E	S-D		1199	F-E	S-D
1075	F-D	S-U		1146	F-E	S-D		1201	F-E	S-D
1076	F-C	S-U		1147	F-E	S-D		1202	F-E	S-E
1077	F-D	S-U		1148	F-E	S-D		1203	F-E	S-E
1078	F-C	S-V		1149	F-E	S-D		1204	F-E	S-D
1079	F-C	S-U		1150	F-E	S-D		1206	F-E	S-D
1080	F-C	S-V		1152	F-E	S-D		1207	F-E	S-D
1081	F-D	S-U		1153	F-E	S-D		1208	F-E	S-D
1082	F-D	S-U		1154	F-E	S-C		1210	F-E	S-D
1083	F-D	S-U		1155	F-E	S-D		1212	F-E	S-D
1085	F-D	S-U		1156	F-E	S-D		1213	F-E	S-D
1086	F-D	S-U		1157	F-E	S-D		1214	F-E	S-C
1087	F-D	S-U		1158	F-E	S-C		1216	F-E	S-D
1088	F-E	S-D		1159	F-E	S-D		1218	F-E	S-D
1089	F-E	S-D		1160	F-E	S-C		1219	F-E	S-D
1090	F-E	S-D		1161	F-E	S-D		1220	F-E	S-D
1091	F-E	S-D		1162	F-E	S-C		1221	F-E	S-C
1092	F-E	S-D		1163	F-E	S-C		1222	F-E	S-D
1093	F-E	S-D		1164	F-E	S-D		1223	F-E	S-E
1098	F-E	S-D		1165	F-E	S-D		1224	F-E	S-D
1099	F-E	S-D		1166	F-E	S-D		1228	F-E	S-D
1100	F-E	S-D		1167	F-E	S-D		1229	F-E	S-D
1104	F-E	S-D		1169	F-E	S-D		1230	F-E	S-D
1105	F-E	S-D		1170	F-E	S-D		1231	F-E	S-D
1106	F-E	S-C		1171	F-E	S-D		1233	F-E	S-D
1107	F-E	S-D		1172	F-E	S-D		1234	F-E	S-D
1108	F-E	S-D		1173	F-E	S-D		1235	F-E	S-C
1109	F-E	S-D		1175	F-E	S-D		1237	F-E	S-D
1110	F-E	S-D		1176	F-E	S-D		1238	F-E	S-C
1111	F-E	S-D		1177	F-E	S-D		1239	F-E	S-D
1112	F-E	S-D		1178	F-E	S-D		1242	F-G	S-O
1113	F-E	S-D		1179	F-E	S-D		1243	F-E	S-D
1114	F-E	S-D		1180	F-E	S-D		1244	F-E	S-C
1120	F-E	S-D		1181	F-E	S-D		1245	F-E	S-D
1123	F-E	S-D		1182	F-E	S-C		1246	F-E	S-D
1125	F-E	S-C		1183	F-G	S-O		1247	F-E	S-D
1126	F-E	S-D		1184	F-E	S-D		1248	F-E	S-D
1127	F-E	S-D		1185	F-E	S-D		1249	F-E	S-D
1128	F-E	S-D		1188	F-E	S-D		1250	F-E	S-C
1129	F-E	S-D		1189	F-E	S-D		1251	F-E	S-C
1130	F-E	S-E		1190	F-E	S-D		1259	F-E	S-D
1131	F-E	S-D		1191	F-E	S-D		1261	F-E	S-D
1133	F-E	S-D		1192	F-E	S-D		1262	F-E	S-E
1134	F-E	S-D		1193	F-E	S-D		1263	F-E	S-E
1135	F-E	S-D		1194	F-E	S-D		1264	F-E	S-D

UN No.	EmS Fire	EmS Spill		UN No.	EmS Fire	EmS Spill		UN No.	EmS Fire	EmS Spill
1265	F-E	S-D		1328	F-A	S-G		1387	F-A	S-J
1266	F-E	S-D		1330	F-A	S-I		1389	F-G	S-N
1267	F-E	S-E		1331	F-A	S-I		1390	F-G	S-O
1268	F-E	S-E		1332	F-A	S-G		1391	F-G	S-N
1272	F-E	S-E		1333	F-G	S-P		1392	F-G	S-N
1274	F-E	S-D		1334	F-A	S-G		1393	F-G	S-N
1275	F-E	S-D		1336	F-B	S-J		1394	F-G	S-N
1276	F-E	S-D		1337	F-B	S-J		1395	F-G	S-N
1277	F-E	S-C		1338	F-A	S-G		1396	F-G	S-O
1278	F-E	S-D		1339	F-G	S-G		1397	F-G	S-N
1279	F-E	S-D		1340	F-G	S-N		1398	F-G	S-N
1280	F-E	S-D		1341	F-A	S-G		1400	F-G	S-O
1281	F-E	S-D		1343	F-G	S-G		1401	F-G	S-O
1282	F-E	S-D		1344	F-B	S-J		1402	F-G	S-N
1286	F-E	S-E		1345	F-A	S-I		1403	F-G	S-N
1287	F-E	S-D		1346	F-A	S-G		1404	F-G	S-O
1288	F-E	S-E		1347	F-B	S-J		1405	F-G	S-N
1289	F-E	S-C		1348	F-B	S-J		1407	F-G	S-N
1292	F-E	S-D		1349	F-B	S-J		1408	F-G	S-N
1293	F-E	S-D		1350	F-A	S-G		1409	F-G	S-L
1294	F-E	S-D		1352	F-A	S-J		1410	F-G	S-M
1295	F-G	S-O		1353	F-A	S-I		1411	F-G	S-M
1296	F-E	S-C		1354	F-B	S-J		1413	F-G	S-O
1297	F-E	S-C		1355	F-B	S-J		1414	F-G	S-N
1298	F-E	S-C		1356	F-B	S-J		1415	F-G	S-N
1299	F-E	S-E		1357	F-B	S-J		1417	F-G	S-N
1300	F-E	S-E		1358	F-G	S-J		1418	F-G	S-O
1301	F-E	S-D		1360	F-G	S-N		1419	F-G	S-N
1302	F-E	S-D		1361	F-A	S-J		1420	F-G	S-L
1303	F-E	S-D		1362	F-A	S-J		1421	F-G	S-L
1304	F-E	S-D		1363	F-A	S-J		1422	F-G	S-L
1305	F-E	S-C		1364	F-A	S-J		1423	F-G	S-N
1306	F-E	S-D		1365	F-A	S-J		1426	F-G	S-O
1307	F-E	S-D		1366	F-G	S-M		1427	F-G	S-O
1308	F-E	S-D		1369	F-A	S-J		1428	F-G	S-N
1309	F-G	S-G		1370	F-G	S-M		1431	F-A	S-L
1310	F-B	S-J		1372	F-A	S-J		1432	F-G	S-N
1312	F-A	S-I		1373	F-A	S-J		1433	F-G	S-N
1313	F-A	S-I		1374	F-A	S-J		1435	F-G	S-O
1314	F-A	S-I		1376	F-G	S-P		1436	F-G	S-O
1318	F-A	S-I		1378	F-H	S-M		1437	F-A	S-G
1320	F-B	S-J		1379	F-A	S-J		1438	F-A	S-Q
1321	F-B	S-J		1380	F-G	S-L		1439	F-H	S-Q
1322	F-B	S-J		1381	F-A	S-J		1442	F-H	S-Q
1323	F-G	S-G		1382	F-A	S-J		1444	F-A	S-Q
1324	F-A	S-I		1383	F-G	S-M		1445	F-H	S-Q
1325	F-A	S-G		1384	F-A	S-J		1446	F-A	S-Q
1326	F-A	S-J		1385	F-A	S-J		1447	F-H	S-Q
1327	F-A	S-I		1386	F-A	S-J		1448	F-H	S-Q

UN No.	EmS Fire	EmS Spill		UN No.	EmS Fire	EmS Spill		UN No.	EmS Fire	EmS Spill
1449	F-G	S-Q		1505	F-A	S-Q		1583	F-A	S-A
1450	F-H	S-Q		1506	F-H	S-Q		1585	F-A	S-A
1451	F-A	S-Q		1507	F-A	S-Q		1586	F-A	S-A
1452	F-H	S-Q		1508	F-H	S-Q		1587	F-A	S-A
1453	F-H	S-Q		1509	F-G	S-Q		1588	F-A	S-A
1454	F-A	S-Q		1510	F-H	S-Q		1589	F-C	S-U
1455	F-H	S-Q		1511	F-A	S-Q		1590	F-A	S-A
1456	F-H	S-Q		1512	F-A	S-Q		1591	F-A	S-A
1457	F-G	S-Q		1513	F-H	S-Q		1593	F-A	S-A
1458	F-H	S-Q		1514	F-H	S-Q		1594	F-A	S-A
1459	F-H	S-Q		1515	F-H	S-Q		1595	F-A	S-B
1461	F-H	S-Q		1516	F-G	S-Q		1596	F-A	S-A
1462	F-H	S-Q		1517	F-B	S-J		1597	F-A	S-A
1463	F-A	S-Q		1541	F-A	S-A		1598	F-A	S-A
1465	F-A	S-Q		1544	F-A	S-A		1599	F-A	S-A
1466	F-A	S-Q		1545	F-E	S-D		1600	F-A	S-A
1467	F-A	S-Q		1546	F-A	S-A		1601	F-A	S-A
1469	F-A	S-Q		1547	F-A	S-A		1602	F-A	S-A
1470	F-H	S-Q		1548	F-A	S-A		1603	F-E	S-D
1471	F-H	S-Q		1549	F-A	S-A		1604	F-E	S-C
1472	F-G	S-Q		1550	F-A	S-A		1605	F-A	S-A
1473	F-H	S-Q		1551	F-A	S-A		1606	F-A	S-A
1474	F-A	S-Q		1553	F-A	S-A		1607	F-A	S-A
1475	F-H	S-Q		1554	F-A	S-A		1608	F-A	S-A
1476	F-G	S-Q		1555	F-A	S-A		1611	F-A	S-A
1477	F-A	S-Q		1556	F-A	S-A		1612	F-C	S-U
1479	F-A	S-Q		1557	F-A	S-A		1613	F-A	S-A
1481	F-H	S-Q		1558	F-A	S-A		1614	F-A	S-U
1482	F-H	S-Q		1559	F-A	S-A		1616	F-A	S-A
1483	F-G	S-Q		1560	F-A	S-A		1617	F-A	S-A
1484	F-H	S-Q		1561	F-A	S-A		1618	F-A	S-A
1485	F-H	S-Q		1562	F-A	S-A		1620	F-A	S-A
1486	F-A	S-Q		1564	F-A	S-A		1621	F-A	S-A
1487	F-A	S-Q		1565	F-A	S-A		1622	F-A	S-A
1488	F-A	S-Q		1566	F-A	S-A		1623	F-A	S-A
1489	F-H	S-Q		1567	F-G	S-G		1624	F-A	S-A
1490	F-H	S-Q		1569	F-E	S-D		1625	F-A	S-A
1491	F-G	S-Q		1570	F-A	S-A		1626	F-A	S-A
1492	F-A	S-Q		1571	F-B	S-J		1627	F-A	S-A
1493	F-A	S-Q		1572	F-A	S-A		1629	F-A	S-A
1494	F-H	S-Q		1573	F-A	S-A		1630	F-A	S-A
1495	F-H	S-Q		1574	F-A	S-A		1631	F-A	S-A
1496	F-H	S-Q		1575	F-A	S-A		1634	F-A	S-A
1498	F-A	S-Q		1577	F-A	S-A		1636	F-A	S-A
1499	F-A	S-Q		1578	F-A	S-A		1637	F-A	S-A
1500	F-A	S-Q		1579	F-A	S-A		1638	F-A	S-A
1502	F-H	S-Q		1580	F-A	S-A		1639	F-A	S-A
1503	F-H	S-Q		1581	F-C	S-U		1640	F-A	S-A
1504	F-G	S-Q		1582	F-C	S-U		1641	F-A	S-A

UN No.	EmS Fire	EmS Spill		UN No.	EmS Fire	EmS Spill		UN No.	EmS Fire	EmS Spill
1642	F-A	S-A		1697	F-A	S-A		1753	F-A	S-B
1643	F-A	S-A		1698	F-A	S-A		1754	F-A	S-B
1644	F-A	S-A		1699	F-A	S-A		1755	F-A	S-B
1645	F-A	S-A		1700	F-A	S-G		1756	F-A	S-B
1646	F-A	S-A		1701	F-A	S-A		1757	F-A	S-B
1647	F-A	S-A		1702	F-A	S-A		1758	F-A	S-B
1648	F-E	S-D		1704	F-A	S-A		1759	F-A	S-B
1649	F-A	S-A		1707	F-A	S-A		1760	F-A	S-B
1649 (if flammable)	F-E	S-D		1708	F-A	S-A		1761	F-A	S-B
				1709	F-A	S-A		1762	F-A	S-B
1650	F-A	S-A		1710	F-A	S-A		1763	F-A	S-B
1651	F-A	S-A		1711	F-A	S-A		1764	F-A	S-B
1652	F-A	S-A		1712	F-A	S-A		1765	F-A	S-B
1653	F-A	S-A		1713	F-A	S-A		1766	F-A	S-B
1654	F-A	S-A		1714	F-G	S-N		1767	F-E	S-C
1655	F-A	S-A		1715	F-E	S-C		1768	F-A	S-B
1656	F-A	S-A		1716	F-A	S-B		1769	F-A	S-B
1657	F-A	S-A		1717	F-E	S-C		1770	F-A	S-B
1658	F-A	S-A		1718	F-A	S-B		1771	F-A	S-B
1659	F-A	S-A		1719	F-A	S-B		1773	F-A	S-B
1660	F-C	S-W		1722	F-E	S-C		1774	F-A	S-B
1661	F-A	S-A		1723	F-E	S-C		1775	F-A	S-B
1662	F-A	S-A		1724	F-E	S-C		1776	F-A	S-B
1663	F-A	S-A		1725	F-A	S-B		1777	F-A	S-B
1664	F-A	S-A		1726	F-A	S-B		1778	F-A	S-B
1665	F-A	S-A		1727	F-A	S-B		1779	F-E	S-C
1669	F-A	S-A		1728	F-A	S-B		1780	F-A	S-B
1670	F-A	S-A		1729	F-A	S-B		1781	F-A	S-B
1671	F-A	S-A		1730	F-A	S-B		1782	F-A	S-B
1672	F-A	S-A		1731	F-A	S-B		1783	F-A	S-B
1673	F-A	S-A		1732	F-A	S-B		1784	F-A	S-B
1674	F-A	S-A		1733	F-A	S-B		1786	F-A	S-B
1677	F-A	S-A		1736	F-A	S-B		1787	F-A	S-B
1678	F-A	S-A		1737	F-A	S-B		1788	F-A	S-B
1679	F-A	S-A		1738	F-A	S-B		1789	F-A	S-B
1680	F-A	S-A		1739	F-A	S-B		1790	F-A	S-B
1683	F-A	S-A		1740	F-A	S-B		1791	F-A	S-B
1684	F-A	S-A		1741	F-C	S-U		1792	F-A	S-B
1685	F-A	S-A		1742	F-A	S-B		1793	F-A	S-B
1686	F-A	S-A		1743	F-A	S-B		1794	F-A	S-B
1687	F-A	S-A		1744	F-A	S-B		1796 I	F-A	S-Q
1688	F-A	S-A		1745	F-A	S-B		1796 II	F-A	S-B
1689	F-A	S-A		1746	F-A	S-B		1798	F-A	S-B
1690	F-A	S-A		1747	F-E	S-C		1799	F-A	S-B
1691	F-A	S-A		1748	F-H	S-Q		1800	F-A	S-B
1692	F-A	S-A		1749	F-C	S-W		1801	F-A	S-B
1693	F-A	S-A		1750	F-A	S-B		1802	F-H	S-Q
1694	F-A	S-A		1751	F-A	S-B		1803	F-A	S-B
1695	F-E	S-C		1752	F-A	S-B		1804	F-A	S-B

UN No.	EmS Fire	EmS Spill		UN No.	EmS Fire	EmS Spill		UN No.	EmS Fire	EmS Spill
1805	F-A	S-B		1862	F-E	S-D		1941	F-A	S-A
1806	F-A	S-B		1863	F-E	S-E		1942	F-H	S-Q
1807	F-A	S-B		1865	F-E	S-D		1944	F-A	S-I
1808	F-A	S-B		1866	F-E	S-E		1945	F-A	S-I
1809	F-A	S-B		1868	F-A	S-G		1950	F-D	S-U
1810	F-A	S-B		1869	F-G	S-G		1951	F-C	S-V
1811	F-A	S-B		1870	F-G	S-O		1952	F-C	S-V
1812	F-A	S-A		1871	F-A	S-G		1953	F-D	S-U
1813	F-A	S-B		1872	F-A	S-Q		1954	F-D	S-U
1814	F-A	S-B		1873	F-A	S-Q		1955	F-C	S-U
1815	F-E	S-C		1884	F-A	S-A		1956	F-C	S-V
1816	F-E	S-C		1885	F-A	S-A		1957	F-D	S-U
1817	F-A	S-B		1886	F-A	S-A		1958	F-C	S-V
1818	F-A	S-B		1887	F-A	S-A		1959	F-D	S-U
1819	F-A	S-B		1888	F-A	S-A		1961	F-D	S-U
1823	F-A	S-B		1889	F-A	S-B		1962	F-D	S-U
1824	F-A	S-B		1891	F-A	S-A		1963	F-C	S-V
1825	F-A	S-B		1892	F-A	S-A		1964	F-D	S-U
1826 I	F-A	S-Q		1894	F-A	S-A		1965	F-D	S-U
1826 II	F-A	S-B		1895	F-A	S-A		1966	F-D	S-U
1827	F-A	S-B		1897	F-A	S-A		1967	F-C	S-U
1828	F-A	S-B		1898	F-A	S-B		1968	F-C	S-V
1829	F-A	S-B		1902	F-A	S-B		1969	F-D	S-U
1830	F-A	S-B		1903	F-A	S-B		1970	F-C	S-V
1831	F-A	S-B		1905	F-A	S-B		1971	F-D	S-U
1832	F-A	S-B		1906	F-A	S-B		1972	F-D	S-U
1833	F-A	S-B		1907	F-A	S-B		1973	F-C	S-V
1834	F-A	S-B		1908	F-A	S-B		1974	F-C	S-V
1835	F-A	S-B		1911	F-D	S-U		1975	F-C	S-W
1836	F-A	S-B		1912	F-D	S-U		1976	F-C	S-V
1837	F-A	S-B		1913	F-C	S-V		1977	F-C	S-V
1838	F-A	S-B		1914	F-E	S-D		1978	F-D	S-U
1839	F-A	S-B		1915	F-E	S-D		1982	F-C	S-V
1840	F-A	S-B		1916	F-E	S-D		1983	F-C	S-V
1841	F-A	S-B		1917	F-E	S-D		1984	F-C	S-V
1843	F-A	S-A		1918	F-E	S-E		1986	F-E	S-D
1845	F-C	S-V		1919	F-E	S-D		1987	F-E	S-D
1846	F-A	S-A		1920	F-E	S-E		1988	F-E	S-D
1847	F-A	S-B		1921	F-E	S-D		1989	F-E	S-D
1848	F-A	S-B		1922	F-E	S-C		1990	F-A	S-A
1849	F-A	S-B		1923	F-A	S-J		1991	F-E	S-D
1851	F-A	S-A		1928	F-G	S-L		1992	F-E	S-D
1854	F-G	S-M		1929	F-A	S-J		1993	F-E	S-E
1855	F-G	S-M		1931	F-A	S-J		1994	F-E	S-D
1856	F-A	S-J		1932	F-G	S-L		1999	F-E	S-E
1857	F-A	S-J		1935	F-A	S-A		2000	F-A	S-I
1858	F-C	S-V		1938	F-A	S-B		2001	F-A	S-I
1859	F-C	S-U		1939	F-A	S-B		2002	F-A	S-J
1860	F-D	S-U		1940	F-A	S-B		2004	F-G	S-M

UN No.	EmS Fire	EmS Spill		UN No.	EmS Fire	EmS Spill		UN No.	EmS Fire	EmS Spill
2005	F-G	S-M		2052	F-E	S-E		2215	F-A	S-B
2006	F-A	S-G		2052	F-E	S-E		2216	F-A	S-J
2008	F-G	S-M		2053	F-E	S-D		2217	F-A	S-J
2009	F-G	S-M		2054	F-E	S-C		2218	F-E	S-C
2010	F-G	S-O		2055	F-E	S-D		2219	F-E	S-D
2011	F-G	S-N		2056	F-E	S-D		2222	F-E	S-D
2012	F-G	S-N		2057	F-E	S-D		2224	F-A	S-A
2013	F-G	S-N		2058	F-E	S-D		2225	F-A	S-B
2014	F-H	S-Q		2059	F-E	S-D		2226	F-A	S-B
2015	F-H	S-Q		2067	F-H	S-Q		2227	F-E	S-D
2016	F-A	S-A		2071	F-H	S-Q		2232	F-A	S-A
2017	F-A	S-B		2073	F-C	S-U		2233	F-A	S-A
2018	F-A	S-A		2074	F-A	S-A		2234	F-E	S-D
2019	F-A	S-A		2075	F-A	S-A		2235	F-A	S-A
2020	F-A	S-A		2076	F-A	S-B		2236	F-A	S-A
2021	F-A	S-A		2077	F-A	S-A		2237	F-A	S-A
2022	F-A	S-B		2078	F-A	S-A		2238	F-E	S-D
2023	F-E	S-D		2079	F-A	S-B		2239	F-A	S-A
2024	F-A	S-A		2187	F-C	S-V		2240	F-A	S-B
2025	F-A	S-A		2188	F-D	S-U		2241	F-E	S-D
2026	F-A	S-A		2189	F-D	S-U		2242	F-E	S-D
2027	F-A	S-A		2190	F-C	S-W		2243	F-E	S-D
2028	F-A	S-B		2191	F-C	S-U		2244	F-E	S-D
2029	F-E	<u>S-C</u>		2192	F-D	S-U		2245	F-E	S-D
2030	F-A	S-B		2193	F-C	S-V		2246	F-E	S-D
2030 (if flammable)	F-E	S-C		2194	F-C	S-U		2247	F-E	S-E
				2195	F-C	S-U		2248	F-E	S-C
2031 I	F-A	S-Q		2196	F-C	S-U		2249	F-E	S-D
2031* II	F-A	S-Q		2197	F-C	S-U		2250	F-A	S-A
2031† II	F-A	S-B		2198	F-C	S-U		2251	F-E	S-D
2032	F-A	S-Q		2199	F-D	S-U		2252	F-E	S-D
2033	F-A	S-B		2200	F-D	S-U		2253	F-A	S-A
2034	F-D	S-U		2201	<u>F-C</u>	S-W		2254	F-A	S-I
2035	F-D	S-U		2202	F-D	S-U		2256	F-E	S-D
2036	F-C	S-V		2203	F-D	S-U		2257	F-G	S-N
2037	F-D	S-U		2204	F-D	S-U		2258	F-E	S-C
2038	F-A	S-A		2205	F-A	S-A		2259	F-A	S-B
2044	F-D	S-U		2206	F-A	S-A		2260	F-E	S-C
2045	F-E	S-D		2208	F-H	S-Q		2261	F-A	S-A
2046	F-E	S-D		2209	F-A	S-B		2262	F-A	S-B
2047	F-E	S-D		2210	F-G	<u>S-L</u>		2263	F-E	S-D
2048	F-E	S-D		2211	F-A	S-I		2264	F-E	S-C
2049	F-E	S-D		2212	F-A	S-A		2265	F-E	S-D
2050	F-E	S-D		2213	F-A	S-G		2266	F-E	S-C
2051	F-E	S-C		2214	F-A	S-B		2267	F-A	S-B

* Applies to NITRIC ACID other than red fuming, with at least 65% but with not more than 70% nitric acid.
† Applies to NITRIC ACID other than red fuming, with less than 65% nitric acid.

UN No.	EmS Fire	EmS Spill		UN No.	EmS Fire	EmS Spill		UN No.	EmS Fire	EmS Spill
2269	F-A	S-B		2320	F-A	S-B		2373	F-E	S-D
2270	F-E	S-C		2321	F-A	S-A		2374	F-E	S-D
2271	F-E	S-D		2322	F-A	S-A		2375	F-E	S-D
2272	F-A	S-A		2323	F-E	S-D		2376	F-E	S-D
2273	F-A	S-A		2324	F-E	S-D		2377	F-E	S-D
2274	F-A	S-A		2325	F-E	S-D		2378	F-E	S-D
2275	F-E	S-D		2326	F-A	S-B		2379	F-E	S-C
2276	F-E	S-C		2327	F-A	S-B		2380	F-E	S-D
2277	F-E	S-D		2328	F-A	S-A		2381	F-E	S-D
2278	F-E	S-D		2329	F-E	S-D		2382	F-E	S-D
2279	F-A	S-A		2330	F-E	S-E		2383	F-E	S-C
2280	F-A	S-B		2331	F-A	S-B		2384	F-E	S-D
2281	F-A	S-A		2332	F-E	S-D		2385	F-E	S-D
2282	F-E	S-D		2333	F-E	S-D		2386	F-E	S-C
2283	F-E	S-D		2334	F-E	S-D		2387	F-E	S-D
2284	F-E	S-D		2335	F-E	S-D		2388	F-E	S-D
2285	F-E	S-D		2336	F-E	S-D		2389	F-E	S-D
2286	F-E	S-D		2337	F-E	S-D		2390	F-E	S-D
2287	F-E	S-D		2338	F-E	S-D		2391	F-E	S-D
2288	F-E	S-D		2339	F-E	S-D		2392	F-E	S-D
2289	F-A	S-B		2340	F-E	S-D		2393	F-E	S-D
2290	F-A	S-A		2341	F-E	S-D		2394	F-E	S-D
2291	F-A	S-A		2342	F-E	S-D		2395	F-E	S-C
2293	F-E	S-D		2343	F-E	S-D		2396	F-E	S-D
2294	F-A	S-A		2344	F-E	S-D		2397	F-E	S-D
2295	F-E	S-D		2345	F-E	S-D		2398	F-E	S-D
2296	F-E	S-D		2346	F-E	S-D		2399	F-E	S-C
2297	F-E	S-D		2347	F-E	S-D		2400	F-E	S-D
2298	F-E	S-D		2348	F-E	S-D		2401	F-E	S-C
2299	F-A	S-A		2350	F-E	S-D		2402	F-E	S-D
2300	F-A	S-A		2351	F-E	S-D		2403	F-E	S-D
2301	F-E	S-D		2352	F-E	S-D		2404	F-E	S-D
2302	F-E	S-D		2353	F-E	S-C		2405	F-E	S-D
2303	F-E	S-D		2354	F-E	S-D		2406	F-E	S-D
2304	F-A	S-H		2356	F-E	S-D		2407	F-E	S-C
2305	F-A	S-B		2357	F-E	S-C		2409	F-E	S-D
2306	F-A	S-A		2358	F-E	S-D		2410	F-E	S-D
2307	F-A	S-A		2359	F-E	S-C		2411	F-E	S-D
2308	F-A	S-B		2360	F-E	S-D		2412	F-E	S-D
2309	F-E	S-D		2361	F-E	S-C		2413	F-E	S-D
2310	F-E	S-D		2362	F-E	S-D		2414	F-E	S-D
2311	F-A	S-A		2363	F-E	S-D		2416	F-E	S-D
2312	F-A	S-A		2364	F-E	S-D		2417	F-C	S-U
2313	F-E	S-D		2366	F-E	S-D		2418	F-C	S-U
2315	F-A	S-A		2367	F-E	S-D		2419	F-D	S-U
2316	F-A	S-A		2368	F-E	S-E		2420	F-C	S-U
2317	F-A	S-A		2370	F-E	S-D		2421	F-C	S-W
2318	F-A	S-J		2371	F-E	S-D		2422	F-C	S-V
2319	F-E	S-D		2372	F-E	S-D		2424	F-C	S-V

UN No.	EmS Fire	EmS Spill		UN No.	EmS Fire	EmS Spill		UN No.	EmS Fire	EmS Spill
2426	F-H	S-Q		2482	F-E	S-D		2547	F-G	S-Q
2427	F-H	S-Q		2483	F-E	S-D		2548	F-C	S-W
2428	F-H	S-Q		2484	F-E	S-D		2552	F-A	S-A
2429	F-H	S-Q		2485	F-E	S-D		2554	F-E	S-D
2430	F-A	S-B		2486	F-E	S-D		2555	F-B	S-J
2431	F-A	S-A		2487	F-E	S-D		2556	F-B	S-J
2432	F-A	S-A		2488	F-E	S-D		2557	F-B	S-J
2433	F-A	S-A		2490	F-A	S-A		2558	F-E	S-D
2434	F-A	S-B		2491	F-A	S-B		2560	F-E	S-D
2435	F-A	S-B		2493	F-E	S-C		2561	F-E	S-D
2436	F-E	S-D		2495	F-A	S-Q		2564	F-A	S-B
2437	F-A	S-B		2496	F-A	S-B		2565	F-A	S-B
2438	F-E	S-C		2498	F-E	S-D		2567	F-A	S-A
2439	F-A	S-B		2501	F-A	S-A		2570	F-A	S-A
2440	F-A	S-B		2502	F-E	S-C		2571	F-A	S-B
2441	F-G	S-M		2503	F-A	S-B		2572	F-A	S-A
2442	F-A	S-B		2504	F-A	S-A		2573	F-H	S-Q
2443	F-A	S-B		2505	F-A	S-A		2574	F-A	S-A
2444	F-A	S-B		2506	F-A	S-B		2576	F-A	S-B
2445	F-G	S-M		2507	F-A	S-B		2577	F-A	S-B
2446	F-A	S-A		2508	F-A	S-B		2578	F-A	S-B
2447	F-A	S-M		2509	F-A	S-B		2579	F-A	S-B
2448	F-A	S-H		2511	F-A	S-B		2580	F-A	S-B
2451	F-C	S-W		2512	F-A	S-A		2581	F-A	S-B
2452	F-D	S-U		2513	F-A	S-B		2582	F-A	S-B
2453	F-D	S-U		2514	F-E	S-D		2583	F-A	S-B
2454	F-D	S-U		2515	F-A	S-A		2584	F-A	S-B
2455	F-C	S-V		2516	F-A	S-A		2585	F-A	S-B
2456	F-E	S-D		2517	F-D	S-U		2586	F-A	S-B
2457	F-E	S-D		2518	F-A	S-A		2587	F-A	S-A
2458	F-E	S-D		2520	F-E	S-D		2588	F-A	S-A
2459	F-E	S-D		2521	F-E	S-D		2589	F-E	S-D
2460	F-E	S-D		2522	F-A	S-A		2590	F-A	S-A
2461	F-E	S-D		2524	F-E	S-D		2591	F-C	S-V
2463	F-G	S-O		2525	F-A	S-A		2599	F-C	S-V
2464	F-A	S-Q		2526	F-E	S-C		2601	F-D	S-U
2465	F-A	S-Q		2527	F-E	S-D		2602	F-C	S-V
2466	F-G	S-Q		2528	F-E	S-D		2603	F-E	S-D
2468	F-A	S-Q		2529	F-E	S-C		2604	F-E	S-C
2469	F-H	S-Q		2531	F-A	S-B		2605	F-E	S-D
2470	F-A	S-A		2533	F-A	S-A		2606	F-E	S-D
2471	F-A	S-A		2534	F-D	S-U		2607	F-E	S-D
2473	F-A	S-A		2535	F-E	S-C		2608	F-E	S-D
2474	F-A	S-A		2536	F-E	S-D		2609	F-A	S-A
2475	F-A	S-B		2538	F-A	S-G		2610	F-E	S-C
2477	F-E	S-D		2541	F-E	S-E		2611	F-E	S-D
2478	F-E	S-D		2542	F-A	S-A		2612	F-E	S-D
2480	F-E	S-D		2545	F-G	S-M		2614	F-E	S-D
2481	F-E	S-D		2546	F-G	S-M		2615	F-E	S-D

UN No.	EmS Fire	EmS Spill		UN No.	EmS Fire	EmS Spill		UN No.	EmS Fire	EmS Spill
2616	F-E	S-D		2685	F-E	S-C		2751	F-A	S-B
2617	F-E	S-D		2686	F-E	S-C		2752	F-E	S-D
2618	F-E	S-D		2687	F-A	S-G		2753	F-A	S-A
2619	F-E	S-C		2688	F-A	S-A		2754	F-A	S-A
2620	F-E	S-D		2689	F-A	S-A		2757	F-A	S-A
2621	F-E	S-D		2690	F-A	S-A		2758	F-E	S-D
2622	F-E	S-D		2691	F-A	S-B		2759	F-A	S-A
2623	F-A	S-I		2692	F-A	S-B		2760	F-E	S-D
2624	F-G	S-O		2693	F-A	S-B		2761	F-A	S-A
2626	F-A	S-Q		2698	F-A	S-B		2762	F-E	S-D
2627	F-A	S-Q		2699	F-A	S-B		2763	F-A	S-A
2628	F-A	S-A		2705	F-A	S-B		2764	F-E	S-D
2629	F-A	S-A		2707	F-E	S-D		2771	F-A	S-A
2630	F-A	S-A		2709	F-E	S-D		2772	F-E	S-D
2642	F-A	S-A		2710	F-E	S-D		2775	F-A	S-A
2643	F-A	S-A		2713	F-A	S-A		2776	F-E	S-D
2644	F-A	S-A		2714	F-A	S-I		2777	F-A	S-A
2645	F-A	S-A		2715	F-A	S-I		2778	F-E	S-D
2646	F-A	S-A		2716	F-A	S-A		2779	F-A	S-A
2647	F-A	S-A		2717	F-A	S-I		2780	F-E	S-D
2648	F-A	S-A		2719	F-H	S-Q		2781	F-A	S-A
2649	F-A	S-A		2720	F-A	S-Q		2782	F-E	S-D
2650	F-A	S-A		2721	F-H	S-Q		2783	F-A	S-A
2651	F-A	S-A		2722	F-A	S-Q		2784	F-E	S-D
2653	F-A	S-A		2723	F-H	S-Q		2785	F-A	S-A
2655	F-A	S-A		2724	F-A	S-Q		2786	F-A	S-A
2656	F-A	S-A		2725	F-A	S-Q		2787	F-E	S-D
2657	F-A	S-A		2726	F-A	S-Q		2788	F-A	S-A
2659	F-A	S-A		2727	F-A	S-Q		2789	F-E	S-C
2660	F-A	S-A		2728	F-A	S-Q		2790	F-A	S-B
2661	F-A	S-A		2729	F-A	S-A		2793	F-G	S-J
2664	F-A	S-A		2730	F-A	S-A		2794	F-A	S-B
2667	F-A	S-A		2732	F-A	S-A		2795	F-A	S-B
2668	F-E	S-D		2733	F-E	S-C		2796	F-A	S-B
2669	F-A	S-A		2734	F-E	S-C		2797	F-A	S-B
2670	F-A	S-B		2735	F-A	S-B		2798	F-A	S-B
2671	F-A	S-A		2738	F-A	S-A		2799	F-A	S-B
2672	F-A	S-B		2739	F-A	S-B		2800	F-A	S-B
2673	F-A	S-A		2740	F-E	S-C		2801	F-A	S-B
2674	F-A	S-A		2741	F-H	S-Q		2802	F-A	<u>S-B</u>
2676	F-D	S-U		2742	F-E	S-C		2803	F-A	S-B
2677	F-A	S-B		2743	F-E	S-C		2805	F-G	S-N
2678	F-A	S-B		2744	F-E	S-C		2806	F-A	S-O
2679	F-A	S-B		2745	F-A	S-B		2809	F-A	<u>S-B</u>
2680	F-A	S-B		2746	F-A	S-B		2810	F-A	S-A
2681	F-A	S-B		2747	F-A	S-A		2811	F-A	S-A
2682	F-A	S-B		2748	F-A	S-B		2813	F-G	S-N
2683	F-E	S-C		2749	F-E	<u>S-D</u>		2814	F-A	S-T
2684	F-E	S-C		2750	F-A	S-A		2815	F-A	S-B

UN No.	EmS Fire	EmS Spill		UN No.	EmS Fire	EmS Spill		UN No.	EmS Fire	EmS Spill
2817	F-A	S-B		2881	F-G	S-M		2968	F-G	S-L
2818	F-A	S-B		2900	F-A	S-T		2969	F-A	S-A
2819	F-A	S-B		2901	F-C	S-W		2977	F-I	S-S
2820	F-A	S-B		2902	F-A	S-A		2978	F-I	S-S
2821	F-A	S-A		2903	F-E	S-D		2983	F-E	S-D
2822	F-A	S-A		2904	F-A	S-B		2984	F-H	S-Q
2823	F-A	S-B		2905	F-A	S-B		2985	F-E	S-C
2826	F-E	S-C		2907	F-B	S-J		2986	F-E	S-C
2829	F-A	S-B		2908	F-I	S-S		2987	F-A	S-B
2830	F-G	S-N		2909	F-I	S-S		2988	F-G	S-N
2831	F-A	S-A		2910	F-I	S-S		2989	F-A	S-G
2834	F-A	S-B		2911	F-I	S-S		2990	F-A	S-V
2835	F-G	S-O		2912	F-I	S-S		2991	F-E	S-D
2837	F-A	S-B		2913	F-I	S-S		2992	F-A	S-A
2838	F-E	S-D		2915	F-I	S-S		2993	F-E	S-D
2839	F-A	S-A		2916	F-I	S-S		2994	F-A	S-A
2840	F-E	S-D		2917	F-I	S-S		2995	F-E	S-D
2841	F-E	S-D		2919	F-I	S-S		2996	F-A	S-A
2842	F-E	S-D		2920	F-E	S-C		2997	F-E	S-D
2844	F-G	S-N		2921	F-A	S-G		2998	F-A	S-A
2845	F-G	S-M		2922	F-A	S-B		3005	F-E	S-D
2846	F-G	S-M		2923	F-A	S-B		3006	F-A	S-A
2849	F-A	S-A		2924	F-E	S-C		3009	F-E	S-D
2850	F-E	S-E		2925	F-A	S-G		3010	F-A	S-A
2851	F-A	S-B		2926	F-A	S-G		3011	F-E	S-D
2852	F-B	S-J		2927	F-A	S-B		3012	F-A	S-A
2853	F-A	S-A		2928	F-A	S-B		3013	F-E	S-D
2854	F-A	S-A		2929	F-E	S-D		3014	F-A	S-A
2855	F-A	S-A		2930	F-A	S-G		3015	F-E	S-D
2856	F-A	S-A		2931	F-A	S-A		3016	F-A	S-A
2857	F-C	S-V		2933	F-E	S-D		3017	F-E	S-D
2858	F-G	S-G		2934	F-E	S-D		3018	F-A	S-A
2859	F-A	S-A		2935	F-E	S-D		3019	F-E	S-D
2861	F-A	S-A		2936	F-A	S-A		3020	F-A	S-A
2862	F-A	S-A		2937	F-A	S-A		3021	F-E	S-D
2863	F-A	S-A		2940	F-A	S-J		3022	F-E	S-D
2864	F-A	S-A		2941	F-A	S-A		3023	F-E	S-D
2865	F-A	S-B		2942	F-A	S-A		3024	F-E	S-D
2869	F-A	S-B		2943	F-E	S-D		3025	F-E	S-D
2870	F-G	S-M		2945	F-E	S-C		3026	F-A	S-A
2871	F-A	S-A		2946	F-A	S-A		3027	F-A	S-A
2872	F-A	S-A		2947	F-E	S-D		3028	F-A	S-B
2873	F-A	S-A		2948	F-A	S-A		3048	F-A	S-A
2874	F-A	S-A		2949	F-A	S-B		3051	F-G	S-M
2875	F-A	S-A		2950	F-G	S-O		3052	F-G	S-M
2876	F-A	S-A		2956	F-B	S-G		3053	F-G	S-L
2878	F-G	S-G		2965	F-G	S-O		3054	F-E	S-D
2879	F-A	S-B		2966	F-A	S-A		3055	F-A	S-B
2880	F-H	S-Q		2967	F-A	S-B		3056	F-E	S-D

UN No.	EmS Fire	EmS Spill		UN No.	EmS Fire	EmS Spill		UN No.	EmS Fire	EmS Spill
3057	F-C	S-U		3118	F-F	S-R		3168	F-D	S-U
3064	F-E	S-D		3119	F-F	S-R		3169	F-C	S-U
3065	F-E	S-D		3120	F-F	S-R		3170	F-G	S-P
3066	F-A	S-B		3121	F-G	S-L		3172	F-A	S-A
3070	F-C	S-V		3122	F-A	S-Q		3174	F-A	S-J
3071	F-E	S-D		3123	F-G	S-N		3175	F-A	S-I
3072	F-A	S-V		3124	F-A	S-J		3176	F-A	S-H
3073	F-E	S-C		3125	F-G	S-N		3178	F-A	S-G
3076	F-G	S-L		3126	F-A	S-J		3179	F-A	S-G
3077	F-A	S-F		3127	F-A	S-J		3180	F-A	S-G
3078	F-G	S-O		3128	F-A	S-J		3181	F-A	S-I
3079	F-E	S-D		3129	F-G	S-N		3182	F-A	S-G
3080	F-E	S-D		3130	F-G	S-N		3183	F-A	S-J
3082	F-A	S-F		3131	F-G	S-L		3184	F-A	S-J
3083	F-C	S-W		3132	F-G	S-N		3185	F-A	S-J
3084	F-A	S-Q		3133	F-G	S-L		3186	F-A	S-J
3085	F-A	S-Q		3134	F-G	S-N		3187	F-A	S-J
3086	F-A	S-Q		3135	F-G	S-N		3188	F-A	S-J
3087	F-A	S-Q		3136	F-C	S-V		3189	F-G	S-J
3088	F-A	S-J		3137	F-G	S-Q		3190	F-A	S-J
3089	F-G	S-G		3138	F-D	S-U		3191	F-A	S-J
3090	F-A	S-I		3139	F-A	S-Q		3192	F-A	S-J
3091	F-A	S-I		3140	F-A	S-A		3194	F-G	S-M
3092	F-E	S-D		3141	F-A	S-A		3200	F-G	S-M
3093	F-A	S-Q		3142	F-A	S-A		3205	F-A	S-J
3094	F-G	S-L		3143	F-A	S-A		3206	F-A	S-J
3095	F-A	S-N		3144	F-A	S-A		3208	F-G	S-N
3096	F-G	S-L		3145	F-A	S-B		3209	F-G	S-N
3097	F-A	S-Q		3146	F-A	S-A		3210	F-H	S-Q
3098	F-A	S-Q		3147	F-A	S-B		3211	F-H	S-Q
3099	F-A	S-Q		3148	F-G	S-N		3212	F-H	S-Q
3100	F-A	S-Q		3149	F-H	S-Q		3213	F-H	S-Q
3101	F-J	S-R		3150	F-D	S-U		3214	F-H	S-Q
3102	F-J	S-R		3151	F-A	S-A		3215	F-A	S-Q
3103	F-J	S-R		3152	F-A	S-A		3216	F-A	S-Q
3104	F-J	S-R		3153	F-D	S-U		3218	F-A	S-Q
3105	F-J	S-R		3154	F-D	S-U		3219	F-A	S-Q
3106	F-J	S-R		3155	F-A	S-A		3220	F-C	S-V
3107	F-J	S-R		3156	F-C	S-W		3221	F-J	S-G
3108	F-J	S-R		3157	F-C	S-W		3222	F-J	S-G
3109	F-J	S-R		3158	F-C	S-V		3223	F-J	S-G
3110	F-J	S-R		3159	F-C	S-V		3224	F-J	S-G
3111	F-F	S-R		3160	F-D	S-U		3225	F-J	S-G
3112	F-F	S-R		3161	F-D	S-U		3226	F-J	S-G
3113	F-F	S-R		3162	F-C	S-U		3227	F-J	S-G
3114	F-F	S-R		3163	F-C	S-V		3228	F-J	S-G
3115	F-F	S-R		3164	F-C	S-V		3229	F-J	S-G
3116	F-F	S-R		3165	F-E	S-C		3230	F-J	S-G
3117	F-F	S-R		3167	F-D	S-U		3231	F-F	S-K

UN No.	EmS Fire	EmS Spill		UN No.	EmS Fire	EmS Spill		UN No.	EmS Fire	EmS Spill
3232	F-F	S-K		3281	F-A	S-A		3330	F-I	S-S
3233	F-F	S-K		3282	F-A	S-A		3331	F-I	S-S
3234	F-F	S-K		3283	F-A	S-A		3332	F-I	S-S
3235	F-F	S-K		3284	F-A	S-A		3333	F-I	S-S
3236	F-F	S-K		3285	F-A	S-A		3336	F-E	S-D
3237	F-F	S-K		3286	F-E	S-C		3337	F-C	S-V
3238	F-F	S-K		3287	F-A	S-A		3338	F-C	S-V
3239	F-F	S-K		3288	F-A	S-A		3339	F-C	S-V
3240	F-F	S-K		3289	F-A	S-B		3340	F-C	S-V
3241	F-J	S-G		3290	F-A	S-B		3341	F-A	S-J
3242	F-J	S-G		3291	F-A	S-T		3342	F-A	S-J
3243	F-A	S-A		3292	F-G	S-P		3343	F-E	S-Y
3244	F-A	S-B		3293	F-A	S-A		3344	F-B	S-J
3245	F-A	S-T		3294	F-E	S-D		3345	F-A	S-A
3246	F-A	S-B		3295	F-E	S-D		3346	F-E	S-D
3247	F-A	S-Q		3296	F-C	S-V		3347	F-E	S-D
3248	F-E	S-D		3297	F-C	S-V		3348	F-A	S-A
3249	F-A	S-A		3298	F-C	S-V		3349	F-A	S-A
3250	F-A	S-B		3299	F-C	S-V		3350	F-E	S-D
3251	F-F	S-G		3300	F-D	S-U		3351	F-E	S-D
3252	F-D	S-U		3301	F-A	S-J		3352	F-A	S-A
3253	F-A	S-B		3302	F-A	S-A		3354	F-D	S-U
3254	F-A	S-M		3303	F-C	S-W		3355	F-D	S-U
3255	F-A	S-M		3304	F-C	S-U		3356	F-H	S-Q
3256	F-E	S-D		3305	F-D	S-U		3357	F-E	S-Y
3257	F-A	S-P		3306	F-C	S-W		3358	F-D	S-U
3258	F-A	S-P		3307	F-C	S-W		3359	F-A	S-D
3259	F-A	S-B		3308	F-C	S-U		3360	F-A	S-I
3260	F-A	S-B		3309	F-D	S-U		3361	F-A	S-B
3261	F-A	S-B		3310	F-C	S-W		3362	F-E	S-C
3262	F-A	S-B		3311	F-C	S-W		3363	F-A	S-P
3263	F-A	S-B		3312	F-D	S-U		3364	F-B	S-J
3264	F-A	S-B		3313	F-A	S-J		3365	F-B	S-J
3265	F-A	S-B		3314	F-A	S-I		3366	F-B	S-J
3266	F-A	S-B		3315	F-A	S-A		3367	F-B	S-J
3267	F-A	S-B		3316	F-A	S-P		3368	F-B	S-J
3268	F-B	S-X		3317	F-B	S-J		3369	F-B	S-J
3269	F-E	S-D		3318	F-C	S-U		3370	F-B	S-J
3270	F-A	S-I		3319	F-B	S-J		3371	F-E	S-D
3271	F-E	S-D		3320	F-A	S-B		3373	F-A	S-T
3272	F-E	S-D		3321	F-I	S-S		3374	F-D	S-U
3273	F-E	S-D		3322	F-I	S-S		3375	F-H	S-Q
3274	F-E	S-C		3323	F-I	S-S		3376	F-B	S-J
3275	F-E	S-D		3324	F-I	S-S		3377	F-A	S-Q
3276	F-A	S-A		3325	F-I	S-S		3378	F-A	S-Q
3277	F-A	S-B		3326	F-I	S-S		3379	F-E	S-Y
3278	F-A	S-A		3327	F-I	S-S		3380	F-B	S-J
3279	F-E	S-D		3328	F-I	S-S		3381	F-A	S-A
3280	F-A	S-A		3329	F-I	S-S		3382	F-A	S-A

UN No.	EmS Fire	EmS Spill		UN No.	EmS Fire	EmS Spill		UN No.	EmS Fire	EmS Spill
3383	F-E	S-D		3416	F-A	S-A		3450	F-A	S-A
3384	F-E	S-D		3417	F-A	S-G		3451	F-A	S-A
3385	F-G	S-N		3418	F-A	S-A		3452	F-A	S-A
3386	F-G	S-N		3419	F-A	S-B		3453	F-A	S-B
3387	F-A	S-Q		3420	F-A	S-B		3454	F-A	S-A
3388	F-A	S-Q		3421	F-A	S-B		3455	F-A	S-B
3389	F-A	S-B		3422	F-A	S-B		3456	F-A	S-B
3390	F-A	S-B		3423	F-A	S-B		3457	F-A	S-A
3391	F-G	S-M		3424	F-A	S-A		3458	F-A	S-A
3392	F-G	S-M		3425	F-A	S-B		3459	F-A	S-A
3393	F-G	S-M		3426	F-A	S-A		3460	F-A	S-A
3394	F-G	S-M		3427	F-A	S-A		3461	F-G	S-M
3395	F-G	S-N		3428	F-A	S-A		3462	F-A	S-A
3396	F-G	S-N		3429	F-A	S-A		3463	F-E	S-C
3397	F-G	S-N		3430	F-A	S-A		3464	F-A	S-A
3398	F-G	S-N		3431	F-A	S-A		3465	F-A	S-A
3399	F-G	S-N		3432	F-A	S-A		3466	F-A	S-A
3400	F-A	S-J		3433	F-G	S-M		3467	F-A	S-A
3401	F-G	S-N		3434	F-A	S-A		3468	F-D	S-U
3402	F-G	S-N		3436	F-A	S-A		3469	F-E	S-C
3403	F-G	S-L		3437	F-A	S-A		3470	F-E	S-C
3404	F-G	S-L		3438	F-A	S-A		3471	F-A	S-B
3405	F-H	S-Q		3439	F-A	S-A		3472	F-A	S-B
3406	F-H	S-Q		3440	F-A	S-A		3473	F-E	S-D
3407	F-H	S-Q		3441	F-A	S-A		3474	F-B	S-J
3408	F-H	S-Q		3442	F-A	S-A		3475	F-E	S-E
3409	F-A	S-A		3443	F-A	S-A		3476	F-G	S-P
3410	F-A	S-A		3444	F-A	S-A		3477	F-A	S-B
3411	F-A	S-A		3445	F-A	S-A		3478	F-D	S-U
3412	F-A	S-B		3446	F-A	S-A		3479	F-D	S-U
3413	F-A	S-A		3447	F-A	S-A		3480	F-A	S-I
3414	F-A	S-A		3448	F-A	S-A		3481	F-A	S-I
3415	F-A	S-A		3449	F-A	S-A				

MEDICAL FIRST AID GUIDE
FOR USE IN ACCIDENTS INVOLVING
DANGEROUS GOODS
(MFAG)

Foreword

The *IMO/WHO/ILO Medical First Aid Guide for Use in Accidents Involving Dangerous Goods (MFAG)* is the Chemicals Supplement to the *International Medical Guide for Ships (IMGS)** which is published by the World Health Organization (WHO), Geneva.

This revised text of the Guide was adopted by the Maritime Safety Committee in May 1998, for use in association with Amendment 30-00 of the IMDG Code, and will be further amended as and when necessary.

---

* *International Medical Guide for Ships*, 3rd edition (World Health Organization, Geneva, 2007), ISBN 978-92-4-154720-8.

Contents

MFAG

Introduction

The IMO/WHO/ILO Medical First Aid Guide for Use in Accidents involving Dangerous Goods (MFAG) refers to the substances, material and articles covered by the International Maritime Dangerous Goods Code (IMDG Code) and the materials covered by Appendix B of the Code of Safe Practice for Solid Bulk Cargoes (BC Code). It is intended to provide advice necessary for initial management of chemical poisoning and diagnosis within the limits of the facilities available at sea.

This Guide should be used in conjunction with the information provided in the IMDG Code, the BC Code, the Emergency Procedures for Ships Carrying Dangerous Goods (EmS), the International Code for the Construction and Equipment of Ships Carrying Dangerous Chemicals in Bulk (IBC Code), and the International Code for the Construction and Equipment of Ships Carrying Liquefied Gases in Bulk (IGC Code).

The MFAG itself gives general information about the particular toxic effects likely to be encountered. **The treatment recommended in this Guide is specified in the appropriate tables and more comprehensive in the appropriate sections of the Appendices.** However, differences exist between countries on certain types of treatment and where these differences occur they are indicated in the relevant national medical guide.

Treatments in this guide cater for the accidental human consequences of the carriage of dangerous goods at sea. Accidental ingestion of toxic substances during voyage is rare. The guide does not cover ingestion by intention.

Minor accidents involving chemicals do not usually cause severe effects provided that the appropriate first aid measures are taken. Although the number of reported serious accidents is small, accidents involving those chemicals which are toxic or corrosive may be dangerous, and must be regarded as being potentially serious until either the affected person has completely recovered, or medical advice to the contrary has been obtained.

Information on the treatment of illnesses which are of a general nature and not predominantly concerned with chemical poisoning may be found in the *ILO/IMO/WHO International Medical Guide for Ships (IMGS)*.

How to use this guide

> **In any case of exposure, start with emergency action and act as advised**

For the convenience of users, and to ensure rapid access to the recommendations in an emergency, this Guide is divided into sections which are grouped to facilitate a three-step approach.

Step 1:	Emergency action and diagnosis	**Start here!**
Step 2:	Tables	The tables give brief instructions for special circumstances
Step 3:	Appendices	The appendices provide comprehensive information, a list of medicines/ drugs, and a list of chemicals referred to in the tables.

NOTE: The **list of chemicals** is limited to those few chemicals requiring special treatment. The list is given both in alphabetical and numerical order (UN No.) in **appendix 15** to this Guide.

MFAG

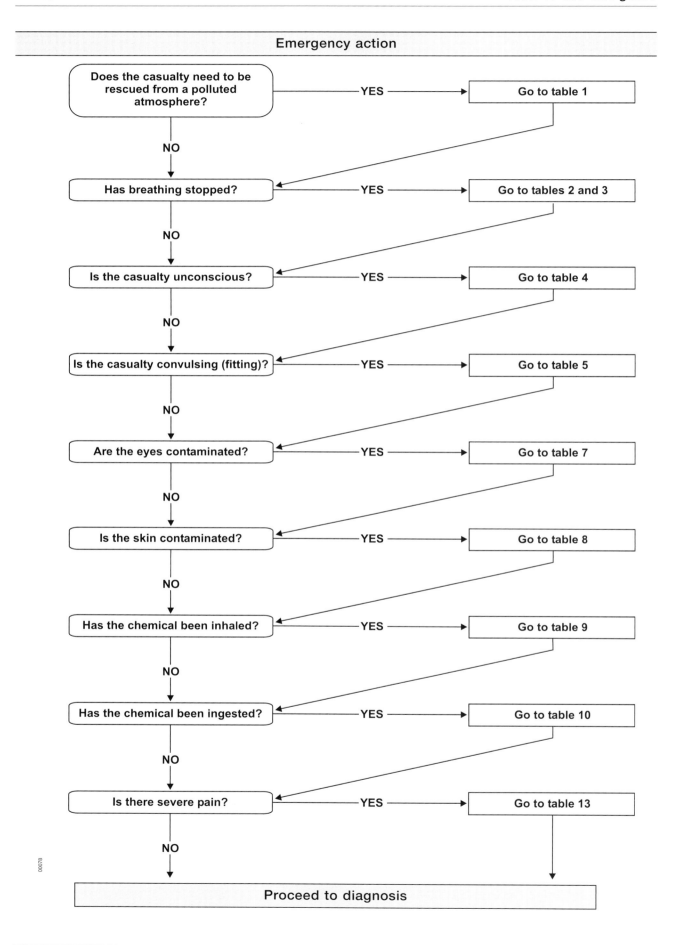

Emergency action

Does the casualty need to be rescued from a polluted atmosphere? ——— YES ———→ Go to table 1

NO

Has breathing stopped? ——— YES ———→ Go to tables 2 and 3

NO

Is the casualty unconscious? ——— YES ———→ Go to table 4

NO

Is the casualty convulsing (fitting)? ——— YES ———→ Go to table 5

NO

Are the eyes contaminated? ——— YES ———→ Go to table 7

NO

Is the skin contaminated? ——— YES ———→ Go to table 8

NO

Has the chemical been inhaled? ——— YES ———→ Go to table 9

NO

Has the chemical been ingested? ——— YES ———→ Go to table 10

NO

Is there severe pain? ——— YES ———→ Go to table 13

NO

Proceed to diagnosis

Diagnosis

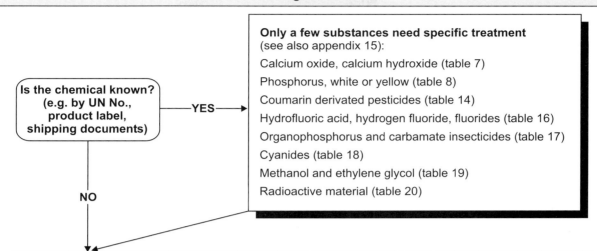

Is the chemical known? (e.g. by UN No., product label, shipping documents)

—YES→

NO

Only a few substances need specific treatment (see also appendix 15):

Calcium oxide, calcium hydroxide (table 7)

Phosphorus, white or yellow (table 8)

Coumarin derivated pesticides (table 14)

Hydrofluoric acid, hydrogen fluoride, fluorides (table 16)

Organophosphorus and carbamate insecticides (table 17)

Cyanides (table 18)

Methanol and ethylene glycol (table 19)

Radioactive material (table 20)

What is the casualty's present state?		
Breathing is rapid, shallow, difficult, irregular or deep:	→	Table 3 and appendix 3
The casualty has a **cough, wheezing, hoarseness or severe breathlessness**:	→	Table 9 and appendix 9
The **pulse** is slow, weak or rapid:	→	Table 11 and appendix 11
Blisters, burns or frost-bite are present:	→	Table 8 and appendix 8
The casualty is in a **coma**:	→	Table 4 and appendix 4
The casualty has **convulsions (seizures, fits)**:	→	Table 5 and appendix 5
The casualty is **vomiting**:	→	Table 10 and appendix 10
The casualty is **restless, excited, confused or hallucinating**:	→	Table 6 and appendix 6
The casualty is **jaundiced** (yellow discoloration of skin or eyes):	→	Table 15
Urine output is decreased or absent:	→	Table 12 and appendix 12
Blood is in the urine, vomit or stool; the gums are bleeding; there are small haemorrhages (petechia) in the skin:	→	Table 14

What is the history of the present illness?

How did the illness start?

What are the symptoms?

Which symptoms are most troublesome?

What illnesses has the casualty suffered previously?

Make a record of any past illnesses, injuries, operations and present drug treatment

00079

Table 1 – Rescue   MFAG

MFAG

Tables

Table 1
RESCUE

Rescuers must be adequately protected from exposure before entering a contaminated area in order to avoid injury. When a chemical is unidentified, worst-case assumptions concerning toxicity must be assumed.

ARRIVAL AT SCENE

- Upon arrival at the scene, an initial assessment of the situation should be made and the size of the incident should be determined.

Rescuers must **NOT**:

- Enter a contaminated area without using a pressure-demand self-contained breathing apparatus and wearing full protective clothing;
- Enter an enclosed space unless they are trained members of a rescue team and follow correct procedures;
- Walk through any spilled materials;
- Allow unnecessary contamination of equipment;
- Attempt to recover shipping papers or manifests from contaminated area unless adequately protected;
- Become exposed while approaching a potentially contaminated area;
- Attempt rescue unless trained and equipped with appropriate personal protective equipment (PPE) and protective clothing for the situation.

QUICKLY ESTABLISH AN EXCLUSION OR HOT ZONE

- Assume that anyone leaving the exclusion zone is contaminated and should be assessed and decontaminated, if necessary.
- Do not remove non-ambulatory casualties from the exclusion zone unless properly trained personnel with the appropriate PPE are available and decontamination has been accomplished.

INITIAL TRIAGE OF CASUALTIES (SORTING AND PRIORITY)

One unconscious casualty

- Give immediate treatment to the unconscious casualty only, and
- Send for help.

Several unconscious casualties

If there is more than one unconscious casualty:

- Send for help, and
- Give appropriate treatment to the worst casualty in the priority order of:
  1 Casualties who have stopped breathing or have no pulse (see **Table 2**).
  2 Casualties who are unconscious (see **Table 4**).

Casualty is unconscious but breathing

If the casualty is unconscious or cyanotic (bluish skin) but breathing, connect to portable oxygen.

Neck or back trauma

Apply neck and back support before moving casualty if there is any question of neck or back trauma.

Priority: Airway, Breathing, Circulation (A-B-C)

Initial management of **A**irway, **B**reathing and **C**irculation (A-B-C, see **table 2**) is all that should be undertaken while there is potential for further injury to the casualty or to response personnel.

Gross decontamination

If the casualty is contaminated with chemicals, gross decontamination should be performed.

- Cut away or remove all suspected contaminated clothing, including jewellery and watches.

- Brush or wipe off any obvious contamination.

- Care should be taken to protect open wounds from contamination.

- Every effort should be made by personnel to avoid contact with potentially contaminated casualties. Rescuers should wear protective clothing, if necessary.

- Cover or wrap casualty to prevent spread of contamination.

Removal of casualties from exclusion zone

Once gross decontamination has been performed, the casualties should be removed from the exclusion zone.

- If casualties can walk, lead them out of the exclusion zone to an area where decontamination and further evaluation can take place.

- If casualties are unable to walk, remove them on stretchers. If stretchers are unavailable, carefully carry or drag casualties to an area where decontamination and further evaluation can take place.

DECONTAMINATION

Decontaminate from head down

- Take care not to introduce contaminants into open wounds.

- Decontaminate exposed wounds and eyes before intact skin areas.

- Cover wounds with a waterproof dressing after decontamination.

For external contamination, begin with the least aggressive methods

- Limit mechanical or chemical irritation of the skin.

- Wash contaminated area gently under a stream of water for at least ten minutes, and wash carefully with soap and warm (never hot) water, scrubbing with a soft brush or surgical sponge.

Reduce level of contaminants

- Remove contaminants to the level that they are no longer a threat to casualty or response personnel.

- Isolate the casualty from the environment to prevent the spread of any remaining contaminants.

Contain runoff; bag contaminated clothing

- If possible, contain all runoff from decontamination procedures for proper disposal.

- Ensure that all potentially contaminated casualty clothing and belongings have been removed and placed in properly labelled bags.

Table 1 – Rescue **MFAG**

SUMMARY OF TREATMENT OF CASUALTIES

- Assign highest priorities to Airway, Breathing, Circulation (ABC) and then decontamination.

- Complete primary and secondary assessments as conditions allow.

- Obtain information on chemical(s) to which the casualty has been exposed from shipping papers, labels or other documents.

- If there are multiple casualties, direct attention to the most seriously affected individuals first.

- Treat symptoms and signs as appropriate and when conditions allow.

- Obtain RADIO MEDICAL ADVICE when conditions allow.

- Perform invasive procedures only in uncontaminated areas.

- Reassess the casualty frequently, because many chemicals have latent physiological effects.

- Delay preventive measures until the casualty is decontaminated.

TRANSFER TO SHIP'S HOSPITAL

Casualties who have been stabilized (airway, breathing and circulation) and decontaminated can be transported to the ship's hospital for further evaluation.

Further advice: ☞ **appendix 1**

Table 2
CPR (CARDIO-PULMONARY RESUSCITATION)

Basic life support comprises the "A-B-C" steps which concern the airway, breathing, and circulation respectively.

Basic life support is indicated for:

Airway obstruction

Breathing (respiratory) arrest

Circulatory or cardiac arrest.

Any inadequacy or absence of breathing or circulation must be determined immediately.

Assessment of breathing

- Tilt the head firmly backwards with one hand while lifting the neck with the other hand to relieve obstructed breathing.

- Pull the tongue forward.

- Suck or swab out excess secretions.

- Clean any vomit from the mouth and back of the throat. Remove any loose dentures.

- Listen and feel for any movement of air, because the chest and abdomen may move in the presence of an obstructed airway, without moving air. The rescuer's face should be placed close to the casualty's nose and mouth so that any exhaled air may be felt against the cheek. Also the rise and fall of the chest can be observed and the exhaled breath heard.

- Look, listen and feel for five seconds before deciding that breathing is absent.

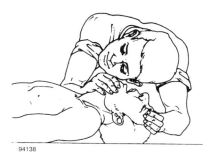

Assessment of heart function

- Check for a pulse. The best pulse to feel in an emergency is the carotid. Feel for five seconds before deciding it is absent. If it cannot be felt or is feeble, there is insufficient circulation.

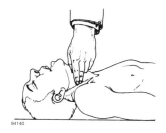

FULL ADVICE ON CPR: ☞ **APPENDIX 2**

Table 2 – CPR (Cardio-pulmonary resuscitation)   **MFAG**

Signs & symptoms	Treatment

Breathing, heart is beating, unconscious

- Place casualty in the recovery position.

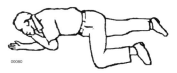

- Remove any loose dentures.
- Clean any vomit from the mouth and back of the throat.

Further advice on the **unconscious casualty:** ☞ **Table 4**

- Once a clear and open airway is established, insert a Guedel airway: ☞ **Appendix 3**

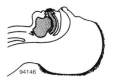

Not breathing but heart is beating

- Begin artificial respiration; mouth-to-mouth or mouth-to-nose respiration.

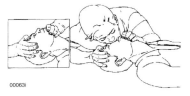

- Give four quick breaths and continue at a rate of 12 inflations per minute.
- Chest should rise and fall. If it does not, check to make sure the casualty's airway is clear and open.

- Do not use mouth-to-mouth respiration if the casualty was exposed to cyanides, organophosphates or radiation to prevent rescuer from being exposed.

Meanwhile, install bag-valve-mask and oxygen supply for continued controlled ventilation. Give oxygen unless there is a danger of fire or explosion.

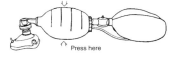

Further advice on **oxygen administration:** ☞ **Table 3**

MFAG

Signs & symptoms	Treatment
Breathing and heart have stopped	■ Begin CPR immediately. If possible, use two rescuers. Don't delay. One rescuer can do the job.

Locate the pressure point (lower half of breast bone: about 4 cm from the tip of the breast bone).

Depress breast bone 4 to 5 cm (80 to 100 times per minute).

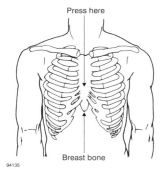

Press here

Breast bone

94135

If one rescuer:
15 heart compressions and 2 very quick lung inflations.

If two rescuers:
5 heart compressions and 1 lung inflation.

MFAG

Table 3
OXYGEN ADMINISTRATION & CONTROLLED VENTILATION

Oxygen is necessary for life. Some intoxications may interfere with normal oxygenation of the blood or tissues. In particular, oxygen can be lifesaving to casualties who have inhaled smoke and other toxic gases but it needs to be given with all speed. **Basic training is required to administer oxygen.**

Diagnosis

- There is difficulty in breathing with an increased rate at first (over 30 per minute). Later it may become slow and stop.

- The pulse is rapid, usually over 100 per minute.

- There is blueness of the skin with purple lips and tongue.

- The casualty may be agitated at first but become apathetic, with muscular weakness. Unconsciousness may follow this.

- The pupils of the eyes will react to light at first. If they become large and do not react to light, life is in danger.

Lack of oxygen is an emergency

Treatment

- Give oxygen by means of a face mask. It makes assisted or controlled ventilation possible. It is better to have the casualty well oxygenated with controlled artificial respiration than to have him poorly oxygenated from breathing spontaneously.

- Place a mask over the nose and mouth. It is essential that the face mask is held firmly in place so as to avoid leakage.

- Check that the equipment is correctly assembled according to the manufacturer's instructions and that sufficient oxygen is contained in the cylinder (a cylinder of 2.5 litre capacity, filled under a pressure of 200 bar, delivers 500 litres oxygen).

Full advice on **oxygen administration:** ☛ **Appendix 3**

The commonest emergency requiring medical assistance on board is **toxic gas inhalation from fires or specific toxic gases.** Combustion in fires on board may well involve substantial release of carbon monoxide and hydrogen cyanide. In these cases, oxygen should be given at a flow rate of 8 litres per minute.

In life-threatening conditions, such as lung oedema or circulatory failure, oxygen should also be given at a flow rate of 8 litres per minute.

Warning: Smoking, a naked flame or light or fires must not be allowed in the same room during the administration of oxygen because of the risk of fire.

Signs & symptoms	Treatment
Not breathing but heart is beating	■ Ensure that a clear airway has been established. ■ A Guedel airway should be inserted. If insertion of an airway cannot be achieved, the chin should be pulled forward throughout the administration of oxygen. If the casualty has seizures due to the lack of oxygen, administration of oxygen may be difficult but is essential. 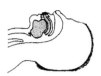 ■ Use a positive-pressure manual operated oxygen resuscitator in accordance with manufacturer's instruction. 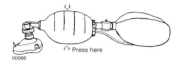 ■ Give oxygen at a flow rate of 8 litres per minute. The bag should be squeezed steadily and firmly and released about 12 times a minute. ■ Always maintain a regular check on the pulse in the neck. The absence of a pulse indicates the need for 15 chest compressions to every two inflations ■ If gagging occurs, remove the airway. ■ Once the casualty is breathing spontaneously, put him in the recovery position.
Breathing is difficult	■ Make sure difficulty in breathing is not due to airway obstruction: ☞ **Table 2** ■ The casualty should be connected to an oxygen-giving set through a simple disposable face mask (non-venturi type) placed securely over the face. ■ Oxygen should be used at a flow rate of 6 to 8 litres per minute. ■ Oxygen should be continued until the casualty no longer has difficulty in breathing and has a normal healthy colour.

Table 4 – Chemical-induced disturbances of consciousness   **MFAG**

Table 4
CHEMICAL-INDUCED DISTURBANCES OF CONSCIOUSNESS

Chemicals, whether inhaled, ingested or absorbed through the skin, can either depress or excite the brain. In cases of severe poisoning, the casualty may not only be unconscious but breathing may also be depressed or absent. Fortunately, in most cases, symptoms usually resolve rapidly when the casualty is removed from the polluted environment.

Signs & symptoms	Treatment
Drowsy but breathing adequately	■ After removal of the casualty from the polluted environment, eye and skin decontamination should be undertaken, if necessary. ■ After decontamination the casualty should be observed in a place of safety for at least eight hours. Usually no specific treatment is necessary.
Increasing loss of consciousness but breathing adequately	■ Place casualty in the recovery position.  ■ Remove any loose dentures. ■ Clean any vomit from the mouth and back of the throat. ■ Turn casualty face down, head to one side as pictured; no pillows should be used under the head. ■ Clear out any vomit in the mouth as soon as vomiting occurs. ■ The casualty must never be left alone or unwatched in case he vomits, has a fit or may fall out of his bunk. ■ Turn the casualty gently every three hours and roll him smoothly from one side to the other.  ■ The head must always be kept back with a chin-up position when actually turning, and, at no time must the head be allowed to bend forwards with the chin sagging. ■ If possible, insert a Guedel airway. ■ **RADIO FOR MEDICAL ADVICE IN ALL CASES**

Signs & symptoms	Treatment

Unconsciousness with less than eight respirations of normal depth per minute

Place the casualty on his back.

- Tilt the head firmly backwards with one hand while lifting the neck with the other hand to relieve obstructed breathing.

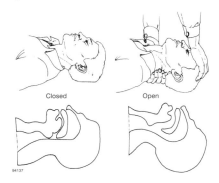

- Once a clear and open airway is established, insert a Guedel airway: ☞ **Appendix 3**

- Administer controlled ventilation.

Further advice on **controlled ventilation:** ☞ **Table 3**

- Check for a pulse. The best pulse to feel in an emergency is the carotid. Feel for five seconds before deciding it is absent. If it cannot be felt or is feeble, there is insufficient circulation.

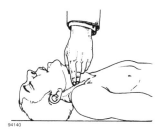

- It should be felt after the first minute of artificial respiration and checked every two minutes thereafter.
- **If morphine has been administered:** ☞ **Table 13**
- **RADIO FOR MEDICAL ADVICE IN ALL CASES**

Prolonged coma with or without breathing difficulty

- **RADIO FOR MEDICAL ADVICE IN ALL CASES**
- Regularly assess that breathing is adequate. Give ventilation support with 8 litres of oxygen per minute if the victim does not breathe adequately.

Further advice on **care of unconscious casualties:** ☞ **Appendix 4**

Signs & symptoms	Treatment
Toxic mental confusion (agitation, hallucinations)	■ If the casualty is difficult to manage, give diazepam 10 mg as rectal solution.

Further advice on treatment of **agitation and hallucinations:** ☞ **Table 6**

Signs & symptoms	Treatment
Convulsions (seizures, fits)	■ Ensure that there are no hard or sharp objects in the vicinity so that the victim will not injure himself. ■ Give diazepam 10 mg as rectal solution. ■ **RADIO FOR MEDICAL ADVICE** ■ If medical advice is unavailable and seizures continue, give a further 10 mg diazepam as rectal solution after 30 minutes.

Further advice on **treatment of convulsions:** ☞ **Table 5**

MFAG

Table 5
CHEMICAL-INDUCED CONVULSIONS (SEIZURES, FITS)

The main risk of convulsions is impaired ventilation (leading to inadequate oxygen supply to tissues). During a convulsion, the casualty may hurt himself. Convulsions may be delayed for hours after exposure to certain chemicals.

FURTHER INFORMATION ON CONVULSIONS: ☞ APPENDIX 5

Signs & symptoms	Treatment
Single convulsions of short duration	▪ Remove the casualty to the ship's hospital.
	▪ Prevent the casualty from hurting himself.
	▪ Never restrain the casualty forcibly, as this may cause injury.
Convulsions may also occur in regular heavy drinkers within about two days after sharply decreased alcohol consumption. Other signs, such as hyperexcitability, sleep disturbances, or generalized tremor, may indicate a withdrawal syndrome.	▪ Ensure that there are no hard or sharp objects in the vicinity so that the victim will not injure himself.
	▪ Surround him with pillows, clothing or other soft material.
	▪ Protect the airway from being blocked by the tongue or secretions.
	▪ After the fit is over, let the casualty sleep it off, as he may be rather confused and dazed when he comes round. Reassure him, and do not leave him until you are sure he is aware of his surroundings, and knows what he is doing.
	▪ **RADIO FOR MEDICAL ADVICE**
Frequent or continuous convulsions	▪ Place casualty in the recovery position.

▪ Give diazepam 10 mg as rectal solution.

▪ **RADIO FOR MEDICAL ADVICE**

▪ If medical advice is unavailable and seizures continue, give a further 10 mg diazepam as rectal solution after 30 minutes.

▪ Stabilize the cervical spine with a collar if trauma is suspected.

Further advice on **convulsions:** ☞ Appendix 5

▪ Give ventilation support with 8 litres of oxygen per minute if the victim does not breathe adequately.

▪ Administer controlled ventilation.

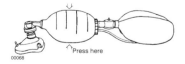

Further advice on **oxygen administration:** ☞ Table 3

▪ After the fit is over, let the casualty sleep it off, as he may be rather confused and dazed when he comes round. Reassure him, and do not leave him until you are sure he is aware of his surroundings, and knows what he is doing.

Table 6
TOXIC MENTAL CONFUSION

Exposure to chemicals and solvents, including alcohol and illicit substances, may result in disorientation in time and space. In these circumstances, the casualty will usually develop the signs and symptoms within 15 to 30 minutes of exposure. Sudden cessation of heavy alcohol consumption may also cause toxic mental confusion.

Signs & symptoms	Treatment
The casualty confuses the day of the week, the month of the year or where they are at that moment in time	■ There is a risk of loss overboard. The person should be kept under close observation in a locked well lit cabin and given repeated reassurance. ■ After removal of the casualty from the polluted atmosphere, no specific treatment is usually necessary.
Agitation (mental agitation, aggressive and sometimes violent behaviour)	■ If the casualty is difficult to manage, give diazepam 10 mg as rectal solution.* ■ Repeat, if necessary, 10 mg diazepam 30 minutes later if medical advice is not immediately available and **SEEK RADIO MEDICAL ADVICE.**
Agitation, convulsions Excessive exposure to chemicals may lead to convulsions (fits).	■ Protect the airway from being blocked by the tongue or secretions. ■ Give diazepam 10 mg as rectal solution.* ■ **RADIO FOR MEDICAL ADVICE**

Further advice on **treatment of convulsions:** ☛ **Table 5**

Signs & symptoms	Treatment
Hallucinations (hearing voices and/or seeing terrifying images) Sometimes mental illness may confuse the issue. Schizophrenia often results in hearing voices that are not there.	■ If the casualty is difficult to manage, give diazepam 10 mg as rectal solution.* ■ Repeat, if necessary, 10 mg diazepam 30 minutes later if medical advice is not immediately available and **SEEK RADIO MEDICAL ADVICE.** ■ If there is a history of previous mental illness: **SEEK RADIO MEDICAL ADVICE.**

* Note: If administration of diazepam as rectal solution is not possible, give haloperidol 5 mg intramuscularly. Haloperidol (e.g. HALDOL™) may be available in the ship's ordinary medicine chest.

Table 7
EYE EXPOSURE TO CHEMICALS

Chemical splashes involving the eye may cause local irritation, inflammation, pain and, in severe cases, blindness. **TREATMENT IS URGENT**

DECONTAMINATION in all cases of eye contact, regardless of symptoms

---

Eye contamination with solid CALCIUM OXIDE and CALCIUM HYDROXIDE (quicklime; slaked lime)

- To avoid "lime burns", try to swab particles mechanically from the eye **before washing**

 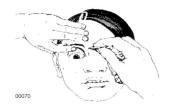

A cotton bud, match or similar object is held over the closed eyelid.

The eyelid is turned inside out over the cotton bud.

Eye contamination with other chemicals

- **IMMEDIATE** washing of the eye with copious amounts of water:
- Keep the eyelids widely apart as illustrated.
- Remove contact lens.
- Direct water flow from inner to outer corner of the eye. Washing must be done thoroughly for ten minutes, timed by the clock.

- If available, use a 1 litre bag of sodium chloride 0.9% with a drip set to irrigate the eye.
- Don't delay. Use water until drip is ready.

Signs & symptoms	Treatment
Pain, redness and watering of the eye	■ Anaesthetic eye drops should be instilled in the eye to ensure adequate irrigation of the eye. ■ If pain is severe, anaesthetic eye drops should be instilled in the eye to relieve pain. ■ If the eye continues to be painful, give two tablets of paracetamol every six hours until the pain is relieved. ■ **RADIO FOR MEDICAL ADVICE**

Table 7 – Eye exposure to chemicals   MFAG

Signs & symptoms	Treatment
Unrelieved severe pain	■ If severe pain continues despite ten minutes irrigation of the eye with water, repeat the eye wash for a further ten minutes after instilling anaesthetic eye drops and **RADIO FOR MEDICAL ADVICE** ■ Give 10 mg morphine sulphate and 10 mg metoclopramide intramuscularly, if advised medically.

Further advice on **pain relief:** ☛ Table 13

Signs & symptoms	Treatment
Loss of vision	■ This is a **MEDICAL EMERGENCY.** ■ Irrigate the eye as described above and seek **URGENT** medical advice.

Further advice on the **treatment of eye injury:** ☛ Appendix 7

Table 8
SKIN EXPOSURE TO CHEMICALS

Skin exposure to chemicals may cause local damage of either chemical burn or frost-bite. Chemical burns resemble thermal burns, with redness, irritation, swelling, pain, blistering and ulceration.

The chemical may be absorbed through the skin, causing general symptoms of poisoning; these symptoms may be delayed for several hours.

Limited exposure to leaking refrigerator gases, compressed gases or solid carbon dioxide (dry ice) may cause local frost-bite that, in principle, will cause the same damage as chemical or thermal burns and is treated accordingly. No special treatment instructions are needed – refer to chemical burns.

In extended burns, fluid loss may be serious.

DECONTAMINATION in all cases of skin exposure, regardless of chemical or symptoms

- Chemical protective gloves and clothing should be used while washing the casualty's skin. After decontamination, it is not necessary to use protective clothing.
- Carefully remove and double-bag contaminated clothing and personal belongings. Cut off the clothes, if necessary.
- If the chemical has affected eyes **and** skin, **the eyes should have PRIOR attention.**
- **IMMEDIATE** washing with copious amounts of water for at least 10 minutes while removing contaminated clothing, rings, wristwatches, etc. **Don't delay.**
- Do not use neutralizing substances.
- Remove the casualty to the ship's hospital.
- Continue washing the skin for additional 10 minutes with soap or shampoo and water.

Exposure to PHOSPHORUS (WHITE OR YELLOW) which ignites in air

- Keep the injured part of the body under water or covered with wet dressings.
- Using chemical protective gloves, remove the phosphorus with a clean spoon or forceps.

Exposure to HYDROFLUORIC ACID

- Using latex gloves, massage exposed area with calcium gluconate gel for at least 15 minutes or until pain is relieved. Leave the gel on the skin. The gel should be re-applied 4 to 6 times daily for 3 to 4 days if a chemical burn is present.

Further advice: ☞ **Table 16**

Signs & symptoms	Treatment
Burning pain with redness and/or swelling of contaminated skin, irritating rash	■ After washing with water, wash exposed areas thoroughly (including skin folds, nail beds and hair) with soap or shampoo and water. Clean away from the burn in every direction. DO NOT use cotton wool for cleaning as it is likely to leave bits in the burn. ■ Dab gently any remaining dirt using a swab soaked in warm water. BE GENTLE as this may cause pain.
Chemical burns	■ Cover burns with a sterile dressing (e.g. perforated silicone dressing or vaseline gauze), overlapping the burn or scald by 5 to 10 cm (2 to 4 inches). Then apply a covering of absorbent material (e.g. a layer of sterile cotton wool) and a suitable bandage.

Further advice on **chemical burns:** ☞ **Appendix 8**

Table 8 – Skin exposure to chemicals   MFAG

Signs & symptoms	Treatment
Blisters	■ Leave blisters intact. ■ If blisters have burst, clip off the dead skin by using a sterilized pair of scissors. Flood area with clean, lukewarm (previously boiled) water from a clean receptacle to remove debris. ■ Cover blisters with a sterile dressing (e.g. perforated silicone dressing or vaseline gauze), overlapping the burn or scald by 5 to 10 cm (2 to 4 inches). Then apply a covering of absorbent material (e.g. a layer of sterile cotton wool) and a suitable bandage.
Pain	■ Give two tablets of paracetamol every six hours until the pain is relieved. ■ If there is very severe pain, give 10 mg morphine sulphate and 10 mg metoclopramide intramuscularly, if advised medically. ■ **SEEK MEDICAL ADVICE** ■ If breakthrough pain persists after 15 minutes or more, give a second injection of 10 mg morphine sulphate intramuscularly.

Further advice on **pain relief:** ☞ **Table 13**

Signs & symptoms	Treatment
Blisters and ulcers	■ Dressings should be left undisturbed for 3 to 4 days unless the dressing becomes smelly or very dirty, or the temperature is raised. Redress such areas as described above). ■ Provide adequate relief for continuing pain (see above).
Blisters, ulcers covering an area exceeding 9% of body surface (corresponding to 9 times the size of the palm of the hand)	■ In addition to normal food and fluid intake give: The **first 24 hours:** For every 10% of the body surface area with burns, give 3 litres of salted water ($1\frac{1}{2}$ teaspoonfuls of table salt in 1 litre) intermittently to help replace fluid loss. **24 to 48 hours:** For every 10% of the body surface area with burns, give $1\frac{1}{2}$ litres of fluids (preferably oral rehydration salt solution – ORS) intermittently. ■ **RADIO FOR MEDICAL ADVICE** **After 48 hours** the fluid intake should in principle be normal. ■ Check for urine output that should be approximately 30 to 50 mℓ per hour (approximately 1 litre per 24 hours).

Further advice on **fluid replacement:** ☞ **Appendix 13**

FOLLOW-UP

■ A patient who has had significant exposure or any symptoms related to exposure should be kept warm in bed and closely observed for 48 hours and **RADIO MEDICAL ADVICE OBTAINED.**

■ Emergency transport for on-shore hospital evaluation will usually be required

Table 9
INHALATION OF CHEMICALS

Inhalation of chemicals may cause suffocation (asphyxia) due to:

- obstruction to breathing in the throat or the air passage through spasm of the air tubes or by swelling of the linings of the voice box due to irritant fumes;
- fluid in the lung air spaces caused by irritant fumes;
- poisoning of the blood which prevents the carriage or use of oxygen in the body caused by, for example, carbon monoxide and cyanide;
- poisoning of the mechanism of breathing in the chest (e.g. by organophosphate pesticides) or the brain (e.g. by chlorinated hydrocarbons);
- gases which do not support life because they replace oxygen in the atmosphere (e.g. carbon dioxide, nitrogen).

Vapours of volatile liquids often have a pleasant or disagreeable odour. They may cause lightheadedness, dizziness, headache or nausea.

A few gases have delayed corrosive effects on the lungs.

For advice on **CPR** in **cases of suffocation:**	☞	**Table 2**
For advice on **chemical hazards of fire:**	☞	**Appendix 9**
For advice on **chemical hazards of welding:**	☞	**Appendix 9**

WARNING: Any casualty who has been gassed and has impaired consciousness must NOT be treated with morphine.

Signs & symptoms	Treatment
Soreness of throat, hoarseness or cough	■ Remove the casualty from the polluted atmosphere, have him rinse his mouth and give one glass of water to drink.
Dry cough, mild breathlessness and wheezing	■ The casualty should be put to bed and placed in the high sitting-up position.

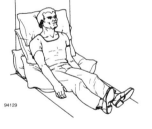 

Signs & symptoms	Treatment
Severe breathlessness and wheezing	■ If breathlessness or wheezing are present, give oxygen at a flow rate of 8 litres per minute until symptoms resolve. ■ Additionally, administer by spacer device: 200 μg salbutamol **or** 500 μg terbutaline **and** 250 μg beclomethasone **or** 400 μg budenoside every 15 minutes for the first hour. ■ At the same time: **RADIO FOR MEDICAL ADVICE.** ■ If breathlessness and wheezing persist after the first hour, continue with oxygen and repeat administration of salbutamol/terbutaline and beclomethasone/budenoside every two hours for the next ten hours, and then four times a day until symptoms resolve.

Table 9 – Inhalation of chemicals   MFAG

Signs & symptoms	Treatment
Severe breathlessness and frothy sputum, blue discoloration of the skin, anxiety and sweating (pulmonary oedema)	■ Casualties must be handled extremely carefully. All strain must be avoided. ■ **RADIO FOR MEDICAL ADVICE.** ■ Arrange for evacuation. The casualty will need to be transferred to a shore hospital as soon as possible.

Further advice on **breathing difficulty:** ☞ **Appendix 9**

- Give oxygen, salbutamol/terbutaline and beclomethasone/budenoside as above.
- Use a sucker, if available, to get rid of the frothy secretions.
- If the casualty is very breathless, give 50 mg furosemide (frusemide) by intramuscular injection to increase the urine output.
- If symptoms persist, continue with oxygen and repeat administration of salbutamol/terbutaline and beclomethasone/budenoside every two hours for the next ten hours, and then four times a day until symptoms resolve.

Signs & symptoms	Treatment
Fever, breathlessness, productive cough, increased pulse rate (over 110 per minute)	■ **RADIO FOR MEDICAL ADVICE** ■ The casualty should be put to bed and placed in the high sitting-up position.

Further advice on **diagnosis of breathing problems:** ☞ **Appendix 9**

- Give 500 mg amoxicillin every eight hours.

Note: Some are allergic to penicillins, including amoxicillin. In such cases, give 500 mg erythromycin four times daily.

- If the patient is breathless, wheezing or blue, oxygen should be given continuously together with 200 μg salbutamol or 500 μg terbutaline four times daily by spacer device, until the symptoms and signs improve.

FOLLOW-UP

A patient who has had significant exposure or any symptoms related to exposure should be kept warm in bed and closely observed for 48 hours and **RADIO MEDICAL ADVICE OBTAINED.**

Table 10
INGESTION OF CHEMICALS

Ingestion of hazardous materials at sea is rare but can occur through attempted suicide, contaminated food or water, or through poor personal hygiene.

Ingestion of a toxic material can cause retching, vomiting (sometimes the vomit is blood-stained), abdominal pain, colic and later diarrhoea. Particularly severe symptoms are caused by corrosives, strong acids, alkalis or disinfectants which burn the lips and mouth and cause intense pain, and rarely perforation of the gut.

Ingested poisons can also produce general toxic effects (e.g. impaired consciousness, convulsions, or heart, liver and acute kidney failure) with or without irritation of the gastrointestinal tract, and such effects can be delayed.

In all cases of ingestion, if the casualty is completely alert and able to swallow, treat as follows:

- Have the casualty rinse mouth with water. Give one glass of water to drink.
- Observe in a place of safety for at least eight hours.
- If a significant amount of material has been ingested and the casualty complains of pain in the mouth or the stomach, give two tablets of paracetamol every six hours until the pain is relieved. **RADIO FOR MEDICAL ADVICE.**

Further advice on **ingestion of chemicals:** ☞ Appendix 10

- **Vomiting should not be induced!**
- Do **not** give salt water to induce vomiting, as it may be dangerous to do so.
- Inducing vomiting by stimulating the back of the throat is usually ineffective and may cause aspiration of the chemical into the lungs, and therefore should not be attempted.
- Dilution with large amounts of water or other liquid is **not** recommended as it may increase the absorption of the chemical.
- Syrup of Ipecac is not recommended, as it may cause aspiration of the chemical into the lungs and there is no evidence of clinical benefit from its use.
- Activated charcoal is usually not recommended at sea because if unconsciousness occurs it may be inhaled into the lungs. Its use in a given case should always be discussed with the Radio Medical Advice.

☞ *IMGS* or equivalent national medical guide

Signs & symptoms	Treatment
Frequent vomiting	- Frequent and prolonged vomiting is a bad sign. Give 10 mg metoclopramide intramuscularly; repeat two hours later if vomiting persists. - Do **not** give solid food.
Bleeding (bright red blood, dark brown "coffee ground" vomit or black, tarry, foul-smelling faeces)	- If severe bleeding occurs, there may be circulatory collapse: ☞ **Table 11** - **RADIO FOR MEDICAL ADVICE**

Table 10 – Ingestion of chemicals   **MFAG**

Signs & symptoms	Treatment

Perforation of the gut (severe pain all over the abdomen, board-like rigidity of the abdominal wall, shock)

Note: no bowel sounds are heard on listening to the abdomen with a stethoscope.

Further advice on **pain relief:** ☞ **Table 13**

- ■ **RADIO FOR MEDICAL ADVICE**
- ■ Arrange for evacuation. The casualty will need to be transferred to a shore hospital as soon as possible.
- ■ Give 10 mg morphine sulphate and 10 mg metoclopramide intramuscularly, if advised medically.

- ■ If advised medically, give cefuroxime 750 mg intramuscularly every eight hours and a metronidazole 1 g suppository every eight hours.
- ■ Institute a rectal infusion with rehydration salts while awaiting the transfer of the casualty to shore hospital.
- ■ The intravenous administration of fluids may be required.

Further advice on **rectal infusion and other fluid replacement:** ☞ **Appendix 13**

FOLLOW-UP

- ■ If the casualty is free of symptoms eight hours after ingestion, no further action is usually required.
- ■ Remember that vomit may be inhaled into the lungs, causing difficulty in breathing; if this occurs, treat as for inhalation: ☞ **Table 9**
- ■ A patient who has had significant exposure or any symptoms related to exposure should be kept warm in bed and closely observed for 48 hours and **RADIO MEDICAL ADVICE OBTAINED.**
- ■ If ingestion was intentional, continuous observation and medical advice is required. Put casualty ashore as soon as possible for hospital evaluation.

Table 11
SHOCK

Chemical burns and chemical-induced bleeding from the gut may cause circulatory collapse and shock with diversion of the blood from the limbs to maintain an adequate blood (and oxygen) supply to the brain and heart. Severe pain from chemical burns may also contribute to shock.

There are also a number of chemicals which are toxic to the heart directly and result in reduced pump action of the heart.

Severe shock may threaten the life of the casualty.

If shock is prolonged, acute kidney failure may result: ☞ **Table 12** and **appendix 12**

Signs & symptoms	Treatment
Pale, cold skin, often moist; later the skin may develop a bluish, ashen colour; rapid and shallow or irregular and deep breathing; rapid, weak but false pulse; anxiety and sweating	■ The casualty should be placed in a horizontal position. His legs should be elevated approximately 30 cm unless there is injury to the head, pelvis, spine, or chest, or difficulty in breathing. ■ Loosen clothing around the neck. ■ Check for a pulse. The best pulse to feel in an emergency is the carotid. Feel for five seconds before deciding it is absent. If it cannot be felt or is feeble, there is insufficient circulation and **CPR may be necessary:** ☞ Table 2 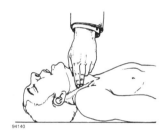 ■ Measure and record pulse and blood pressure every 15 minutes. ■ Give oxygen at a flow rate of 8 litres per minute until symptoms resolve. ■ Keep the casualty warm.
Shock due to chemical burns	■ Within the first 24 hours, give for every 10% of the body surface area with burns 3 litres of salted water ($1\frac{1}{2}$ teaspoonfuls of table salt in 1 litre) intermittently as often as the casualty tolerates (e.g. one glass every ten minutes). ■ Liquids should not be given by mouth if the patient is drowsy, convulsing, or about to have surgery.
Shock due to chemical-induced bleeding from the gut	■ The intravenous or rectal administration of fluids may be required. ■ **RADIO FOR MEDICAL ADVICE**

Further advice on **fluid replacement:** ☞ **Table 8, appendix 13**

Further advice on **pain relief:** ☞ **Table 13**

Breathing has stopped, no pulse	■ Institute CPR: ☞ Table 2

Table 11 – Shock   MFAG

FOLLOW-UP

A reduction in the amount of urine passed	This may be due to the onset of acute kidney failure.

- Measure and keep a record of the urine passed. Adjust the fluid intake until transfer to hospital is possible:

☛ **Table 12**

No urine is passed	

- **RADIO FOR MEDICAL ADVICE** in all cases.
- Seek **URGENT RADIO MEDICAL ADVICE.** Arrange for evacuation. The casualty will need to be transferred to a shore hospital as soon as possible

MFAG

Table 12
ACUTE KIDNEY FAILURE

Most chemicals are excreted by the kidneys, which may be damaged in the process. In severe poisoning, acute kidney failure may develop after 24 hours, and if it does not improve, the casualty may die after 7 to 14 days.

- Acute kidney failure must not be confused with retention of urine in the bladder.
- Acute kidney failure may arise for reasons other than chemical poisoning.

Further advice on **acute kidney failure:** ☞ Appendix 12

Signs & symptoms	Treatment
A steady reduction in the amount of urine passed	This may be a warning of the onset of acute kidney failure. ■ Record casualty's fluid intake and urine output carefully on a chart as shown in **appendix 12.** ■ Volume of urine passed, if any, should be measured and recorded every two hours. ■ If less than 125 mℓ of urine is passed in six hours, check whether bladder is over-full. ■ If not full, then acute kidney failure is present.
No urine is passed	■ This may be due either to an over-full bladder or acute kidney failure. ■ **RADIO FOR MEDICAL ADVICE** ■ If medical advice is not available, insert a urinary catheter into the bladder: 　☞ *IMGS* or equivalent national medical guide ■ If bladder is over-full (retention), leave the catheter in place and **SEEK RADIO MEDICAL ADVICE.** ■ If there is less than 125 mℓ of urine in the bladder and the casualty has not passed urine for more than six hours, **SEEK URGENT RADIO MEDICAL ADVICE.**

Table 13 – Pain relief   MFAG

Table 13
PAIN RELIEF

The use of analgesics (pain-killing drugs) is a very important step in the treatment of poisoning associated with severe tissue damage. Pain relief calms the casualty and stabilizes his condition. Paracetamol is a mild analgesic and morphine is used to treat severe pains. As morphine often causes vomiting, it should be combined with an anti-emetic such as metoclopramide.

Mild to moderate pain

- Give two tablets of paracetamol every six hours until the pain is relieved.

Severe pain

Casualty is breathing normally:

- **RADIO FOR MEDICAL ADVICE**

- If advice is not available:

  1 give morphine sulphate 10 mg and metoclopramide 10 mg intramuscularly.

  2 If breakthrough pain persists after 15 minutes or more, give a second injection of 10 mg of morphine sulphate intramuscularly.

  3 After four hours, if pain persists or recurs, give 10 to 20 mg morphine sulphate with a further dose of 10 mg metoclopramide intramuscularly.

  4 Where pain persists, the third and subsequent doses of 10 to 20 mg morphine sulphate must not be given more frequently than every four hours with metoclopramide 10 mg but the total dose of metoclopramide must not exceed 30 mg each 24 hours.

- Follow medical advice if available.

Casualty is breathing poorly:

- Administer oxygen at a flow rate of 6 to 8 litres per minute.

- **RADIO FOR MEDICAL ADVICE.** Evacuation to shore hospital is likely to be needed.

- If medical advice is not available and the pain is excruciating, give morphine sulphate 10 mg and metoclopramide 10 mg intramuscularly.

- If breakthrough pain persists after 15 minutes or more, give a second injection of 10 mg of morphine sulphate intramuscularly. **OBSERVE CAREFULLY FOR FURTHER DETERIORATION.**

- **RADIO FOR MEDICAL ADVICE** if not received previously.

Slow irregular breathing after morphine

- The following signs may indicate over-treatment with morphine:

  - Irregular breathing pattern;

  - Shallow and slow breathing;

  - Development of unconsciousness if the casualty was conscious at first;

  - Small pin-point pupils.

- If breathing is inadequate, give ventilation support and administer oxygen: ☞ **Table 3**

- **RADIO FOR MEDICAL ADVICE**

- If medical advice is not available, give 0.4 mg naloxone intramuscularly. Naloxone counteracts the side effects of morphine.

- Repeat the dose within 15 minutes if the casualty's condition does not improve and medical advice is not available.

- If there is no improvement after these two injections (total dose of 0.8 mg) of naloxone, it is very unlikely the deterioration is due to an overdose of morphine.
- If there is a response, and then further deterioration occurs, give a further dose of 0.4 mg of naloxone.

Morphine is a controlled substance as it is an addiction-producing drug

- Obtain RADIO MEDICAL ADVICE if at all possible prior to the use of morphine. Keep an exact record of morphine use.
- Keep stock locked away.
- Discontinue as soon as the pain can be relieved by paracetamol.
- If, under certain radio conditions, radio medical advice is not feasible, it is up to the master's discretion to ensure that adequate morphine is administered when pain is excruciating.

Table 14 – Chemical-induced bleeding   MFAG

Table 14
CHEMICAL-INDUCED BLEEDING

Some anti-coagulant pesticides ("super-warfarine") inhibit the normal blood clotting and lead to bleeding which may rarely be life-threatening, particularly if it occurs from the stomach. These effects may be delayed for 24 to 48 hours after exposure and can last for several weeks.

Signs & symptoms	Treatment
Bleeding from the nose and gums, blood in the urine, vomiting blood, vomiting "coffee grounds", black and tarry diarrhoea	■ Remove the casualty to the ship's hospital. ■ **RADIO FOR MEDICAL ADVICE** Arrange for evacuation. The casualty will need to be transferred to a shore hospital as soon as possible. ■ Give 10 mg phytomenadione (vitamin K_1) intramuscularly, if there is any delay in evacuation. ■ If bleeding persists **RADIO FOR MEDICAL ADVICE** and give a further 10 mg phytomenadione intramuscularly, if advised. ■ Massive bleeding can only be counteracted by infusion of plasma expanders.

Further advice on **fluid replacement:** ☞ **Appendix 13**

Table 15
CHEMICAL-INDUCED JAUNDICE

Jaundice refers to the yellow discoloration of the skin and eyes. The condition can be caused by liver disease or the breakdown of red blood cells (haemolysis).

LIVER DISEASE

The liver is the chemical factory where the body attempts to destroy all poisons. The most common cause of liver injury is the excessive intake of ethyl alcohol. Infectious agents can also cause liver disease (hepatitis) and jaundice.

The liver can rarely be damaged by certain chemicals, e.g. chlorinated hydrocarbons, metal salts and phosphorus. Chemical-induced liver injury does not show itself until two to three days after poisoning.

In severe cases, rapid and progressive failure of the liver can lead to increasing drowsiness followed by loss of consciousness and death after several days.

HAEMOLYSIS

Haemolysis of red blood cells can occur when there is either mechanical destruction of the cells (e.g. in certain heart conditions) or in certain types of blood disorders. Rarely, haemolysis can also result from overexposure to certain chemicals. There is no specific therapy of haemolysis on board a marine vessel but potential complications of kidney dysfunction due to the heavy overload of haemolytic products should be mitigated by high fluid intake. Urine output should be closely monitored.

Signs & symptoms	Treatment
Yellowing of skin and eyes; pain or tenderness in the right upper abdomen; urine becomes dark brown, and the stool pale in colour	■ RADIO FOR MEDICAL ADVICE. ■ The casualty should be transferred to a shore hospital as soon as possible. ■ The casualty should rest in bed and be kept warm. ■ Although the casualty may be feeling sick, he should be encouraged to take a high-carbohydrate diet in the form of liquids and bread. Liquids should contain at least two teaspoonfuls of sugar in a glass of water every two hours. ■ No drugs should be given unless there is severe vomiting, in which case give 10 mg metoclopramide intramuscularly; repeat two hours later if vomiting persists. ■ Alcoholic beverages should be completely avoided until on-shore clinical evaluation is obtained.

FOLLOW-UP

If there is a rapid onset of the symptoms and signs, associated with drowsiness or coma, then the damage is likely to be severe: **RADIO FOR MEDICAL ADVICE.** Arrange for evacuation. The casualty will need to be transferred to a shore hospital as soon as possible.

Table 16 – Hydrofluoric acid and hydrogen fluoride   **MFAG**

Table 16
HYDROFLUORIC ACID AND HYDROGEN FLUORIDE

These chemicals are corrosive to living tissue. They may cause deep, slowly healing, and painful burns. Systemically, damage to the heart and convulsions may occur. Several fluorides react with water forming hydrogen fluoride.

The onset of local reactions, pain and other symptoms may be delayed up to 24 hours after exposure to lower concentrations. The surface of the skin may not be destroyed for several hours, but the increasing pain and redness indicate a continuing destruction of tissues underneath the skin.

Treatment for EYE CONTACT in all cases of exposure, regardless of symptoms

- **IMMEDIATE** washing of the eye with copious amounts of water.
- Remove contact lens.
- Keep the eyelids widely apart as illustrated.
- Direct water flow from inner to outer corner of the eye. Washing must be done thoroughly for ten minutes, timed by the clock.

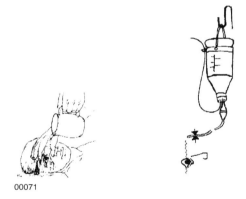

00071

- Anaesthetic eye drops should be instilled in the eye to ensure adequate irrigation of the eye.

Further advice on **eye treatment:** ☞ Table 7

Treatment for SKIN CONTACT in all cases of exposure, regardless of symptoms

- Chemical protective gloves and clothing should be used while washing the casualty's skin. After decontamination, it is not necessary to use protective clothing.
- Cut, if necessary, the clothes by using shears.
- **IMMEDIATE** washing with copious amounts of water for at least 10 minutes while removing contaminated clothing, rings, wristwatches, etc.
- After washing with water for 10 minutes, dry skin.
- Using latex gloves, massage exposed area with calcium gluconate gel for at least 15 minutes or until pain is relieved. Leave the gel on the skin. The gel should be re-applied 4 to 6 times daily for 3 to 4 days if a chemical burn is present.

If skin exposure exceeds 1% of body surface (approximately the size of the palm of the hand) and local symptoms (redness, pain, blisters)

- Give 5 g calcium gluconate, as effervescent tablets in 250 mℓ ($\frac{1}{2}$ pint) of water, to drink immediately and repeat two hours later.

  If calcium gluconate is not available, give milk.

- **RADIO FOR MEDICAL ADVICE.**

Further advice on **treatment of skin burns:** ☞ Table 8

MFAG

Treatment for INHALATION in all cases of exposure, regardless of symptoms

- Remove the casualty from the polluted atmosphere, have him rinse his mouth and give one glass of water to drink.
- If breathlessness or wheezing are present, give oxygen at a flow rate of 8 litres per minute until symptoms resolve.
- **RADIO FOR MEDICAL ADVICE**

Further advice on **breathing problems:** ☞ Table 9

Treatment for INGESTION in all cases of exposure, regardless of symptoms

- **RADIO FOR MEDICAL ADVICE**
- Have the casualty rinse mouth with water.
- Give 5 g calcium gluconate, as effervescent tablets in 250 ml ($\frac{1}{2}$ pint) of water, to drink immediately and repeat two hours later.

  If calcium gluconate is not available, give milk.

Signs & symptoms	Treatment
Vomiting, abdominal pain, diarrhoea	■ RADIO FOR MEDICAL ADVICE and ☞ Table 10
Shock	■ RADIO FOR MEDICAL ADVICE and ☞ Table 11
Convulsions (seizures, fits)	☞ Table 5

Table 17 – Organophosphate and carbamate insecticides   MFAG

Table 17
ORGANOPHOSPHATE AND CARBAMATE INSECTICIDES

Organophosphorus and carbamate insecticides cause disturbances in the transmission of nerve impulses to target organs such as muscles and glands by inhibiting the enzyme acetylcholinesterase.

Signs and symptoms may include:

- Headache, nausea, dizziness, fatigue
- Blurred vision, pin-point pupils
- Confusion
- Vomiting, abdominal cramps and diarrhoea
- Sweating, salivation, watering of the eyes, and increased nasal and lung secretions
- Muscle twitching, weakness, tremor, convulsions
- Tightness in the chest, wheezing, slow pulse, respiratory and cardiac arrest.

Symptoms usually develop during exposure or within 12 hours after contact. The acute intoxication stage usually does not last longer than 48 hours unless exposure has been prolonged or the insecticide has been ingested. Recovery from exposure to carbamate insecticides usually occur within 24 hours.

Treatment for EYE CONTACT in all cases of exposure, regardless of symptoms

- **IMMEDIATE** washing of the eye with copious amounts of water.

Further advice on **eye treatment:** ☞ Table 7

Treatment for SKIN CONTACT in all cases of exposure, regardless of symptoms

- **IMMEDIATE** washing with soap or shampoo and copious amounts of water for at least 10 minutes while removing contaminated clothing, rings, wristwatches, etc.
- The casualty should shower thoroughly.
- Chemical protective gloves should be worn by those attending the exposed individual to prevent self-contamination.

Further advice in cases of **skin burns:** ☞ Table 8

- Contaminated clothing should be kept in properly labelled bags until washing.
- Remove the casualty to the ship's hospital.
- **RADIO FOR MEDICAL ADVICE** if symptoms develop.

Treatment for INHALATION in all cases of exposure, regardless of symptoms

(toxic effects may be expected particularly after inhalation of dust and mist)

- Remove the casualty from the polluted atmosphere, have him rinse his mouth and give one glass of water to drink.
- Remove clothes and shower thoroughly.
- **RADIO FOR MEDICAL ADVICE** if symptoms develop.

Treatment for INGESTION in all cases of exposure, regardless of symptoms

- Have the casualty rinse his mouth thoroughly with water.
- **RADIO FOR MEDICAL ADVICE**

Signs & symptoms irrespective of routes of exposure	Treatment
Blurred vision, headache, nausea, fatigue or dizziness	■ Observe in a place of safety. ■ RADIO FOR MEDICAL ADVICE ■ If the casualty becomes free of symptoms, no further action is required.
Vomiting, cramp-like abdominal pains, excessive sweating and salivation, tightness in the chest or twitching of the muscles	■ **RADIO FOR MEDICAL ADVICE** ■ Inject 1 mg atropine intramuscularly. If the skin and mouth have not become dry within 30 minutes, give a further dose of 1 mg atropine intramuscularly. In casualties severely poisoned with an organophosphorus insecticide, very large doses (10 to 15 mg) of atropine may be required. ■ CAUTION: Overdosage of atropine may lead to fever, restlessness, hallucinations and disorientation, followed by depression, respiratory arrest and death. If atropine toxicity is suspected, discontinue further treatment with atropine.
Respiratory difficulty with excessive lung secretions, paralysis with complete loss of muscle function, slow pulse, or unconsciousness	■ Administer controlled ventilation with oxygen at a flow rate of 8 litres per minute and heart compression as warranted. ■ If a medically trained individual is available, atropine should be given intravenously as follows: 1 to 2 mg repeated every 15 minutes until lung secretions have dried up.

Further advice: ☞ **Tables 2 and 3**

■ Transfer to shore hospital is **URGENT**

FOLLOW-UP

■ A patient who has had significant exposure or any symptoms related to exposure should be kept warm in bed and closely observed for 48 hours and **RADIO MEDICAL ADVICE OBTAINED.**

■ Since atropine has a short action, vomiting, cramp-like pains, excessive sweating and salivation or tightness of the chest may reappear after initial improvement with atropine therapy.

■ If these symptoms recur, repeat injection of atropine as described above. In very severe poisoning this may be necessary for 24 to 48 hours.

■ Some organophosphorus insecticides may damage the nerves in the limbs after the casualty's recovery from acute poisoning. The muscles controlled by those nerves may become weak, and paralysis with complete loss of muscle function may occur.

■ RADIO FOR MEDICAL ADVICE AND TRANSFER THE CASUALTY TO A SHORE HOSPITAL AS SOON AS POSSIBLE.

Table 18 – Cyanides   **MFAG**

Table 18
CYANIDES

Cyanides are fast acting, highly poisonous materials. They may be fatal if inhaled, swallowed, or absorbed through the skin and are extremely hazardous when in liquid and vapour form under pressure.

Signs and symptoms may include:

- Headache, nausea and dizziness
- Drowsiness, drop in blood pressure, rapid pulse
- Convulsions, unconsciousness
- Impaired respiration

With prompt rescue and treatment following exposure, recovery is normally quick and complete. Mouth-to-mouth resuscitation should be avoided in CPR to prevent the rescuer from being exposed.

Treatment for EYE CONTACT in all cases of exposure, regardless of symptoms

- **IMMEDIATE** washing of the eye with copious amounts of water.

Further advice on **eye treatment:** ☞ Table 7

Treatment for SKIN CONTACT in all cases of exposure, regardless of symptoms

- **IMMEDIATE** washing with soap or shampoo and copious amounts of water for at least 10 minutes while removing contaminated clothing, rings, wristwatches, etc.
- Remove the casualty to the ship's hospital.

Treatment for INHALATION in all cases of exposure, regardless of symptoms

- Remove the casualty from the polluted atmosphere. Ensure that rescuers are equipped with respiratory protection so that they do not become poisoned also.
- After removal of the casualty from the polluted atmosphere, usually no specific treatment is necessary unless breathing is depressed or absent.

If breathing is absent, give **CPR and oxygen:** ☞ Tables 2 and 3

Treatment for INGESTION in all cases of exposure, regardless of symptoms

- Have the casualty rinse his mouth with water.
- **RADIO FOR MEDICAL ADVICE**

Signs & symptoms irrespective of routes of exposure	Treatment
Nausea or dizziness; slurred speech, confusion or drowsiness; difficulty in breathing and impaired consciousness	<ul><li>Give oxygen at a flow rate of 8 litres per minute until symptoms resolve.</li><li>Observe in a place of safety for eight hours.</li><li>**RADIO FOR MEDICAL ADVICE**</li><li>If the casualty becomes free of symptoms within eight hours after exposure, no further action is required.</li></ul>

Table 19
METHANOL (METHYL ALCOHOL) AND ETHYLENE GLYCOL

Methanol and ethylene glycol ("antifreeze") are particularly dangerous when swallowed. Poisoning by methanol absorption through the intact skin may also occur if methanol-soaked clothes are worn. The administration of alcohol (ethyl alcohol, ethanol) will reduce the risk of toxicity.

Signs and symptoms may include:

- Drunkenness, headache, nausea
- Blurred vision, avoidance of daylight (in methanol poisoning)
- Unconsciousness, impaired breathing

Onset of signs and symptoms may be delayed, particularly if alcohol (ethyl alcohol, ethanol) has been drunk at the same time.

Treatment for SKIN CONTACT in all cases of exposure, regardless of symptoms

- The casualty should remove contaminated clothing and wash with soap and water.

INGESTION

Signs & symptoms	Treatment
If a mouthful or more is swallowed, regardless of symptoms	■ **RADIO FOR MEDICAL ADVICE** in all cases. ■ Give 25 mℓ of ethyl alcohol 99.5% in 250 to 300 mℓ water or soft drink. ■ This is a **MEDICAL EMERGENCY**. The casualty should be transferred to a shore hospital as soon as possible.
Drunkenness, headache, fatigue, blurred vision, photophobia (avoidance of daylight)	■ Continue to give water or soft drink with ethyl alcohol as above every three hours until the casualty can be evacuated.
Unconsciousness with less than eight respirations of normal depth per minute or respiratory arrest	■ Administer controlled ventilation with oxygen at a flow rate of 8 litres per minute and heart compression as warranted.

Further advice on **CPR and oxygen administration:** ☞ Tables 2 and 3

FOLLOW-UP

- If the casualty cannot be evacuated, and if medically advised, continue treatment with alcohol (ethyl alcohol).

Further advice on **prolonged unconsciousness:** ☞ Table 4

- If ingestion was intentional, continuous observation and medical advice is required. Put casualty ashore as soon as possible for hospital evaluation.

Table 20 – Radioactive material MFAG

Table 20
RADIOACTIVE MATERIAL

Hazards may come from either the radioactive nature of the material or its chemical nature. The radioactive nature of the material may result in external radiation or internal radiation if the substance is inhaled, ingested or absorbed through the skin.

The acute effects of radiation exposure may include:

- Vomiting
- Weakness
- Headache
- Diarrhoea

Onset and severity of signs indicate the course of illness. After a period of one to three weeks with few symptoms, loss of hair, complicating infections, diffuse bleeding and uncontrollable diarrhoea may be seen in severe cases. **LIFE IS IN DANGER.**

- **Rescue personnel should wear full chemically protective clothing and breathing apparatus.**

In all cases of contamination, treat the casualty as follows:

- Remove persons from the source of radiation as far away as possible.

- Give first aid to any immediate life-threatening problems such as not breathing, heart stopped or serious bleeding.

- Institute CPR, if necessary. Use an oxygen resuscitator. **Do not use mouth-to-nose** or **mouth-to-mouth resuscitation** to prevent the rescuer from being exposed.

- Wrap stabilised or less injured casualties in blankets to contain contamination whilst you treat any seriously injured casualties.

- Remove the casualty's clothing and personal items which may be contaminated and place them in a plastic bag or sealed box. Label and hold it in a secure place that is not near any occupied space on board until the assistance of radiation experts is available to evaluate them. Treat non-life-threatening injuries at this time. Allow wounds/cuts that are not life-threatening to bleed briefly and then treat.

- Have the casualty blow his nose and gently swab the nasal passages and ears to remove any contaminated particles. Save swabs and nose blows, treat as if contaminated. Rinse the mouth thoroughly.

- If the injuries of an exposed person do not prevent it, have the casualty shower or wash thoroughly, including body hair and eyes, as soon as possible after being removed from the affected area. Hair shampoo may be used during the showering. Take care not to damage the skin when washing.

- Care should be taken to prevent the spread of contaminated washing water. Store any towels, blankets, brushes, etc., used in the decontamination.

- Apply first aid dressings to minor injuries after the decontamination washing.

- Rescue personnel wearing protective clothing and breathing apparatus should be hosed down with water for 10 minutes and should remove and store their clothing, as above, and thoroughly shower, using shampoo, after completing assistance to casualties.

- As soon as possible, take a specimen of urine from every person who has been in direct or indirect contact with the radioactive substance. Keep the urine in a closed receptacle for further analysis.

- **RADIO FOR MEDICAL ADVICE**

- Do not give any treatment for possible ingestion, inhalation or absorption through the skin of radioactive material except on the advice of a physician.

Signs & symptoms	Treatment
Nausea, weakness, sleepiness, loss of appetite	- **RADIO FOR MEDICAL ADVICE** - The casualty should be kept at rest under observation in a warm cabin or in the ship's hospital. - If no vomiting occurs during 2 to 3 days, the casualty should be put under medical supervision at the next port of call.

MFAG

Signs & symptoms	Treatment
Vomiting within 2 to 3 days after exposure	■ Give 10 mg metoclopramide intramuscularly; repeat two hours later if vomiting persists. An earlier onset of frequent and prolonged vomiting is a bad sign. ■ Be prepared to administer shock treatment. ■ **RADIO FOR MEDICAL ADVICE AND TRANSFER THE CASUALTY TO A SHORE HOSPITAL AS SOON AS POSSIBLE.**

Appendices

Appendix 1
RESCUE

Integrated response

The potential for hazardous chemical exposures and subsequent injury to personnel exists on board ships that carry hazardous materials. While occurring infrequently, chemical incidents are capable of endangering the health of exposed individuals and emergency personnel directed to assist them. People who have been seriously injured by a hazardous material have a greater chance of recovery without complications when appropriate emergency treatment is provided by trained personnel at the scene, and when the casualty is safely transported to an area where further care can be given. This requires an integrated emergency medical response involving the ship's master and all individuals who may be called upon to rescue and provide medical assistance after an exposure incident.

Emergency response plan

A common characteristic of the successful management of chemical incidents is adequate contingency planning. Planning requires the involvement of all personnel on board the ship who might be called upon to provide emergency response and first aid to injured individuals.

Every ship carrying dangerous goods should have an emergency response plan which includes the following:

◆ A listing of individuals who are trained to respond to an exposure incident and administer first aid.

◆ Methods and procedures for response which are specific for the particular ship, including procedures and equipment for casualty decontamination.

◆ Location of personal protective equipment and transport equipment.

◆ Content and frequency of training programmes and drills.

◆ Location of Material Safety Data Sheets (MSDS), papers related to ship inventories and other documents that might help identify chemicals present at an incident.

Arrival at the scene

Many first responders are accustomed to immediately attending an injured casualty and may disregard the possibility of danger to themselves. Without proper protection, a rescuer entering a contaminated area risks exposure and the potential for becoming a casualty. Even though rescue of any casualty is important, it should only be attempted after it is certain that the responders, themselves, will not become injured.

Whenever a chemical is unidentified, worst-case assumptions concerning toxicity must be assumed.

Rescuers therefore must **NOT**:

◆ Enter a contaminated area without using a pressure-demand self-contained breathing apparatus and wearing full protective clothing;

◆ Enter an enclosed space unless they are trained members of a rescue team and follow correct procedures;

◆ Walk through any spilled materials;

◆ Allow unnecessary contamination of equipment;

◆ Attempt to recover shipping papers or manifests from contaminated area unless adequately protected;

◆ Become exposed while approaching a potentially contaminated area;

◆ Attempt rescue unless trained and equipped with appropriate personal protective equipment (PPE) and protective clothing for the situation.

Establishment of an exclusion or hot zone

The **first rescuer** at the site should establish an exclusion zone that encompasses all contaminated areas, but should not become exposed in doing so. No one should be allowed to cross into the zone without wearing a self-contained breathing apparatus and full protective clothing.

Assessment, decontamination and initial treatment of casualties

Primary goals for emergency personnel in a hazardous materials incident include termination of exposure to the casualty, removal of the casualty from danger, and casualty treatment – while not jeopardizing the safety of rescue personnel.

Termination of exposure can best be accomplished by removing the casualty from the exposure area and removing contaminates from the casualty. If the casualty is removed from the possibility of additional exposure or other dangers and the casualty is no longer contaminated, the level of protection for personnel can be downgraded to a level that will better facilitate the provision of casualty care.

The potential for additional danger to casualty and responder prohibits any medical treatment inside the exclusion zone other than basic life support. The probability of contact with hazardous substances either by subsequent release of materials still in the area, along with dangers of fire or explosion, and the restriction of movement by necessary PPE outweigh the time saved by attempting casualty care in the exclusion or hot zone.

Priority should be given to the **A**irway, **B**reathing, and **C**irculation (ABC, see **table 2**). Once life-threatening matters have been addressed, rescue personnel can then direct attention to secondary casualty assessment. It is important to remember that appropriate personal protective equipment and clothing must be worn until the threat of secondary exposure is no longer a danger. Therefore, the sooner the casualty becomes decontaminated the sooner response personnel may reduce protective measures or downgrade the level of protection.

During initial casualty stabilization, a gross decontamination should simultaneously be performed. This consists of cutting away or otherwise removing all suspected contaminated clothing, including jewellery and watches, and the brushing or wiping off any obvious contamination. Care should be taken to protect any open wounds from contamination. Every effort should be made by personnel to avoid contact with any potentially hazardous substance.

Decontamination

Decontamination includes the reduction of external contamination, containment of the contamination that is present, and prevention of the further spread of potentially dangerous substances. In other words, remove what you can and contain what you can't.

Table 7 (EYE EXPOSURE TO CHEMICALS) and **table 8** (SKIN EXPOSURE TO CHEMICALS) provide detailed instructions for decontamination.

With a few exceptions, intact skin is less absorptive than injured flesh, mucous membranes, or eyes. Therefore, decontamination should begin at the head of the casualty and proceed downward with initial attention to contaminated eyes and open wounds. Once wounds have been cleaned, care should be exercised so as not to recontaminate them. This can be aided by covering the wounds with a waterproof dressing. For some chemicals, such as strong alkali, it may be necessary to flush exposed eyes with water or normal saline for extended period of time.

External decontamination should be performed using the least aggressive methods. Mechanical or chemical irritation to the skin should be limited to prevent increased permeability. Contaminated areas should be carefully cleaned under a gentle spray of water with a soft sponge and a mild soap such as dishwashing liquid. Warm water (never hot) should be used. The degree of decontamination should be completed based on the nature of the contaminant, the form of contaminant, the casualty's condition, environmental conditions, and resources available.

Responders should try to contain all runoff from decontamination procedures for proper disposal. The casualty should be isolated from the environment to prevent the spread of any remaining contaminants.

All potentially contaminated casualty clothing and belongings should be removed and placed within properly labelled bags.

Considerations for casualty treatment

A contaminated casualty is like any other casualty and may be treated as such except that responders must protect themselves and others from dangers due to contamination. Response personnel must first address life-threatening issues and then decontamination and supportive measures. The initial assessment can be accomplished simultaneously with decontamination and additional management completed as conditions allow. The chemical-specific information which is obtained from shipping papers and labels should be incorporated into the proper casualty treatment procedures.

When more than one casualty is involved, proper triage procedures should be implemented.

◆ If there is only one unconscious casualty (irrespective of the total number of casualties):
1 Give immediate treatment to the unconscious casualty only; and
2 Send for help.

◆ If there is more than one unconscious casualty:
1 Send for help, and
2 Give appropriate treatment to the worst casualty in the priority order of:
a Casualties who have stopped breathing or have no pulse (see **table 2**),
b Casualties who are unconscious (see **table 4**).

◆ If the casualty is unconscious or cyanotic (bluish skin) but breathing, connect to portable oxygen.

Presenting signs and symptoms can then be treated as appropriate and when conditions allow. The sooner a casualty has been decontaminated the sooner he or she can be treated like a "normal" casualty. Unless required by life-threatening conditions, preventive invasive procedures, such as intravenous injections, should be performed only in fully decontaminated areas where conditions permit. These procedures may create a direct route for introducing the hazardous material into the casualty.

Oxygen should be given using a bag valve mask with reservoir device (rebreather). The contaminated atmosphere should not mix with the oxygen if possible.

The casualty should be frequently reassessed because many hazardous materials have latent physiological effects. While some cases may require treatment with antidotes, most cases will be handled with symptomatic care.

Transport of casualty to medical area of ship

The casualty should be as clean as possible before transport, and further contact with contaminants should be avoided. Special care should be exercised in preventing contamination of stretchers and others who will subsequently come in contact with the casualty. Protective clothing should be worn by response personnel as appropriate. If decontamination cannot be performed adequately, responders should make every attempt to prevent the spread of contamination and at the very least remove casualty clothing, wrap the casualty in blankets, followed by body bags or plastic or rubber sheets to lessen the likelihood of contamination to equipment and others. Minimize contamination from shoes.

If casualties can walk, lead them out of contaminated area.

If casualties are unable to walk, remove them on backboards or stretchers. Fibreglass backboards and disposable sheeting are recommended.

If a wood backboard is used, it should be covered with disposable sheeting or it may have to be discarded afterwards. Equipment that comes in contact with the casualty should be segregated for disposal or decontamination.

If no other means of removal are available, carefully carry or drag casualties to safety.

Medical management of casualty

If the route of exposure to the casualty is known, the appropriate table should be consulted for guidance.

If the chemical has a specific treatment procedure (see **appendix 15**), the appropriate table should be consulted.

If the casualty has signs or symptoms, the appropriate table should be consulted.

Appendix 2
CPR (CARDIO-PULMONARY RESUSCITATION)

ASSESSMENT OF BREATHING

◆ Tilt the head firmly backwards with one hand while lifting the neck with the other hand to relieve obstructed breathing.

◆ Pull the tongue forward.

◆ Suck or swab out excess secretions.

◆ Clean any vomit from the mouth and back of the throat.

◆ Remove any loose dentures.

◆ Listen and feel for any movement of air, because the chest and abdomen may move in the presence of an obstructed airway, without moving air. The rescuer's face should be placed close to the casualty's nose and mouth so that any exhaled air may be felt against the cheek. Also the rise and fall of the chest can be observed and the exhaled breath heard.

◆ Look, listen and feel for five seconds before deciding that breathing is absent.

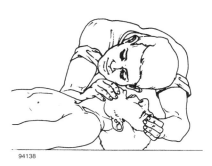

94138

ASSESSMENT OF HEART FUNCTION

◆ Check for a pulse. The best pulse to feel in an emergency is the carotid. Feel for five seconds before deciding it is absent. If it cannot be felt or is feeble, there is insufficient circulation.

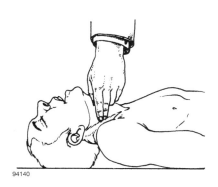

94140

BREATHING, HEART IS BEATING, UNCONSCIOUS

◆ Insert a Guedel airway (see **appendix 3**) to prevent the tongue slipping back and obstructing the upper air passage; it should be left in place until the casualty becomes conscious again.

◆ Place casualty in the recovery position; no pillows should be used under the head:

▶ Place the arm nearest to you out at right angles to his body, elbow bent with the hand palm uppermost.

▶ Bring the far arm across the chest and place the hand, palm down, on the shoulder nearest to you.

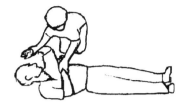

▶ Grasp the far leg just above the knee and pull it up, keeping the foot on the ground.

▶ With your other hand on the far shoulder, pull on the leg to roll the casualty towards you onto his side.

▶ Adjust the upper leg so that both the hip and knee are bent at right angles.

▶ Tilt the head back to make sure the airway remains open.

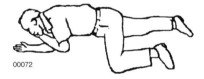

00072

GUIDELINES FOR RESUSCITATION:
European Resuscitation Council 1996

◆ If the casualty has breathing difficulties and his lips turn blue, give oxygen at a flow rate of 6 to 8 litres per minute until symptoms resolve (see **appendix 3**).

◆ Keep the casualty warm.

RADIO FOR MEDICAL ADVICE

Further advice on **subsequent treatment for an unconscious person:** ☞ Appendix 4

NOT BREATHING BUT HEART IS BEATING

Airway

Establishing an OPEN AIRWAY IS THE MOST IMPORTANT STEP IN ARTIFICIAL RESPIRATION. Spontaneous breathing may occur as a result of this simple measure.

◆ Place the casualty in a face-up position on a hard surface.

◆ Put one hand beneath the casualty's neck and the other hand on the forehead. Lift the neck with the one hand, and apply pressure to the forehead with the other to tilt the head backward.

This extends the neck and moves the base of the tongue away from the back of the throat. The head should be maintained in this position during the entire artificial respiration and heart compression procedure.

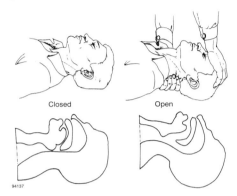

Closed   Open

94137

◆ If only one rescuer is available, the head should be fixed in the shown position by means of a rolled blanket or similar object pushed under the casualty's shoulders.

◆ If the airway is still obstructed, any foreign material in the mouth or throat should be removed immediately with the fingers.

Artificial respiration

If the casualty does not resume adequate, spontaneous breathing promptly after his head has been tilted backward, artificial respiration should be given by the mouth-to-mouth or mouth-to-nose method or other techniques. Regardless of the method used, preservation of an open airway is essential.

Before starting artificial respiration, the casualty's clothes should be removed as far as feasible. Otherwise, the rescuer might become poisoned by inhaling vapour or gases emanating from contaminated clothes.

In some circumstances, mouth-to-mouth respiration should be used cautiously. The rescuer should be aware of getting in touch with toxic and caustic materials around the casualty's mouth.

As the artificial respiration must be continued as long as there are signs of life, a resuscitator should be made available as soon as possible.

Mouth-to-mouth respiration

◆ Keep the casualty's head at a maximum backward tilt *with one hand* under the neck.

◆ Place the heel of *the other hand* on the forehead, with the thumb and index finger towards the nose. Pinch together the casualty's nostrils with the thumb and index finger to prevent air from escaping. Continue to exert pressure on the forehead with the palm of the hand to maintain the backward tilt of the head.

94141

◆ Take a deep breath, then form a tight seal with your mouth over and around the casualty's mouth.

◆ Blow in until the casualty's chest rises.

◆ Watch the casualty's chest while inflating the lungs. If adequate respiration is taking place, the chest should rise and fall.

◆ Remove your mouth and allow the casualty to exhale passively. If in the right position, the casualty's exhalation will be felt on your cheek.

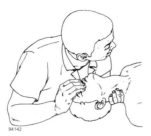

◆ Take another deep breath, form a tight seal around the casualty's mouth and blow into the mouth again. Repeat this procedure 10 to 12 times a minute, once every 5 seconds.

◆ If there is no air exchange, and an airway obstruction exists, reach into the casualty's mouth and throat to remove any foreign matter with your fingers; and resume artificial respiration. A foreign body should be suspected if you are unable to inflate the lungs, despite proper positioning and a tight air-seal around the mouth or nose.

Mouth-to-nose respiration

The mouth-to-nose technique should be used when it is impossible to open the casualty's mouth, when the mouth is severely injured, or a tight seal around the lips cannot be obtained.

◆ Keep the casualty's head tilted back with one hand. Use the other hand to lift up the casualty's lower jaw to seal the lips.

◆ Take a deep breath, seal your lips around the casualty's nose, and blow in until the casualty's chest rises.

◆ Remove your mouth and allow the casualty to exhale passively.

◆ Repeat the cycle 10 to 12 times per minute.

Artificial respiration should be continued for 2 hours if necessary; longer if there are signs of life.

BREATHING AND HEART HAVE STOPPED

Heart compression (external cardiac compression) should be applied together with artificial respiration throughout any attempt to resuscitate a casualty whose breathing and heart have stopped. Unless circulation is restored, the brain will be without oxygen and the person will suffer cerebral damage within 4 to 6 minutes, and may die.

Artificial respiration will bring oxygen-containing air to the lungs of the casualty. From there, oxygen is transported with circulating blood to the brain and to other organs, and the effective heart compression will – for some time – artificially restore the blood circulation, until the heart starts beating.

Technique for heart compression

Compression of the breast bone produces some artificial ventilation, but not enough for adequate oxygenation of the blood. For this reason, artificial respiration is always required whenever heart compression is used.

MFAG

Effective heart compression requires sufficient pressure to depress the casualty's lower breast bone about 4 to 5 cm (in an adult). *For heart compression to be effective, the casualty must be on a firm surface. If he is in bed, a board or improvised support should be placed under his back. However, chest compression must not be delayed to look for a firmer support.*

◆   Kneel close to the side of the casualty and place only the heel of one hand over the lower half of the breast bone. Avoid placing the hand over the tip of the breast bone which extends down over the upper abdomen. Pressure on the tip may tear the liver and lead to severe internal bleeding.

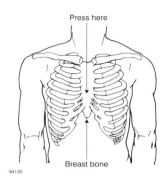

◆   Feel the tip of the breast bone and place the heel of the hand about 4 cm towards the head of the casualty. Your fingers must never rest on the casualty's ribs during compression. This increases the possibility of rib fractures.

◆   Place the heel of the other hand on top of the first one.

◆   Rock forward so that your shoulders are almost directly above the casualty's chest.

◆   Keep your arms straight and exert adequate pressure almost directly downward to depress an adult's lower sternum 4 to 5 cm.

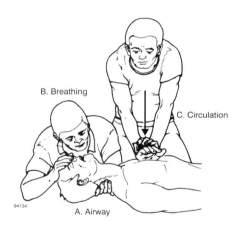

◆   Depress the sternum 80 to 100 times per minute for an adult (when two rescuers are used). This is usually rapid enough to maintain blood flow, and slow enough to allow the heart to fill with blood. The compression should be regular, smooth, and uninterrupted, with compression and relaxion being of equal duration. **Under no circumstances should compression be interrupted for more than 5 seconds.**

Two-rescuer heart compressions and artificial respiration:

◆   Five heart compressions:

   ▶   at a rate of 80 to 100 per minute

   ▶   no pause for ventilation.

◆   One respiration:

   ▶   after each 5 compressions

   ▶   interposed between compressions.

It is preferable to have two rescuers because artificial circulation must be combined with artificial respiration. The most effective artificial respiration and heart compression are achieved by giving one lung inflation quickly after each five heart compressions (5:1 ratio). *The compression rate should be 80 to 100 per minute for two rescuers.*

One rescuer performs heart compression while the other remains at the casualty's head, keeps it tilted back, and continues rescue breathing (artificial respiration). **Supplying the breaths without any pauses in heart compression is important, because every interruption in this compression results in a drop of blood flow and blood pressure to zero.**

Single-rescuer heart compressions and artificial respiration:

A single rescuer must perform both artificial respiration and artificial circulation using a 15:2 ratio. The head should be kept in the shown position by means of a rolled blanket or similar object pushed under the casualty's shoulders. *Two very quick lung inflations should be delivered after each 15 chest compressions, without waiting for full exhalation of the casualty's breath.*

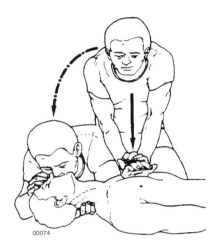

00074

- ◆ Fifteen heart compressions at a rate of 80 to 100 per minute.

- ◆ Two very quick lung inflations

Checking effectiveness of heart compression: pupils and pulse

Check the reaction of the pupils: a pupil that narrows when exposed to light indicates that the brain is receiving adequate oxygen and blood. If the pupils remain widely dilated and do not react to light, serious brain damage is likely to occur soon or has occurred already. Dilated but reactive pupils are a less serious sign.

The carotid (neck) pulse should be felt after the first minute of the heart compression and artificial respiration, and every 2 minutes thereafter. The pulse will indicate the effectiveness of the heart compression or the return of a spontaneous effective heartbeat.

Other indicators of this effectiveness are the following:

- ◆ Expansion of the chest each time the operator blows air into the lung.
- ◆ A pulse which can be felt each time the chest is compressed.
- ◆ Return of colour to the skin.
- ◆ A spontaneous gasp for breath.
- ◆ Return of a spontaneous heartbeat.

Terminating heart compression

Deep unconsciousness, the absence of spontaneous respiration, and fixed, dilated pupils for 15 to 30 minutes indicate cerebral death of the casualty, and further efforts to restore circulation and breathing are usually futile, unless it is a case of hypothermia in which cerebral death can be delayed.

In the absence of a physician, artificial respiration and heart compression should be continued until:

- ◆ The heart of the casualty starts beating again and breathing is restored.
- ◆ The casualty is transferred to the care of the doctor, or other health personnel responsible for emergency care.
- ◆ The rescuer is unable to continue because of fatigue.

Appendix 3
OXYGEN ADMINISTRATION AND CONTROLLED VENTILATION

Suffocation

Suffocation (asphyxia) causes a lack of tissue oxygen in the blood. It has many causes other than those arising from chemical poisoning. The latter are principally:

◆ The air passage may be blocked by vomit, blood or secretions.

◆ Obstruction to breathing in the throat or the air passage through spasm of the air tubes or by swelling of the linings of the voice box due to irritant fumes.

◆ Fluid in the lung air spaces (pulmonary oedema) caused by irritant fumes, e.g. by ammonia or chlorine.

◆ Poisoning of the blood which prevents the carriage or use of oxygen in the body caused by, for example, carbon monoxide, cyanides, or aniline.

◆ Poisoning of the mechanisms of breathing in the chest (e.g. by organophosphate insecticides) or the brain (chlorinated hydrocarbons).

◆ Gases which do not support life because they replace oxygen in the atmosphere, e.g. carbon dioxide, nitrogen, hydrogen.

Diagnosis

◆ There is difficulty in breathing with an increased rate at first (over 30 per minute). Later it may become slow and stop.

◆ The pulse is rapid, usually over 100 per minute.

◆ There is blueness of the skin with purple lips and tongue.

◆ The casualty may be agitated at first but become apathetic, with muscular weakness. Unconsciousness may follow this.

◆ The pupils of the eyes will react to light at first. If they become large and do not react to light, life is in danger.

Dangers of oxygen

◆ Spontaneous combustion occurs in the presence of oxygen. For example, a glowing cigarette will burst into flames in an oxygen atmosphere. **Smoking, naked lights or fires must not be allowed in any place where oxygen is being administered because of the fire risk.**

◆ Oxygen treatment prolonged over many hours can be particularly dangerous to persons with chronic breathing disorders. Too much oxygen impedes the breathing time clock that triggers the natural breathing bellows mechanism.

Radio medical advice should always be sought when giving oxygen treatment. Prolonged oxygen treatment should only be given in a shore hospital where laboratory blood gas analysis can be undertaken. Therefore all cases requiring prolonged oxygen treatment should be hospitalized ashore as soon as possible.

Oxygen resuscitation kits

Valve and bag oxygen resuscitation kits are primarily applicable to people who are not breathing. They are intended for use only by trained persons. There are a number of manufacturers marketing these products and training must be related to the manufacturers' instructions relating to the specific model carried on board.

The basic parts of the kit need to be stored assembled correctly in accordance with the manufacturers' instructions and ready for use. Generally they comprise:

◆ face mask (sizes varying depending on the size of the face, but for adults usually there are only two sizes, large and small).

◆ the bag with valve to which the oxygen intake is attached.

◆ the oxygen reservoir also attached to the bag and valve.

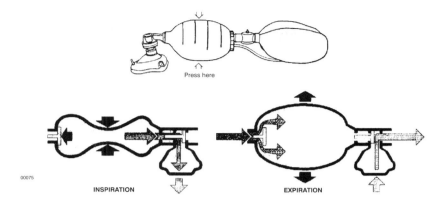

The oxygen supply needs to comprise:

◆ A cylinder containing medical oxygen (industrial oxygen may contain unsafe impurities).

◆ A reducing valve with wheel control.

◆ A pressure gauge and valve with "on" "off" knob.

◆ Hose connecting the bag to the "on" "off" knob for the valve.

Note: When the kit is operating successfully, oxygen will be heard to be flowing through the tubing. If the cylinder is empty or there is a kink in the oxygen supply tube, the casualty receives air only (21% oxygen). But this is similar to giving ordinary mouth-to-mouth ventilation.

Insertion of Guedel airway

This airway is for use in an unconscious casualty. Select the appropriate size; males usually require the largest size. The function of the airway is to ensure a clear passage between the lips and the back of the throat.

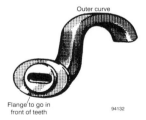

◆ First remove any dentures and any debris or vomit from the mouth with the fingers. If an electric or manual suction pump with catheter attached is immediately available, use this to clear the air passage. Then, with the head fully back, slide the airway gently into the mouth with the outer curve of the airway towards the tongue. This operation will be easier if the airway is wetted.

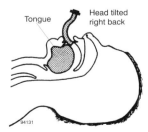

◆ If there is any attempt by the casualty to gag, retch or vomit, it is better not to proceed with the insertion of the airway. If necessary, try again later to insert it.

◆ Continue to slide the airway in until the flange of the airway reaches the lips. Then rotate the airway through 180° so that the outer curve is towards the roof of the mouth.

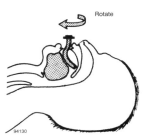

◆ Bring the jaw upwards and push the airway in until the flange at the end of the airway is outside the teeth (or gums) and inside the lips. If necessary, tape one or both lips so that the end of the airway is not covered by them.

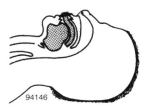

Oxygen for the casualty who is not breathing

◆ If the casualty does not have a pulse or heart beat, CPR should be performed immediately by a second rescuer. Administration of oxygen as soon as possible is critical.

◆ A Guedel airway should be inserted. If insertion of an airway cannot be achieved, the chin should be pulled forward throughout the administration of oxygen. If the casualty has seizures due to the lack of oxygen, administration of oxygen may be difficult but is essential.

◆ Use a positive-pressure manual operated oxygen resuscitator in accordance with manufacturer's instruction. It makes assisted or controlled ventilation possible.

◆ Oxygen should be used at a flow rate of 8 litres per minute. The bag should be squeezed steadily and firmly and released about 12 times a minute. As the bag is squeezed, watch the chest rise and listen for the sound of escaping air which indicates that the face mask seal needs adjusting. It is essential that the face mask is held firmly in place so as to avoid leakage.

◆ If gagging occurs, remove the airway. Always maintain a regular check on the pulse in the neck. The absence of a pulse indicates the need for 15 chest compressions to every two inflations. Once the casualty is breathing spontaneously, put him in the recovery position.

Oxygen for the casualty who has difficulty in breathing

◆ Make sure difficulty in breathing is not due to airway obstruction (see **appendix 2**).

◆ The casualty should be connected to an oxygen-giving set through a simple disposable face mask (non-venturi type) placed securely over the face.

◆ Oxygen should be used at a flow rate of 6 to 8 litres per minute (see appropriate table for recommended setting).

◆ Oxygen should be continued until the casualty no longer has difficulty in breathing and has a normal healthy colour.

Appendix 4
CHEMICAL-INDUCED DISTURBANCES OF CONSCIOUSNESS

Some chemicals, particularly if inhaled, can act rapidly on the brain to cause either depression of consciousness (coma) or toxic mental confusion (see **table 6**). Prolonged skin contact or accidental ingestion can cause similar effects, though they are more gradual in onset.

Symptoms will usually resolve very quickly when the casualty is removed from the polluted atmosphere.

Other causes of unconsciousness include:

◆ Serious traumatic injury

◆ Fits

◆ Diabetes

◆ Stroke.

Immediate danger to life is from failure of, or obstruction to, breathing.

Diagnosis

Symptoms and signs include:

◆ No reactions to rousing stimuli;

◆ Weak or irregular pulse in serious cases;

◆ Breathing is often slow and shallow;

◆ If pupils are large and do not react to light, **LIFE IS IN DANGER**.

Watch for any signs of difficulty in breathing, which may be due to:

◆ Suffocation (asphyxia)

◆ Chemical irritation or infection of the lungs

◆ Heart failure.

DO NOT GIVE ALCOHOL OR INJECT MORPHINE OR ANY STIMULANT.

The unconscious position

Turn casualty face down, head to one side; no pillows should be used under the head.

▶ Place the arm nearest to you out at right angles to his body, elbow bent with the hand palm uppermost.

▶ Bring the far arm across the chest and place the hand, palm down, on the shoulder nearest to you.

▶ Grasp the far leg just above the knee and pull it up, keeping the foot on the ground.

▶ With your other hand on the far shoulder, pull on the leg to roll the casualty towards you onto his side.

▶ Adjust the upper leg so that both the hip and knee are bent at right angles.

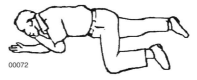

▶ Tilt the head back to make sure the airway remains open.

00072

GUIDELINES FOR RESUSCITATION:
European Resuscitation Council 1996

Unconscious casualties:

◆ Must have a clear air passage;

◆ Must have their loose dentures removed;

◆ Must have any vomit removed from the mouth and back of the throat.

◆ Should have a Guedel airway inserted, if possible;

◆ Should be kept in the unconscious position;

◆ Must not be left alone or unwatched in case vomiting or a fit occur, or they fall out of their bunk;

◆ Should be turned from one side to the other at least every three hours to prevent bedsores. Turn the casualty gently and roll him smoothly from one side to the other;

◆ When being turned, should always have their heads kept back with a chin-up position. At no time must their heads be allowed to bend forwards with the chin sagging;

◆ Should have their breathing checked. Ensure that the Guedel airway is securely in place after the casualty has been turned;

◆ Make sure that all limb joints are neither fully straight nor fully bent. Ideally they should all be kept in mid-position. Place pillows under and between the bent knees and between the feet and ankles;

◆ Use a bed-cage (a large stiff cardboard box will make a good improvised cage) to keep the bedclothes from pressing on the feet and ankles;

◆ Check that elbows, wrists and fingers are in a relaxed mid-position after turning. Do not pull, strain or stretch any joint at any time;

◆ Make quite sure that the eyelids are closed and that they remain closed at all times, otherwise preventable damage to the eyeball can easily occur.

◆ Moisten the eyes every two hours with saline (sodium chloride 0.9%) by opening the lids slightly and dripping some saline solution gently into the corner of each eye in such a way that the saline will run across each eye and drain from the inner to outer corner. If available, use a 1 litre bag of sodium chloride 0.9% with a drip set to irrigate the eyes (a saline solution can be made by dissolving one teaspoonful of salt in half a litre (one pint) of boiled water which has been allowed to cool).

After 12 hours of unconsciousness, further problems will arise:

◆ Unconscious casualties must be given nothing by mouth in case it chokes them and they suffer from obstructed breathing. However, after 12 hours of unconsciousness fluid will have to be given *per rectum* (see **appendix 13**), particularly in hot climates and/or if the casualty is obviously sweating.

◆ The mouth, cheeks, tongue and teeth should be moistened every three hours, using a small swab moistened with water. Carry out mouth care every time the casualty is turned.

After 48 hours of unconsciousness, move the limb joints at least once a day:

◆ All the joints in all the limbs should be moved very gently in such a way as to put each joint through a *full range* of movements, provided that other considerations such as fracture do not prevent this. Watch that the exercise of the arms does not interfere unduly with the casualty's breathing;

◆ Do the job systematically. Begin on the side of the casualty which is most accessible. Start with the fingers and thumb, then move the wrist, the elbow and the shoulder. Now move the toes, the foot and the ankle. Then bend the knee and move the hip round;

◆ Next, turn the casualty, if necessary with the help of another person, and move the joints on the other side;

◆ Remember that unconscious casualties may be very relaxed and floppy – so do not let go of their limbs until you have placed the limbs safely back on the bed. Hold the limbs firmly but not tightly and do everything slowly and with the utmost gentleness. Take your time in moving each joint fully before going on to the next.

Appendix 5
CHEMICAL-INDUCED CONVULSIONS (SEIZURES, FITS)

Chemically induced convulsions may occur in poisoning by substances directly irritating the brain. They may be preceded by mental agitation.

Convulsions are involuntary contractions of the muscles. There is a variation in severity from twitching of the muscles to general heaving of the body. During a seizure the casualty is often unconscious for a short time and then confused with a headache – sleep usually follows. In severe cases, the casualty does not regain consciousness between attacks.

Convulsions may occur at any time after poisoning and recur several times. The more frequent and longer the attacks, the greater the danger to life. After exposure to certain chemicals, convulsions may occur after a time delay of hours, especially after skin exposure.

The main risk of convulsions is impaired ventilation (leading to inadequate oxygen supply to tissues).

◆ Give ventilation support with 8 litres of oxygen per minute if the victim does not breathe adequately.

◆ Administer controlled ventilation.

◆ The casualty may hurt himself during convulsions. Never restrain him forcibly, as this may cause injury, but remove hard objects and surround him with pillows, clothing or other soft material.

◆ After the fit is over, let the casualty sleep it off, as he may be rather confused and dazed when he comes round. Reassure him, and do not leave him until you are sure he is aware of his surroundings, and knows what he is doing.

Appendix 6
TOXIC MENTAL CONFUSION

Mental confusion state is the name given to the condition where a casualty becomes confused and disoriented after being poisoned by a chemical, including alcohol and illicit substances. Even hallucinations (hearing voices and/or seeing terrifying images) can occur either as a direct result of the chemical on the brain, e.g. chlorinated hydrocarbons, or indirectly, when the function of vital organs such as heart, liver, or kidney is severely disturbed by poisons.

Diagnosis

◆ If the mental confusion state is due to a direct action of the chemical on the brain, the casualty will develop the signs and symptoms within 15 to 30 minutes after exposure.

◆ The casualty may be disorientated as to the date, time and place, and be unable to speak coherently. He may be unable to recognize friends, or perform simple tasks which he does in everyday life.

◆ On occasions, the casualty may appear drowsy and can only be roused with difficulty.

Look for signs of

▶ Suffocation (see **table 9**)

▶ Shock (see **table 11**)

▶ Jaundice (see **table 15**)

▶ Acute kidney failure (see **table 12**)

and treat for these if appropriate.

◆ In severe cases, the casualty may become unconscious.

◆ Some chemicals may cause confusion with mental agitation and aggressive violent behaviour.

Appendix 7
EYE EXPOSURE TO CHEMICALS

After a chemical injury, and if advised medically, it can be useful to stain the eye with fluorescein to highlight any area of corneal or conjunctival damage.

◆ The paper strip, which contains the dye, should be drawn gently across the everted (rolled back) lower lid with the casualty looking upwards;

◆ If there is an area of the eye which stains green with fluorescein, apply antibiotic eye ointment to prevent the eyelid sticking to the eyeball.

RADIO FOR MEDICAL ADVICE

00077

▶ Apply antibiotic eye ointment every two hours and cover the eye with a dry sterile eye dressing pad. Hold in place securely by using sticking plaster.

▶ Treatment should be continued for 24 hours after the eye is no longer inflamed, and is white.

After 48 hours, reapply the fluorescein paper strip as above. If there is an area of the eye which continues to stain green, reapply antibiotic eye ointment and a sterile eye dressing pad, and **urgently evacuate the casualty to a hospital with eye treatment facilities**.

Appendix 8
SKIN EXPOSURE TO CHEMICALS

Many chemicals may produce burns when in contact with the skin or eyes or mucous membranes. These are very similar to burns from fire or electricity.

Moreover, the chemical may be absorbed through the skin, causing general symptoms of poisoning such as nausea, vomiting, headache, breathing difficulties, cramps and gradual loss of consciousness.

Diagnosis

Depending on the chemical, the site and duration of contact, symptoms and signs may include:

◆ Irritating rash.

◆ Burning pain with redness and/or swelling of contaminated skin.

◆ Blistering or a loss of skin and/or underlying tissue.

Decontamination

In all cases of skin exposure, decontamination must be performed.

Further advice: ☛ **Table 8**

Treatment

If exposure was to **hydrofluoric acid or hydrogen fluoride** ☛ **Table 16**

If exposure was to **anything else:** ☛ **Table 8**

In general, after decontamination has been performed, treatment of burns should be undertaken as follows:

◆ Wash your hands and forearms thoroughly and then remove the first-aid dressing to expose either a single burned area (in multiple burns) or a portion of a large single burn. The aim is to limit the areas of burned skin exposed at any one time to lessen both the risk of infection and the seepage of fluid. Clean the skin around the edges of the burn with soap, water and swabs. Clean away from the burn in every direction. **DO NOT** use cotton wool for cleaning as it is likely to leave bits in the burn.

◆ Leave blisters intact but clip off the dead skin by using a sterilized pair of scissors if blisters have burst. Flood the area with clean, lukewarm (previously boiled) water from a clean receptacle to remove debris. With a soaked swab, dab gently at any remaining dirt or foreign matter in the burned area. *Be gentle* as this will inevitably cause pain.

◆ Next cover the burn with a sterile dressing (e.g. perforated silicone dressing or vaseline gauze), overlapping the burn or scald by 5 to 10 cm (2 to 4 inches). Now apply a covering of absorbent material, e.g. a layer of sterile cotton wool, to absorb any fluid leaking from the burn. This is held in place by a suitable bandage – tubular dressings or crepe bandage are useful for limbs and elastic net dressings for other areas.

◆ Thoroughly wash hands and arms before proceeding to deal as above with the remainder of a large burn, or with another burn in the case of multiple burns.

◆ Dressings should be left undisturbed for 3 to 5 days unless the dressing becomes smelly or very dirty, or the temperature is raised. Redress such areas as described above.

◆ If there is persistent pain, give two tablets of paracetamol every six hours until the pain is relieved.

◆ If there is severe pain, not relieved by the paracetamol, give 10 mg morphine sulphate and 10 mg metoclopramide intramuscularly, if advised medically.

Further advice on **pain relief:** ☛ **Table 13**

◆ If the burn is other than small in area (i.e. more than nine times the size of the palm of the hand), give a full glass of water (preferably oral rehydration salt solution) every ten minutes to help replace fluid loss.

Further advice on **fluid replacement:** ☛ **Appendix 13**

Appendix 9
INHALATION OF CHEMICALS

Suffocation (asphyxia)

THIS IS AN EMERGENCY

It may be due to:

◆ Obstruction to breathing in the throat or the air passage through spasm of the air tubes or by swelling of the linings of the voice box due to irritant fumes;

◆ Fluid in the lung air spaces caused by irritant fumes;

◆ Poisoning of the blood which prevents the carriage or use of oxygen in the body, caused, for example, by carbon monoxide and cyanide;

◆ Poisoning of the mechanism of breathing in the chest (e.g. by organophosphorus insecticides) or the brain (e.g. by chlorinated hydrocarbons);

◆ Gases which do not support life because they replace oxygen in the atmosphere (e.g. carbon dioxide, nitrogen).

Diagnosis

Symptoms and signs include:

◆ Difficulty in breathing with an increased rate at first (over 30 per minute). Later it may become slow and stop;

◆ A rapid pulse, usually over 100 per minute;

◆ Blueness of the skin with purple lips and tongue;

◆ Agitation at first but later the casualty becomes apathetic, with muscular weakness. Unconsciousness may follow this;

◆ Large pupils which will not react to light. **LIFE IS IN DANGER.**

Further advice: ☞ **Tables 2, 3 and 4**

Chemical irritation of the lungs: dry cough, breathlessness and wheezing

Shortly after exposure to smoke, fumes or some gases, the casualty may develop irritation and inflammation of the throat, windpipe and bronchi (the branches of the windpipe inside the lungs). Sometimes this inflammation is delayed for several hours or, rarely, for some days after exposure.

Diagnosis

Symptoms and signs include:

◆ A harsh, dry cough;

◆ A feeling of rawness in the windpipe in the neck and under the breastbone, which is made worse by coughing;

◆ Breathlessness and wheezing.

Further advice: ☞ **Table 9**

Usually, these symptoms subside within a few hours of exposure. If they do not, **RADIO FOR MEDICAL ADVICE.**

Chemical irritation and oedema of the lungs: severe breathlessness and frothy sputum

This occurs after inhalation of some irritant gases and fumes, and may be delayed for up to 48 hours after exposure, and rarely, for longer. The lung air spaces become filled with tissue fluid so that the casualty is drowning in his own secretions.

THIS IS AN EMERGENCY. RADIO FOR MEDICAL ADVICE in all cases. Every effort should be made to get medical help on board, or to transfer the casualty to hospital if there is not rapid improvement in symptoms.

Diagnosis

Symptoms and signs include:

- Severe difficulty in breathing;
- Increase in breathing rate to 30 to 40 per minute;
- Cough with the production of frothy sputum, which is sometimes pink in colour with flecks of blood;
- Difficulty in lying flat;
- Gurgling noise in the throat when the casualty is breathing;
- Blue discoloration of the skin;
- Anxiety and sweating;
- In severe cases, acute circulatory collapse, unconsciousness, and convulsions may occur. Breathing and the heart may both stop suddenly.

Further advice: ☞ **Table 9**

Chemical irritation and secondary infection of the lungs: productive cough (sticky white, yellow or green phlegm [sputum])

In cases of significant exposure to smoke, fumes or some gases, secondary infection may occur several days later.

Diagnosis

Symptoms and signs include:

- Fever (usually mild);
- Productive cough. Phlegm (sputum, spit) is coughed up, at first sticky, white and difficult to bring up, later greenish yellow, thicker and more copious. The phlegm is occasionally tinged with blood;
- Breathlessness and wheezing;
- A pulse rate over 110 per minute with blueness of the skin, ears and lips indicates severe infection.

Further advice: ☞ **Table 9**

The chemical hazards from fire

Combustion of many chemicals may produce a wide range of substances which are toxic. These may be present at a distance from the main site of the fire, and may have no odour. Self-contained breathing apparatus should be used in approaching chemical fires.

The main toxic chemicals which may be produced are:

- ▶ Carbon dioxide
- ▶ Carbon monoxide
- ▶ Hydrogen chloride (hydrochloric acid fumes)
- ▶ Hydrogen cyanide
- ▶ Nitrogen oxides (particularly produced in smouldering fires.)

Hypoxia due to "consumption" of oxygen by fire may occur. Oxygen must only be administered to a casualty in a place of safety.

Further advice: ☞ **Tables 2 and 3**

Diagnosis

Symptoms and signs include:

◆ Dizziness

◆ Headache

◆ Nausea and vomiting

◆ A persistent cough and difficulty in breathing

◆ Unconsciousness

Inhalation of fumes may result in rapid collapse and unconsciousness.

Further advice on **disturbed consciousness:** ☞ Table 4

Further advice on **inhalational injuries:** ☞ Table 9

Chemical hazards from welding

If adequate precautions are not taken, symptoms of poisoning may arise during welding in confined spaces.

The main danger is from nitrogen oxides.

Certain metal alloys, in particular those containing zinc or cadmium, also give off fumes, causing characteristic symptoms known as "metal fume fever". These usually do not develop for a period of 6 to 12 hours after exposure, and comprise:

◆ Shivering

◆ Fever, headache and muscle pains

◆ Nausea

◆ A dry cough

These symptoms usually resolve spontaneously without any treatment over the following 12 hours. Lung oedema, however, may occur as a very rare complication.

Further advice on **lung oedema:** ☞ Table 9

Chemical hazards from explosive chemicals

The main hazard is injury from explosion.

Contact with explosives does not normally cause a medical problem from the chemicals themselves, unless they are in a decomposed state, when they may produce fumes, particularly of nitrogen oxides, which may be inhaled.

Appendix 10
INGESTION OF CHEMICALS

The swallowing of a chemical is one of the less probable events on board a ship. In general, it happens by mistake, such as after drinking from the wrong bottle. Usually this mistake is noticed at once.

Chemicals may act as local irritants on the stomach and intestines. The more severe corrosive chemicals, e.g. acids and alkalis, may cause bleeding or perforation of the gut. Remember that other illnesses, e.g. food poisoning, peptic ulcer, alcohol excess, may cause similar symptoms.

Chemicals may also be absorbed, and cause general symptoms.

Diagnosis

◆ There may be chemical burns around the lips and the mouth and throat.

◆ Nausea and vomiting usually occur, but there may be symptoms of more general poisoning.

◆ Diarrhoea may occur; it is important to note whether the faeces become black, tarry, foul smelling after poisoning since this is likely to be caused by **BLEEDING** from the gut.

◆ The casualty may vomit up bright red blood, or dark brown "coffee grounds" which is blood that has been altered in the stomach.

◆ If an intense pain develops in the stomach accompanied by a rigid abdomen when touched, then a **PERFORATION OF THE GUT** may have occurred.

◆ Thirst may become intense after severe diarrhoea and vomiting.

◆ There may also be general symptoms which may occur after a time delay.

RADIO FOR MEDICAL ADVICE

Further advice: ☞ **Table 10**

Perforation of the gut and peritonitis

If an intense pain develops in the stomach and the abdomen is rigid when touched, then perforation of the gut may have occurred.

This causes peritonitis, which is an inflammation of the thin layer of tissue (the peritoneum) which covers the intestines and lines the inside of the abdomen.

Diagnosis

◆ The onset of peritonitis may be assumed when there is a general worsening of the condition of a casualty already seriously ill following ingestion of corrosive chemicals.

◆ Peritonitis commences with severe pain all over the abdomen – pain which is made worse by the slightest movement. The abdomen becomes hard and extremely tender, and the casualty draws up his knees to relax the abdominal muscles.

◆ Vomiting occurs and becomes progressively more frequent, large quantities of brown fluid being brought up without any effort.

◆ The temperature is raised (up to 39.40°C [103°F]).

◆ The pulse is feeble and rapid (110 to 120 per minute), gradually increasing in rate.

◆ The pallid anxious face, the sunken eyes and extreme general weakness all confirm the gravely ill state of the casualty.

◆ If hiccoughs begin, this must be regarded as a very serious sign.

RADIO FOR MEDICAL ADVICE

Further advice: ☞ **Table 10**

Appendix 11
SHOCK

Fainting

Fainting is the emotional response of some individuals to trivial injuries so that they feel week and nauseated and may faint. This reaction is not serious and will disappear quickly if the casualty lies down.

Diagnosis

Symptoms and signs include:

◆ Pale, waxy skin which is cold and clammy to the touch;

◆ Pulse is usually slow at first and then becomes rapid during recovery;

◆ Unconsciousness lasts only a few minutes, and the casualty recovers rapidly after he lies down.

Circulatory collapse and shock

Circulatory collapse is a disturbed distribution of blood within the body. Severe circulatory disturbances are called "shock" and result in serious impairment of vital organ functions due to an insufficient supply of blood.

Chemical burns and chemically induced bleeding from the gut may cause circulatory collapse and shock.

There are also a number of chemicals which are toxic to the heart directly and result in reduced pump action of the heart and shock within a few hours; acute kidney failure may result.

Diagnosis

Symptoms and signs include:

◆ Pale, waxy skin which is cold and clammy to the touch;

◆ Rapid, weak pulse;

◆ Agitation at first but later the casualty becomes apathetic. Unconsciousness may follow this;

◆ Large pupils which do not react to light. **LIFE IS IN DANGER;**

◆ A reduction in the amount of urine passed, if this condition persists for more than one or two hours.

Further advice: ☛ **Table 11**

Heart failure

Heart failure may occur within a few hours of chemical poisoning or may develop gradually over a period of 24 to 48 hours following exposure to an irritant gas.

It should be remembered that a casualty may already be under treatment for a heart condition.

Diagnosis

Symptoms and signs include:

◆ Weakness, apathy and headache;

◆ Breathing rapid and shallow;

◆ Sweating and restlessness with a rapid pulse;

◆ Blue lips, tongue and ears;

◆ Swelling of feet and legs;

◆ Prominent veins in the neck in severe cases;

◆ A reduction in the amount of urine passed, if this condition persists for more than one or two hours.

Further advice: ☛ **Table 11**

Appendix 12
ACUTE KIDNEY FAILURE

Acute kidney failure is a disorder characterized by an abrupt decline in the amount of urine passed. That impairs the kidney's capacity to maintain metabolic balance.

It is important to distinguish acute kidney failure from urinary retention. Urinary retention occurs when the bladder becomes over-full and is common in cases of prolonged unconsciousness, but it may also occur in a conscious casualty. If retention is present, the bladder becomes increasingly distended, with the casualty complaining of pain in the lower abdomen.

Chemical-induced acute kidney failure may be caused directly by a variety of chemicals, including ethylene glycol and halogenated hydrocarbons. In addition, it may occur secondary to shock due to severe chemical burns or chemical-induced bleeding.

DIAGNOSIS

Symptoms and signs include:

◆ A steady reduction in the amount of urine passed;

Insert a urinary catheter into the bladder. If there is less than 125 mℓ of urine in the bladder, or the casualty has not passed urine for more than six hours, the casualty is in acute kidney failure.

◆ Nausea, vomiting, diarrhoea;

◆ Persistent hiccoughing;

◆ Fatigue.

RADIO FOR MEDICAL ADVICE. Arrange for evacuation. The casualty will need to be transferred to a shore hospital as soon as possible.

Record casualty's fluid intake and output carefully on a chart as follows (amounts given in millilitres):

Date & time	Type of fluid	In* Mouth	Out Urine	Vomit	Other
12/8/96					
11.00	Clear soup	250			
11.15				200	very sweaty for 1 hour
12.00			500	60	
12.30	Milk	125			
13.00				120	runny diarrhoea
14.00	Oral rehydration salt (ORS) solution	180			
17.00	ORS solution	200			
20.00	ORS solution	200			
20.15			20		
23.00	ORS solution	200			
12-hourly balance:		1155	520 + 380		?
			900		
		difference: plus 255 mℓ (but the casualty lost fluid by sweating and diarrhoea, probably more than 255 mℓ)			

* Fluid given intravenously or by rectum also counts for input.

Appendix 13
FLUID REPLACEMENT

An average daily intake of fluids from food and drink is about 2.5 litres. Body fluid is lost through unseen perspiration, obvious sweating, the breath, the urine and the faeces. In temperate climates it is possible to manage for a short time on as little as one litre (just under 2 pints). In very hot climates where there is a large fluid loss through sweating, an intake of 6 litres per day may be necessary.

If extensive chemical burns (see **table 8**) are present or chemical-induced bleeding (see **table 14**) from the gut occurs, there will be substantial loss of fluid (more than 3 litres/day). If this fluid is not replaced, circulatory collapse, shock (see **table 11**) and acute kidney failure (see **table 12**) may follow. Although fluid may be replaced orally in the case of chemical burns, intravenous fluid replacement is preferable in all cases if a person is trained in the technique. Alternatively, rectal fluid replacement may be used.

ORAL FLUIDS

Use oral rehydration salts, which, when reconstituted with water according to instruction, will provide all necessary salts to maintain metabolic balance.

◆ In mild cases of fluid loss, give intermittently 1 litre of the solution each day;

◆ In more severe cases, give 2 litres each day;

◆ In very severe cases of fluid loss, give at least 3 litres each day.

Monitor pulse and blood pressure regularly.

In **cases of extended chemical burns:**

the first 24 hours: give – in addition to normal food and fluid intake – for every 10% of the body surface area with burns, 3 litres of salted water ($1\frac{1}{2}$ teaspoonfuls of table salt in 1 litre) intermittently.

24 to 48 hours: For every 10% of the body surface area with burns, give $1\frac{1}{2}$ litres of fluids (preferably oral rehydration salt solution – ORS) intermittently.

After 48 hours the fluid intake should, in principle, be normal.

Check for urine output, that should be approximately 30 to 50 mℓ per hour (approximately 1 litre per 24 hours).

INTRAVENOUS FLUIDS

If advised medically and a trained person is available, give 1 to 3 (or more) litres of sodium chloride (0.9%) intravenous infusion via an infusion set, depending on the severity of fluid loss and the **RADIO MEDICAL ADVICE**.

In very severe cases of shock, a gelatine-based plasma expander may be advised:

◆ Give 500 mℓ plasma expander via an infusion set and monitor pulse and blood pressure regularly.

◆ Seek **RADIO MEDICAL ADVICE** again.

◆ If advised, give a further 500 mℓ plasma expander and monitor pulse and blood pressure regularly.

RECTAL FLUIDS

Fluid may also be given via rectum, though it is difficult to administer more than 1 litre of fluid per day by this route.

To prepare the bed, place two pillows, one on top of the other, across the middle of the undersheet. Protect the pillows with a width of rubber or plastic sheeting covered by a wide clean towel. Allow the ends of the sheeting and towel to hang over the side of the bed to drain any possible leakage. The casualty should be placed lying on his left side with his buttocks raised on the pillows and with his right knee flexed. He should be made comfortable but only one pillow should be allowed to support his head so that the tilt can be maintained. He should then be covered by a sheet, leaving only the buttocks exposed.

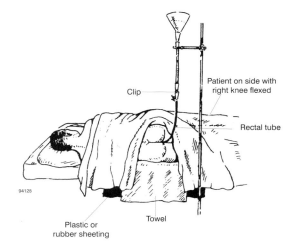

The importance of the treatment should have been explained to the casualty and he should be encouraged to relax and not to resist. The buttocks should be separated gently, then a catheter (26 French gauge) well lubricated with petroleum jelly (vaseline) should be passed slowly and gently through the anus into the rectum for a distance of about 23 cm (9 inches). After the catheter has been inserted, its external end should be taped to the skin in a convenient position to attach to a tube and drip set.

Give 200 mℓ of water slowly through the tube, taking about 10 to 15 minutes to drip the water in. This amount will usually be retained. Leave the catheter in position and block its end with a spigot, or small cork, or compression clip.

Give the casualty a further 200 mℓ of water every 3 to 4 hours. This should give a fluid intake of about 1000 mℓ (1 litre) per day. The rectum will not retain large amounts of fluid, and fluid must be retained in order to be absorbed. Occasionally the rectum will not accept fluid readily, especially if it is loaded with faeces. Smaller quantities at more frequent intervals should be tried in these cases. Careful observation will show whether the fluid is being retained.

Aim to give at least 1 litre of fluid per day if possible. Giving fluid by rectum should be continued until the casualty can safely take fluid by mouth, or medical assistance becomes available.

Appendix 14
LIST OF MEDICINES AND EQUIPMENT

Preamble

1   Medicines and equipment already available in the ship's medicine chest may be counted towards the MFAG numerical requirements outlined below.

2   In some cases, alternatives are given. This means that one of the given alternatives should be chosen.

3   Not all drugs and antidotes on the list may be licensed as pharmaceutical specialities in all Member States and thus available for general purchase. In such cases, the national authorities may issue a modified list, also in English, where drugs on the below list not available are substituted with analogous drugs in corresponding quantities.

4   In countries with official lists on contents of ship's medicine chests, the national authorities can decide to substitute some of the drugs on the below list with analogous drugs available in the ordinary ship's medicine chest.

5   The recommended minimum quantities are based on an estimate of risk to persons on board and the time within which full treatment on shore can be given.

6   National authorities can decide on exemption from carrying these medicines for vessels making short regular voyages of ten minutes or less.

Labelling, storage and dispensing should, in general, conform to the relevant specifications in the *IMGS*. Contents and storage conditions should be checked at least once a year, taking account of manufacturers expiry date and instructions. Medicines used should be replaced as soon as possible.

Column A   of the following table shows the recommended minimum requirements for ships when casualties **cannot** be hospitalized on shore within 24 hours.

Column B   shows the recommended minimum requirements for ships when casualties can be hospitalized on shore within 24 hours.

Column C   shows the recommended minimum requirements for ships when casualties can be hospitalized on shore within 2 hours.

Medicine	Format/ Standard unit	Recommended minimum quantity			Dosage	Reference
		A	B	C		
amoxycillin	capsules 500 mg	30 capsules	*none*	*none*	500 mg × 3	Table 9
anaesthetic eye drops	eye drops (bottle)	5 bottles	5 bottles	5 bottles	several drops × several	Table 7
antibiotic eye ointment	eye ointment (tube)	5 tubes	5 tubes	*none*	apply 2 to 4 times daily or more frequently if required	Appendix 7
atropine	injection fluid 1 (or 0.5) mg/mℓ (1 mℓ ampoule)	15 (or 30) × 1 mℓ	15 (or 30) × 1 mℓ	*none*	1 mg × several	Table 17
beclomethasone (including inhalation device)	inhalation aerosol 50 µg/dose (200 doses) **or** 250 µg/dose (200 doses)	5 × 200 doses	5 × 200 doses	*none*	250 µg × several (5 puffs of 50 µg/dose) **or** (1 puff of 250 µg/dose)	Table 9
or budenoside (including inhalation device)	inhalation aerosol 200 µg/dose (100 doses)	5 × 100 doses	5 × 100 doses	*none*	400 µg × several (2 puffs of 200 µg/dose)	
calcium gluconate gel	gel 2% (25 g tube)	5 tubes	5 tubes	5 tubes	apply several times	Tables 8, 16
calcium gluconate	effervescent tablets 1 g	20 tablets	20 tablets	*none*	5 g × 2	Table 16
cefuroxime	injection substance 750 mg (750 mg bottle)	10 × 750 mg	*none*	*none*	750 mg × 3	Table 10

Medicine	Format/ Standard unit	Recommended minimum quantity			Dosage	Reference
		A	B	C		
charcoal, activated	powder (50 g bottle) or effervescent granules (5 g sachet)	2 × 50 g or 10 × 5 g	2 × 50 g or 10 × 5 g	*none*	50 g × 1	Table 10
diazepam	rectal solution 10 mg (ampoule)	5 × 10 mg	5 × 10 mg	*none*	10 mg × 1 to 5	Tables 4, 5, 6
erythromycin	tablets 500 mg	30 × 500 mg	*none*	*none*	500 mg × 4	Table 9
ethyl alcohol	solution 99.5% (500 mℓ bottle)	3 × 500 mℓ	1 × 500 mℓ	*none*	25 mℓ × 8 (25 mℓ 99.5% in 250 to 300 mℓ water or soft drink)	Table 19
fluorescein	eye test strip	1 package	*none*	*none*	1 test strip × 2	Appendix 7
furosemide (frusemide)	injection fluid 10 mg/mℓ (5 mℓ ampoule)	5 × 5 mℓ	*none*	*none*	50 mg × 3	Tables 2, 9
metoclopramide	injection fluid 5 mg/mℓ (2 mℓ ampoule)	30 × 2 mℓ	10 × 2 mℓ	5 × 2 mℓ	10 mg × 3	Tables 7, 8, 10, 13, 15, 20
metronidazole	suppositories 1 g	10 × 1 g	*none*	*none*	1 g × 3	Table 10
morphine sulphate	injection fluid 10 mg/mℓ (1 mℓ ampoule)	40 × 1 mℓ	10 × 1 mℓ	5 × 1 mℓ	10 to 20 mg × 6 or 7	Tables 7, 8, 10, 13
naloxone	injection fluid 0.4 mg/mℓ (1 mℓ ampoule)	5 × 1 mℓ	5 × 1 mℓ	2 × 1 mℓ	0.4 mg × 1 to 5	Tables 4, 13
oral rehydration salts (ORS)	sachets or tablets to dissolve in water	ORS to give 18 litres solution	ORS to give 6 litres solution	*none*	1 litre × 3 or more	Tables 8, 10, 11
paracetamol	tablets 0.5 g	200 tablets	100 tablets	20 tablets	1 g × 4	Tables 7, 8, 13
phytomenadione	injection fluid 10 mg/mℓ (1 mℓ ampoule)	10 × 1 mℓ	*none*	*none*	10 mg × 2 or more	Table 14
plasma expander (gelatine-based)	infusion fluids (500 mℓ bottles)	3 × 500 mℓ	3 × 500 mℓ	*none*	500 mℓ × 1 to 3	Appendix 13
rehydration salts – *see* oral rehydration salts						Tables 8, 10, 11
salbutamol (including inhalation device) **or** terbutaline (including inhalation device)	inhalation aerosol 100 μg/dose (200 doses) / inhalation aerosol 500 μg/dose (50 doses)	5 × 200 doses / 5 × 50 doses	5 × 200 doses / 5 × 50 doses	1 × 200 doses / 1 × 50 doses	200 μg × several (2 puffs of 100 μg/dose) / 500 μg × several (1 puff of 500 μg/dose)	Table 9
sodium chloride, isotonic (saline)	9 mg/mℓ (0.9%) (1 ℓ bottle)	5 × 1 ℓ	3 × 1 ℓ	1 × 1 ℓ	1 ℓ × 1 to 3	Table 7
terbutaline – *see* salbutamol						

LIST OF EQUIPMENT

Column A   of the following table shows the recommended minimum requirements for ships when casualties **cannot** be hospitalized on shore within 24 hours.

Column B   shows the recommended minimum requirements for ships when casualties can be hospitalized on shore within 24 hours.

Column C   shows the recommended minimum requirements for ships when casualties can be hospitalized on shore within 2 hours.

Equipment	Recommended minimum quantity			Reference
	A	B	C	
Guedel airway				Appendix 3
size 2	2	2	2	
size 3	2	2	2	
size 4	2	2	2	
iv cannula (size 1.2)	10	10	*none*	Appendix 13
iv set	10	10	*none*	Appendix 13
needles size 0.8	100	50	10	
simple face mask (allowing up to 60% oxygen), disposable	10	10	2	Appendix 3
valve and bag manual resuscitator	2	2	2	Appendix 3
oxygen cylinder	40 ℓ/200 bar*	40 ℓ/200 bar*	none	Appendix 3
portable oxygen-giving set ready for use	1* (2 ℓ/200 bar)	1* (2 ℓ/200 bar)	1	
spare portable oxygen cylinder	1* (2 ℓ/200 bar)	1* (2 ℓ/200 bar)	1	
rectal infusion set catheter (26 French gauge)	1 6	*none* *none*	*none* *none*	Appendix 13
syringes				
2 mℓ	100	50	10	
5 mℓ	10	10	*none*	

* A minimum of 44 litres/200 bar oxygen of which there should be at least:

   ▪ one complete portable set with 2 ℓ/200 bar oxygen ready for use with a spare cylinder of 2 ℓ/200 bar and

   ▪ one oxygen cylinder of 40 ℓ/200 bar (at ship's hospital, assembled for direct use) with one flowmeter unit (two ports) for supplying of oxygen for two persons at the same time. If more than one non-portable oxygen cylinder is used, there must be two flowmeter units for supplying of oxygen for two persons at the same time.

Appendix 15
LIST OF SUBSTANCES

Chemicals allocated to specific treatment may be found under the following UN entries:

UN No.		Substance	Table No.
1008		BORON TRIFLUORIDE	16
1051	1614	HYDROGEN CYANIDE, STABILIZED, . . .	18
1052		HYDROGEN FLUORIDE, ANHYDROUS	16
1171		ETHYLENE GLYCOL MONOETHYL ETHER	19
1172		ETHYLENE GLYCOL MONOETHYL ETHER ACETATE	19
1188		ETHYLENE GLYCOL MONOMETHYL ETHER	19
1189		ETHYLENE GLYCOL MONOMETHYL ETHER ACETATE	19
1230		METHANOL	19
1381	2447	PHOSPHORUS, WHITE or YELLOW, . . .	8
1565		BARIUM CYANIDE	18
1575		CALCIUM CYANIDE	18
1587		COPPER CYANIDE	18
1613		HYDROCYANIC ACID, AQUEOUS SOLUTION, . . .	18
1620		LEAD CYANIDE	18
1626		MERCURIC POTASSIUM CYANIDE	18
1636		MERCURY CYANIDE	18
1679		POTASSIUM CUPROCYANIDE	18
1680		POTASSIUM CYANIDE	18
1689		SODIUM CYANIDE	18
1732		ANTIMONY PENTAFLUORIDE	16
1749		CHLORINE TRIFLUORIDE	16
1786		HYDROFLUORIC ACID AND SULPHURIC ACID MIXTURES	16
1790		HYDROFLUORIC ACID, SOLUTION	16
1859		SILICON TETRAFLUORIDE	16
1910		CALCIUM OXIDE	7
2198		PHOSPHORUS PENTAFLUORIDE	16
2417		CARBONYL FLUORIDE	16
2495		IODINE PENTAFLUORIDE	16
2548		CHLORINE PENTAFLUORIDE	16
2604		BORON TRIFLUORIDE DIETHYL ETHERATE	16
2851		BORON TRIFLUORIDE DIHYDRATE	16
2908	2908–2919, 2977, 2978, 3321–3333	RADIOACTIVE MATERIAL	20
2965		BORON TRIFLUORIDE DIMETHYL ETHERATE	16
2991	2992, 2757, 2758	CARBAMATE PESTICIDE, . . .	17
3017	3018, 2783, 2784	ORGANOPHOSPHORUS PESTICIDE, . . .	17
3024	3025, 3026, 3027	COUMARIN DERIVATIVE PESTICIDE, . . .	14
3294		HYDROGEN CYANIDE, SOLUTION IN ALCOHOL, . . .	18

ALPHABETIC SORTATION

UN No.		Substance	Table No.
1732		ANTIMONY PENTAFLUORIDE	16
1565		BARIUM CYANIDE	18
1008		BORON TRIFLUORIDE	16
2604		BORON TRIFLUORIDE DIETHYL ETHERATE	16
2851		BORON TRIFLUORIDE DIHYDRATE	16
2965		BORON TRIFLUORIDE DIMETHYL ETHERATE	16
1575		CALCIUM CYANIDE	18
1910		CALCIUM OXIDE	7
2991	2992, 2757, 2758	CARBAMATE PESTICIDE, . . .	17
2417		CARBONYL FLUORIDE	16
2548		CHLORINE PENTAFLUORIDE	16
1749		CHLORINE TRIFLUORIDE	16
1587		COPPER CYANIDE	18
3024	3025, 3026, 3027	COUMARIN DERIVATIVE PESTICIDE, . . .	14
1171		ETHYLENE GLYCOL MONOETHYL ETHER	19
1172		ETHYLENE GLYCOL MONOETHYL ETHER ACETATE	19
1188		ETHYLENE GLYCOL MONOMETHYL ETHER	19
1189		ETHYLENE GLYCOL MONOMETHYL ETHER ACETATE	19
1613		HYDROCYANIC ACID, AQUEOUS SOLUTION, . . .	18
1786		HYDROFLUORIC ACID AND SULPHURIC ACID MIXTURES	16
1790		HYDROFLUORIC ACID, SOLUTION	16
3294		HYDROGEN CYANIDE, SOLUTION IN ALCOHOL, . . .	18
1051	1614	HYDROGEN CYANIDE, STABILIZED, . . .	18
1052		HYDROGEN FLUORIDE, ANHYDROUS	16
2495		IODINE PENTAFLUORIDE	16
1620		LEAD CYANIDE	18
1626		MERCURIC POTASSIUM CYANIDE	18
1636		MERCURY CYANIDE	18
1230		METHANOL	19
3017	3018, 2783, 2784	ORGANOPHOSPHORUS PESTICIDE, . . .	17
2198		PHOSPHORUS PENTAFLUORIDE	16
1381	2447	PHOSPHORUS, WHITE or YELLOW, . . .	8
1679		POTASSIUM CUPROCYANIDE	18
1680		POTASSIUM CYANIDE	18
2908	2908–2919, 2977, 2978, 3321–3333	RADIOACTIVE MATERIAL	20
1859		SILICON TETRAFLUORIDE	16
1689		SODIUM CYANIDE	18

REPORTING PROCEDURES
GENERAL PRINCIPLES FOR SHIP REPORTING SYSTEMS AND SHIP REPORTING REQUIREMENTS INCLUDING GUIDELINES FOR REPORTING INCIDENTS INVOLVING DANGEROUS GOODS, HARMFUL SUBSTANCES AND/OR MARINE POLLUTANTS

Foreword

The International Convention for the Prevention of Pollution from Ships, 1973, was adopted by the International Conference on Marine Pollution convened by IMO from 8 November to 2 December 1973. This Convention was subsequently modified by a Protocol adopted by the International Conference on Tanker Safety and Pollution Prevention convened from 6 to 17 February 1978. The 1973 Convention, as modified by the 1978 Protocol, is known as MARPOL 73/78.

The MARPOL Convention recognizes that a vessel casualty or an accidental discharge from a ship may give rise to serious pollution or a threat of pollution to the marine environment and provides, therefore, that such incidents should be reported without delay and to the fullest extent possible, in order to facilitate necessary counter-pollution actions by coastal States that might be affected.

The reporting of incidents involving harmful substances and/or marine pollutants is regulated by Protocol I to MARPOL 73/78, as revised by the 1985 and 1996 amendments, which entered into force on 6 April 1987 and 1 January 1998. To supplement the requirements of Protocol I, the IMO Assembly, at its twentieth session, adopted resolution A.851(20) on general principles for ship reporting systems and ship reporting requirements, including guidelines for reporting incidents involving dangerous goods, harmful substances and/or marine pollutants. These general principles supersede all previous guidelines adopted by the Maritime Safety Committee and the Marine Environment Protection Committee in this regard (resolution A.598(15), resolution A.648(16), resolution MEPC.30(25) and MSC/Circ.360/Rev.1).

The list of agencies or officials of Administrations responsible for receiving and processing such reports is now distributed by means of an MSC/MEPC.6 circular issued annually. The updated circular can also be found on the IMO website.

Contents

Reporting

General principles for ship reporting systems and ship reporting requirements, including guidelines for reporting incidents involving dangerous goods, harmful substances and/or marine pollutants*

1 General principles

1.1 Ship reporting systems and reporting requirements are used to provide, gather or exchange information through radio reports. The information is used to provide data for many purposes, including search and rescue, vessel traffic services, weather forecasting and prevention of marine pollution. Ship reporting systems and reporting requirements should, as far as practicable, comply with the following principles:

.1 reports should contain only information essential to achieve the objectives of the system;

.2 reports should be simple and use the standard international ship reporting format and procedures; where language difficulties may exist, the languages used should include English, using where possible the Standard Marine Navigational Vocabulary, or alternatively the International Code of Signals. The standard reporting format and procedures to be used are given in the appendix to this annex;

.3 the number of reports should be kept to a minimum;

.4 no charge should be made for communication of reports;

.5 safety or pollution-related reports should be made without delay; however, the time and place of making non-urgent reports should be sufficiently flexible to avoid interference with essential navigational duties;

.6 information obtained from the system should be made available to other systems when required for distress, safety and pollution purposes;

.7 basic information (ship's particulars, on-board facilities and equipment, etc.) should be reported once, be retained in the system and be updated by the ship when changes occur in the basic information reported;

.8 the purpose of the system should be clearly defined;

.9 Governments establishing a ship reporting system should notify mariners of full details of the requirements to be met and procedures to be followed. Details of types of ships and areas of applicability, of times and geographical positions for submitting reports, of shore establishments responsible for operation of the system and of the services provided should be clearly specified. Chartlets depicting boundaries of the system and providing other necessary information should be made available to mariners;

.10 the establishment and operation of a ship reporting system should take into account:

.10.1 international as well as national responsibilities and requirements;

.10.2 the cost to ship operators and responsible authorities;

.10.3 navigational hazards;

.10.4 existing and proposed aids to safety; and

.10.5 the need for early and continuing consultation with interested parties, including a sufficient period to allow for trial, familiarization and assessment to ensure satisfactory operation and to allow necessary changes to be made to the system;

.11 Governments should ensure that shore establishments responsible for operation of the system are manned by properly trained persons;

.12 Governments should consider the interrelationship between ship reporting systems and other systems;

---

* This is the annex to resolution A.851(20). See page 177.

.13 ship reporting systems should preferably use a single operating radio frequency; where additional frequencies are necessary, the number of frequencies should be restricted to the minimum required for the effective operation of the system;

.14 information provided by the system to ships should be restricted to that necessary for the proper operation of the system and for safety;

.15 ship reporting systems and requirements should provide for special reports from ships concerning defects or deficiencies with respect to their hull, machinery, equipment or manning, or concerning other limitations which could adversely affect navigation and for special reports concerning incidents of actual or probable marine pollution;

.16 Governments should issue instructions to their shore establishments responsible for the operation of ship reporting systems to ensure that any reports involving pollution, actual or probable, are relayed without delay to the officer or agency nominated to receive and process such reports, and to ensure that such an officer or agency relays these reports without delay to the flag State of the ship involved and to any other State which may be affected;

.17 States which are affected or likely to be affected by pollution incidents and may require information relevant to the incident should take into account the circumstances in which the master is placed, and should endeavour to limit their requests for additional information; and

.18 the appendix to this annex does not apply to danger messages referred to under regulation V/2 of the 1974 SOLAS Convention, as amended. The present practice of transmitting such messages should remain unchanged.

2 Guidelines for reporting incidents involving dangerous goods

2.1 The intent of these Guidelines and those contained in the appendix is to enable coastal States and other interested parties to be informed without delay when any incident occurs involving the loss, or likely loss, overboard of packaged dangerous goods into the sea.

2.2 Reports should be transmitted to the nearest coastal State. When the ship is within or near an area for which a ship reporting system has been established, reports should be transmitted to the designated shore station of that system.*

3 Guidelines for reporting incidents involving harmful substances and/or marine pollutants

3.1 The intent of these Guidelines and those contained in the appendix is to enable coastal States and other interested parties to be informed without delay of any incident giving rise to pollution, or threat of pollution, of the marine environment, as well as of assistance and salvage measures, so that appropriate action may be taken.

3.2 In accordance with article V(1) of Protocol I of MARPOL 73/78, a report shall be made to the nearest coastal State.

3.3 Whenever a ship is engaged in or requested to engage in an operation to render assistance to or undertake salvage of a ship involved in an incident referred to in 1(a) or (b) of article II of Protocol I of MARPOL 73/78, as amended, the master of the former ship should report, without delay, the particulars of the action undertaken or planned. The coastal States should also be kept informed of developments.

3.4 The probability of a discharge resulting from damage to the ship or its equipment is a reason for making a report.

---

* Refer to the List of national contact points for safety and pollution prevention. This List is issued by IMO as an MSC/MEPC.6 circular and is also available on the IMO website. The list on the website is regularly updated; the printed list will be updated annually.

Appendix

1   Procedures

Reports should be sent as follows:

Sailing plan (SP)   –   Before or as near as possible to the time of departure from a port within a system or when entering the area covered by a system.

Position report (PR)   –   When necessary to ensure effective operation of the system.

Deviation report (DR)   –   When the ship's position varies significantly from the position that would have been predicted from previous reports, when changing the reported route, or as decided by the master.

Final report (FR)   –   On arrival at destination and when leaving the area covered by a system.

Dangerous goods report (DG) –   When an incident takes place involving the loss or likely loss overboard of packaged dangerous goods, including those in freight containers, portable tanks, road and rail vehicles and shipborne barges, into the sea.

Harmful substances report (HS) – When an incident takes place involving the discharge or probable discharge of oil (Annex I of MARPOL 73/78) or noxious liquid substances in bulk (Annex II of MARPOL 73/78).

Marine pollutants report (MP) –   In the case of loss or likely loss overboard of harmful substances in packaged form, including those in freight containers, portable tanks, road and rail vehicles and shipborne barges, identified in the International Maritime Dangerous Goods Code as marine pollutants (Annex III of MARPOL 73/78).

Any other report   –   Any other report should be made in accordance with the system procedures as notified in accordance with paragraph 9 of the General Principles.

2   Standard reporting format and procedures

2.1   Sections of the ship reporting format which are inappropriate should be omitted from the report.

2.2   Where language difficulties may exist, the languages used should include English, using where possible the Standard Marine Navigational Vocabulary. Alternatively, the International Code of Signals may be used to send detailed information. When the International Code is used, the appropriate indicator should be inserted in the text, after the alphabetical index.

2.3   For route information, latitude and longitude should be given for each turn point, expressed as in C below, together with type of intended track between these points, for example "RL" (rhumb line), "GC" (great circle) or "coastal", or, in the case of coastal sailing, the estimated date and time of passing significant points expressed by a 6-digit group as in B below.

Telegraphy	Telephone (alternative)	Function	Information required
Name of system (e.g. AMVER/ AUSREP/MAREP/ ECAREG/JASREP	Name of system (e.g. AMVER/AUSREP/ MAREP/ECAREG/ JASREP)	System identifier	Ship reporting system or nearest appropriate coast radio station
	State in full	Type of report	Type of report:
SP			Sailing plan
PR			Position report
DR			Deviation report
FR			Final report
DG			Dangerous goods report
HS			Harmful substances report
MP			Marine pollutants report
Give in full			Any other report
A	Ship (alpha)	Ship	Name, call sign or ship station identity, and flag
B	Time (bravo)	Date and time of event	A 6-digit group giving day of month (first two digits), hours and minutes (last four digits). If other than UTC, state time zone used
C	Position (charlie)	Position	A 4-digit group giving latitude in degrees and minutes suffixed with N (north) or S (south) and a 5-digit group giving longitude in degrees and minutes suffixed with E (east) or W (west); or
D	Position (delta)	Position	True bearing (first 3 digits) and distance (*state distance*) in nautical miles from a clearly identified landmark (*state landmark*)
E	Course (echo)	True course	A 3-digit group
F	Speed (foxtrot)	Speed in knots and tenths of knots	A 3-digit group
G	Departed (golf)	Port of departure	Name of last port of call
H	Entry (hotel)	Date, time and point of entry into system	Entry time expressed as in (B) and entry position expressed as in (C) or (D)
I	Destination and ETA (India)	Destination and expected time of arrival	Name of port and date and time group expressed as in (B)
J	Pilot (juliet)	Pilot	State whether a deep-sea or local pilot is on board
K	Exit (kilo)	Date, time and point of exit from system or arrival at the ship's destination	Exit time expressed as in (B) and exit position expressed as in (C) or (D)

Telegraphy	Telephone (alternative)	Function	Information required
L	Route (lima)	Route information	Intended track
M	Radiocommunications (mike)	Radiocommunications	State in full names of stations/ frequencies guarded
N	Next report (november)	Time of next report	Date and time group expressed as in (B)
O	Draught (oscar)	Maximum present static draught in metres	4-digit group giving metres and centimetres
P	Cargo (papa)	Cargo on board	Cargo and brief details of any dangerous cargoes as well as harmful substances and gases that could endanger persons or the environment (See detailed reporting requirements)
Q	Defect, damage, deficiency, limitations (quebec)	Defects/damage/deficiencies/ other limitations	Brief details of defects, damage, deficiencies or other limitations (See detailed reporting requirements)
R	Pollution/dangerous goods lost overboard (romeo)	Description of pollution or dangerous goods lost overboard	Brief details of type of pollution (oil, chemicals, etc.) or dangerous goods lost overboard; position expressed as in (C) or (D) (See detailed reporting requirements)
S	Weather (sierra)	Weather conditions	Brief details of weather and sea conditions prevailing
T	Agent (tango)	Ship's representative and/or owner	Details of name and particulars of ship's representative or owner or both for provision of information (See detailed reporting requirements)
U	Size and type (uniform)	Ship size and type	Details of length, breadth, tonnage, and type, etc., as required
V	Medic (victor)	Medical personnel	Doctor, physician's assistant, nurse, personnel without medical training
W	Persons (whiskey)	Total number of persons on board	State number
X	Remarks (x-ray)	Miscellaneous	Any other information – including, as appropriate, brief details of incident and of other ships involved either in incident, assistance or salvage (See detailed reporting requirements)
Y	Relay (yankee)	Request to relay report to another system, e.g., AMVER, AUSREP, JASREP, MAREP, etc.	Content of report
Z	End of report (zulu)	End of report	No further information required

Reporting

3   Guidelines for detailed reporting requirements

3.1   Dangerous goods reports (DG)

3.1.1   Primary reports should contain items A, B, C (or D), M, Q, R, S, T, U, X of the standard reporting format; details for R should be as follows:

R   1   Correct technical name or names of goods.

2   UN number or numbers.

3   IMO hazard class or classes.

4   Names of manufacturers of goods when known, or consignee or consignor.

5   Types of packages, including identification marks. Specify whether portable tank or tank vehicle, or whether vehicle or freight container or other cargo transport unit containing packages. Include official registration marks and numbers assigned to the unit.

6   An estimate of the quantity and likely condition of the goods.

7   Whether lost goods floated or sank.

8   Whether loss is continuing.

9   Cause of loss.

3.1.2   If the condition of the ship is such that there is danger of further loss of packaged dangerous goods into the sea, items P and Q of the standard reporting format should be reported; details for P should be as follows:

P   1   Correct technical name or names of goods.

2   UN number or numbers.

3   IMO hazard class or classes.

4   Names of manufacturers of goods when known, or consignee or consignor.

5   Types of packages, including identification marks. Specify whether portable tank or tank vehicle, or whether vehicle or freight container or other cargo transport unit containing packages. Include official registration marks and numbers assigned to the unit.

6   An estimate of the quantity and likely condition of the goods.

3.1.3   Particulars not immediately available should be inserted in a supplementary message or messages.

3.2   Harmful substances reports (HS)

3.2.1   In the case of actual discharge, primary HS reports should contain items A, B, C (or D), E, F, L, M, N, Q, R, S, T, U, X of the standard reporting format. In the case of probable discharge (see 3.4), item P should also be included. Details for P, Q, R, T and X should be as follows:

P   1   Type of oil or the correct technical name of the noxious liquid substances on board.

2   UN number or numbers.

3   Pollution category (A, B, C or D), for noxious liquid substances.

4   Names of manufacturers of substances, if appropriate, when known, or consignee or consignor.

5   Quantity.

Q   1   Condition of the ship as relevant.

2   Ability to transfer cargo/ballast/fuel.

R   1   Type of oil or the correct technical name of the noxious liquid discharged into the sea.

     2   UN number or numbers.

     3   Pollution category (A, B, C or D), for noxious liquid substances.

     4   Names of manufacturers of substances, if appropriate, when known, or consignee or consignor.

     5   An estimate of the quantity of the substances.

     6   Whether lost substances floated or sank.

     7   Whether loss is continuing.

     8   Cause of loss.

     9   Estimate of the movement of the discharge or lost substances, giving current conditions if known.

    10   Estimate of the surface area of the spill if possible.

T   1   Name, address, telex and telephone number of the ship's owner and representative (charterer, manager or operator of the ship or their agent).

X   1   Action being taken with regard to the discharge and the movement of the ship.

     2   Assistance or salvage efforts which have been requested or which have been provided by others.

     3   The master of an assisting or salvaging ship should report the particulars of the action undertaken or planned.

3.2.2   After the transmission of the information referred to above in the initial report, as much as possible of the information essential for the protection of the marine environment as is appropriate to the incident should be reported in a supplementary report as soon as possible. That information should include items P, Q, R, S and X.

3.2.3   The master of any ship engaged in or requested to engage in an operation to render assistance or undertake salvage should report, as far as practicable, items A, B, C (or D), E, F, L, M, N, P, Q, R, S, T, U, X of the standard reporting format. The master should also keep the coastal State informed of developments.

3.3   Marine pollutants reports (MP)

3.3.1   In the case of actual discharge, primary MP reports should contain items A, B, C (or D), M, Q, R, S, T, U, X of the standard reporting format. In the case of probable discharge (see 3.4), item P should also be included. Details for P, Q, R, T and X should be as follows:

P   1   Correct technical name or names of goods.

     2   UN number or numbers.

     3   IMO hazard class or classes.

     4   Names of manufacturers of goods when known, or consignee or consignor.

     5   Types of packages, including identification marks. Specify whether portable tank or tank vehicle, or whether vehicle or freight container or other cargo transport unit containing packages. Include official registration marks and numbers assigned to the unit.

     6   An estimate of the quantity and likely condition of the goods.

Q   1   Condition of the ship as relevant.

     2   Ability to transfer cargo/ballast/fuel.

R   1   Correct technical name or names of goods.

     2   UN number or numbers.

     3   IMO hazard class or classes.

     4   Names of manufacturers of goods when known, or consignee or consignor.

     5   Types of packages, including identification marks. Specify whether portable tank or tank vehicle, or whether vehicle or freight container or other cargo transport unit containing packages. Include official registration marks and numbers assigned to the unit.

     6   An estimate of the quantity and likely condition of the goods.

     7   Whether lost goods floated or sank.

     8   Whether loss is continuing.

     9   Cause of loss.

T   1   Name, address, telex and telephone number of the ship's owner and representative (charterer, manager or operator of the ship or their agent).

X   1   Action being taken with regard to the discharge and the movement of the ship.

2   Assistance or salvage efforts which have been requested or which have been provided by others.

3   The master of an assisting or salvaging ship should report the particulars of the action undertaken or planned.

3.3.2   After the transmission of the information referred to above in the initial report, as much as possible of the information essential for the protection of the marine environment as is appropriate to the incident should be reported. That information should include items P, Q, R, S and X.

3.3.3   The master of any ship engaged in or requested to engage in an operation to render assistance or undertake salvage should report, as far as practicable, items A, B, C (or D), M, P, Q, R, S, T, U, X of the standard reporting format. The master should also keep the coastal State informed of developments.

3.4   Probability of discharge

3.4.1   The probability of a discharge resulting from damage to the ship or its equipment is a reason for making a report. In judging whether there is such a probability and whether the report should be made, the following factors, among others, should be taken into account:

.1   the nature of the damage, failure or breakdown of the ship, machinery or equipment; and

.2   sea and wind state and also traffic density in the area at the time and place of the incident.

3.4.2   It is recognized that it would be impracticable to lay down precise definitions of all types of incidents involving probable discharge which would warrant an obligation to report. Nevertheless, as a general guideline the master of the ship should make reports in cases of:

.1   damage, failure or breakdown which affects the safety of ships; examples of such incidents are collision, grounding, fire, explosion, structural failure, flooding, cargo shifting; and

.2   failure or breakdown of machinery or equipment which results in impairment of the safety of navigation; examples of such incidents are failure or breakdown of steering gear, propulsion plant, electrical generating system, essential shipborne navigational aids.

Resolution A.851(20)

Adopted on 27 November 1997

GENERAL PRINCIPLES FOR SHIP REPORTING SYSTEMS AND SHIP REPORTING REQUIREMENTS, INCLUDING GUIDELINES FOR REPORTING INCIDENTS INVOLVING DANGEROUS GOODS, HARMFUL SUBSTANCES AND/OR MARINE POLLUTANTS

THE ASSEMBLY,

RECALLING Article 15(j) of the Convention on the International Maritime Organization concerning the functions of the Assembly in relation to regulations and guidelines concerning maritime safety and the prevention and control of marine pollution from ships,

RECALLING ALSO resolution 3 of the International Conference on Maritime Search and Rescue, 1979, on the need for an internationally agreed format and procedure for ship reporting systems,

CONSIDERING that current national ship reporting systems may use different procedures and reporting formats,

REALIZING that such different procedures and reporting formats could cause confusion to masters of ships moving from one area to another covered by different ship reporting systems,

BELIEVING that such confusion could be alleviated if ship reporting systems and reporting requirements were to comply as far as practicable with relevant general principles and if reports were made in accordance with a standard format and procedures,

RECALLING the General Principles for Ship Reporting Systems and Ship Reporting Requirements, including Guidelines for Reporting Incidents Involving Dangerous Goods, Harmful Substances and/or Marine Pollutants, adopted by resolution A.648(16),

RECOGNIZING that States Parties to the International Convention relating to Intervention on the High Seas in Cases of Oil Pollution Casualties (1969) and the Protocol relating to Intervention on the High Seas in Cases of Marine Pollution by Substances other than Oil (1973) may take such measures on the high seas as may be necessary to prevent, mitigate or eliminate grave and imminent danger to their coastline or related interests from pollution or threat of pollution of the sea by oil and substances other than oil following upon a maritime casualty or acts related to such a casualty, which may reasonably be expected to result in major harmful consequences,

RECOGNIZING ALSO the need for coastal States to be informed by the master of an assisting ship, or of a ship undertaking salvage, of particulars of the incident and of action taken,

RECOGNIZING FURTHER that an incident involving damage, failure or breakdown of the ship, its machinery or equipment could give rise to a significant threat of pollution to coastlines or related interests,

HAVING CONSIDERED the recommendation made by the Maritime Safety Committee at its sixty-seventh session and the Marine Environment Protection Committee at its thirty-ninth session,

1.   ADOPTS the General Principles for Ship Reporting Systems and Ship Reporting Requirements, including Guidelines for Reporting Incidents Involving Dangerous Goods, Harmful Substances and/or Marine Pollutants, set out in the annex to the present resolution;

2.   URGES Governments to ensure that ship reporting systems and reporting requirements comply as closely as possible with the general principles specified in the annex* to the present resolution;

3.   URGES ALSO Governments to bring the reporting format and procedures to the notice of shipowners and seafarers as well as of the designated authorities concerned;

4.   RECOMMENDS Governments and States Parties to MARPOL 73/78 to implement the Guidelines, in accordance with paragraph (2) of article V of Protocol I thereof;

5.   REVOKES resolution A.648(16).

---

* See page 169.

Protocol I to MARPOL 73/78

Provisions concerning Reports on Incidents Involving Harmful Substances

(in accordance with article 8 of the Convention)

Article I – *Duty to report*

(1) The master or other person having charge of any ship involved in an incident referred to in article II of this Protocol shall report the particulars of such incident without delay and to the fullest extent possible in accordance with the provisions of this Protocol.

(2) In the event of the ship referred to in paragraph (1) of this article being abandoned, or in the event of a report from such a ship being incomplete or unobtainable, the owner, charterer, manager or operator of the ship, or their agent shall, to the fullest extent possible, assume the obligations placed upon the master under the provisions of this Protocol.

Article II – *When to make reports*

(1) The report shall be made when an incident involves:

    (a) a discharge above the permitted level or probable discharge of oil or of noxious liquid substances for whatever reason including those for the purpose of securing the safety of the ship or for saving life at sea; or

    (b) a discharge or probable discharge of harmful substances in packaged form, including those in freight containers, portable tanks, road and rail vehicles and shipborne barges; or

    (c) damage, failure or breakdown of a ship of 15 metres in length or above which:

        (i) affects the safety of the ship; including but not limited to collision, grounding, fire, explosion, structural failure, flooding, and cargo shifting; or

        (ii) results in impairment of the safety of navigation; including but not limited to, failure or breakdown of steering gear, propulsion plant, electrical generating system, and essential shipborne navigational aids; or

    (d) a discharge during the operation of the ship of oil or noxious liquid substances in excess of the quantity or instantaneous rate permitted under the present Convention.

(2) For the purposes of this Protocol:

    (a) *Oil* referred to in subparagraph 1(a) of this article means oil as defined in regulation 1(1) of Annex I of the Convention.

    (b) *Noxious liquid substances* referred to in subparagraph 1(a) of this article means noxious liquid substances as defined in regulation 1(6) of Annex II of the Convention.

    (c) *Harmful substances* in packaged form referred to in subparagraph 1(b) of this article means substances which are identified as marine pollutants in the International Maritime Dangerous Goods Code (IMDG Code).

Article III – *Contents of report*

    Reports shall in any case include:

    (a) identity of ships involved;

    (b) time, type and location of incident;

    (c) quantity and type of harmful substance involved;

    (d) assistance and salvage measures.

Article IV – *Supplementary report*

    Any person who is obliged under the provisions of this Protocol to send a report shall, when possible:

    (a) supplement the initial report, as necessary, and provide information concerning further developments; and

    (b) comply as fully as possible with requests from affected States for additional information.

Article V – *Reporting procedures*

(1)   Reports shall be made by the fastest telecommunications channels available with the highest possible priority to the nearest coastal State.

(2)   In order to implement the provisions of this Protocol, Parties to the present Convention shall issue, or cause to be issued, regulations or instructions on the procedures to be followed in reporting incidents involving harmful substances, based on guidelines developed by the Organization.*

Reporting

---

* Refer to the General Principles for Ship Reporting Systems and Ship Reporting Requirements, including Guidelines for Reporting Incidents Involving Dangerous Goods, Harmful Substances and/or Marine Pollutants adopted by the Organization by resolution A.851(20).

Article 8 of MARPOL 73/78

Reports on incidents involving harmful substances

(1)   A report of an incident shall be made without delay to the fullest extent possible in accordance with the provisions of Protocol I to the present Convention.

(2)   Each Party to the Convention shall:

(a)   make all arrangements necessary for an appropriate officer or agency to receive and process all reports on incidents; and

(b)   notify the Organization with complete details of such arrangements for circulation to other Parties and Member States of the Organization.

(3)   Whenever a Party receives a report under the provisions of the present article, that Party shall relay the report without delay to:

(a)   the Administration of the ship involved; and

(b)   any other State which may be affected.

(4)   Each Party to the Convention undertakes to issue instructions to its maritime inspection vessels and aircraft and to other appropriate services, to report to its authorities any incident referred to in Protocol I to the present Convention. That Party shall, if it considers it appropriate, report accordingly to the Organization and to any other Party concerned.

IMO/ILO/UNECE GUIDELINES FOR PACKING OF CARGO TRANSPORT UNITS (CTUs)

Foreword

The Maritime Safety Committee of IMO, at its sixty-seventh session (2 to 6 December 1996), approved the IMO/ILO/UNECE Guidelines for Packing of Cargo Transport Units (CTUs) which were prepared by the Working Group on Ship/Port Interface (SPI Working Group) in co-operation with the UNECE Working Party on Combined Transport (WP.24), subject to editorial improvements by the UNECE, ILO and IMO Secretariats, if necessary. The Committee instructed the IMO Secretariat to publish the Guidelines, in co-operation with the UNECE and ILO, after endorsement by these two organizations. The Guidelines were subsequently endorsed by the Inland Transport Committee of the UNECE in January 1997 and by the Governing Body of the ILO in March 1997 and circulated as MSC/Circ.787 dated 2 May 1997.

These Guidelines, which have been based on the existing IMO/ILO Guidelines for Packing Cargo in Freight Containers or Vehicles, are applicable to transport operations by all surface and water modes of transport and the whole intermodal transport chain, and supersede the previous IMO/ILO Guidelines.

This edition has been amended to conform with Amendment 31-02 of the IMDG Code.

Contents

Packing

Guidelines for the packing of cargo, other than bulk cargo, into or onto cargo transport units (CTUs) applicable to transport operations by all surface and water modes of transport

Preamble

While the use of freight containers, swap-bodies, vehicles or other cargo transport units substantially reduces the physical hazards to which cargoes are exposed, improper or careless packing of cargoes into/onto such units, or lack of proper blocking, bracing and securing, may be the cause of personnel injury when they are handled or transported. In addition, serious and costly damage may occur to the cargo or to the equipment. The person who packs and secures cargo into/onto the cargo transport unit (CTU) may be the last person to look inside the unit until it is opened by the consignee at its final destination.

Consequently, a great many people in the transport chain will rely on the skill of such persons, including:

- road vehicle drivers and other highway users when the unit is transported;
- rail workers, and others, when the unit is transported by rail;
- crew members of inland waterway vessels when the unit is transported on inland waterways;
- handling staff at inland terminals when the unit is transferred from one transport mode to another;
- dock workers when the unit is loaded or discharged;
- crew members of the ship which may be taking the unit through its most severe conditions during the transport operation; and
- those who unpack the unit.

All persons, such as the above and passengers, may be at risk from a poorly packed container, swap-body or vehicle, particularly one which is carrying dangerous cargoes.

Scope

These Guidelines, which are not all-inclusive, are essential to the safe packing of CTUs by those responsible for the packing and securing of the cargo and by those whose task it is to train people to pack such units. Training is essential if safety standards are to be maintained.

These Guidelines are not intended to conflict with, or to replace or supersede, any existing regulations or recommendations which may concern the carriage of cargo in CTUs. They do not cover the filling or emptying of tank containers, portable tanks or road tank vehicles, or the transport of any bulk cargo in bulk packagings.

Definitions

For the purposes of these Guidelines, *cargo transport unit (CTU)* has the same meaning as *intermodal transport unit (ITU)* and the following definitions apply:

- *bulk cargoes* means cargoes which are intended to be transported without any intermediate form of containment in bulk packagings or portable tanks;
- *block train* means a number of permanently coupled railway wagons, normally running directly between two selected terminals or entities without shunting;
- *cargo* means any goods, wares, merchandise and articles of any kind which are intended to be transported;
- *cargo transport unit (CTU)* means a freight container, swap-body, vehicle, railway wagon or any other similar unit;
- *dangerous cargoes* means packaged dangerous, hazardous or harmful substances, materials or articles, including environmentally hazardous substances (marine pollutants) and wastes, covered by

the International Maritime Dangerous Goods (IMDG) Code; the term *dangerous cargoes* includes any empty uncleaned packagings;

- *freight container* means an article of transport equipment that is of a permanent character and accordingly strong enough to be suitable for repeated use; it is designed to transport a number of receptacles, packages, unit loads or overpacks together from the packing point to its final destination by road, rail, inland waterway and/or sea without intermediate separate handling of each package, unit load or overpack. The word "freight" is not repeated throughout these Guidelines;

- *handling* includes the operation of loading or unloading/discharging of a ship, railway wagon, vehicle or other means of transport;

- *intermediate bulk container (IBC)* means a rigid, semi-rigid or flexible portable packaging that:

  .1 has a capacity of not more than 3.0 m^3 (3,000 ℓ) for solids and liquids;

  .2 is designed for mechanical handling; and

  .3 is resistant to the stresses produced in handling and transport, as determined by tests;

- *intermodal transport unit (ITU)* means a container, swap-body or semi-trailer suitable for intermodal transport;

- *lift truck* means a truck equipped with devices such as arms, forks, clamps, hooks, etc. to handle any kind of cargo, including cargo that is unitized, overpacked or packed in CTUs;

- *maximum payload* means the maximum permissible weight of cargo to be packed into or onto a CTU. It is the difference between the maximum operating gross weight or rating and the tare weight, which are normally marked on CTUs as appropriate;

- *overpack* means an enclosure used by a single shipper to contain one or more packages and to form one unit for convenience of handling and stowage during transport.

  Examples of overpacks are a number of packages either:

  .1 placed or stacked on to a load board such as a pallet and secured by strapping, shrink-wrapping, stretch-wrapping or other suitable means; or

  .2 placed in a protective outer packaging such as a box or crate;

- *packing* means the packing of packaged and/or unitized or overpacked cargoes into CTUs;

- *unpacking* means the removal of cargo from CTUs;

- *packaging(s)* means receptacles and any other components or materials necessary for the receptacle to perform its containment function;

- *packages* means the complete product of the packing operation, consisting of the packaging and its contents as prepared for transport;

- *responsible person* means a person appointed by a shore-side employer who is empowered to take all decisions relating to his/her specific task, having the necessary current knowledge and experience for that purpose, and who, where required, is suitably certificated or otherwise recognized by the regulatory authority;

- *ship* means a seagoing or non-seagoing watercraft, including those used on inland waters;

- *shunting* means the operation when single railway wagons or groups of railway wagons are pushed to run against each other and be coupled together;

- *stowage* means the positioning of packages, IBCs, containers, swap-bodies, tank-containers, vehicles or other CTUs on board ships, in warehouses and sheds or in other areas such as terminals;

- *swap-body* means a CTU not permanently attached to an underframe and wheels or to a chassis and wheels, with at least four twist-locks that take into account ISO standard 1161:1984. A swap-body need not be stackable but is usually equipped with support legs, designed especially for combined road–rail transport;

- *transport* means movement of cargo by one or more modes of transport;

- *unit load* means a number of packages that are:

  .1 placed or stacked on and secured by strapping, shrink-wrapping or other suitable means to a load board such as a pallet; or

  .2 placed in a protective outer enclosure such as a pallet box; or

  .3 permanently secured together in a sling;

- *vehicle* means a road vehicle or railway freight wagon, permanently attached to an underframe and wheels or to a chassis and wheels, which is loaded and unloaded as a unit. It also includes a trailer, semi-trailer or similar mobile unit except those used solely for the purposes of loading and unloading.

1   General conditions

1.1   Sea voyages are made in a variety of weather conditions which are likely to exert a combination of forces upon the ship and its cargo over a prolonged period. Such forces may arise from pitching, rolling, heaving, surging, yawing or swaying or a combination of any two or more.

1.2   Packing and securing of cargo into/onto a CTU should be carried out with this in mind. It should never be assumed that the weather will be calm and the sea smooth or that securing methods used for land transport will always be adequate at sea.

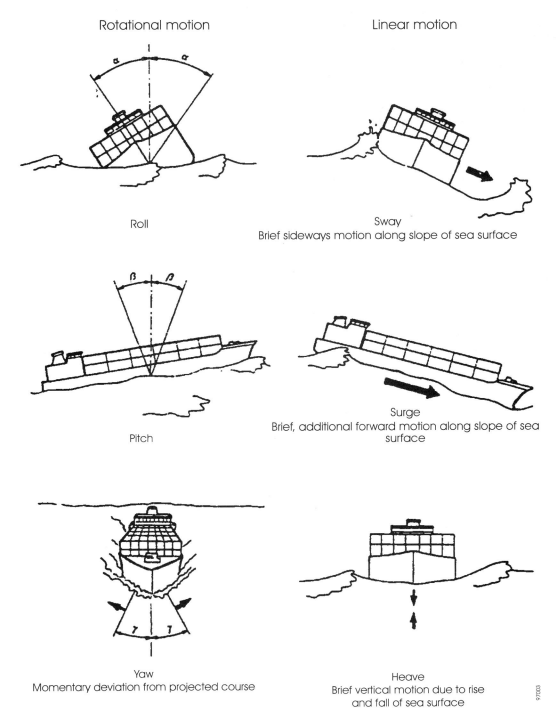

Rotational motion   Linear motion

Roll

Sway
Brief sideways motion along slope of sea surface

Pitch

Surge
Brief, additional forward motion along slope of sea surface

Yaw
Momentary deviation from projected course

Heave
Brief vertical motion due to rise and fall of sea surface

Figure 1 – *Examples of ship movement at sea*

1.3   During longer voyages, climatic conditions (temperature, humidity, etc.) are likely to vary considerably. These may affect the internal conditions in a CTU which may give rise to condensation (sweating)* on cargo or internal surfaces. Where cargo is liable to damage from condensation, expert advice should be sought.

1.4   Road transport operations may generate short-term longitudinal forces upon the cargo and the CTU. They may also cause vibrations that may vary considerably due to different suspension systems, different road surface conditions and different driving habits.

1.5   Rail transport, in addition to subjecting cargo to vibrations (16 Hz), may also lead to shocks as a result of shunting operations. Many railways have organised their operations in such a way as to avoid shunting of railway wagons incurring high forces (e.g., by operating dedicated block trains) or by moving CTUs on wagons with high-performance shock absorbers that are normally able to reduce shunting shock forces. It may be advisable to ensure that such operational features have been established for the rail journey.

1.6   Inland river and waterway transport is generally smooth. It will not normally exert any forces higher than those of road transport on the cargo and the CTU. Diesel engines of inland river and waterway vessels may create some low-frequency vibrations which under normal conditions should not give reason for any concern.

1.7   The following[†] table provides an example of the accelerations in g,s which could arise during transport operations; however, national legislation or recommendations may require the use of other values.

Mode of transport	Forwards	Backwards	Sideways
ROAD	1.0g	0.5g	0.5g
RAILWAY Wagons subject to shunting[1] Combined transport[2]	 4.0g 1.0g	 4.0g 1.0g	 0.5g (a) 0.5g (a)
SEA Baltic Sea North Sea Unrestricted	 0.3g (b) 0.3g (c) 0.4g (d)	 0.3g (b) 0.3g (c) 0.4g (d)	 0.5g 0.7g 0.8g

[1] The use of specifically equipped rolling stock is advisable (e.g., long shock absorbers, instructions for shunting restrictions).

[2] *Combined transport* means wagons with containers, swap-bodies, semi-trailers and trucks, and also "block trains" (UIC and RIV).

1g = 9.81 m/s^2

The above values should be combined with static gravity force of 1.0g acting downwards and a dynamic variation of:

(a) $\pm 0.3g$

(b) $\pm 0.5g$

(c) $\pm 0.7g$

(d) $\pm 0.8g$

1.8   Container movements by terminal tractors may be subject to differing forces as terminal trailers are not equipped with suspension. Additionally, ramps can be very steep, causing badly stowed cargo inside CTUs to be thrown forward or backward.

1.9   Considerable forces may also be exerted on CTUs and their cargoes during terminal transfer. Especially in sea-ports, containers are transferred by shore-side gantry cranes that lift and lower containers, applying considerable acceleration forces and creating pressure on the packages in containers. Lift trucks and straddle carriers may take containers, lift them, tip them and move them across the terminal ground.

---

* See annex 1.

[†] References:
– Swedish, Finnish and Norwegian national road regulations.
– Code of Practice – Safety of Loads on Vehicles, United Kingdom Department of Transport.
– UIC prescription – Regolamento Internazionale Veicoli (RIV) – Loading of Wagons.
– Swedish national regulations on securing of cargo in CTUs for sea transportation.
– The Safety of Passenger Ro–Ro Vessels – Results of the North West European Research and Development Project.
– IMO Code of Safe Practice for Cargo Stowage and Securing (CSS Code).

Braking – forces acting forward

Turning – forces acting sideways

Speed increase – forces acting backwards

Figure 2 – *Forces acting on the cargo during road transport*

Shunting – forces acting forwards or backwards

Figure 3 – *Forces acting on the cargo during rail transport*

Forces acting forwards, backwards and sideways.
The sideways forces are normally the most troublesome

Figure 4 – *Forces acting on the cargo during sea transport*

2   Visual inspections prior to packing

A CTU should be thoroughly inspected before it is packed with cargo. The following may be used as a guide to inspecting a unit before packing.

2.1   Exterior inspection

2.1.1   The structural strength of a container depends to a great extent on the integrity of its main framework comprising the corner posts, corner fittings, main longitudinal and the top and bottom end transverse members which form the end frame. If there is evidence that the container is weakened, it should not be used.

2.1.2   The walls, floor and roof of a CTU should be in good condition, and not significantly distorted.

2.1.3   The doors of a CTU should work properly and be capable of being securely locked and sealed in the closed position, and properly secured in the open position. Door gaskets and weather strips should be in good condition.

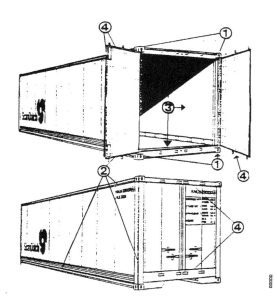

1   Corner castings
2   Welding on framework and walls
3   Walls, floor and roof
4   Door closures

Figure 5 – *Inspection of a container*

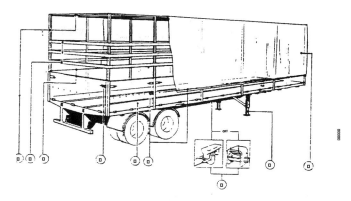

1 Load platform
2 Sideboards
3 Locking device
4 Support leg
5 Cargo securing device
6 Cover stanchions
7 Cover batten
8 Canopy
9 Canopy seal

Figure 6 – *Inspection of a semi-trailer*

2.1.4 A container on international voyages should be affixed with a current International Convention for Safe Containers (CSC)* Safety Approval Plate. A swap-body may be required to have a yellow code plate, fixed at its side wall (for details see UIC[†] leaflet 596), which proves that it has been codified in conformity with the safety rules of European railways. Such swap-bodies need not be affixed with a CSC plate, but many of them will have one in addition to the yellow code plate.

2.1.5 Irrelevant labels, placards, marks or signs should be removed or masked.

2.1.6 A vehicle should be provided with points for securing it aboard ships (refer to ISO 9367-1: Lashing and securing arrangements on road vehicles for sea transportation on Ro/Ro ships – General requirements – Part 1: Commercial vehicles and combinations of vehicles, semi-trailers excluded, and to ISO 9367-2: Lashing and securing arrangements on road vehicles for sea transportation on Ro/Ro ships – General requirements – Part 2: Semi-trailers).

2.1.7 When canvas covers are used, they should be checked as being in satisfactory condition and capable of being secured. Loops or eyes in such canvas which take the fastening ropes, as well as the ropes themselves, must be in good condition.

2.1.8 When loading swap-bodies, it should be borne in mind that in most cases, the bottom and floor of swap-bodies are the main areas of their structural strength.

2.2 **Interior inspection**

2.2.1 A CTU should be weatherproof unless it is so constructed that this is obviously not feasible. Previous patches or repairs should be carefully checked for possible leakage. Potential points of leakage may be detected by observing if any light enters a closed unit. In carrying out this check, care should be taken to ensure that no person becomes locked inside a unit.

2.2.2 A CTU should be free from major damage, with no broken flooring or protrusions such as nails, bolts, special fittings, etc. which could cause injury to persons or damage to the cargo.

2.2.3 Cargo tie-down cleats or rings, where provided, should be in good condition and well anchored. If heavy items of cargo are to be secured in a CTU, the forwarder or shipping agent should be contacted for information about the cleat strength and appropriate action taken.

2.2.4 A CTU should be clean, dry and free of residue and persistent odours from previous cargo.

---

* International Convention for Safe Containers (CSC), published by the International Maritime Organization (IMO).
[†] International Union of Railways (UIC).

2.2.5   A folding CTU with movable or removable main components should be correctly assembled. Care should be taken to ensure that removable parts not in use are packed and secured inside the unit.

3   Packing and securing of cargo

3.1   Before packing

3.1.1   Before packing a CTU, careful consideration should be given as to how the unit will be presented during the packing operation. The same applies for unpacking. The CTU may be presented for packing or unpacking as follows:

- loaded on a semi-trailer chassis together with a truck;
- loaded on a semi-trailer chassis, but without a truck;
- loaded on a rigid truck or chassis;
- standing on the ground;
- standing on its supporting legs (in case of class C swap-bodies);
- loaded on a rail-car;
- loaded on an inland barge; or
- loaded on a seagoing vessel.

Any of these configurations is possible. The actual packing or unpacking situation often depends on site and facility considerations. However, whenever the CTU is presented on a chassis or on supporting legs, special care should be taken in planning the packing or unpacking operation.

3.1.2   A CTU to be packed should rest on level and firm ground or on a trailer or a rail-car. If a CTU is on a trailer, care should be taken to ensure the trailer cannot tip while the container is being packed, especially if a lift truck is being used. If necessary, the trailer should be propped. Brakes should be securely applied and the wheels chocked.

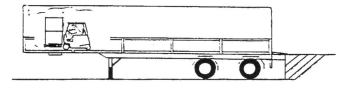

Figure 7 – *Inadequate support of the trailer when working in the forward part*

3.1.3   When a swap-body standing on its supporting legs is packed, particular care should be taken to ensure that the swap-body does not tip when a lift truck is used for packing. It should be checked that the supporting legs of the swap-body rest firmly on the ground and cannot shift, slump or move when forces are exerted to the swap-body during packing.

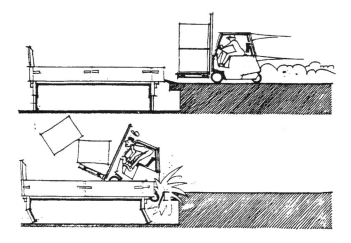

Figure 8 – *Don't drive a lift truck onto a swap-body too fast*

3.1.4   Packing should be planned before it is started. This should make it possible to segregate incompatible cargoes and produce either a tight or secured stow, in which the compatibility of all items of cargo and the nature, i.e. type and strength, of any packages or packaging involved are taken into account. The possibility of cross-contamination by odour or dust, as well as physical or chemical compatibility, should be considered.

3.1.5   The planned cargo should not weigh more than the maximum payload of the CTU. In the case of containers, this ensures that the permitted maximum gross weight of the container (which includes the payload) marked on the CSC Safety Approval Plate* will never be exceeded (see also annex 3). For CTUs not marked with their maximum permissible gross weight, tare weight or other features, any of these values should be known before packing starts. According to CEN[†] standards, a swap-body of class C (7.15 m to 7.82 m) will have a maximum gross mass of 16,000 kg and a swap-body of class A (12.2 m to 13.6 m) will have a gross mass of up to 32,000 kg.

3.1.6   Notwithstanding the foregoing, any height or weight limitation along the projected route that may be dictated by regulations or other circumstances (such as lifting, handling equipment, clearances and surface conditions) should be complied with. Such weight limits may be considerably less than the permitted gross weight already referred to.

3.1.7   Stowage planning should take account of the fact that CTUs are generally designed and handled assuming the cargo to be evenly distributed over the entire floor area. Where substantial deviations from uniform packing occur, special advice for preferred packing should be sought.

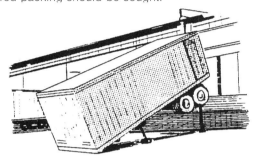

Figure 9 – *Nose-heavy trailer*

3.1.8   When a heavy indivisible load is to be shipped in a CTU, due regard should be given to the localized weight-bearing capability of the unit. If necessary, the weight should be spread over a larger area than the actual bearing surface of the load, for example by use of properly secured baulks of timber. In such a case the method of securing the load should be planned before packing is started and any necessary preparations should be made.

3.1.9   If the planned cargo of an open-topped or open-sided CTU will project beyond the overall dimensions of the unit, special arrangements should be made. It should be borne in mind that road traffic regulations may not allow such overhangs. Furthermore, CTUs are often loaded door-to-door and side by side, thus not permitting any overhang.

3.1.10   The centre of gravity of the packed cargo should be at or near the longitudinal centreline of the CTU and below half the height of the cargo space of the unit (see also 3.2.5 and 3.2.6).

3.1.11   When planning the packing of a CTU, consideration should be given to potential problems which may be created for those who unpack it, e.g., cargo falling when doors are opened.

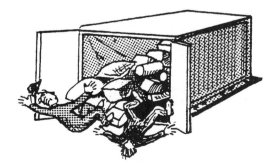

Figure 10 – *Secure the cargo to prevent it falling when the doors are opened*

---

* International Convention for Safe Containers (CSC), published by the International Maritime Organization (IMO).
[†] European Standardization Committee (CEN).

3.1.12   Before a CTU is packed, it should be ensured that the personnel responsible for the packing are fully informed about all the risks and dangers involved. As a minimum requirement some sketches showing the basic rules of CTU packing should be available. The present Guidelines should also be readily available. If necessary, the shipper and the packing personnel should consult each other regarding any special feature of the cargo to be packed into the units. In particular, information on possible dangerous cargoes should be considered very carefully. Consideration should also be given to the provision of appropriate training for personnel involved in packing CTUs.

3.1.13   When packing a CTU, the shipper and persons responsible for packing should bear in mind that any failure to pack and secure the cargo correctly may result in additional costs that they will have to bear. If, for example in railway transport, a unit is found not to be properly packed and secured, the rail-car may be marshalled out of the train into a siding and the transport can only be continued once the cargo has been properly secured. The shipper may have to pay for this work, especially for the repacking and resecuring operation, as well as for the additional time during which the rail-car has been used. In addition, he may be held responsible for any delay of the transport operation.

3.1.14   Not all handling equipment is suitable for container packing. Lift trucks used for container packing and unpacking should have a short lifting mast and a low driver's overhead guard. If the lift truck operates inside the container, equipment with electric power supply should be used. Container floors are built to withstand a maximum wheel pressure corresponding to an axle load of a lift truck of 5,460 kg or 2,730 kg per wheel. Such an axle load is usually found on lift trucks with a lifting capacity of 2.5 t.

3.1.15   If the CTU floor is at a different height level than the loading ramp, a bridging unit may need to be used. This may result in sharp bends between the loading ramp and the bridging unit as well as between the bridging unit and the CTU floor. In such cases the lift truck used should have sufficient ground clearance to ensure that the chassis does not touch the ramp when passing these bends.

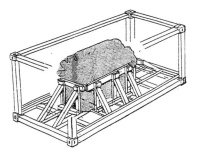

Figure 11 – *Blocking against the framework in a container*

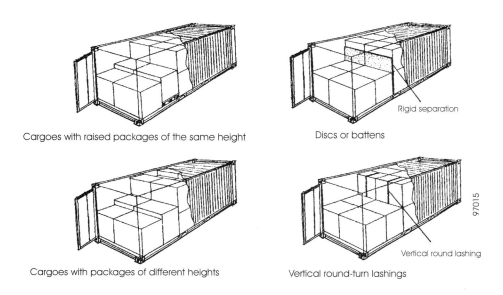

Figure 12 – *Blocking a second layer*

3.2   Packing and securing

3.2.1   It is essential to make the cargo in a CTU secure to prevent cargo movement inside the unit. However, the method of securing the cargo should not itself cause damage or deterioration to the cargo or the unit. A number of "DO's" and "DON'Ts" relating to cargo packing are illustrated in annex 5.

3.2.2   It should not be assumed that because cargo is heavy it will not move during transport. All items of cargo should be secured to ensure they cannot move during transport.

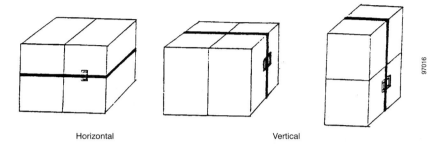

Horizontal   Vertical

Figure 13 – *Round-turn lashing*

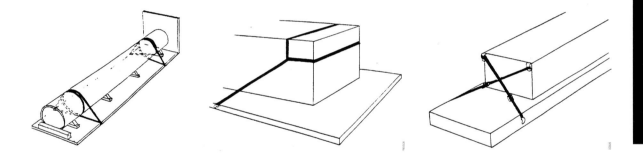

Figure 14 – *Loop-lashing*   Figure 15 – *Spring lashing*   Figure 16 – *Cross lashing*

3.2.3   Where cargo of regular shape and size is loaded, a tight stow from wall to wall should be sought. However, in many instances some void spaces may occur. If the spaces between the packages are too large, then the stow should be secured by using dunnage, folded cardboard, air bags or other suitable means.

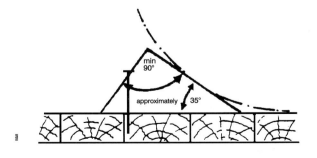

Figure 17 – *Blocking rolling cargo by wedges*

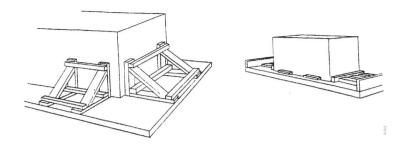

Figure 18 – *Blocking by battens*

Figure 19 – *Blocking against the headboard in a trailer*

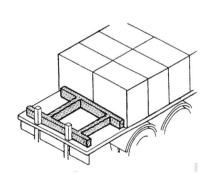

Figure 20 – *Blocking by an H-block*

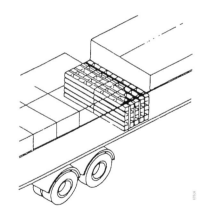

Figure 21 – *Blocking by empty vertical pallets*

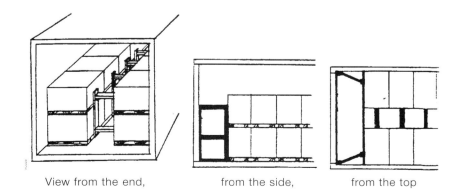

View from the end,   from the side,   from the top

Figure 22 – *Blocking cargoes in a strong-walled cargo unit*

Packing

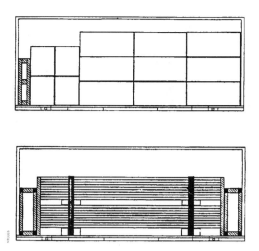

Figure 23 – *Fill all spaces between load and unit wall, e.g., by blocking*

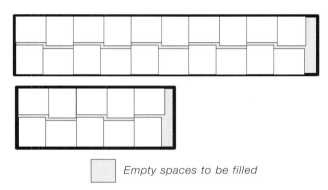

☐ *Empty spaces to be filled*

Figure 24 – *Packing 1000 × 1200 mm unit loads in 20 ft and 40 ft containers*

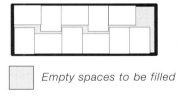

☐ *Empty spaces to be filled*

Figure 25 – *Packing 800 × 1200 mm unit loads in 20 ft containers*

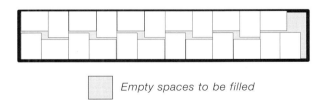

☐ *Empty spaces to be filled*

Figure 26 – *Packing 800 × 1200 mm unit loads in 40 ft containers*

3.2.4   If air bags are used, the manufacturer's instructions on filling pressure should be scrupulously observed. Allowance should be made for the possibility of a considerable rise in the internal temperature of the CTU above the temperature at the time of packing. This may cause the bags to expand and burst, thereby making them ineffectual as a means of securing the cargo. Air bags should not be used as a means of filling space at the doorway unless precautions are taken to ensure that they cannot cause the door to open violently when the locking bars are released (see also 3.3.1).

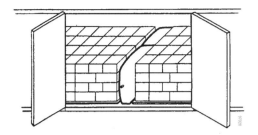

Figure 27 – *Blocking by air bags*

3.2.5 The weight of the cargo should be evenly distributed over the floor of a container. Where cargo items of a varying weight are to be packed into a container or where a container will not be full (either because of insufficient cargo or because the maximum weight allowed will be reached before the container is full), the stow should be so arranged and secured that the approximate centre of gravity of the cargo is close to the mid-length of the container. If it is not, then special handling of the container may be necessary. In no case should more than 60% of the load be concentrated in less than half of the length of a container measured from one end. For vehicles, special attention should be paid to axle loads.

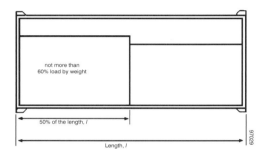

Figure 28 – *Even load distribution: not more than 60% in one half of the container*

3.2.6 Heavy cargoes should not be placed on top of lighter cargoes and liquids should not be placed on top of solids. When it is intended that packages are to be stacked on top of each other, attention should be paid to the strength of pallets and the shape and condition of the packages. Attention is drawn to part 6 of the IMDG Code on stacking tests.* It may be necessary in some cases to ensure stability of such a stack by introducing dunnage or solid flooring between tiers of the stow. When doubt exists, especially with heavier packages such as intermediate bulk containers (IBCs) for liquids, it should be ascertained from the shipper or manufacturer of such packages whether or not they are designed and strong enough to be stacked on top of one another, especially where part of the transport will involve a sea voyage. The centre of gravity should be below the half-height of the cargo space.

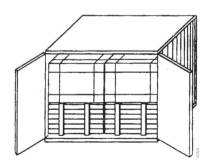

Figure 29 – *Do load lightweight items on top of heavy ones*

---

* The stacking test requires that test samples be stacked with a load equal to that which they would be subjected to in transit, with a stacking height of at least 3 m. The packages must not leak or show deterioration or distortion after a specified time. The minimum time is 24 h, with 28 days being required for some types of packages. The test is intended for all types of packages other than bags.

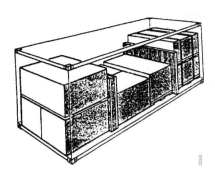

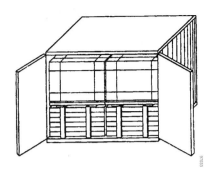

Figure 30 – *Securing load by vertical separator* Figure 31 – *Securing load by intermediate floor layers*

3.2.7 In order to avoid cargo damage from moisture, wet cargoes, moisture-inherent cargoes or cargoes liable to leak should not be packed with cargoes susceptible to damage by moisture. Wet dunnage, pallets or packaging should not be used. In certain cases, damage to equipment and cargo can be prevented by the use of protective material such as polythene sheeting.

3.2.8 Damaged packages should not be packed into a CTU unless precautions have been taken against harm from spillage or leakage (see 4.2.7 and 4.3.1 for dangerous cargoes).

3.2.9 Permanent securing equipment incorporated into a CTU should be used wherever necessary to prevent cargo movement.

3.2.10 Where open or curtain-sided units are concerned, particular care should be taken to secure cargo against side forces, including those likely to arise from the rolling of the ship or in traffic. A check should be made to ensure that all side battens are fitted where appropriate or other adequate precautions are taken.

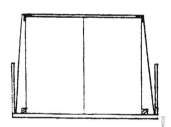

Figure 32 – *Over-top lashing*

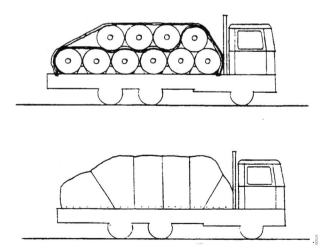

Figure 33 – *Conventional securing by tarpaulin*

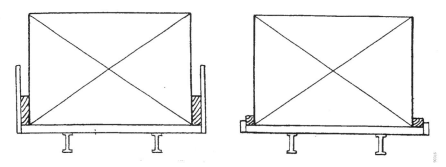

Figure 34 – *Blocking against sideboards or side edges*

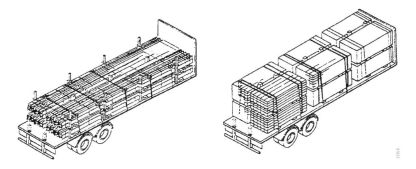

Figure 35 – *Blocking by stanchions*

3.2.11   Any special instructions on packages, or otherwise available, should be followed, e.g.:

- cargoes marked "protect from frost" should be packed away from the walls of a CTU;

- cargoes marked "this way up" should be packed accordingly;

- maximum stacking height marked should not be exceeded; and

where practicable, markings on packagings should conform to ISO 780:1985.

3.2.12   When deciding on packaging and cargo-securing material, it should be borne in mind that some countries enforce a garbage- and litter-avoidance policy. This may lead to limitations on the use of certain materials and imply fees for the recovery of packaging at the reception point as well as similar problems for the shipper of the cargo. In such cases, reusable packaging and securing material should be used. Increasingly, countries are requiring timber dunnage and packaging materials to be debarked.

3.3   **On completion of packing**

3.3.1   During the final stages of packing a CTU, care should be taken, so far as is practicable, to build a secure face of the cargo so as to prevent "fall out" when the doors are opened. Where there is any doubt as to the security of the cargo, further steps should be taken to ensure security, e.g., by weaving strapping between securing points or placing timber between the rear posts.

Two factors should be borne in mind:

- that a container on a trailer usually inclines towards the doors; and

- that cargo may move against the doors due to jolts, etc., during transport.

3.3.2   If a CTU is destined for a country with wood treatment quarantine regulations, care should be taken that all wood in the unit, packaging and cargo complies with the regulations. It is a useful practice to place a copy of the wood treatment certificate in a conspicuous place inside and, where appropriate, outside the unit in a weatherproof pouch.

3.3.3   After closing the doors, it should be ensured that all closures are properly engaged and secure. Usually a seal is applied to a container. Care should be taken that sealing procedures are carried out properly.

3.3.4   Where CTUs have hinged or detachable fittings, a check should be made that they are properly secured, with no loose equipment likely to cause a hazard during transport.

4   Additional advice on the packing and securing of dangerous cargoes

4.1   General

4.1.1   The advice of this section applies to CTUs in which dangerous cargoes are packed. It should be followed in addition to the advice given elsewhere in these Guidelines.

4.1.2   International (and often national) transport of dangerous cargoes may be subject to several dangerous cargoes transport regulations, depending on the final destination and the modes of transport used.

4.1.3   For combined transport, involving several modes of transport other than by sea, the rules and regulations applicable depend on whether it is a national movement or international transport or transport within a political or economic union or trading zone, such as the European Union.

4.1.4   International transport of dangerous cargoes by road, rail or inland waterways is subject to the following Agreements in Europe:

- European Agreement concerning the International Carriage of Dangerous Goods by Road (ADR);

- Regulations concerning the International Carriage of Dangerous Goods by Rail (RID); and

- Regulations for the Carriage of Dangerous Substances on the Rhine (ADNR) based on the provisions contained in the European Agreement concerning the International Carriage of Dangerous Goods by Inland Waterways (ADN).

4.1.5   The provisions of ADR, RID, ADNR and ADN are harmonized. Most national and international regulations are based on the United Nations Recommendations on the Transport of Dangerous Goods (Orange Book). However, national rules, applicable to domestic transport, may differ from international regulations.

4.1.6   For maritime transport, the provisions of the International Maritime Dangerous Goods (IMDG)* Code apply. The IMDG Code provides detailed guidance on all aspects of the transport of packaged dangerous goods by sea. Special attention is drawn to part 5 (Consignment procedures) of the IMDG Code, which comprises the following chapters:

- chapter 5.1   General provisions;

- chapter 5.2   Marking and labelling of packages including IBCs;

- chapter 5.3   Placarding and marking of cargo transport units;

- chapter 5.4   Documentation; and

- chapter 5.5   Special provisions.

4.1.7   Dangerous goods are divided into the following classes:

- Class 1 – Explosives

  Class 1 is divided into six divisions:

    Division 1.1: Substances and articles which have a mass explosion hazard

    Division 1.2: Substances and articles which have a projection hazard but not a mass explosion hazard

    Division 1.3: Substances and articles which have a fire hazard and either a minor blast hazard or a minor projection hazard or both, but not a mass explosion hazard

    Division 1.4: Substances and articles which present no significant hazard

    Division 1.5: Very insensitive substances which have a mass explosion hazard

    Division 1.6: Extremely insensitive articles which do not have a mass explosion hazard

- Class 2 – Gases: compressed, liquefied or dissolved under pressure

    Class 2.1: Flammable[†] gases

    Class 2.2: Non-flammable, non-toxic gases

    Class 2.3: Toxic[‡] gases

- Class 3 – Flammable liquids

---

* International Maritime Dangerous Goods (IMDG) Code, published by the International Maritime Organization.
[†] *Inflammable* has the same meaning as *flammable*.
[‡] *Poisonous* has the same meaning as *toxic*.

- Class 4 – Flammable solids, substances liable to spontaneous combustion, substances which in contact with water emit flammable gases

    Class 4.1 – Readily combustible solids and solids which may cause fire through friction; Self-reactive (solids and liquids) and related substances; Desensitized explosives.

    Class 4.2 – Substances liable to spontaneous combustion

    Class 4.3 – Substances which, in contact with water, emit flammable gases

- Class 5 – Oxidizing substances (agents) and organic peroxides

    Class 5.1: Oxidizing substances (agents)

    Class 5.2: Organic peroxides

- Class 6 – Toxic and infectious substances

    Class 6.1: Toxic substances

    Class 6.2: Infectious substances

- Class 7 – Radioactive material

- Class 8 – Corrosive substances

- Class 9 – Miscellaneous dangerous substances and articles

Class 9 comprises:

.1 substances and articles not covered by other classes which experience has shown, or may show, to be of such a dangerous character that the provisions of part A of chapter VII of SOLAS, 1974, as amended, shall apply; these include substances that are transported or offered for transport at temperatures equal to, or exceeding, 100°C, in a liquid state, and solids that are transported or offered for transport at temperatures equal to or exceeding 240°C; and

.2 substances not subject to the provisions of part A of chapter VII of the aforementioned Convention, but to which the provisions of Annex III of MARPOL 73/78, as amended, apply. The properties or characteristics of each substance are given in the Dangerous Goods List in chapter 3.2 pertaining to the substance or article.

4.2 Before packing

4.2.1 Information should be provided by the shipper about the properties of the dangerous cargoes to be handled and their quantities. The basic items of information necessary for each dangerous substance, material or article to be transported by any mode of transport are the following:

- the Proper Shipping Name (correct technical name);

- the class and/or division (and the compatibility group letter for cargo of class 1);

- the UN Number and the packing/packaging group; and

- the total quantity of dangerous cargoes (by volume or mass, and for explosives the net explosive content).

Other items of information may be required, depending on the mode of transport (flashpoint for transport by sea, instructions to be followed in case of incident for road transport under the ADR regime, special certificates, e.g., for radioactive materials, etc.). The various items of information required under each regulation and applicable during combined transport operations should be provided so that appropriate documentation may be prepared for each shipment.

4.2.2 The shipper should also ensure that dangerous cargoes are packaged, packed, marked, labelled, placarded and provided with the required signs, in accordance with the applicable regulations. A declaration that this has been carried out is normally required. Such a declaration may be incorporated into or attached to the transport documents.

4.2.3 The shipper should also ensure that the cargoes to be transported are authorized for transport by the modes to be used during the transport operation. For example, self-reacting substances and organic peroxides requiring temperature control are not authorized for transport by rail under the RID regime. Certain types of dangerous cargoes are not authorized to be transported on board passenger ships and therefore the requirements of the IMDG Code should be carefully studied, particularly before the consolidation of several shipments of dangerous cargoes in a CTU which may need to be segregated "away from" each other. These shipments may only be carried in the same unit with the approval of the competent authority concerned.

4.2.4 Current versions of all applicable regulations (IMDG Code, ADR, RID, ADN and ADNR) should be easily accessible during packing to ensure appropriate checking.

4.2.5   Dangerous cargoes should only be handled, packed and secured under direct and identifiable supervision of a responsible person who is familiar with the legal requirements and the risks involved and who knows the measures that should be taken in an emergency.

4.2.6   Suitable measures to prevent fires should be taken, including the prohibition of smoking in the vicinity of dangerous cargoes.

4.2.7   Packages of dangerous cargoes should be examined and any found to be damaged, leaking or sifting should not be packed into a CTU. Packages showing evidence of staining, etc. should not be packed without first determining that it is safe and acceptable to do so. Water, snow, ice or other matter adhering to packages should be removed before packing. Liquids that have accumulated on drum heads should initially be treated with caution in case they are the result of leakage of contents. If pallets have been contaminated by spilt dangerous cargoes they should be destroyed by appropriate disposal methods to prevent use at a later date.

4.2.8   If dangerous cargoes are palletised or otherwise unitised they should be compacted so as to be regularly shaped, with approximately vertical sides and level at the top. They should be secured in a manner unlikely to damage the individual packages comprising the unit load. The materials used to bond a unit load together should be compatible with the substances unitised and retain their efficiency when exposed to moisture, extremes of temperature and sunlight.

4.2.9   The packing and method of securing of dangerous cargoes in a CTU should be planned before packing is started.

4.3   **Packing and securing**

4.3.1   Special care should be taken during handling to avoid damage to packages. However, if a package containing dangerous cargoes is damaged during handling so that the contents leak out, the immediate area should be evacuated until the hazard potential can be assessed. The damaged package should not be shipped. It should be moved to a safe place in accordance with instructions given by a responsible person who is familiar with the risks involved and knows the measures that should be taken*in an emergency.

4.3.2   If a leakage of dangerous cargoes presents safety or health hazards such as explosion, spontaneous combustion, poisoning or similar danger, personnel should immediately be moved to a safe place and the Emergency Response Organization notified.

4.3.3   Dangerous cargoes should not be packed in the same CTU with incompatible cargoes. In some instances even cargoes of the same class are incompatible with each other and should not be packed in the same unit. The requirements of the IMDG Code concerning the segregation of dangerous cargoes inside CTUs are usually more stringent than those for road and rail transport. Whenever a combined transport operation does not include transport by sea, compliance with the respective inland transport regulations, such as ADR, RID, ADN and ADNR, may be sufficient. However, if it cannot be guaranteed that no part of the transport operation will be by sea, the segregation requirements of the IMDG Code should be strictly complied with.

4.3.4   When dangerous cargoes are being handled, the consumption of food and drink should be prohibited.

4.3.5   Vented packages should be packed with the vents in an upright position and in such a way that the vents will not be blocked.

4.3.6   Drums containing dangerous cargoes should always be stowed in an upright position unless otherwise authorized by the competent authority.

4.3.7   Dangerous cargoes consignments which form only part of the load of a CTU should, whenever possible, be packed adjacent to the doors with markings and labels visible. Particular attention is drawn to 3.3.1 concerning the securing of cargo by the doors of a unit.

---

* The *Emergency Response Procedures for Ships Carrying Dangerous Goods (EmS Guide)* and the *Medical First Aid Guide for Use in Accidents Involving Dangerous Goods (MFAG)* in the Supplement of the IMDG Code give further useful advice, but it should be borne in mind that the former may not be appropriate for use on land. Emergency response handbooks, giving emergency response information cross-referenced to the substance's United Nations identification number (UN Number), are usually available at the national level.

4.4   On completion of packing

4.4.1   *Placarding*

4.4.1.1   Placards (enlarged labels) (minimum size 250 mm × 250 mm) and, if applicable for maritime transport, "MARINE POLLUTANT" marks (minimum size of a side 250 mm) and other signs should be affixed to the exterior surfaces of a CTU or unit load or overpack to provide a warning that the contents of the unit are dangerous cargoes and present risks, unless the labels, marks or signs affixed to the packages are clearly visible from the exterior of the unit.

4.4.1.2   CTUs containing dangerous cargoes or residues of dangerous cargoes should clearly display placards and, if applicable for maritime transport, "MARINE POLLUTANT" marks or other signs as follows:

.1   *a cargo transport unit, semi-trailer or portable tank*, one on each side and one on each end of the unit;

.2   *a railway wagon*, at least one on each side;

.3   *a multiple-compartment tank containing more than one dangerous substance or their residues*, along each side at the positions of the relevant compartments; and

.4   *any other cargo transport unit*, at least one on both sides and on the back of the unit.

Placards on the sides of a CTU should be affixed in such a position that they are not obscured when the unit doors are opened. For international road transport under the ADR regime, the display of enlarged labels on vehicles is only required for transport in bulk.

4.4.1.3   Whenever dangerous cargoes present several risks, subsidiary risk placards should be displayed in addition to primary risk placards. CTUs containing cargoes of more than one class, however, need not bear a subsidiary risk placard if the hazard represented is already indicated by the primary risk placard.

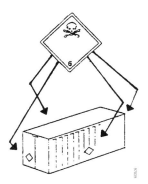

Figure 36 – *Placards on a container*

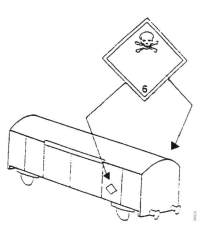

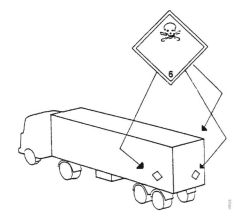

Figure 37 – *Placards on a railway wagon*   Figure 38 – *Placards on a trailer*

4.4.1.4 Where individual schedules in the IMDG Code indicate that no hazard label or class marking is necessary on individual packages, then no placard or class marking is required on the CTU, provided the UN Number is displayed on the unit in accordance with 4.4.1.6.

4.4.1.5 For maritime cargo, any CTU containing packaged dangerous cargoes of a single commodity which constitute a full load and for which no placard is required should be durably marked with the Proper Shipping Name of the contents.

4.4.1.6 Consignments of packaged dangerous cargoes of a single commodity, other than cargoes of class 1, which constitute a full load for the CTU should have the UN Number for the commodity displayed in black digits not less than 65 mm high either against a white background in the lower half of the class placard or on an orange rectangular panel not less than 120 mm high and 300 mm wide, with a 10 mm black border, to be placed immediately adjacent to the placard or Marine Pollutant mark (see section 5.3.2.1 of the IMDG Code). In those cases the UN Number should be displayed immediately adjacent to the Proper Shipping Name.

4.4.1.7 For radioactive materials special requirements apply (see, for example, section 5.3.1.2.2 of the IMDG Code).

4.4.1.8 When solid carbon dioxide (CO_2 – dry ice) or other expendable refrigerant is used for cooling purposes, a warning sign should be affixed to the outside of the doors so that it is clearly visible to any person operating the doors. The sign should warn of the possibility of an asphyxiating atmosphere. An example of such a warning sign is given in annex 2.

4.4.1.9 As CTUs offered for shipment under fumigation may require special precautions, they should only be accepted with the agreement of the carrier and they should be identified to him prior to loading. CTUs under fumigation are now included in class 9 of the IMDG Code.

4.4.1.10 When a closed CTU or its contents has been fumigated and is to be shipped under fumigation, a warning sign should be affixed to the outside of the doors so that it is clearly visible to any person operating the doors. An example of such a warning sign is given in annex 2. The sign should state the fumigant, the method of fumigation employed and the date and time when it took place. The sign should only be removed when the unit has been ventilated after fumigation, to ensure that no harmful concentration of gas remains.

4.4.2 *Certification*

4.4.2.1 For transport by sea, regulation 4 of chapter VII of SOLAS 1974, as amended, requires that the person responsible for the packing of dangerous cargoes into a container or road vehicle shall provide a signed Container Packing Certificate or Vehicle Declaration stating that the cargo in the unit has been properly packed and secured and that all applicable transport requirements are met.

4.4.2.2 The IMDG Code states the following declaration:

.1 The container/vehicle was clean, dry and apparently fit to receive the goods;

.2 Packages which need to be segregated in accordance with applicable segregation requirements have not been packed together onto or in the container/vehicle (unless approved by the competent authority concerned in accordance with 7.2.2.3);

.3 All packages have been externally inspected for damage, and only sound packages have been loaded;

.4 Drums have been stowed in an upright position, unless otherwise authorized by the competent authority, and all goods have been properly loaded and, where necessary, adequately braced with securing material to suit the mode(s) of transport for the intended journey;

.5 Goods loaded in bulk have been evenly distributed within the container/vehicle;

.6 For consignments including goods of class 1 other than division 1.4, the container/vehicle is structurally serviceable in accordance with 7.4.6;

.7 The container/vehicle and packages are properly marked, labelled and placarded, as appropriate;

.8 When solid carbon dioxide (CO_2 – dry ice) is used for cooling purposes, the container/vehicle is externally marked or labelled in a conspicuous place, such as, at the door end, with the words: "DANGEROUS CO_2 (DRY ICE) INSIDE. VENTILATE THOROUGHLY BEFORE ENTERING"; and

.9 A dangerous goods transport document, as indicated in 5.4.1, has been received for each dangerous goods consignment loaded in the container/vehicle.

Note: The container/vehicle packing certificate is not required for tanks.

4.4.2.3 A Container Packing Certificate/Vehicle Declaration is not required under the RID, ADR, ADN or ADNR regimes, even though they may be required for inland domestic transport in certain countries. However, such certificates will be needed if the transport operation includes sea voyages. They will then need to be provided prior to loading, as port authorities, berth operators and shipmasters may wish to sight them (or a copy) before accepting containers or vehicles packed with dangerous cargoes into their premises or aboard their ship.

Packing

4.4.2.4	For international road transport under the ADR regime, when several items of dangerous cargoes are packed together in a single CTU, the shipper should declare that such mixed packing is not prohibited.

4.4.2.5	The functions of the dangerous goods declaration (see 4.2.2) and of the Container Packing Certificate/Vehicle Declaration may be incorporated into a single document; if not, these documents should be attached one to the other. If these functions are incorporated into a single document, e.g., a Dangerous Goods Declaration, a shipping note, etc., the inclusion of a phrase such as "it is declared that the packing of the cargoes into the vehicle or freight container has been carried out in accordance with the applicable provisions" (see section 5.4.2.2 of the IMDG Code). Where both declarations are included in a single document, separate signatures are required for the two declarations.

4.4.3	If the doors of containers or vehicles are locked, the means of locking should be of such a construction that, in case of emergency, the doors can be opened without delay.

4.4.4	Where dangerous cargoes are kept in combined transport terminals in port areas, reference should be made to the IMO Recommendations on the Safe Transport of Dangerous Cargoes and Related Activities in Port Areas.

4.4.5	CTUs packed with dangerous cargoes should only be collected from terminals by a driver who has been properly trained and instructed. The driver should possess a driver training certificate proving that he is allowed to drive a vehicle carrying dangerous cargoes of the classes contained in the unit. Before departure, he should be provided with all relevant documentation for the dangerous cargoes, as well as with written instructions on the action to be taken in the case of incidents involving the dangerous cargoes.

## 5	Advice on receipt of CTUs

5.1	When receiving a CTU, the receiver should ascertain that the unit is externally in good condition and without damage. If there is any damage, the receiver should document and notify it as appropriate. Specific attention should be paid to damage that may have influenced the condition of the cargo within the unit. If the receiver detects any damage during the discharge of the unit, this should be documented and notified as appropriate. If a package containing dangerous cargoes is found to be so damaged that the contents leak out, the immediate area should be evacuated until the hazard potential can be assessed.

5.2	Persons opening a CTU should be aware of the risk of cargo falling out. Doors, when opened, should be secured in the fully opened position.

5.3	A CTU which carries dangerous cargoes, or in which expendable refrigerants have been used, or which has been shipped under fumigation may present a special risk of a dangerous atmosphere, which may be flammable, explosive, toxic or asphyxiant. In such a case the CTU should be ventilated by leaving it open for a sufficient time, or other steps taken to ensure that no harmful concentration of gas remains before allowing personnel to enter. Where a flammable cargo is concerned, there should be no sources of ignition in the vicinity.

5.4	If there is a particular reason to suspect danger, e.g., because of damage to packages or the presence of fumigants, expert advice should be sought before unpacking of the unit is started.

5.5	After a CTU with dangerous cargoes has been unpacked, particular care should be taken to ensure that no hazard remains. This may require special cleaning, particularly if spillage of a toxic substance has occurred or is suspected. When the CTU offers no further hazard, the dangerous goods placards, orange panels, "MARINE POLLUTANT" marks and any other marks or signs should be removed, masked or otherwise obliterated.

5.6	If a CTU shows signs of abnormally high temperatures it should be moved to a safe place and the fire services notified. Care should be taken to ensure that the fire-fighting methods used are suitable for the cargo in the unit.

5.7	Attention is drawn to the fact that the receiver is normally obliged to return a CTU, after discharge, clean and suitable for the transport of every kind of cargo. This applies especially when dangerous cargoes or obnoxious cargoes have been transported. Pamphlets on this subject have been published by ICHCA* and IICL.[†]

5.8	The receiver shall keep in mind that he may be held responsible for all damage to the CTU, other than those that have been officially observed and endorsed by the operator prior to the transfer of the unit to the receiver.

---

* International Cargo Handling Co-ordination Association (ICHCA).
[†] Institute of International Container Lessors (IICL).

6 Basic principles for the safe handling and securing of CTUs

6.1 General

Before handling a CTU, the handling staff should make certain whether it is empty or loaded. Unless otherwise known, it should be treated as being loaded.

6.2 Lifting

6.2.1 Before lifting a CTU, the handling staff should ensure that the lifting equipment is safely and securely attached to it and that the unit is free-standing (i.e. all securing, fixing and lashing devices have been released).

6.2.2 Not all lifting equipment is suitable for all types and all sizes of CTUs. Before using any such equipment, the lifting staff should ensure that the equipment selected is suitable for use with the unit. International Standard ISO 3874:1988 gives all necessary details for such a decision for containers.

6.2.3 Some methods of lifting CTUs may only be used when the unit is empty ("tare weight"). This relates particularly to the use of lift trucks or four leg slings. Such limitations have to be strictly observed, otherwise very severe accidents may occur.

6.2.4 Under no circumstances should containers be lifted with forks applied under the base of the container. This applies equally to containers with or without fork-lift pockets.

6.2.5 Under no circumstances should CTUs without a grappler lifting area be lifted by means of grappler arms.

6.3 Containers on the ground

6.3.1 When a container is standing on the ground, a firm, flat and drained surface should be provided, clear of obstructions and projections. On the ground, the container should be supported by the four bottom corner fittings only.

6.3.2 When stacking containers, the bottom surfaces of the lower corner fittings of the upper container should have complete contact with upper surfaces of the top corner fittings of the lower container. A shift of up to 25 mm laterally and 38 mm longitudinally may be tolerated.

6.3.3 A container stack may be subject to forces by heavy winds. This might lead to sliding and toppling of containers. Stacks of empty containers will be more subject to such dangers than stacks of loaded containers. The higher the stack, the greater the danger.

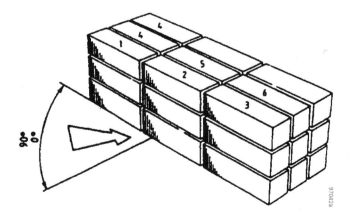

Container 1: most likely to be displaced by wind
Container 2: second most likely to be displaced by wind

Figure 39 – *Wind effect on container stacks*

6.4 CTUs on vehicles

6.4.1 CTUs should be firmly secured on vehicles before the vehicle is moved. The most appropriate points for fixing containers and swap-bodies are the bottom corner fittings of the unit. Before and during transport, it should be checked that the unit is properly secured on the vehicle.

6.4.2 For transport on public roads or by rail, containers and swap-bodies should be secured to the road or rail vehicle by all bottom corner fittings, in the absence of which, appropriate alternative measures should be taken. The main forces during the transport operation should be transferred to the unit through these bottom corner fittings. Some additional forces may be transferred between the road vehicle chassis or rail-car surface and the unit bottom through load-transfer areas in the unit bottom and in the vehicle surface. The securing devices on the vehicle may be twist-locks, securing cones, or securing guides. All such securing devices should be designed in such a way that the "open" or "locked" position of such securing devices is readily apparent.

6.5 CTUs on ships

6.5.1 Securing of CTUs on board ships should be carried out in accordance with instructions in the ship's Cargo Securing Manual.*

6.5.2 Whenever practicable, overheight, soft-top and tank containers should be stowed so that access for securing or cargo-handling operations is provided.

6.5.3 Handling of CTUs with a high centre of gravity should be carried out carefully. Such units may need extra lashings.

7 Training in packing of cargo in CTUs

7.1 Regulatory authorities

7.1.1 The regulatory authority should establish minimum requirements for training and, where appropriate, qualifications for each person involved, directly or indirectly, in the packing of cargo in CTUs, particularly in relation to dangerous cargoes.

7.1.2 Regulatory authorities involved in the development or enforcement of legal requirements relating to the supervision of the safety of the transport by road, rail and sea should ensure that their personnel are adequately trained, commensurate with their responsibilities.

7.2 Management

Management should ensure that all personnel involved in the packing of cargo in CTUs or in the supervision thereof are adequately trained and appropriately qualified, commensurate with their responsibilities within their organization.

7.3 Personnel

All persons engaged in the transport or packing of cargo in CTUs should receive training on the safe packing of cargo in CTUs, commensurate with their responsibilities.

7.4 Training

7.4.1 *General awareness/familiarization training*

All persons should receive training on the safe transport and packing of cargo, commensurate with their duties. The training should be designed to provide an appreciation of the consequences of badly packed and secured cargo in CTUs, the legal requirements, the magnitude of forces which may act on cargo during road, rail and sea transport, as well as basic principles of packing and securing of cargoes in CTUs.

7.4.2 *Function-specific training*

All persons should receive detailed training concerning specific requirements for the transport and packing of cargo in CTUs which are applicable to the functions that they perform.

7.4.3 *Verification*

The adequacy of the knowledge of any person to be employed in work involving the packing of cargo in CTUs should be verified or appropriate training provided. This should be supplemented by periodic training, as deemed appropriate by the regulatory authority.

---

* Reference is made to MSC/Circ.745, Guidelines for the preparation of the Cargo Securing Manual, approved by the International Maritime Organization (IMO).

7.5   Recommended course syllabus – overview

The adequacy of the knowledge of any persons to be employed in work involving the packing of cargo in CTUs should be verified, in the absence of which appropriate training is considered essential and should be provided. The function-specific training should be commensurate with the duties required to be performed by an individual in the packing and securing of cargo in CTUs. Topics for consideration, to be included in the training as appropriate, are given in annex 6.

Packing

ANNEX 1
Condensation

1   Cargoes in transit may be affected by the conditions to which they are subjected. These conditions may include changes in temperature and humidity and particularly cyclic changes that may be encountered. An understanding of condensation phenomena is desirable because condensation may lead to such damage as rust, discoloration, dislodging of labels, collapse of fibreboard packages or mould formation.

2   Solar radiation can produce air temperatures under the inner surfaces of a CTU which are significantly higher than external air temperatures. The combination of these effects can result in a range of day and night cyclic temperature variations in the air adjacent to the inner surfaces of a CTU which is greater than the corresponding range of temperatures just outside.

3   Cargoes closest to the walls or roof will be more affected by external temperature variations than those in the centre of a CTU. If the possible extent of temperature variations or their full significance is not known, advice should be obtained from specialists.

4   Under the circumstances described, condensation may occur either on the surface of the cargo (cargo sweat) or on the inside surfaces of a CTU (container sweat) either during transport or when the unit is opened for discharge.

5   The main factors leading to condensation inside a CTU are:

   .1   sources of moisture inside the unit which, depending on ambient temperature conditions, will affect the moisture content of the atmosphere in the unit;

   .2   a difference between the temperature of the atmosphere within the unit and the surface temperature of either the cargo or the inner surfaces of the unit itself; and

   .3   changes in the temperature of the outer surface of the unit which affect the two factors above.

6   Warming the air in a CTU causes it to absorb moisture from packagings or any other source. Cooling the air below its dewpoint* causes condensation.

7   If, after high humidity has been established inside a CTU, the outside of the unit is cooled, then the temperature of the unit surface may fall below the dewpoint of the air inside it. Under these circumstances moisture will form on the inner surfaces of the unit. After forming under the roof, the moisture may drop onto the cargo. Cyclical repetition of cargo or container sweat phenomena can result in a greater degree of damage.

8   Condensation can also occur immediately after a CTU is opened if the air inside the unit is humid and the outside air is relatively cool. Such conditions can produce a fog and even precipitation but, because this phenomenon usually occurs only once, it seldom results in serious damage.

9   The risk of damage and dangerous situations[†] can be minimized if the moisture content of the packaging and securing materials is kept low.

---

* The dewpoint is the temperature at which air saturated with moisture at the prevailing atmospheric pressure will start to shed moisture by condensation.

† For example, when dangerous cargoes of class 4.3 (dangerous when wet) are packed in a container.

ANNEX 2
Labels, placards, marks and signs*

Hazard labels and placards

Labels of class

1

The appropriate division number and compatibility group are to be placed in this location for divisions 1.1, 1.2 and 1.3, e.g., **1.1 D**.

The appropriate compatibility group is to be placed in this location, e.g., **D** or **N**. For goods of class 1 in division 1.4, compatibility group S, each package may alternatively be marked **1.4 S**.

Labels of class

2

Class 2.1   Class 2.2   Class 2.3

Label of class

3

Labels of class

4

Class 4.1   Class 4.2   Class 4.3

---

* These relate to Amendments 30-00 and later of the IMDG Code. These Guidelines are under review. Users should refer to chapters 5.2 and 5.3 of Amendment 34-08 to the IMDG Code for the correct labels, placards, marks and signs.

Labels of class

Class 5.1   Class 5.2

Labels of class

Class 6.1   Class 6.2

Labels of class

Category I   Category II   Category III   Class 7 fissile material

PLACARD

Labels of class

Labels of class

UN Number on cargo transport units

ALTERNATIVE 1   ALTERNATIVE 2

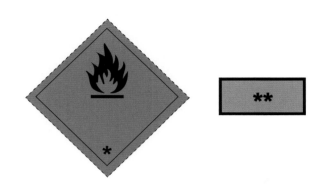

*   Location of class number
** Location of UN number

The MARINE POLLUTANT mark

The ELEVATED TEMPERATURE mark

The FUMIGATION WARNING sign

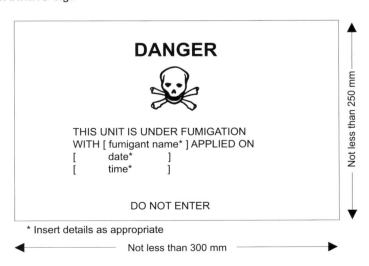

* Insert details as appropriate

Warning label for dry ice or other expendable refrigerant used for cooling purposes

Note: The text under "WARNING" should refer to the refrigerant gas used.

ANNEX 3
Consequences of overloading of CTUs

1　Occupational safety hazards caused by overweight CTUs in a multimodal transport chain include hazards:

.1　to ship- and shore-side handlers in the event of structural failure of the unit;

.2　to unit handlers and plant operators, particularly lift truck drivers whose vehicles may be damaged or may become unstable;

.3　of accidents to road and rail vehicles when the overloaded container exceeds the maximum permissible weight of the vehicles. The hazards are aggravated by the fact that the road vehicle driver is often not aware that his vehicle is overloaded and does not adjust his driving habits accordingly. A further hazard can arise from the special conditions in intermodal road/rail transport in Europe, as rail-car design does not provide for a large overweight safety margin.

2　The principal hazard is of accidents involving loading or unloading a CTU on or off a ship or vehicle and container-handling equipment in the terminal area, especially when units are to be stacked pending shipment or dispatch to consignees.

　Note: When high-density goods, such as heavy machinery or metal ingots, are packed into a CTU, the selection of the type and capacity of the unit should be taken into account to prevent overloading.

3　Most cranes can be expected to have weight limit controls but, as these are designed to prevent overstressing of the crane, they will not necessarily assist in the detection of overweight CTUs.

4　When an overweight CTU is offloaded from a ship or vehicle, its condition may only be discovered upon being removed for stacking in the terminal area and the handling equipment being found to have inadequate lifting capacity. Handling equipment, in some ports, may not be available for handling heavy units.

5　The problem of overweight CTUs should be properly addressed at the initial phase of packing the unit. Packing of units, either at the manufacturing or producing premises, consolidation depots, or consignor's warehouse, should be under the supervision of trained operatives who are provided with adequate information on the cargo to be packed and who possess sufficient authority to control the operation to prevent overloading.

6　In view of the above, all measures should be taken to prevent overloading of CTUs. However, if a container is found to be overloaded, it should be removed from service until it can be repacked within its maximum gross weight.

ANNEX 4
List of relevant international organizations

Further information, particularly on regulations and legal provisions at the international level, can be obtained from the organizations listed below:

United Nations Conference on Trade and Development (UNCTAD)
Palais des Nations
1211 Geneva 10
Switzerland
Fax: + 41-22-907-0050

United Nations Economic Commission for Europe (ECE)
Transport Division
Palais des Nations
1211 Geneva 10
Switzerland
Fax: + 41-22-917-0039

International Labour Office (ILO)
Maritime Industries Branch
4, route des Morillons
1211 Geneva
Switzerland
Fax: + 41-22-799-7050

International Maritime Organization (IMO)
Cargoes and Facilitation Section
4 Albert Embankment
London SE1 7SR
United Kingdom
Tel: +44 20 7735 7611
Fax: + 44-20-7587-3240
email: info@imo.org

International Organization for Standardization (ISO)
1–3, rue de Varembé
1211 Geneva 20
Switzerland
Fax: + 41-22-733-3430

International Cargo-Handling Co-ordination Association (ICHCA)
Suite 2,
85 Western Road
Romford
Essex RM1 3LS
United Kingdom
Tel: +44 1708 734787
Fax: +44 1708 734877
email: postmaster@ichca.org.uk

Institute of International Container Lessors (IICL)
Bedford Consultants Building, Box 605
Bedford, NY 10506
USA
Fax: +1-914-234-3641

Central Commission of Navigation on the Rhine (CCNR)
2, place de la République
67082 Strasbourg
France
Fax: + 33-88-32 10 72

Danube Commission (CD)
25, rue Benczur
1068 Budapest
Hungary
Fax: + 36-1-268-1980

European Standardization Committee (CEN)
Rue de Strassart 36
1050 Bruxelles
Belgium
Fax: + 32-2-519-6819

International Union of Railways (UIC)
16, rue Jean Rey
75015 Paris
France
Fax: + 33-1-44-49-20-29

International Road Transport Union (IRU)
Centre international
3, rue de Varembé – B.P. 44
1211 Geneva 20
Switzerland
Fax: + 41-22-733-0660

Packing

ANNEX 5
Illustrations of "DOs" and "DON'Ts"

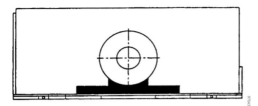

DO distribute heavy loads over a large floor area

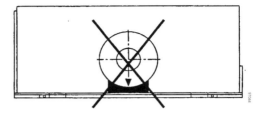

DON'T concentrate heavy loads on small areas of the floor

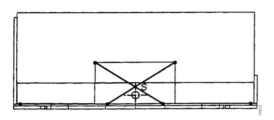

DO load with the centre of gravity in the centre of the container

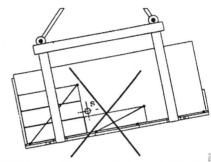

DON'T load with excentric load distribution

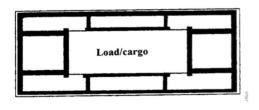

DO secure loads in a way that forces are distributed over a large area of a unit

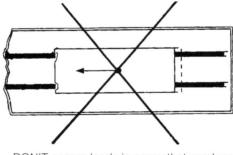

DON'T secure loads in a way that produces heavy forces on small areas of the inside structure of a unit

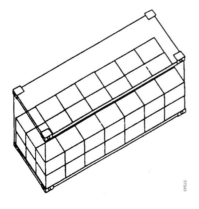

DO use a block stow when packing cargo

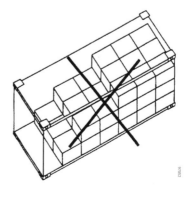

DON'T build up irregular layers of packages

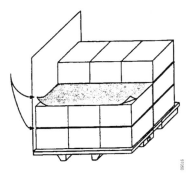

DO use non-slip surface material
to prevent sliding of packages

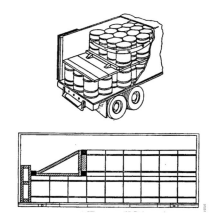

DO secure the upper layer adequately

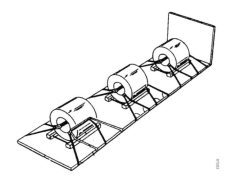

DO secure each single loaded item independently

Packing

ANNEX 6
Topics to be included in a training programme for the packing and securing of cargoes in cargo transport units (CTUs)

1   Consequences of badly packed and secured cargo

1.1   Injuries to persons and damage to the environment

1.2   Damage to ships and CTUs

1.3   Damage to cargo

1.4   Economic consequences

2   Liabilities

2.1   Different parties involved in cargo transport

2.2   Legal responsibility

2.3   Goodwill responsibility

2.4   Quality assurance

3   Forces acting on the cargo during transport

3.1   Road transport

3.2   Rail transport

3.3   Sea transport

4   Basic principles for cargo packing and securing

4.1   Prevention from sliding

4.2   Prevention from tipping

4.3   Influence of friction

4.4   Basic principles for cargo securing

4.5   Dimensions of securing arrangements for combined transportation

5   CTUs – types

5.1   Containers

5.2   Flats

5.3   Swap-bodies

5.4   Road vehicles

5.5   Rail-cars/wagons

6   Cargo care consciousness and cargo planning

6.1   Choice of transport means

6.2   Choice of CTU type

6.3   Check of CTU prior to packing

6.4   Cargo distribution in CTUs

6.5   Requirements from the receiver of cargo regarding cargo packing

6.6   Condensation risks in CTUs

6.7   Symbols for cargo handling

7   Different methods for cargo packing and securing

7.1   Lashing

7.2   Blocking and bracing

7.3   Increasing friction

8   Equipment for securing and protection of cargo

8.1   Fixed equipment on CTUs

8.2   Reusable cargo-securing equipment

8.3   One-way equipment

8.4   Inspection and rejection of securing equipment

9   Packing and securing of unitized cargo (bulk)

9.1   Cases

9.2   Palletized cargoes

9.3   Bales and bundles

9.4   Bags on pallets

9.5   Big bags

9.6   Slabs and panels

9.7   Barrels

9.8   Pipes

9.9   Cartons

10   Packing and securing of non-unitized cargo (break-bulk)

10.1   Different types of packaged cargoes loaded together

10.2   Packing of heavy and light cargoes together

10.3   Packing of rigid and non-rigid cargoes together

10.4   Packing of long and short cargoes together

10.5   Packing of high and low cargoes together

10.6   Packing of liquid and dry cargoes together

11   Packing and securing of paper products

11.1   General guidelines for the packing and securing of paper products

11.2   Vertical rolls

11.3   Horizontal rolls

11.4   Sheet paper on pallets

12   Packing and securing of cargo requiring special techniques

12.1   Steel coils

12.2   Cable drums

12.3   Wire rolls

12.4   Steel slabs

12.5   Steel plates

12.6   Big pipes

12.7   Stone blocks

12.8   Machines

13   Packing and securing of dangerous cargoes

13.1   Regulations for the transport of dangerous cargoes

13.2   Definitions

13.3   Packing regulations

13.4   Packing, separation and securing

13.5   Labelling and placarding

13.6   Information transfer when transporting dangerous cargoes

13.7   Liabilities

Packing

LIST OF REFERENCES

- International Maritime Dangerous Goods (IMDG) Code
- UIC prescription – Regolamento Internazionale Veicoli (RIV) – Loading of Wagons
- Code of Safe Practice for Cargo Stowage and Securing (CSS Code)
- International Convention for Safe Containers, 1972 (CSC)
- United Nations Recommendations on the Transport of Dangerous Goods (Orange Book)
- Regulations for the Carriage of Dangerous Substances on the Rhine (ADNR)
- European Agreement concerning the International Carriage of Dangerous Goods by Road (ADR)
- Regulations concerning the International Carriage of Dangerous Goods by Rail (RID)
- European Provisions concerning the International Carriage of Dangerous Goods by Inland Waterways (ADN)
- International Convention for the Safety of Life at Sea (SOLAS), 1974, as amended
- International Convention for the Prevention of Pollution from Ships, 1973, as modified by the Protocol of 1978 relating thereto (MARPOL 73/78)
- Emergency Procedures for Ships Carrying Dangerous Goods (EmS)
- Medical First Aid Guide for Use in Accidents Involving Dangerous Goods (MFAG)
- Recommendations on the Safe Transport of Dangerous Cargoes and Related Activities in Port Areas
- Guidelines for the Preparation of the Cargo Securing Manual
- ISO Standard No. 1161:1984
- ISO Standard No. 780:1985
- ISO Standard No. 3874:1988
- ISO Standard No. 9367-1:1989
- ISO Standard No. 9367-2:1994
- UIC leaflet 596
- Swedish, Finnish and Norwegian national road regulations
- Code of Safe Practice – Safety of Loads on Vehicles, UK Department of Transport
- Swedish national regulations on securing of cargo in CTUs for sea transportation
- The Safety of Passenger Ro–Ro Vessels – Results of the North West European Research and Development Project

RECOMMENDATIONS ON THE SAFE USE OF PESTICIDES IN SHIPS

Foreword

The *Recommendations on the Safe Use of Pesticides in Ships* are intended as a guide to competent authorities, mariners, fumigators, fumigant and pesticide manufacturers, and others concerned. They were first circulated in September 1971 and revised by the Maritime Safety Committee in 1984, 1993, 1995, 1996 and 2008. The Maritime Safety Committee, at its eighty-fourth session, revised those aspects of the Recommendations relating to the fumigation of cargo holds and cargo transport units and approved:

.1 The Recommendations on the Safe Use of Pesticides in Ships applicable to the Fumigation of Cargo Holds, MSC.1/Circ.1264, which supersedes the relevant provisions of the Recommendations on the Safe Use of Pesticides in Ships with regard to the fumigation of cargo holds; and

.2 The Recommendations on the Safe Use of Pesticides in Ships applicable to the Fumigation of Cargo Transport Units, MSC.1/Circ.1265, which supersedes the relevant provisions of Recommendations on the Safe Use of Pesticides in Ships with regard to the fumigation of cargo transport units.

RECOMMENDATIONS

The *Recommendations on the Safe Use of Pesticides in Ships*, the *Recommendations on the Safe Use of Pesticides in Ships applicable to the Fumigation of Cargo Holds* and the *Recommendations on the Safe Use of Pesticides in Ships applicable to the Fumigation of Cargo Transport Units* are recommended to governments in pursuance of their obligations under chapter VI of the 1974 SOLAS Convention as amended.

Pesticides

Contents

Recommendations on the safe use of pesticides in ships

Pesticides

1 Introduction

1.1 These Recommendations have been compiled by the Sub-Committee on the Carriage of Dangerous Goods and the Sub-Committee on Containers and Cargoes, both of which have been amalgamated into the Sub-Committee on Dangerous Goods, Solid Cargoes and Containers since 1995, under the direction of the Maritime Safety Committee of the International Maritime Organization (IMO).

1.2 Insects and rodents on ships are objectionable for various reasons. In addition to aesthetic and nuisance aspects, pests may damage equipment and spread disease and infection, contaminate food in galleys and food stores, and cause damage to cargoes that will result in commercial or other losses. Very few pesticides are suitable for use against all kinds of pests that may occur aboard or in different parts of ships. It is therefore necessary to consider the main categories of pesticides individually.

1.2.1 *Insects in cargo spaces and cargoes*

1.2.1.1 Insect and mite pests of plant and animal products may be carried into the cargo spaces with goods (*introduced infestation*); they may move from one kind of product to another (*cross-infestation*) and may remain to attack subsequent cargoes (*residual infestation*). Their control may be required to comply with phytosanitary requirements to prevent spread of pests and for commercial reasons to prevent infestation and contamination of, or damage to, cargoes of human and animal food.* In severe cases of infestation of bulk cargoes such as cereals, excessive heating may occur.

1.2.2 *Rodents*

1.2.2.1 Rodents should be controlled not only because of the damage they may do to cargo or the ship's equipment, but also, as required by the International Health Regulations, to prevent the spread of disease.

1.3 The following sections provide guidance to shipmasters in the use of pesticides† with a view to safety of personnel and to avoidance of excessive residues of toxic agents in human and animal food. They cover pesticides used for the control of insect‡ and rodent pests in empty and loaded cargo spaces, in crew and passenger accommodation and in food stores. Account has been taken of existing recommendations of the World Health Organization (WHO), the International Labour Office (ILO), and the Food and Agriculture Organization of the United Nations (FAO) in regard to pesticide residues and occupational safety.

2 Prevention of infestation

2.1 Maintenance and sanitation

2.1.1 Ship cargo spaces, tank top ceilings and other parts of the ship should be kept in a good state of repair to avoid infestation. Many ports of the world have rules and by-laws dealing specifically with the maintenance of ships intended to carry grain cargoes; for example, boards and ceilings should be completely grain-tight.

2.1.2 Cleanliness, or good housekeeping, is as important a means of controlling pests on a ship as it is in a home, warehouse, mill or factory. Since insect pests on ships become established and multiply in debris, much can be done to prevent their increase by simple, thorough cleaning. Box beams and stiffeners, for example, become filled with debris during discharge of cargo and unless kept clean can become a source of heavy infestation. It is important to remove *thoroughly* all cargo residue from deckhead frames and longitudinal deck girders at the time of discharge, preferably when the cargo level is suitable for convenient cleaning. Where available, industrial vacuum cleaners are of value for the cleaning of cargo spaces and fittings.

2.1.3 The material collected during cleaning should be disposed of, or treated, immediately so that the insects cannot escape and spread to other parts of the ship or elsewhere. In port it may be burnt or treated with a pesticide, but in many countries such material may only be landed under phytosanitary supervision. Where destruction ashore is not practicable, the sweepings should be jettisoned well out to sea. If any part of the ship is being fumigated the material may be left exposed to the gas.

2.2 Main sites of infestation

2.2.1 *Tank top ceiling:* If, as often happens, cracks appear between the ceiling boards, food material may be forced down into the underlying space and serve as a focus of infestation for an indefinite period. Insects bred in this space can readily move out to attack food cargoes and establish their progeny in them.

---

* References to human and animal food include both raw and processed materials.
† The word *pesticide* as used throughout the text means insecticides, fumigants and rodenticides.
‡ The word *insect* as used throughout the text includes mites.

2.2.2 *'Tween-deck centre lines, wooden feeders and bins* are often left in place for several voyages and because of their construction are a frequent source of infestation. After unloading a grain cargo, burlap and battens covering the narrow spaces between the planks should be removed and discarded before the holds are cleaned or washed down. These coverings should be replaced by new material in preparation for the next cargo.

2.2.3 *Transverse beams and longitudinal deck girders* which support the decks and hatch openings may have an L-shaped angle-bar construction. Such girders provide ledges where grain may lodge when bulk cargoes are unloaded. The ledges are often in inaccessible places overlooked during cleaning operations.

2.2.4 *Insulated bulkheads near engine-rooms:* When the hold side of an engine-room bulkhead is insulated with a wooden sheathing, the airspace and the cracks between the boards often become filled with grain and other material. Sometimes the airspace is filled with insulating material which may become heavily infested and serves as a place for insect breeding. Temporary wooden bulkheads also provide an ideal place for insect breeding, especially under moist conditions, such as when green lumber is used.

2.2.5 *Cargo battens:* The crevices at the sparring cleats are ideal places for material to lodge and for insects to hide.

2.2.6 *Bilges:* Insects in accumulations of food material are often found in these spaces.

2.2.7 *Electrical conduit casings:* Sometimes the sheet-metal covering is damaged by general cargo and when bulk grain is loaded later, the casings may become completely filled. This residual grain has often been found to be heavily infested. Casings that are damaged should be repaired immediately or, where possible, they should be replaced with steel strapping, which can be cleaned more easily.

2.2.8 Other places where material accumulates and where insects breed and hide include:

The area underneath burlap, which is used to cover limber boards and sometimes to cover tank top ceilings.

Boxing around pipes, especially if it is broken.

Corners, where old cereal material is often found.

Crevices at plate landings, frames and chocks.

Wooden coverings of manholes or wells leading to double-bottom tanks or other places.

Cracks in the wooden ceiling protecting the propeller shaft tunnel.

Beneath rusty scale and old paint on the inside of hull plates.

Shifting boards.

Dunnage material, empty bags and used separation cloths.

Inside lockers.

3 Chemical control of insect infestation

3.1 Methods of chemical disinfestation

3.1.1 *Types of pesticides and methods of insect control*

3.1.1.1 To avoid insect populations becoming firmly established in cargo spaces and other parts of a ship, it is necessary to use some form of chemical toxicant for control. The materials available may be divided conveniently into two classes: contact insecticides and fumigants. The choice of agent and method of application depend on the type of commodity, the extent and location of the infestation, the importance and habits of the insects found, and the climatic and other conditions. Recommended treatments are altered or modified from time to time in accordance with new developments.

3.1.1.2 The success of chemical treatments does not lie wholly in the pesticidal activity of the agents used. In addition, an appreciation of the requirements and limitations of the different available methods is required. Crew members can carry out small-scale or "spot" treatments if they adhere to the manufacturer's instructions and take care to cover the whole area of infestation. However, extensive or hazardous treatments including fumigation and spraying near human and animal food should be placed in the hands of professional operators, who should inform the master of the identity of the active ingredients used, the hazards involved and the precautions to be taken.

3.1.2 *Contact insecticides*

3.1.2.1 *Space treatments:* Insecticides may be discharged into the air as fine particles of liquid or solid. There are a number of types of equipment for producing and distributing such particles. This method of treatment kills flying insects and deals with superficial infestation where exposed insects come into contact with the particles, whilst there may be a limited residual pesticidal effect on surfaces on which the particles settle.

3.1.2.2 For use in cargo spaces, space sprays and fogs can be produced in several different ways. These include fog generators in which an insecticide in the form of a liquid or coarse spray is vaporized. Such vaporized insecticides may condense into fine particles on reaching cool air. Alternatively, fine particles may be produced mechanically from suitable formulations by dispersing nozzles, venturi systems or centrifugal force. Insecticidal smokes are evolved from generators simply by igniting the material and such generators are a convenient form of application for use by ships' personnel.

3.1.2.3 Tests have shown that these insecticidal smokes and sprays can be very effective against insects moving freely in the open, in spaces such as holds. However, no appreciable penetration or control of insects can be obtained in deep crevices, or between or under deck boards, tank top ceilings and limber boards, places where infestation commonly occurs. Where insects are deep-seated, it is usually necessary to use a fumigant.

3.1.2.4 *Surface sprays:* Spraying with a suitable insecticide can also be used to control residual infestation. Within the limitations of the technique this is a convenient way to control insects as it does not require evacuation of spaces not being treated. Various formulations are available:

.1 emulsifiable concentrates and water-dispersible powder concentrates for dilution with water; and

.2 oil concentrates for dilution with a suitable carrier oil and, for small-scale use, ready-to-use formulations, usually in a light oil.

3.1.2.5 Hand-operated or mechanically operated sprayers may be used according to the size of the job to be done. To reach the heights of some ships' holds, power equipment is required which will develop enough pressure to get the spray material where it is needed. Hand sprayers are rarely adequate: "knapsack" sprayers which develop enough pressure to reach infested areas may be used. Such surface sprays produce a deposit toxic to insects present at the time and also to those that subsequently crawl over or settle on treated surfaces.

3.1.2.6 As with fogging, a disadvantage of spraying is that the insecticide does not kill insects hidden in inaccessible parts of cargo spaces. Insecticidal sprays applied in oil solutions or water emulsions take some time to dry and may be hazardous to persons moving about the ship. No cargo should be loaded until spray deposits have dried.

3.1.2.7 In addition to the methods described above, insecticidal lacquers may be painted on to boundary junctures in accommodation and galley areas in accordance with the manufacturers' instructions, to provide control of pests. Hand sprayers and hand-held aerosols may also be effective in these areas.

3.1.2.8 During the application of contact insecticides by any method, all personnel not directly involved should be evacuated from the areas being treated for a period of time not less than that recommended by the manufacturer of the specific pesticide used on the label or package itself.

3.1.3 *Fumigants*

3.1.3.1 Fumigants are used where contact insecticides will not give control. Fumigants act in a gaseous phase even though they may be applied as solid or liquid formulations from which the gas arises. Effective and safe use requires that the space being treated be rendered gastight for the period of exposure, which may vary from a few hours to several days, depending on the fumigant type and concentration used, the pests, the commodities treated and the temperature. Additional information is provided on two of the most widely used fumigants, methyl bromide and phosphine (hydrogen phosphide), in annex 1 (D).

3.1.3.2 Since fumigant gases are poisonous to humans and require special equipment and skills in application, they should be used by specialists and not by the ship's crew.

3.1.3.3 Evacuation of the space under gas treatment is mandatory and in some cases it will be necessary for the whole ship to be evacuated (see 3.4.2 and 3.4.3 below).

3.1.3.4 A "fumigator-in-charge" should be designated by the fumigation company, government agency or appropriate authority. He should be able to provide documentation to the master proving his competence and authorization. The master should be provided with written instructions by the fumigator-in-charge on the type of fumigant used, the hazards involved, the threshold limit values (TLV)* and the precautions to be taken, and in view of the highly toxic nature of all commonly used fumigants these should be followed carefully. Such instructions should be written in a language readily understood by the master or his representative.

---

* For definition of *threshold limit value* (TLV) see annex 2.

Safe Use of Pesticides in Ships

3.2 Disinfestation of empty cargo spaces

3.2.1 An empty cargo space may be treated by any of the methods described, excepting the use of insecticidal lacquers. Care should be taken to avoid contamination and taint to subsequent cargoes. Examples of some commonly used pesticides are listed in annex 1. (For precautions before, during and after fumigation of cargo spaces see 3.4 below.)

3.3 Disinfestation of food stores, galleys and crew and passenger accommodation

3.3.1 In general, only those insecticides suitable for use in cargo spaces should be used in dry-food stores in ships. A wider range of insecticides may be needed for treatments in galleys and in passenger and crew accommodation, especially against pests such as cockroaches, ants, flies and bedbugs. Examples of some commonly used pesticides are listed in annex 1.

3.4 Disinfestation of cargoes and surrounds

3.4.1 *Fumigation of cargo spaces and cargoes*

3.4.1.1 Apart from space and surface treatments with contact pesticides, the principal method of treatment of cargo spaces or their contents for the control of insects is by fumigation.

3.4.2 *Fumigation with aeration (ventilation) in port*

3.4.2.1 Fumigation and aeration (ventilation) of empty cargo spaces should always be carried out in port (alongside or at anchorage). Ships should not be permitted to leave port until gas-free certification has been received from the fumigator-in-charge.

3.4.2.2 Prior to the application of fumigants to cargo spaces, the crew should be landed and remain ashore until the ship is certified "gas-free", in writing, by the fumigator-in-charge or other authorized person. During this period a watchman should be posted to prevent unauthorized boarding or entry, and warning signs* should be prominently displayed at gangways and at entrances to accommodation.

3.4.2.3 The fumigator-in-charge should be retained throughout the fumigation period and until such time as the ship is declared gas-free.

3.4.2.4 At the end of the fumigation period the fumigator will take the necessary action to ensure that the fumigant is dispersed. If crew members are required to assist in such actions, for example in opening hatches, they should be provided with adequate respiratory protection and adhere strictly to instructions given by the fumigator-in-charge.

3.4.2.5 The fumigator-in-charge should notify the master in writing of any spaces determined to be safe for re-occupancy by essential crew members prior to the aeration of the ship.

3.4.2.6 In such circumstances the fumigator-in-charge should monitor, throughout the fumigation and aeration periods, spaces to which personnel have been permitted to return, to ensure that the TLV for the fumigant is not exceeded. Should the concentration in any such area exceed the TLV, crew members should wear adequate respiratory protection or should be evacuated from the area until measurements show re-occupancy to be safe.

3.4.2.7 No unauthorized persons should be allowed on board until all parts of the ship have been determined gas-free, warning signs removed and clearance certificates issued by the fumigator-in-charge.

3.4.2.8 Clearance certificates should only be issued when tests show that all residual fumigant has been dispersed from empty cargo spaces and adjacent working spaces and any residual fumigant material has been removed.

3.4.2.9 Entry into a space under fumigation should never take place except in the event of an extreme emergency. If entry is imperative the fumigator-in-charge and at least one other person should enter, each wearing adequate protective equipment appropriate for the fumigant used and a safety harness and lifeline. Each lifeline should be tended by a person outside the space, who should be similarly equipped.

3.4.2.10 If a clearance certificate cannot be issued after the fumigation of cargo in port, the provisions of 3.4.3 should apply.

3.4.3 *Fumigation continued in transit*

3.4.3.1 Fumigation in transit should only be carried out at the discretion of the master. This should be clearly understood by owners, charterers, and all other parties involved when considering the transport of cargoes that may be infested. Due consideration should be taken of this when assessing the options of fumigation. The master should

---

* A specimen of such a warning sign is given in annex 3.

be aware of the regulations of the flag State Administration with regard to in-transit fumigation. The application of the process should be with the agreement of the port State Administration. The process may be considered under two headings:

.1 fumigation in which treatment is intentionally continued in a sealed space during a voyage and in which no aeration has taken place before sailing; and

.2 in-port cargo fumigation where some aeration is carried out before sailing, but where a clearance certificate for the cargo space(s) cannot be issued because of residual gas and the cargo space(s) has been re-sealed before sailing.

3.4.3.2 Before a decision on sailing with a fumigated cargo is made it should be taken into account that, due to operational conditions, the circumstances outlined in 3.4.3.1.2 may arise unintentionally, e.g., a ship may be required to sail at a time earlier than anticipated when the fumigation was started. In such circumstances the potential hazards may be as great as with a planned in-transit fumigation and all the precautions in the following paragraphs should be observed.

3.4.3.3 Before a decision is made as to whether a fumigation treatment planned to be commenced in port and continued at sea should be carried out, special precautions are necessary. These include the following:

.1 at least two members of the crew (including one officer) who have received appropriate training (see 3.4.3.6) should be designated as the trained representatives of the master responsible for ensuring that safe conditions in accommodation, engine-room and other working spaces are maintained after the fumigator-in-charge has handed over that responsibility to the master (see 3.4.3.12); and

.2 the trained representatives of the master should brief the crew before a fumigation takes place and satisfy the fumigator-in-charge that this has been done.

3.4.3.4 Empty cargo spaces are to be inspected and/or tested for leakage with instruments so that proper sealing can be done before or after loading. The fumigator-in-charge, accompanied by a trained representative of the master or a competent person, should determine whether the cargo spaces to be treated are or can be made sufficiently gastight to prevent leakage of the fumigant to the accommodation, engine-rooms and other working spaces in the ship. Special attention should be paid to potential problem areas such as bilge and cargo line systems. On completion of such inspection and/or test, the fumigator-in-charge should supply to the master for his retention a signed statement that the inspection and/or test has been performed, what provisions have been made and that the cargo spaces are or can be made satisfactory for fumigation. Whenever a cargo space is found not to be sufficiently gastight, the fumigator-in-charge should issue a signed statement to the master and the other parties involved.

3.4.3.5 Accommodation, engine-rooms, areas designated for use in navigation of the ship, frequently visited working areas and stores, such as the forecastle head spaces, adjacent to cargo spaces being subject to fumigation in transit should be treated in accordance with the provisions of 3.4.3.13. Special attention should be paid to gas concentration safety checks in problem areas referred to in 3.4.3.4.

3.4.3.6 The trained representatives of the master designated in 3.4.3.3 should be provided and be familiar with:

.1 the information in the relevant Material Safety Data Sheet, if available; and

.2 the instructions on the fumigant label or package itself, such as the recommendations of the fumigant manufacturer concerning methods of detection of the fumigant in air, its behaviour and hazardous properties, symptoms of poisoning, relevant first aid and special medical treatment and emergency procedures.

3.4.3.7 The ship should carry:

.1 gas-detection equipment and adequate fresh supplies of service items for the fumigant(s) concerned as required by 3.4.3.12, together with instructions for its use and the TLVs for safe working conditions;

.2 instructions on disposal of residual fumigant material;

.3 at least four sets of adequate respiratory protective equipment appropriate for the fumigant used;

.4 the necessary medicines and medical equipment; and

.5 a copy of the latest version of the *Medical First Aid Guide for Use in Accidents Involving Dangerous Goods (MFAG)*.

3.4.3.8 The fumigator-in-charge should notify the master in writing of the spaces containing the cargo to be fumigated and also of any other spaces that are considered unsafe to enter during the fumigation. During the application of the fumigant the fumigator-in-charge should ensure that the surrounding areas are checked for safety.

3.4.3.9 If cargo spaces containing cargo are to be fumigated in transit:

.1 After application of the fumigant, an initial check should be made by the fumigator-in-charge together with trained representatives of the master for any leak which, if detected, should be effectively sealed. When the master is satisfied that all precautions detailed in 3.4.3.1 to 3.4.3.12 have been fulfilled (refer to model

Pesticides

checklist in annex 4) then the vessel may sail. Otherwise, provisions outlined in 3.4.3.9.2 or 3.4.3.9.3 are to be followed.

If the provisions of 3.4.3.9.1 are not satisfied,

either:

.2 After application of fumigants, the ship should be delayed in port alongside at a suitable berth or at anchorage for such a period as to allow the gas in the fumigated cargo spaces to reach sufficiently high concentrations to detect any possible leakage. Special attention should be paid to those cases where fumigants in a solid or liquid form have been applied which may require a long period (normally from 4 to 7 days unless a recirculation or similar distribution system is used) to reach such a high concentration that leakages can be detected. If leakages are detected, the ship should not sail until the source(s) of such leakages are determined and eliminated. After ascertaining that the ship is in a safe condition to sail, i.e. no gas leakages are present, the fumigator-in-charge should furnish the master with a written statement that:

.2.1 the gas in the cargo space(s) has reached sufficiently high concentrations to detect any possible leakages;

.2.2 spaces adjacent to the treated cargo space(s) have been checked and found gas-free; and

.2.3 the ship's representative is fully conversant with the use of the gas-detection equipment provided.

or:

.3 After application of the fumigants and immediately after the sailing of the ship, the fumigator-in-charge should remain on board for such a period as to allow the gas in the fumigated cargo space or spaces to reach sufficiently high concentrations to detect any possible leakage, or until the fumigated cargo is discharged (see 3.4.3.20), whichever is the shorter, to check and rectify any gas leakages. Prior to his leaving the ship, he should ascertain that the ship is in a safe condition, i.e. no gas leakages are present, and he should furnish the master with a written statement to the effect that the provisions of 3.4.3.9.2.1, 3.4.3.9.2.2 and 3.4.3.9.2.3 have been carried out.

3.4.3.10 On application of the fumigant, the fumigator-in-charge should post warning signs at all entrances to places notified to the master as in 3.4.3.8. These warning signs should indicate the identity of the fumigant and the date and time of fumigation.*

3.4.3.11 At an appropriate time after application of the fumigant, the fumigator-in-charge, accompanied by a representative of the master, should check that accommodation, engine-rooms and other working spaces remain free of harmful concentrations of gas.

3.4.3.12 Upon discharging his agreed responsibilities, the fumigator-in-charge should formally hand over to the master in writing responsibility for maintaining safe conditions in all occupied spaces. The fumigator-in-charge should ensure that gas-detection and respiratory protection equipment carried on the ship is in good order, and that adequate fresh supplies of consumable items are available to allow sampling as required in 3.4.3.13.

3.4.3.13 Gas concentration safety checks at all appropriate locations, which should at least include the spaces indicated in 3.4.3.5, should be continued throughout the voyage at least at eight-hour intervals or more frequently if so advised by the fumigator-in-charge. These readings should be recorded in the ship's log-book.

3.4.3.14 Except in extreme emergency, cargo spaces sealed for fumigation in transit should never be opened at sea or entered. If entry is imperative, at least two persons should enter, wearing adequate protection equipment and a safety harness and lifeline tended by a person outside the space, similarly equipped with protective, self-contained breathing apparatus.

3.4.3.15 If it is essential to ventilate a cargo space or spaces, every effort should be made to prevent a fumigant from accumulating in accommodation or working areas. Those spaces should be carefully checked to that effect. If the gas concentration in those areas at any time exceeds the TLV they should be evacuated and the cargo space or cargo spaces should be re-sealed. If a cargo space is re-sealed after ventilation it should not be assumed that it is completely clear of gas and tests should be made and appropriate precautions taken before entering.

3.4.3.16 Prior to the arrival of the ship, generally not less than 24 hours in advance, the master should inform the appropriate authorities of the country of destination and ports of call that fumigation in transit is being carried out. The information should include the type of fumigant used, the date of fumigation, the cargo spaces which have been fumigated, and whether ventilation has commenced. Upon arrival at the port of discharge, the master should also provide information as required in 3.4.3.6.2 and 3.4.3.7.2.

---

* A specimen of such a warning sign is given in annex 3.

3.4.3.17 On arrival at the port of discharge, the requirements of receiving countries regarding handling of fumigated cargoes should be established. Before entry of fumigated cargo spaces, trained personnel from a fumigation company or other authorized persons, wearing respiratory protection, should carry out careful monitoring of the spaces to ensure the safety of personnel. The monitored values should be recorded in the ship's log-book. In case of need or emergency the master may commence ventilation of the fumigated cargo spaces under the conditions of 3.4.3.15, having due regard for the safety of personnel on board. If this operation is to be done at sea, the master should evaluate weather and sea conditions before proceeding.

3.4.3.18 Only mechanical unloading that does not necessitate entry of personnel into the cargo spaces of such fumigated cargoes should be undertaken. However, when the presence of personnel in cargo spaces is necessary for the handling and operation of unloading equipment, continuous monitoring of the fumigated spaces should be carried out to ensure the safety of the personnel involved. When necessary, these personnel should be equipped with adequate respiratory protection.

3.4.3.19 During the final stages of discharge, when it becomes necessary for personnel to enter the cargo spaces, such entry should only be permitted subsequent to verification that such cargo spaces are gas-free.

3.4.3.20 Upon completion of discharge and when the ship is found free of fumigants and certified as such, all warning signs should be removed. Any action in this respect should be recorded in the ship's log-book.

3.5   Carriage of fumigated freight containers, barges and other cargo transport units on a ship

3.5.1   *Loaded without ventilation after fumigation*

3.5.1.1 If it is intended that freight containers, barges or cargo transport units containing cargo under fumigation should be taken on board ship without preliminary ventilation, their shipment must be considered as a Class 9 Hazard under the IMDG Code and as such the procedures should conform to the provisions as specified in the entries for FUMIGATED UNIT (UN 3359) of the Code. The following special precautions, incorporating the IMDG provisions, are necessary:

.1   A freight container, barge or cargo transport unit containing cargo under fumigation should not be allowed on board until sufficient time has elapsed to allow the attainment of a reasonably uniform gas concentration throughout the cargo. Because of variations due to types and amounts of fumigants and commodities and temperature levels, it is recommended that the period to elapse between fumigant application and loading should be determined locally for each country. Twenty-four hours is normally adequate for this purpose.

.2   The master should be informed prior to loading of freight containers, barges and cargo transport units under fumigation. These should be identified with suitable warning signs* incorporating the identity of the fumigant and the date and time of fumigation. Any freight container under fumigation must have the doors substantially secured before loading onto a ship. Plastic or lightweight metal seals are not sufficient for this purpose. The securing arrangement must be such as to allow only authorized entry to the freight container. If container doors are to be locked, the means of locking should be of such a construction that, in case of emergency, the doors could be opened without delay. Adequate instructions for disposal of any residual fumigant material should be provided.

.3   Shipping documents for freight containers, barges or cargo transport units concerned should show the date of fumigation and the type and amount of fumigant used.

.4   Stowage *on deck* should be at least 6 m away from vent intakes, crew quarters and regularly occupied spaces.

.5   Stowage *under deck* should only be undertaken when unavoidable and then in a cargo space equipped with mechanical ventilation sufficient to prevent the build-up of fumigant concentrations above the TLV. The ventilation rate of the mechanical ventilation system should be at least two air changes per hour, based on the empty cargo space. The provisions of 3.4.3.13 should apply.

.6   Equipment suitable for detecting the fumigant gas or gases used should be carried on the ship, with instructions for its use.

.7   Where the stowage requirements in 3.5.1.1.5 cannot be met, cargo spaces carrying fumigated freight containers, barges or cargo transport units should be treated as if under fumigation and the provisions of 3.4.3.3 to 3.4.3.13 should apply.

---

* A specimen of such a warning sign is given in annex 3.

3.5.1.2   Prior to the arrival of the ship, generally not less than 24 hours in advance, the master should inform the appropriate authorities of the country of destination and ports of call that fumigation in transit is being carried out. The information should include the type of fumigant used, the date of fumigation and cargo spaces carrying fumigated freight containers, barges or cargo transport units. Upon arrival at the port of discharge, the master should also provide information as required in 3.4.3.6.2 and 3.4.3.7.2.

3.5.2   *Fumigated freight containers, barges or other cargo transport units ventilated before loading*

3.5.2.1   Freight containers, barges or cargo transport units that have been ventilated after fumigation to ensure that no harmful concentration of gas remains should have the warning signs removed and, whether empty or loaded, may be taken on board a ship without the precautions in 3.5.1.1.1 to 3.5.1.1.7.

3.5.3   *Fumigation after loading on board a ship*

3.5.3.1   No person should fumigate the contents of a freight container, barge or cargo transport unit once it has been loaded on board a ship.

4   Control of rodent pests

4.1   General

4.1.1   In regard to rodent control, ships are subject to the provisions of the WHO's International Health Regulations.

4.1.2   Rodents may be controlled by fumigation, by the use of a bait incorporating a poison which acts within a few minutes (*acute poison*) or one which acts over a period (*chronic poison*), or by trapping.

4.2   Fumigation and baiting

4.2.1   Fumigation against rodents is normally done at dosages and periods of exposure much less than those required for insect control. It follows that an insect fumigation also controls rodents in areas that are treated. However, rodent control often requires fumigation of accommodation and working spaces that may not normally be treated for insect control.

4.2.2   Fumigation against rodents alone should be undertaken in port and ventilation completed in port. The precautions in 3.4.2 should be observed.

4.2.3   Methods involving fumigation or the use of acute poisons should be employed only by qualified personnel of pest control servicing firms or appropriate authorities (e.g., port health authorities). Baits containing acute poisons should be collected and disposed of by such personnel when the treatment is completed. Chronic poisons should be used strictly in accordance with the manufacturer's instructions contained on the label or on the package itself.

4.3   Rodent baits (Chronic poisons permitted for use by ship's personnel)

4.3.1   Careless use may cause injury to ship's personnel.

4.3.2   For rodenticides to be efficient, they should be placed where the rodents are moving. Runways are usually detected by evidence of marking, debris and dirt. The use of rodenticides, however, is no substitute for high standards of hygiene and the rodent-proofing of equipment whenever possible.

4.3.2.1   Baits should be protected from accidental consumption by humans or domestic animals and from contact with human and animal food.

4.3.2.2   Where practicable, cereal baits should be replaced within 30 days to avoid providing a source of insect infestation.

4.3.3   A record should be kept of the locations in which baits are set, particular care being taken to search for and remove all baits from cargo spaces prior to the loading of bulk foodstuffs and livestock cargoes.

5   Regulations for the use of pesticides

5.1   National and international controls on pesticide usage

5.1.1   In many countries the sale and use of pesticides are regulated by governments to ensure safety in application and prevention of contamination of foodstuffs. Among the factors taken into account in such regulations are the recommendations made by international organizations such as FAO and WHO, especially in regard to maximum limits of pesticide residues in food and foodstuffs.

5.1.2   Examples of some commonly used pesticides are listed in annex 1. Pesticides should be used strictly in accordance with the manufacturer's instructions as given on the label or package itself. National regulations and requirements vary from one country to another; therefore particular pesticides which may be used for treatment of cargo spaces and accommodation in ships may be limited by the regulations and requirements of:

   .1   the country where the cargo is loaded or treated;

   .2   the country of destination of the cargo, especially in regard to pesticide residues in foodstuffs; and

   .3   the country of registration of the ship.

5.1.3   Ships' masters should ensure that they have the necessary knowledge of the above regulations and requirements.

6   Safety precautions – general

6.1   Pesticide materials

6.1.1   Pesticides are often at least as poisonous to humans as to the pests against which they are used. The instructions given on the label or package itself, particularly those relating to safety and disposal of residual material, should be strictly followed.

6.1.2   Pesticides should be stored in strict compliance with national regulations and requirements or the manufacturer's instructions.

6.1.3   Smoking, eating or drinking while using pesticides should always be avoided.

6.1.4   Empty pesticide receptacles and packaging should never be re-used.

6.1.5   Hands should always be washed after applying pesticides.

6.2   Space and surface spraying (See also 3.1.2)

6.2.1   When spraying is being carried out by professional operators they are responsible for taking the necessary safety precautions. If operations are carried out by the crew, the master should ensure that the following safeguards are observed, both in the preparation and the application of the pesticides:

   .1   wear protective clothing, gloves, respirators and eye protection appropriate to the pesticides being used;

   .2   do not remove clothes, gloves, respirators or eye protection whilst applying pesticides, even under hot conditions; and

   .3   avoid excessive application and run-off on surfaces and avoid contamination of foodstuffs.

6.2.2   If clothing becomes contaminated:

   .1   stop work immediately and leave the area;

   .2   remove clothing and footwear;

   .3   take a shower and wash skin thoroughly;

   .4   wash clothing and footwear, and wash skin again; and

   .5   seek medical advice.

6.2.3   After work:

   .1   remove and wash clothing, footwear and other equipment; and

   .2   take a shower, using plenty of soap.

6.3   Fumigation

6.3.1   Ship's personnel should not handle fumigants and such operations should be carried out only by qualified operators. Personnel allowed to remain in the vicinity of a fumigation operation for a particular purpose should follow the instructions of the fumigator-in-charge implicitly.

6.3.2   Aeration of treated cargo spaces should be completed and a clearance certificate issued as in 3.4.2.8 or 3.4.2.10 before personnel are permitted to enter.

6.4   **Contact insecticides in the cargo space, admixture with raw grain**

6.4.1   When a contact insecticide is to be applied to grain during the loading of a ship, the master should be provided by the grain contractors with written instructions on the type and amount of insecticide used and on the precautions to be taken. Ship's personnel and those unloading cargo should not enter cargo spaces containing treated grains without taking general safety precautions as provided by the manufacturer of the insecticide.

6.5   **Exposure to pesticides resulting in illness**

6.5.1   In the case of exposure to pesticides and subsequent illness, medical advice should be sought immediately. Information on poisoning by specific compounds may be found in the *Medical First Aid Guide for Use in Accidents Involving Dangerous Goods (MFAG)* or on the package (manufacturer's instructions and safety precautions on the label or the package itself).

ANNEX 1
Pesticides suitable for shipboard use

The materials listed should be used strictly in accordance with the manufacturer's instructions and safety precautions given on the label or package itself, especially in respect of flammability, and with regard to any further limitations applied by the law of the country of loading, destination or flag of the ship, contracts relating to the cargo, or the shipowner's instructions.

Materials may be used by ship's personnel unless the contrary is indicated. A space-application insecticide may be used in conjunction with a residual insecticide.

It should be especially noted that some materials listed may taint sensitive commodities, e.g., coffee and cocoa, and special care should be taken when stowing these commodities in order to prevent this. The reason for naming purified grades in the list below is to minimize tainting.

A   Contact insecticides in a cargo space

A1   *Fast-acting insecticides for space application, e.g., against flying insects:*

Pyrethrins (with or without synergist)

Bioresmethrin

Dichlorvos

A2   *Slower-acting residual insecticides for surface application:*

Malathion (premium grade)

Bromophos

Carbaryl

Fenitrothion

Chlorpyriphos-methyl

Pirimiphos-methyl

B   Contact insecticides and baits in accommodation

B1   *Fast-acting insecticides for space application, e.g., against flying insects:*

Pyrethrins (with or without synergist)

Bioresmethrin

Dichlorvos

B2   *Slower-acting residual pesticides:*

Malathion (premium grade)

Diazinon

Fenitrothion

Propoxur

Pirimiphos-methyl

Chlorpyriphos-ethyl

Chlorpyriphos-methyl

Bendiocarb

Permethrin

B3   *Insecticides for use against particular pests and as an additional treatment:*

Diazinon, as an aerosol spray or lacquer against ants, cockroaches and flies

Dieldrin and Aldrin, in lacquers for control of ants and cockroaches

Methoprene bait, for control of Pharoah's ants

Chlorpyriphos-ethyl, as a bait and as a lacquer

C   Rodenticides

C1   *Chronic poisons in baits:*

      Calciferol

      Any anticoagulant in the following two classes:

      Hydroxycoumarins (e.g., Warfarin, Fumarin, Coumatetralyl, Difenacoum, Brodifacoum)

      Indanediones (e.g., Pival, Diphacinone, Chlorophacinone)

C2   *Acute poisons in baits or liquids:*

TO BE USED ONLY IN PORT AND BY QUALIFIED OPERATORS

      Barium fluoroacetate

      Fluoroacetamide

      Sodium fluoroacetate

      Zinc phosphide

D   Fumigants

TO BE APPLIED ONLY BY QUALIFIED OPERATORS

Additional information on methyl bromide and phosphine (hydrogen phosphide) to be read in conjunction with 3.1.3

Methyl bromide

Methyl bromide is used in situations where a rapid treatment of commodities or space is required. It should not be used in spaces where ventilation systems are not adequate for the removal of all gases from the free space. **In-ship in-transit fumigations with methyl bromide should not be carried out.** Fumigation with methyl bromide should be permitted only when the ship is in the confines of a port (either at anchor or alongside) and to disinfest before discharge, once crew members have disembarked (see 3.1.3.3). Prior to discharge, ventilation must be done, forced if necessary, to reduce the gaseous residues below the TLV in the free spaces. (See procedures for ventilation in 3.4.3.17 to 3.4.3.19).

Phosphine (hydrogen phosphide)

A variety of phosphine-generating formulations are used for in-ship in-transit or at-berth fumigations. Application methods vary widely and include surface-only treatment, probing, perforated tubing laid at the bottom of spaces, recirculation systems and gas-injection systems or their combinations. Treatment times will vary considerably depending on the temperature, depth of cargo and on the application method used. **Clear written instructions must be given to the master of the ship, to the receiver of the cargo and to the authorities at the discharging port as to how any powdery residues are to be disposed of.** These will vary with each formulation and the method of application. Prior to discharge, ventilation must be done, forced if necessary, to reduce the gaseous residues below the TLV in the free spaces (see procedures for ventilation in 3.4.3.17 to 3.4.3.19). For safety aspects during the voyage see 3.4.3.3.

D1   *Fumigants against insects in empty cargo spaces and against rodents anywhere aboard ship:*

      Carbon dioxide

      Nitrogen

      Methyl bromide and carbon dioxide mixture

      Methyl bromide

      Hydrogen cyanide

      Phosphine (hydrogen phosphide)

D2   *Fumigants against insects in loaded or partially loaded cargo spaces:*

CARE IS NEEDED IN SELECTING TYPES AND AMOUNTS OF FUMIGANTS FOR TREATMENT OF PARTICULAR COMMODITIES

      Carbon dioxide

      Nitrogen

      Methyl bromide and carbon dioxide mixture

      Methyl bromide

      Phosphine (hydrogen phosphide)

Pesticides

ANNEX 2
Threshold limit values (TLV) for vapours in air

The threshold limit value (TLV) for a substance in air has been defined* as the time-weighted average concentration for a normal eight-hour working day to which nearly all workers may be repeatedly exposed, day after day, without adverse effect. Certain fumigants, including dichlorvos, methyl bromide and hydrogen cyanide, have the ability to penetrate the intact skin and thus become absorbed into the body. In the case of ships at sea, it may be considered that personnel cannot be limited to eight hours' exposure in their particular environment in the course of each 24-hour period. However, these recommendations make clear that, in the event of excessive vapour concentrations being measured in any occupied space, steps should be taken to avoid unprotected respiration in that space and action initiated to vacate and ventilate the space. It should be emphasized that the registering of gas concentrations above the TLV in an occupied space arising from the use of fumigants on a ship should be an exceptional occurrence which would constitute the need for immediate countermeasures. In those circumstances, and in the absence of any alternative guidelines based on scientific principles, it is considered that the safe limits for the working environment accepted by a number of countries should be observed on ships.

The recommended levels* are as follows

	TLV	
	ppm	mg/m^3
Dichlorvos†	0.1	0.9
Hydrogen cyanide†	10	11
Phosphine (hydrogen phosphide)	0.3	0.4
Methyl bromide†	5	20

---

* The latest edition of the *Recommendations of the American Conference of Governmental Industrial Hygienists* or other appropriate national recommendations or regulations should be consulted.

† Materials absorbed through the skin.

ANNEX 3
Fumigation warning sign

The markings should be black print on a white background with lettering not less than 25 mm high.

DANGER

THIS UNIT IS UNDER FUMIGATION
WITH [fumigant name*] APPLIED ON
[date*   ]
[time*   ]

DO NOT ENTER

Not less than 250 mm

* Insert details as appropriate

Not less than 300 mm

ANNEX 4
Model checklist for in-transit fumigation with phosphine

Date: . . . .

Port: . . . . Terminal/Quay: . . . .

Ship's name:. . . . .

Type of fumigant: . . . . Method of application:. . . . .

Date & time fumigation commenced:. . . . .

Name of fumigator/company:. . . . .

The master and fumigator-in-charge, or their representatives, should complete the checklist jointly. The purpose of this checklist is to ensure that the responsibilities and requirements of 3.4.3.11, and 3.4.3.12 are carried out fully for in-transit fumigation under section 3.4.3.9.

Safety of operations requires that all questions should be answered affirmatively by ticking the appropriate boxes. If this is not possible, the reason should be given and agreement reached upon precautions to be taken between ship and fumigator-in-charge. If a question is considered to be not applicable, write "n/a", explaining why if appropriate.

PART A: BEFORE FUMIGATION

		SHIP	FUMIGATOR-IN-CHARGE
1	The inspection required before loading has been performed (3.4.3.4)	☐	☐
2	All the cargo spaces to be fumigated are satisfactory for fumigation	☐	☐
3	Spaces, where found not be satisfactory, have been sealed	☐	☐
4	The master or his trained representatives have been made aware of the specific areas to be checked for gas concentrations throughout the fumigation period	☐	☐
5	The master or his trained representatives have been made familiar with the fumigant label, detection methods, safety procedures and emergency procedures (refer to 3.4.3.6)	☐	☐
6	The fumigator-in-charge has ensured that gas-detection and respiratory protection equipment carried on the ship is in good order, and that adequate fresh supplies of consumable items for this equipment are available to allow sampling as required by 3.4.3.13.	☐	☐
7	The master has been notified in writing of:		
(a)	the spaces containing cargo to be fumigated	☐	☐
(b)	any other spaces that are considered unsafe to enter during the fumigation	☐	☐

PART B: AFTER FUMIGATION

The following procedure should be carried out after application of fumigant and closing and sealing of cargo spaces.

		SHIP	FUMIGATOR-IN-CHARGE
8	Presence of gas has been confirmed inside each hold under fumigation	☐	☐
9	Each hold has been checked for leakage and sealed properly	☐	☐
10	Spaces adjacent to the treated cargo spaces have been checked and found gas-free	☐	☐
11	The responsible crew members have been shown how to take gas readings properly when gas is present and they are fully conversant with the use of gas-detection equipment provided	☐	☐
12	Methods of application:		
	(a) *Surface application method* Initial rapid build-up of the gas in the upper regions of hold airspace with subsequent penetration downward of the gas over a longer period	☐	☐
	or		
	(b) *Deep probing* More rapid dispersion of gas than in (a) with lower concentrations in upper regions of airspace in the hold	☐	☐
	or		
	(c) *Recirculation* Rapid dispersion of gas throughout hold but at lower initial gas levels with subsequent build-up of gas levels which, however, may be lower due to even distribution	☐	☐
	or		
	(d) *Other*	☐	☐
13	The master or trained representatives have been briefed fully on the method of application and the spread of the gas throughout the hold	☐	☐
14	The master or trained representatives have been made:	☐	☐
	(a) aware that even though the initial check may not indicate any leaks, it is essential that monitoring is to be continued in the accommodation, engine-room, etc. because gas concentrations may reach their highest levels after several days	☐	☐
	(b) aware of the possibility of the spreading of gas throughout the duct keel and/or ballast tanks	☐	☐
15	The fumigator-in-charge has supplied a signed statement to the master conforming to the requirements of 3.4.3.12 for his retention	☐	☐

The above has been agreed:

Time: . . . .   Date: . . . .

For ship: . . . .   Fumigator-in-charge: . . . .

Rank: . . . .

RECOMMENDATIONS ON THE SAFE USE OF PESTICIDES IN SHIPS

APPLICABLE TO THE FUMIGATION OF CARGO HOLDS

RECOMMENDATIONS ON THE SAFE USE OF PESTICIDES IN SHIPS APPLICABLE TO THE FUMIGATION OF CARGO HOLDS

1   The Maritime Safety Committee, at its sixty-second session (24 to 28 May 1993), approved the Recommendations on the safe use of pesticides in ships (MSC/Circ.612), proposed by the Sub-Committee on Containers and Cargoes at its thirty-second session.

2   The Maritime Safety Committee, at its eighty-fourth session (7 to 16 May 2008), approved the Recommendations on the safe use of pesticides in ships applicable to the fumigation of cargo holds, which apply to carriage of solid bulk cargoes including grain in pursuance of the requirement of SOLAS regulation VI/4, proposed by the Sub-Committee on Dangerous Goods, Solid Cargoes and Containers at its twelfth session, set out in the annex.*

3   The Committee agreed that the Recommendations should not apply to the carriage of fresh food produce under controlled atmosphere.

4   Member Governments are invited to bring the Recommendations to the attention of competent authorities, mariners, fumigators, fumigant and pesticide manufacturers and others concerned.

5   The present circular supersedes MSC/Circ.612, as amended by MSC/Circ.689 and MSC/Circ.746, with regard to the fumigation of cargo holds.

---

* The text of the annex begins on page 247.

Contents

Recommendations on the safe use of pesticides in ships applicable to the fumigation of cargo holds

Pesticides

1 Introduction

1.1 Insect and mite pests of plant and animal products may be carried into the cargo holds with goods (introduced infestation); they may move from one kind of product to another (cross-infestation) and may remain to attack subsequent cargoes (residual infestation). Their control may be required to comply with phytosanitary requirements to prevent spread of pests and for commercial reasons to prevent infestation and contamination of, or damage to, cargoes of human and animal food, both raw and processed materials. Although fumigants may be used to kill rodent pests, the control of rodents on board ships is dealt with separately. In severe cases of infestation of bulk cargoes such as cereals, excessive heating may occur.

1.2 The following sections provide guidance to shipmasters in the use of pesticides* with a view to safety of personnel. They cover pesticides used for the control of insect† and rodent pests in empty and loaded cargo holds.

2 Prevention of infestation

2.1 Maintenance and sanitation

2.1.1 Ship cargo holds, tank top ceilings and other parts of the ship should be kept in a good state of repair to avoid infestation. Many ports of the world have rules and by-laws dealing specifically with the maintenance of ships intended to carry grain cargoes; for example, boards and ceilings should be completely grain-tight.

2.1.2 Cleanliness, or good housekeeping, is as important a means of controlling pests on a ship as it is in a home, warehouse, mill or factory. Since insect pests on ships become established and multiply in debris, much can be done to prevent their increase by simple, thorough cleaning. Box beams and stiffeners, for example, become filled with debris during discharge of cargo and unless kept clean can become a source of heavy infestation. It is important to remove thoroughly all cargo residue from deckhead frames and longitudinal deck girders at the time of discharge, preferably when the cargo level is suitable for convenient cleaning. Where available, industrial vacuum cleaners are of value for the cleaning of cargo holds and fittings.

2.1.3 The material collected during cleaning should be disposed of, or treated, immediately so that the insects cannot escape and spread to other parts of the ship or elsewhere. In port it may be burnt or treated with a pesticide, but in many countries such material may only be landed under phytosanitary supervision. If any part of the ship is being fumigated, the material may be left exposed to the gas.

2.2 Main sites of infestation

2.2.1 *Tank top ceiling:* If, as often happens, cracks appear between the ceiling boards, food material may be forced down into the underlying space and serve as a focus of infestation for an indefinite period. Insects bred in this space can readily move out to attack food cargoes and establish their progeny in them.

2.2.2 *'Tween-deck centre lines, wooden feeders* and *bins* are often left in place for several voyages and because of their construction are a frequent source of infestation. After unloading a grain cargo, burlap and battens covering the narrow spaces between the planks should be removed and discarded before the holds are cleaned or washed down. These coverings should be replaced by new material in preparation for the next cargo.

2.2.3 *Transverse beams* and *longitudinal deck girders* which support the decks and hatch openings may have an L-shaped angle-bar construction. Such girders provide ledges where grain may lodge when bulk cargoes are unloaded. The ledges are often in inaccessible places overlooked during cleaning operations.

2.2.4 *Insulated bulkheads near engine-rooms:* When the hold side of an engine-room bulkhead is insulated with a wooden sheathing, the airspace and the cracks between the boards often become filled with grain and other material. Sometimes the airspace is filled with insulating material which may become heavily infested and serves as a place for insect breeding. Temporary wooden bulkheads also provide an ideal place for insect breeding, especially under moist conditions, such as when green lumber is used.

2.2.5 *Cargo battens:* The crevices at the sparring cleats are ideal places for material to lodge and for insects to hide.

2.2.6 *Bilges:* Insects in accumulations of food material are often found in these spaces.

---

* The word *pesticide* as used throughout the text means fumigants. Examples of some commonly used pesticides are listed in appendix 1.
† The word *insect* as used throughout the text includes mites.

2.2.7 *Electrical conduit casings:* Sometimes the sheet-metal covering is damaged by general cargo and when bulk grain is loaded later, the casings may become completely filled. This residual grain has often been found to be heavily infested. Casings that are damaged should be repaired immediately or, where possible, they should be replaced with steel strapping, which can be cleaned more easily.

2.2.8 Other places where material accumulates and where insects breed and hide include:

The area underneath burlap, which is used to cover limber boards and sometimes to cover tank top ceilings.

Boxing around pipes, especially if it is broken.

Corners, where old cereal material is often found.

Crevices at plate landings, frames and chocks.

Wooden coverings of manholes or wells leading to double-bottom tanks or other places.

Cracks in the wooden ceiling protecting the propeller shaft tunnel.

Beneath rusty scale and old paint on the inside of hull plates.

Shifting boards.

Dunnage material, empty bags and used separation cloths.

Inside lockers.

3 Chemical control of insect infestation

3.1 Methods of chemical disinfestation

3.1.1 *Types of pesticides and methods of insect control*

3.1.1.1 To avoid insect populations becoming firmly established in cargo holds and other parts of a ship, it is necessary to use some form of chemical toxicant for control. The materials available may be divided conveniently into two classes: contact insecticides and fumigants. The choice of agent and method of application depend on the type of commodity, the extent and location of the infestation, the importance and habits of the insects found, and the climatic and other conditions. Recommended treatments are altered or modified from time to time in accordance with new developments.

3.1.1.2 The success of chemical treatments does not lie wholly in the pesticidal activity of the agents used. In addition, an appreciation of the requirements and limitations of the different available methods is required. Crew members can carry out small-scale or "spot" treatments if they adhere to the manufacturer's instructions and take care to cover the whole area of infestation. However, extensive or hazardous treatments, including fumigation and spraying near human and animal food, should be placed in the hands of professional operators, who should inform the master of the identity of the active ingredients used, the hazards involved and the precautions to be taken.

3.1.2 *Fumigants*

3.1.2.1 Fumigants act in a gaseous phase even though they may be applied as solid or liquid formulations from which the gas arises. Effective and safe use requires that the space being treated be rendered gastight for the period of exposure, which may vary from a few hours to several days, depending on the fumigant type and concentration used, the pests, the commodities treated and the temperature. Additional information is provided on two of the most widely used fumigants, methyl bromide and phosphine, in appendix 1.

3.1.2.2 Since fumigant gases are poisonous to humans and require special equipment and skills in application, they should be used by specialists and not by the ship's crew.

3.1.2.3 Evacuation of the space under gas treatment is mandatory and in some cases it will be necessary for the whole ship to be evacuated (see 3.3.1 and 3.3.2 below).

3.1.2.4 A "fumigator-in-charge" should be designated by the fumigation company, government agency or appropriate authority. He should be able to provide documentation to the master proving his competence and authorization. The master should be provided with written instructions by the fumigator-in-charge on the type of fumigant used, the hazards to human health involved and the precautions to be taken, and, in view of the highly toxic nature of all commonly used fumigants, these should be followed carefully. Such instructions should be written in a language readily understood by the master or his representative.

3.2 Disinfestation of empty cargo holds

3.2.1 An empty cargo hold may be fumigated. Examples of some commonly used pesticides are listed in appendix 1. (For precautions before, during and after fumigation of cargo holds, see 3.3 below.)

3.3 Disinfestation of cargoes and surrounds

3.3.1 *Fumigation with aeration (ventilation) in port*

3.3.1.1 Fumigation and aeration (ventilation) of empty cargo holds should always be carried out in port (alongside or at anchorage). Ships should not be permitted to leave port until gas-free certification has been received from the fumigator-in-charge.

3.3.1.2 Prior to the application of fumigants to cargo holds, the crew should be landed and remain ashore until the ship is certified "gas-free", in writing, by the fumigator-in-charge or other authorized person. During this period a watchman should be posted to prevent unauthorized boarding or entry, and warning signs should be prominently displayed at gangways and at entrances to accommodation. A specimen of such a warning sign is given in appendix 2.

3.3.1.3 The fumigator-in-charge should be retained throughout the fumigation period and until such time as the ship is declared gas-free.

3.3.1.4 At the end of the fumigation period the fumigator will take the necessary action to ensure that the fumigant is dispersed. If crew members are required to assist in such actions, for example in opening hatches, they should be provided with adequate respiratory protection and adhere strictly to instructions given by the fumigator-in-charge.

3.3.1.5 The fumigator-in-charge should notify the master, in writing, of any spaces determined to be safe for re-occupancy by essential crew members prior to the aeration of the ship.

3.3.1.6 In such circumstances the fumigator-in-charge should monitor, throughout the fumigation and aeration periods, spaces to which personnel have been permitted to return. Should the concentration in any such area exceed the occupational exposure limit values set by the flag State regulations, crew members should be evacuated from the area until measurements show re-occupancy to be safe.

3.3.1.7 No unauthorized persons should be allowed on board until all parts of the ship have been determined gas-free, warning signs removed and clearance certificates issued by the fumigator-in-charge.

3.3.1.8 Clearance certificates should only be issued when tests show that all residual fumigant has been dispersed from empty cargo holds and adjacent working spaces and any residual fumigant material has been removed.

3.3.1.9 Entry into a space under fumigation should never take place except in the event of an extreme emergency. If entry is imperative, the fumigator-in-charge and at least one other person should enter, each wearing adequate protective equipment appropriate for the fumigant used and a safety harness and lifeline. Each lifeline should be tended by a person outside the space, who should be similarly equipped.

3.3.1.10 If a clearance certificate cannot be issued after the fumigation of cargo in port, the provisions of 3.3.2 should apply.

3.3.2 *Fumigation continued in transit*

3.3.2.1 Fumigation in transit should only be carried out at the discretion of the master. This should be clearly understood by owners, charterers, and all other parties involved when considering the transport of cargoes that may be infested. Due consideration should be taken of this when assessing the options of fumigation. The master should be aware of the regulations of the flag State Administration with regard to in-transit fumigation. The application of the process should be with the agreement of the port State Administration. The process may be considered under two headings:

.1 fumigation in which treatment is intentionally continued in a sealed space during a voyage and in which no aeration has taken place before sailing; and

.2 in-port cargo fumigation where some aeration is carried out before sailing, but where a clearance certificate for the cargo hold(s) cannot be issued because of residual gas and the cargo hold(s) has been re-sealed before sailing.

3.3.2.2 Before a decision on sailing with a fumigated cargo hold(s) is made, it should be taken into account that, due to operational conditions, the circumstances outlined in 3.3.2.1.2 may arise unintentionally, e.g., a ship may be required to sail at a time earlier than anticipated when the fumigation was started. In such circumstances the potential hazards may be as great as with a planned in-transit fumigation and all the precautions in the following paragraphs should be observed.

3.3.2.3 Before a decision is made as to whether a fumigation treatment planned to be commenced in port and continued at sea should be carried out, special precautions are necessary. These include the following:

.1 at least two members of the crew (including one officer) who have received appropriate training (see 3.3.2.6) should be designated as the trained representatives of the master responsible for ensuring that safe conditions in accommodation, engine-room and other working spaces are maintained after the fumigator-in-charge has handed over that responsibility to the master (see 3.3.2.12); and

.2 the trained representatives of the master should brief the crew before a fumigation takes place and satisfy the fumigator-in-charge that this has been done.

3.3.2.4 Empty cargo holds are to be inspected and/or tested for leakage with instruments so that proper sealing can be done before or after loading. The fumigator-in-charge, accompanied by a trained representative of the master or a competent person, should determine whether the cargo holds to be treated are or can be made sufficiently gastight to prevent leakage of the fumigant to the accommodation, engine-rooms and other working spaces in the ship. Special attention should be paid to potential problem areas such as bilge and cargo line systems. On completion of such inspection and/or test, the fumigator-in-charge should supply to the master, for his retention, a signed statement that the inspection and/or test has been performed, what provisions have been made and that the cargo holds are or can be made satisfactory for fumigation. Whenever a cargo hold is found not to be sufficiently gastight, the fumigator-in-charge should issue a signed statement to the master and the other parties involved.

3.3.2.5 Accommodation, engine-rooms, areas designated for use in navigation of the ship, frequently visited working areas and stores, such as the forecastle head spaces, adjacent to cargo holds being subject to fumigation in transit should be treated in accordance with the provisions of 3.3.2.13. Special attention should be paid to gas concentration safety checks in problem areas referred to in 3.3.2.4.

3.3.2.6 The trained representatives of the master designated in 3.3.2.3 should be provided and be familiar with:

.1 the information in the relevant Safety Data Sheet; and

.2 the instructions for use, e.g., on the fumigant label or package itself, such as the recommendations of the fumigant manufacturer concerning methods of detection of the fumigant in air, its behaviour and hazardous properties, symptoms of poisoning, relevant first aid and special medical treatment and emergency procedures.

3.3.2.7 The ship should carry:

.1 gas-detection equipment and adequate fresh supplies of service items for the fumigant(s) concerned as required by 3.3.2.12, together with instructions for its use and the occupational exposure limit values set by the flag State regulations for safe working conditions;

.2 instructions on disposal of residual fumigant material;

.3 at least four sets of adequate respiratory protective equipment; and

.4 a copy of the latest version of the *Medical First Aid Guide for Use in Accidents Involving Dangerous Goods (MFAG)*, including appropriate medicines and medical equipment.

3.3.2.8 The fumigator-in-charge should notify the master, in writing, of the spaces containing the cargo to be fumigated and also of any other spaces that are considered unsafe to enter during the fumigation. During the application of the fumigant, the fumigator-in-charge should ensure that the surrounding areas are checked for safety.

3.3.2.9 If cargo holds are to be fumigated in transit:

.1 After application of the fumigant, an initial check should be made by the fumigator-in-charge together with trained representatives of the master for any leak which, if detected, should be effectively sealed. When the master is satisfied that all precautions detailed in 3.3.2.1 to 3.3.2.12 have been fulfilled (refer to model checklist in appendix 3), then the vessel may sail. Otherwise, provisions outlined in 3.3.2.9.2 or 3.3.2.9.3 are to be followed.

If the provisions of 3.3.2.9.1 are not satisfied,

either:

.2 After application of fumigants, the ship should be delayed in port alongside at a suitable berth or at anchorage for such a period as to allow the gas in the fumigated cargo holds to reach sufficiently high concentrations to detect any possible leakage. Special attention should be paid to those cases where fumigants in a solid or liquid form have been applied which may require a long period (normally from 4 to 7 days unless a recirculation or similar distribution system is used) to reach such a high concentration that leakages can be detected. If leakages are detected, the ship should not sail until the source(s) of such leakages are determined and eliminated. After ascertaining that the ship is in a safe condition to sail, i.e. no gas leakages are present, the fumigator-in-charge should furnish the master with a written statement that:

.2.1 the gas in the cargo hold(s) has reached sufficiently high concentrations to detect any possible leakages;

.2.2   spaces adjacent to the treated cargo hold(s) have been checked and found gas-free; and

.2.3   the ship's representative is fully conversant with the use of the gas-detection equipment provided.

or:

.3   After application of the fumigants and immediately after the sailing of the ship, the fumigator-in-charge should remain on board for such a period as to allow the gas in the fumigated cargo hold or spaces to reach sufficiently high concentrations to detect any possible leakage, or until the fumigated cargo is discharged (see 3.3.2.20), whichever is the shorter, to check and rectify any gas leakages. Prior to his leaving the ship, he should ascertain that the ship is in a safe condition, i.e. no gas leakages are present, and he should furnish the master with a written statement to the effect that the provisions of 3.3.2.9.2.1, 3.3.2.9.2.2 and 3.3.2.9.2.3 have been carried out.

3.3.2.10   On application of the fumigant, the fumigator-in-charge should post warning signs at all entrances to places notified to the master as in 3.3.2.8. These warning signs should indicate the identity of the fumigant and the date and time of fumigation. A specimen of such a warning sign is given in appendix 2.

3.3.2.11   At an appropriate time after application of the fumigant, the fumigator-in-charge, accompanied by a representative of the master, should check that accommodation, engine-rooms and other working spaces remain free of harmful concentrations of gas.

3.3.2.12   Upon discharging his agreed responsibilities, the fumigator-in-charge should formally hand over to the master, in writing, responsibility for maintaining safe conditions in all occupied spaces. The fumigator-in-charge should ensure that gas-detection and respiratory protection equipment carried on the ship is in good order, and that adequate fresh supplies of consumable items are available to allow sampling as required in 3.3.2.13.

3.3.2.13   Gas concentration safety checks at all appropriate locations, which should at least include the spaces indicated in 3.3.2.5, should be continued throughout the voyage at least at eight-hour intervals or more frequently if so advised by the fumigator-in-charge. These readings should be recorded in the ship's log-book.

3.3.2.14   Except in extreme emergency, cargo holds sealed for fumigation in transit should never be opened at sea or entered. If entry is imperative, at least two persons should enter, wearing adequate protection equipment and a safety harness and lifeline tended by a person outside the space, similarly equipped with protective, self-contained breathing apparatus.

3.3.2.15   If it is essential to ventilate a cargo hold or holds, every effort should be made to prevent a fumigant from accumulating in accommodation or working areas. Those spaces should be carefully checked to that effect. If the gas concentration in those areas at any time exceeds the occupational exposure limit values set by the flag State regulations, they should be evacuated and the cargo hold or cargo holds should be re-sealed. If a cargo hold is re-sealed after ventilation, it should not be assumed that it is completely clear of gas and tests should be made and appropriate precautions taken before entering.

3.3.2.16   Prior to the arrival of the ship, generally not less than 24 hours in advance, the master should inform the appropriate authorities of the country of destination and ports of call that fumigation in transit is being carried out. The information should include the type of fumigant used, the date of fumigation, the cargo holds which have been fumigated, and whether ventilation has commenced. Upon arrival at the port of discharge, the master should also provide information as required in 3.3.2.6.2 and 3.3.2.7.2.

3.3.2.17   On arrival at the port of discharge, the requirements of receiving countries regarding handling of fumigated cargoes should be established. Before entry of fumigated cargo holds, trained personnel from a fumigation company or other authorized persons, wearing respiratory protection, should carry out careful monitoring of the spaces to ensure the safety of personnel. The monitored values should be recorded in the ship's log-book. In case of need or emergency, the master may commence ventilation of the fumigated cargo holds under the conditions of 3.3.2.15, having due regard for the safety of personnel on board. If this operation is to be done at sea, the master should evaluate weather and sea conditions before proceeding.

3.3.2.18   Only mechanical unloading that does not necessitate entry of personnel into the cargo holds of such fumigated cargoes should be undertaken. However, when the presence of personnel in cargo holds is necessary for the handling and operation of unloading equipment, continuous monitoring of the fumigated spaces should be carried out to ensure the safety of the personnel involved. When necessary, these personnel should be equipped with adequate respiratory protection.

3.3.2.19   During the final stages of discharge, when it becomes necessary for personnel to enter the cargo holds, such entry should only be permitted subsequent to verification that such cargo holds are gas-free.

3.3.2.20   Upon completion of discharge and when the ship is found free of fumigants and certified as such, all warning signs should be removed. Any action in this respect should be recorded in the ship's log-book.

Pesticides

4 Regulations for the use of pesticides

4.1 National and international controls on pesticide usage

4.1.1 In many countries the sale and use of pesticides are regulated by governments to ensure safety in application and prevention of contamination of foodstuffs. Among the factors taken into account in such regulations are the recommendations made by international organizations such as FAO and WHO, especially in regard to maximum limits of pesticide residues in food and foodstuffs.

4.1.2 Examples of some commonly used pesticides are listed in appendix 1. Pesticides should be used strictly in accordance with the manufacturer's instructions as given on the label or package itself. National regulations and requirements vary from one country to another; therefore particular pesticides which may be used for treatment of cargo holds and accommodation in ships may be limited by the regulations and requirements of:

    .1   the country where the cargo is loaded or treated;

    .2   the country of destination of the cargo, especially in regard to pesticide residues in foodstuffs; and

    .3   flag State of the ship.

4.1.3 Ships' masters should ensure that they have the necessary knowledge of the above regulations and requirements.

5 Safety precautions – general

5.1 Fumigation

5.1.1 Ship's personnel should not handle fumigants and such operations should be carried out only by qualified operators. Personnel allowed to remain in the vicinity of a fumigation operation for a particular purpose should follow the instructions of the fumigator-in-charge implicitly.

5.1.2 Aeration of treated cargo holds should be completed and a clearance certificate issued as in 3.3.1.8 or 3.3.1.10 before personnel are permitted to enter.

5.2 Exposure to pesticides resulting in illness

5.2.1 In the case of exposure to pesticides and subsequent illness, medical advice should be sought immediately. Information on poisoning may be found in the *Medical First Aid Guide for Use in Accidents Involving Dangerous Goods (MFAG)* or on the package (manufacturer's instructions and safety precautions on the label or the package itself).

Pesticides

APPENDIX 1
Fumigants suitable for shipboard use

The materials listed should be used strictly in accordance with the manufacturer's instructions and safety precautions given on the label or package itself, especially in respect of flammability, and with regard to any further limitations applied by the law of the country of loading, destination or flag of the ship, contracts relating to the cargo, or the shipowner's instructions.

1 Fumigants against insects in empty cargo holds

TO BE APPLIED ONLY BY QUALIFIED OPERATORS

Carbon dioxide

Nitrogen

Methyl bromide and carbon dioxide mixture

Methyl bromide

Hydrogen cyanide

Phosphine

2 Fumigants against insects in loaded or partially loaded cargo holds

CARE IS NEEDED IN SELECTING TYPES AND AMOUNTS OF FUMIGANTS FOR TREATMENT OF PARTICULAR COMMODITIES

Carbon dioxide

Nitrogen

Methyl bromide and carbon dioxide mixture

Methyl bromide

Phosphine

3 Fumigant information

3.1 Methyl bromide

Methyl bromide is used in situations where a rapid treatment of commodities or space is required. It should not be used in spaces where ventilation systems are not adequate for the removal of all gases from the free space. In-ship in-transit fumigations with methyl bromide should not be carried out. Fumigation with methyl bromide should be permitted only when the ship is in the confines of a port (either at anchor or alongside) and to disinfest before discharge, once crew members have disembarked (see 3.1.2.3). Prior to discharge, ventilation must be done, forced if necessary, to reduce the gaseous residues below the occupational exposure limit values set by the flag State regulations in the free spaces. (See procedures for ventilation in 3.3.2.17 to 3.3.2.19).

3.2 Phosphine

3.2.1 A variety of phosphine-generating formulations are used for in-ship in-transit or at-berth fumigations. Application methods vary widely and include surface-only treatment, probing, perforated tubing laid at the bottom of spaces, recirculation systems and gas-injection systems or their combinations. Treatment times will vary considerably depending on the temperature, depth of cargo and on the application method used.

3.2.2 Any discharge of active packages producing phosphine gas represents a significant risk to the public who may encounter them at sea. It should therefore be ensured that all waste and residues are disposed of in an appropriate manner, either by incineration or by disposal on shore, as recommended by the manufacturer. **Clear written instructions must be given to the master of the ship, to the receiver of the cargo and to the authorities at the discharging port as to how any powdery residues are to be disposed of.**

3.2.3 These will vary with each formulation and the method of application. Prior to discharge, ventilation must be done, forced if necessary, to reduce the gaseous residues below the occupational exposure limit values set by the flag State regulations in the free spaces (see procedures for ventilation in 3.3.2.17 to 3.3.2.19). For safety aspects during the voyage, see 3.3.2.3.

Pesticides

APPENDIX 2
Fumigation warning sign

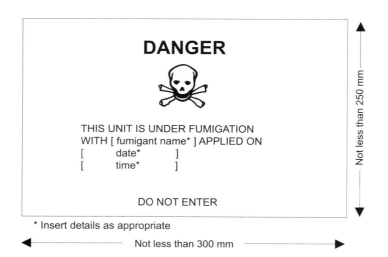

* Insert details as appropriate

Not less than 300 mm

APPENDIX 3
Model checklist for in-transit fumigation

Date: . . . .

Port: . . . . Terminal/Quay: . . . .

Ship's name:. . . . .

Type of fumigant: . . . . Method of application: . . . .

Date & time fumigation commenced:. . . . .

Name of fumigator/company:. . . . .

The master and fumigator-in-charge, or their representatives, should complete the checklist jointly. The purpose of this checklist is to ensure that the responsibilities and requirements of 3.3.2.11, and 3.3.2.12 are carried out fully for in-transit fumigation under section 3.3.2.9.

Safety of operations requires that all questions should be answered affirmatively by ticking the appropriate boxes. If this is not possible, the reason should be given and agreement reached upon precautions to be taken between ship and fumigator-in-charge. If a question is considered to be not applicable, write "n/a", explaining why, if appropriate.

PART A: BEFORE FUMIGATION

		SHIP	FUMIGATOR-IN-CHARGE
1	The inspection required before loading has been performed (3.3.2.4)	☐	☐
2	All the cargo holds to be fumigated are satisfactory for fumigation	☐	☐
3	Spaces, where found not be satisfactory, have been sealed	☐	☐
4	The master or his trained representatives have been made aware of the specific areas to be checked for gas concentrations throughout the fumigation period	☐	☐
5	The master or his trained representatives have been made familiar with the fumigant label, detection methods, safety procedures and emergency procedures (refer to 3.3.2.6)	☐	☐
6	The fumigator-in-charge has ensured that gas-detection and respiratory protection equipment carried on the ship is in good order, and that adequate fresh supplies of consumable items for this equipment are available to allow sampling as required by 3.3.2.13.	☐	☐
7	The master has been notified in writing of:		
	(a) the spaces containing cargo to be fumigated	☐	☐
	(b) any other spaces that are considered unsafe to enter during the fumigation	☐	☐

PART B: AFTER FUMIGATION

The following procedure should be carried out after application of fumigant and closing and sealing of cargo holds.

		SHIP	FUMIGATOR-IN-CHARGE
8	Presence of gas has been confirmed inside each hold under fumigation	☐	☐
9	Each hold has been checked for leakage and sealed properly	☐	☐
10	Spaces adjacent to the treated cargo holds have been checked and found gas-free	☐	☐
11	The responsible crew members have been shown how to take gas readings properly when gas is present and they are fully conversant with the use of gas-detection equipment provided	☐	☐
12	Methods of application:		
	(a) *Surface application method* Initial rapid build-up of the gas in the upper regions of hold airspace with subsequent penetration downward of the gas over a longer period	☐	☐
	or		
	(b) *Deep probing* More rapid dispersion of gas than in (a) with lower concentrations in upper regions of airspace in the hold	☐	☐
	or		
	(c) *Recirculation* Rapid dispersion of gas throughout hold but at lower initial gas levels with subsequent build-up of gas levels, which, however, may be lower due to even distribution	☐	☐
	or		
	(d) *Other*	☐	☐
13	The master or trained representatives have been briefed fully on the method of application and the spread of the gas throughout the hold	☐	☐
14	The master or trained representatives have been made:	☐	☐
	(a) aware that even though the initial check may not indicate any leaks, it is essential that monitoring is to be continued in the accommodation, engine-room, etc. because gas concentrations may reach their highest levels after several days	☐	☐
	(b) aware of the possibility of the spreading of gas throughout the duct keel and/or ballast tanks	☐	☐
15	The fumigator-in-charge has supplied a signed statement to the master, conforming to the requirements of 3.3.2.12, for his retention	☐	☐

The above has been agreed:

Time: . . . .   Date: . . . .

For ship: . . . .   Fumigator-in-charge: . . . .

Rank: . . . .

RECOMMENDATIONS ON THE SAFE USE OF PESTICIDES IN SHIPS

APPLICABLE TO THE FUMIGATION OF CARGO TRANSPORT UNITS

RECOMMENDATIONS ON THE SAFE USE OF PESTICIDES IN SHIPS APPLICABLE TO THE FUMIGATION OF CARGO TRANSPORT UNITS

1   The Maritime Safety Committee, at its sixty-second session (24 to 28 May 1993), approved the Recommendations on the safe use of pesticides in ships (MSC/Circ.612), proposed by the Sub-Committee on Containers and Cargoes at its thirty-second session.

2   The Maritime Safety Committee, at its eighty-fourth session (7 to 16 May 2008), approved the Recommendations on the safe use of pesticides in ships applicable to the fumigation of cargo transport units, which apply to carriage of packaged dangerous goods in pursuance of the requirements of SOLAS regulation VI/4 and the relevant parts of the IMDG Code, proposed by the Sub-Committee on Dangerous Goods, Solid Cargoes and Containers at its twelfth session, as set out in the annex.*

3   The Committee agreed that the Recommendations should not apply to the carriage of fresh food produce under controlled atmosphere.

4   Member Governments are invited to bring the Recommendations to the attention of competent authorities, mariners, fumigators, fumigant and pesticide manufacturers and others concerned.

5   The present circular supersedes MSC/Circ.612, as amended by MSC/Circ.689 and MSC/Circ.746, with regard to the fumigation of cargo transport units.

---

* The text of the annex begins on page 261.

Contents

Recommendations on the safe use of pesticides in ships applicable to the fumigation of cargo transport units

Pesticides

1 Introduction

1.1 These recommendations address the hazards to personnel arising from the operations involved in the carriage of fumigated containers. This guidance is aimed at everyone involved in the supply chain. Although the contents of the container may not be subject to the provisions of the International Maritime Dangerous Goods (IMDG) Code, the process of fumigating such a container may bring it into the scope of the Code. If the container comes within the scope of the Code, hazard communication provisions are mandatory. Hazard communication measures required by the IMDG Code include:

.1 warning signs on containers;

.2 transport documents describing the fumigation method and, if appropriate, ventilation date; and

.3 requirements to declare fumigated containers on ships' manifests.

1.2 It is generally acknowledged, however, that there is widespread non-compliance with these requirements. Before entering the container, all personnel should assess the risk as to whether it is safe to enter and, if appropriate, determine the level of fumigant present. The use of gas-detection equipment may be required.

2 Reasons for fumigation

2.1 The presence of insects and rodents on ships is clearly undesirable for various reasons, and in addition to aesthetic and nuisance aspects, they may damage equipment and spread disease and infection, contaminate food in galleys and food stores, and cause damage to cargoes that will result in commercial or other losses.

2.2 The same highly toxic chemicals are used in containers as on board bulk ships. However, when a container that contains fumigant chemicals leaves the place at which it was fumigated, no-one can practically supervise the hazard unless they are aware of the presence of the fumigant. Any person who later enters the container can therefore be unknowingly exposed to dangerous levels of highly toxic chemicals.

2.3 Insects in containers

2.3.1 Grubs and larvae of insects and other species can infest cargo, as well as packaging, dunnage, etc., associated with the cargo, at any stage during harvesting, manufacture, processing, storage, packing or transport. These can spoil foodstuffs, textiles, leather goods, furniture, art and antiques, affect electronic equipment, contaminate sterile goods or deface consumer packaging or labelling, making the goods unfit for sale and therefore valueless.

2.3.2 Insect and mite pests of plant and animal products may be carried into the containers with goods (introduced infestation); they may move from one kind of product to another (cross-infestation) and may remain to attack subsequent cargoes (residual infestation). Their control may be required to comply with phytosanitary requirements to prevent spread of pests and for commercial reasons to prevent infestation and contamination of, or damage to, cargoes of human and animal food.

2.4 Rodents

2.4.1 Rodents should be controlled not only because of the damage they may do to cargo or the ship's equipment, but also, as required by the International Health Regulations, to prevent the spread of disease. Importers, particularly those that operate food processing plants, make great efforts to eliminate infestation in order to prevent the invasion of the importer's local storage or processing plant from infestation carried in incoming cargo. Consequently, they regularly fumigate their premises and may insist that goods delivered to their premises are certified free of infestation by means of fumigation.

3 Shore-side fumigation operations – fumigated containers

3.1 Fumigated containers which have been ventilated

3.1.1 It is important to ensure that freight containers are properly ventilated by opening the doors and allowing the gas to escape. This can be a natural process or can be accelerated by mechanical means such as blowers or extractors. The ventilation process can take many hours.

3.1.2 Freight containers or cargo transport units that have been completely ventilated after fumigation to ensure that no harmful concentration of gas remains should have the warning signs marked to show that it has been ventilated and the date of ventilation (in accordance with Special Provision 902 and column 17 of the Dangerous Goods List for UN 3359 Fumigated Unit) is not subject to the other requirements of the IMDG Code.

3.1.3   Care should be taken even after a container has been declared as ventilated. Gas can be held in packages of cargo, then desorbed over a long period of time, even over many days, raising the level of gas inside the container to above the safe exposure level. Bagged cereals and cartons with large air spaces are likely to produce this effect. Alternatively, gas and the fumigant sachets or tablets can become 'trapped' at the far end of a container by tightly packed cargo.

3.2   **Containers loaded without ventilation after fumigation (fumigation in transit)**

3.2.1   A freight container or cargo transport unit containing cargo under fumigation should not be allowed on board until sufficient time has elapsed to allow the attainment of a reasonably uniform gas concentration throughout the cargo. Because of variations due to types and amounts of fumigants and commodities and temperature levels, it is recommended that the period to elapse between fumigant application and loading should be determined locally for each country. Twenty-four hours is normally adequate for this purpose.

3.2.2   Carriage of fumigated containers which have not been ventilated before loading must be carried in accordance with the IMDG Code; the text below is reproduced from the 33rd amendment to the IMDG Code. A container which is carried under fumigation is classified as Class 9, assigned a UN Number (UN 3359) and a Proper Shipping Name (Fumigated Unit). The Dangerous Goods List of the IMDG Code also specifies the following for fumigated units. It assigns two Special Provisions:

Special Provision SP302

In the Proper Shipping Name, the word "UNIT" means a cargo transport unit.

Special Provision SP910

A FUMIGATED UNIT is a closed cargo transport unit containing goods or materials that either are or have been fumigated within the unit. The fumigant gases used are either poisonous or asphyxiant. The gases are usually evolved from solid or liquid preparations distributed within the unit. Fumigated units are subject to the following provisions:

1   Cargo transport units shall be fumigated and handled taking into account the provisions of the IMO publication *Recommendations on the Safe Use of Pesticides in Ships*, as amended.

2   Only cargo transport units that can be closed in such a way that the escape of gas is reduced to a minimum shall be used for the transport of fumigated cargo.

3   Class 9 placards shall not be affixed to a fumigated unit, except as required for other class 9 substances or articles packed therein (see 5.3.1.3).

4   Fumigated units shall be marked with a warning sign affixed to the access door(s) identifying the type and amount of fumigant used and the date and time of fumigation (see 5.3.2.5).

5   The transport document for a fumigated unit shall show the type and amount of fumigant used and the date and time of fumigation (see 5.4.4.2). In addition, instructions for disposal for any residual fumigant, including fumigation devices if used, shall be provided.

6   A closed cargo transport unit that has been fumigated is not subject to the provisions of this Code if it has been completely ventilated either by opening the doors of the unit or by mechanical ventilation after fumigation and if the date of ventilation is marked on the fumigation warning sign. When the fumigated goods or materials have been unloaded, the fumigation warning sign(s) shall be removed (see also 7.4.3).

7   When fumigated units are stowed under deck, equipment for detecting fumigant gas(es) shall be carried on the ship with instructions for their use.

8   Fumigants shall not be applied to the contents of a cargo transport unit once it has been loaded aboard the ship.

3.2.3   In column 17 (Properties and observations) of the Dangerous Goods List for UN 3359, the following information is given:

A 'FUMIGATED UNIT' is a closed cargo transport unit containing goods or materials that either are or have been fumigated within the unit. The fumigant gases used are either poisonous or asphyxiant. The gases are usually evolved from solid or liquid preparations distributed within the unit. Fumigants shall not be applied to the contents of a cargo transport unit once it has been loaded aboard the ship. A closed cargo transport unit that has been fumigated is not subject to the provisions of this Code if it has been completely ventilated either by opening the doors of the unit or by mechanical ventilation after fumigation and the date of ventilation is marked on the fumigation warning sign (see also Special Provision 910).

3.2.4 *Marking of the cargo transport unit*

3.2.4.1 To meet the requirements of the IMDG Code, the container has to be marked in accordance with chapter 5.3 of the IMDG Code; the relevant text is reproduced below:

Paragraph 5.3.2.5 Fumigated units

.1 The marking of the Proper Shipping Name (FUMIGATED UNIT) and the UN Number (UN 3359) is not required on fumigated units. However, if a fumigated unit is loaded with dangerous goods, any mark required by the provisions in 5.3.2.0 to 5.3.2.4 shall be marked on the fumigated unit.

.2 A fumigated unit shall be marked with the warning sign, as specified in .3, affixed in a location where it will be easily seen by persons attempting to enter the interior of the unit. The marking, as required by this paragraph, shall remain on the unit until the following provisions are met:

   .1 the fumigated unit has been ventilated to remove harmful concentrations of fumigant gas; and

   .2 the fumigated goods or materials have been unloaded.

.3 The fumigation warning sign shall be rectangular and shall be not less than 300 mm wide and 250 mm high. The markings shall be in black print on a white background with lettering not less than 25 mm high. An illustration of this sign is given below:

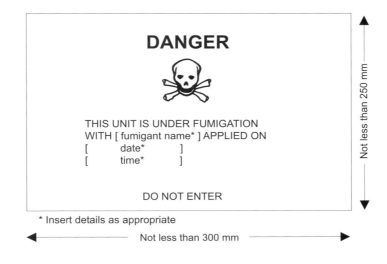

* Insert details as appropriate

Transport documentation for the fumigated cargo transport unit

3.2.5 To meet the requirements of the IMDG Code, the container must be documented in accordance with chapter 5.4 of the Code; the relevant text is reproduced below:

Paragraph 5.4.4.2 Fumigated units

The transport document for a fumigated unit shall show the type and amount of fumigant used and the date and time of fumigation. In addition, instructions for disposal of any residual fumigant, including fumigation devices, if used, shall be provided.

4   Fumigants used

There are a number of chemicals that are used as fumigants, such as phosphine and methyl bromide.

4.1   Phosphine UN 2199

4.1.1 This process requires a long period of time to work completely. This can be applied with little technical training as it is supplied in sachets, tablets or pressed plates containing magnesium phosphide or aluminium phosphide. These generate phosphine gas when exposed to the moisture in the air. The gas has a slight "fishy garlic" smell and breaks down into a powdery grey residue.

4.1.2 The rate of generation of phosphine depends on the temperature, the airborne moisture and the degree the generating material is exposed to the air.

4.1.3 Symptoms of poisoning by inhalation of phosphine include nausea, vomiting, headache, feeling weak, fainting, pain in chest, cough, chest tightness and difficulty breathing. Pulmonary oedema (the presence of excess fluid in the lungs usually due to heart failure) can follow, usually within 24 hours, but sometimes this is delayed for some days.

4.2 Methyl bromide UN 1062

4.2.1 Fumigation with methyl bromide is a relatively rapid process that can normally be completed in less than 48 hours. So these containers are not usually presented for shipment with gas above the toxicity levels (threshold limits) set by national agencies.

4.2.2 Symptoms of poisoning by inhalation of methyl bromide include headaches, dizziness, and eye irritation; coughing, nausea, abdominal discomfort, and numbness of feet. Higher exposure will bring about unconsciousness to central nervous system, convulsions, and loss of vision, balance and hearing.

4.2.3 Methyl bromide is supplied as a gas. So, during application, expertise is required to carry out the operation.

5 Ship-side operations

5.1 Fumigation after loading on board a ship

5.1.1 No person should be allowed by the master to fumigate the contents of a freight container or cargo transport unit once it has been loaded on board a ship.

5.2 Containers loaded without ventilation after fumigation (fumigation in transit)

5.2.1 If it is intended that freight containers or cargo transport units containing cargo under fumigation should be taken on board ship without preliminary ventilation, their shipment must be considered as a Class 9 Hazard under the IMDG Code and as such the procedures should conform to the provisions as specified in the entries for FUMIGATED UNIT (UN 3359) of the Code. The following special precautions, incorporating the IMDG provisions, are necessary:

.1 A freight container or cargo transport unit containing cargo under fumigation should not be allowed on board until sufficient time has elapsed to allow the attainment of a reasonably uniform gas concentration throughout the cargo. Because of variations due to types and amounts of fumigants and commodities and temperature levels, it is recommended that the period to elapse between fumigant application and loading should be determined locally for each country. Twenty-four hours is normally adequate for this purpose. Before loading, the container should be checked for leaks and any leakage sealed.

.2 The master should be informed prior to loading of freight containers and cargo transport units under fumigation. These should be identified with suitable warning signs, incorporating the identity of the fumigant and the date and time of fumigation. Any freight container under fumigation must have the doors substantially secured before loading onto a ship. Plastic or lightweight metal seals are not sufficient for this purpose. The securing arrangement must be such as to allow only authorized entry to the freight container. If container doors are to be locked, the means of locking should be of such a construction that, in case of emergency, the doors could be opened without delay. Adequate instructions for disposal of any residual fumigant material should be provided.

.3 Shipping documents for freight containers or cargo transport units concerned should show the date of fumigation and the type and amount of fumigant used.

.4 Stowage on deck should be at least 6 m away from vent intakes, crew quarters and regularly occupied spaces.

.5 Stowage under deck should only be undertaken when unavoidable and then only in a cargo space equipped with mechanical ventilation sufficient to prevent the build-up of fumigant concentrations above the toxicity levels (threshold limits) set by national agencies. The threshold limit for occupational exposure to the fumigant can be found on the Safety Data Sheet. The ventilation rate of the mechanical ventilation system should be at least two air changes per hour, based on the empty cargo space.

.6 Equipment suitable for detecting the fumigant gas or gases used should be carried on the ship, with instructions for its use.

.7 Where the stowage requirements above cannot be met, cargo spaces carrying fumigated freight containers or cargo transport units should be treated as if under fumigation and the provisions below should apply.

5.2.2 Before a fumigated container is loaded to a vessel below deck, special precautions are necessary. This includes the following:

.1 At least an officer and one other are to receive appropriate training and will be designated as the trained representatives of the master. The master, through his representative, is responsible for ensuring safe conditions in the occupied spaces of the vessel.

.2 The trained representatives should brief the crew before the container is loaded.

5.2.3 The fumigant gas is heavier than air, so care should be taken in the holds, particularly when working on the tank tops.

5.2.4 The trained representatives of the master should be provided and be familiar with:

.1 The information in the relevant Safety Data Sheet (SDS), if available.

.2 The instructions on the packaging itself, such as the recommendations of the fumigant manufacturer concerning methods of detection of the fumigant in air, its behaviour and hazardous properties, symptoms of poisoning, relevant first aid and special medical treatment and emergency procedures.

5.2.5 The ship should carry:

.1 adequate gas-detection equipment for the fumigant concerned, together with instructions for its use;

.2 instructions on disposal of residual fumigant material;

.3 at least four sets of adequate respiratory protective equipment; and

.4 a copy of the latest version of the *Medical First Aid Guide for Use in Accidents Involving Dangerous Goods (MFAG)*, including appropriate medicines and medical equipment.

5.2.6 Prior to the arrival of the ship, generally not less than 24 hours in advance, the master should inform the appropriate authorities of the country of destination and ports of call that fumigation in transit is being carried out. The information should include the type of fumigant used, the date of fumigation and cargo spaces carrying fumigated freight containers or cargo transport units.

5.2.7 The instructions on the fumigant label or package itself, such as the recommendations of the fumigant manufacturer concerning methods of detection of the fumigant in air, its behaviour and hazardous properties, symptoms of poisoning, relevant first aid and special medical treatment.

5.2.8 Disposal of any residual fumigant material should be in accordance with supplier's instructions.

6   Hazards to personnel

6.1 If, for any reason, the ship's crew or other personnel have to open a container declared as being under fumigation, they must be very careful.

6.2 There are no obvious signs when methyl bromide has been used as a fumigant (e.g., by sight or smell). The container should be left open as long as possible and then checked with the equipment available and should be declared gas-free before entry is allowed. In the case of an emergency, entry may be allowed, with full confined space precautions, if there is any gas found to be present.

6.3 If the container is fumigated with phosphine there are normally visual signs inside the container of the fumigant in the form of sachets, tablets, pressed plates or powder. The state of the packaging depends on the time these have been exposed and the atmosphere that they have been exposed in. It is also possible that the fumigants have moved between cargo items and may not be immediately visible.

6.4 As moisture is required for the reaction to take place, when a container is opened at sea the level of moisture in the air may re-start the reaction.

6.5 After the magnesium or aluminium phosphide reacts with moisture to generate phosphine, a residue of magnesium or aluminium hydroxide remains. This is a light powdery grey substance like ash. Hopefully, this has been retained in some kind of packaging so that it can be removed safely. If, however, there is a residue over the cargo, the crew must avoid breathing in this residue or getting it into their eyes or mouth. If not, they are still at risk of being poisoned by the residue, which may still be able to generate some phosphine.

6.6 It should be noted that there are certain commodities (e.g., edible nuts) where a small amount of fumigant is put in cotton wool and placed inside each bag. These items are then dangerous because their handling brings the fumigant close to the face.

6.7 Personnel should be made aware that not every fumigated container is declared and, hence, not marked as such. There are indicators for fumigated containers like tapes on vents or the door joints, a possible "fishy garlic" smell of phosphine and packets or piles of powdery residue inside the container.

7   Fumigation detection

7.1   The most effective method of protection is to carry out gas tests when the container doors are opened. As a minimum, it is recommended to test for phosphine and methyl bromide as the two most common fumigants used. If gas is found, the container should be put aside for ventilation.

7.1.1   *Stain tube gas test equipment*

7.1.1.1   Glass stain tube equipment is simple in design and use, robust and reliable. A test for phosphine and methyl bromide can be carried out by a person standing outside the container using a lance inserted into the container doorway. In practice, air is drawn by small hand-held bellows through a glass tube containing impregnated crystals which react with the gas for which the test is being done. If the air is contaminated by the gas in question, the crystals change colour. The function is not affected by moisture, but care has to be taken to warm the tubes to above 0°C in sub-zero temperatures. Also, a reasonable degree of light is required to detect the colour change of the crystals. The tubes should be used in accordance with the manufacturer's instructions. In particular, they must not be used after their expiry date.

7.1.2   *Electronic (photo-ionisation gas testing equipment)*

7.1.2.1   Gas tests can be carried out that detect the presence of gases and their concentration levels. Similarly, equipment can confirm that there is a safe level of oxygen within the container. At the present time, the technology is such that both the quantification and discrimination are poor. There are frequent false positives due to cross-sensitivities, and readings are not accurate enough for determining safe exposure levels. Therefore the use of these instruments at the present time is not recommended.

7.2   Personal monitors

7.2.1   Small electronic personal monitors are available for phosphine, but not for methyl bromide. Phosphine monitors can be placed inside the container while unloaders are working, or worn by individuals on outer garments. The location of an independent monitor is important both to ensure that any fumigant is detected and ensure that the reading is not compromised by ventilation at the door or external contaminants. Monitors issue an audible signal if phosphine levels reach the pre-set level and are useful as warning devices. However, they should not be used for the initial fumigation detection and measurement process. Also, electronic monitors have the disadvantage that they can respond to a range of harmless substances, giving misleading alarm signals.

7.2.2   Personal monitors are also available to show the level of oxygen within the container. This would indicate a deoxygenated atmosphere but would not necessarily indicate that the atmosphere is free from fumigant.

APPENDIX
Aide memoire for fumigation of containers

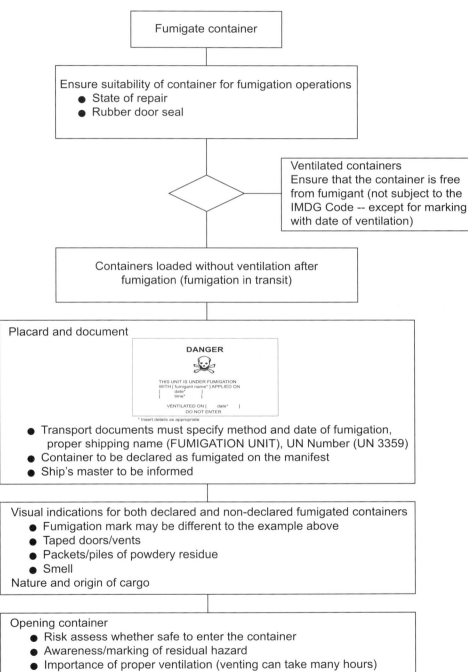

INTERNATIONAL CODE FOR THE SAFE CARRIAGE OF PACKAGED IRRADIATED NUCLEAR FUEL, PLUTONIUM AND HIGH-LEVEL RADIOACTIVE WASTES ON BOARD SHIPS

(INF CODE)

INF Code

Foreword

The International Code for the Safe Carriage of Packaged Irradiated Nuclear Fuel, Plutonium and High-Level Radioactive Wastes on board Ships (INF Code) was adopted by resolution MSC.88(71) on 27 May 1999 after the Maritime Safety Committee had considered earlier resolutions A.748(18) (Code for the Safe Carriage of Irradiated Nuclear Fuel, Plutonium and High-Level Radioactive Wastes in Flasks on board Ships (INF Code)), A.790(19) (Review of the INF Code), A.853(20) (Amendments to the INF Code), and A.854(20) (Guidelines for developing shipboard emergency plans for ships carrying materials subject to the INF Code).

The International Code is mandatory under SOLAS 1974 and entered into force 1 January 2001.

The Code was amended by resolution MSC.118(74) on 6 June 2001 to align it with Amendment 30 of the IMDG Code. The amendment was accepted, and came into force on 1 January 2003. The Code was also amended by resolution MSC.135(76) on 12 December 2002 to align it with amendments to chapter VII of SOLAS. This amendment was accepted, and entered into force on 1 July 2004. The Code was further amended by resolution MSC.178(79). The amendment to the International Certificate of Fitness was accepted and came into force on 1 July 2006. This publication has been amended appropriately.

Further amendments to the Code have been adopted by resolution MSC.241(83) in October 2007. The acceptance date for these amendments, which are appended to this text, is 1 January 2009. If accepted by an appropriate number of Member States, these will enter into force on 1 July 2009.

Contents

INF Code

Chapter 1 – General

1.1 Definitions

1.1.1 For the purpose of this Code:

.1 *Administration* means the Government of the State whose flag the ship is entitled to fly.

.2 *Convention* means the International Convention for the Safety of Life at Sea, 1974, as amended.

.3 *INF cargo* means packaged irradiated nuclear fuel, plutonium and high-level radioactive wastes carried as cargo in accordance with class 7 of the IMDG Code.

.4 *Irradiated nuclear fuel* means material containing uranium, thorium and/or plutonium isotopes which has been used to maintain a self-sustaining nuclear chain reaction.

.5 *Plutonium* means the resultant mixture of isotopes of that material extracted from irradiated nuclear fuel from reprocessing.

.6 *High-level radioactive wastes* means liquid wastes resulting from the operation of the first stage extraction system or the concentrated wastes from subsequent extraction stages, in a facility for reprocessing irradiated nuclear fuel, or solids into which such liquid wastes have been converted.

.7 *IMDG Code* means the International Maritime Dangerous Goods Code defined in regulation VII/1.1 of the Convention.

.8 *IBC Code* means the International Code for the Construction and Equipment of Ships Carrying Dangerous Chemicals in Bulk, as defined in regulation VII/8.1 of the Convention.

.9 *Incident* means any occurrence or series of occurrences, including loss of container integrity, having the same origin which results or may result in a release, or probable cargo release, of INF cargo.

.10 *Release* means the escape of INF cargo from its containment system or the loss of an INF cargo package.

1.1.2 For the purpose of this Code, ships carrying INF cargo are assigned to the following three classes, depending on the total activity of INF cargo which is carried on board:

Class INF 1 ship – Ships which are certified to carry INF cargo with an aggregate activity less than 4,000 TBq.

Class INF 2 ship – Ships which are certified to carry irradiated nuclear fuel or high-level radioactive wastes with an aggregate activity less than 2×10^6 TBq and ships which are certified to carry plutonium with an aggregate activity less than 2×10^5 TBq.

Class INF 3 ship – Ships which are certified to carry irradiated nuclear fuel or high-level radioactive wastes and ships which are certified to carry plutonium with no restriction of the maximum aggregate activity of the materials.

1.2 Application

1.2.1 This Code applies to ships engaged in the carriage of INF cargo as prescribed in regulation VII/15 of the Convention.

1.2.2 In addition to the requirements of this Code, the provisions of the IMDG Code shall apply to the carriage of INF cargo.

1.2.3 INF cargo that would be required to be carried on Class INF 3 ships shall not be allowed on passenger ships.

1.3 Survey and certification

1.3.1 Before the carriage of INF cargo takes place, a ship intended to carry INF cargo shall be subject to an initial survey which shall include a complete examination of its structure, equipment, fittings, arrangements and material in so far as the ship is covered by this Code.

1.3.2 The Administration, or an organization recognized by it in accordance with regulation I/6 of the Convention, shall, after the initial survey as required in 1.3.1, issue the ship with the International Certificate of Fitness for the Carriage of INF Cargo, the form of which is set out in the appendix.

1.3.3 A ship certified for the carriage of INF cargo shall be subject to inspections and surveys under the applicable provisions of chapter I of the Convention in order to ensure that the structure, equipment, fittings, arrangements and material comply with the provisions of this Code.

1.3.4 The International Certificate of Fitness for the Carriage of INF Cargo shall cease to be valid if the survey required by 1.3.3 has not been carried out or has shown that the ship does not comply with the provisions of this Code, or when a certificate of that ship required by the Convention has expired.

Chapter 2 – Damage stability

2.1 The damage stability of a Class INF 1 ship shall be to the satisfaction of the Administration.

2.2 A Class INF 2 ship shall:

.1 if it is built to the standards for a passenger ship, comply with the damage stability requirements of part B of chapter II-1 of the Convention; or

.2 if it is built to the standards for a cargo ship, comply with the damage stability requirements of part B-1 of chapter II-1 of the Convention, regardless of the length of the ship.

2.3 A Class INF 3 ship shall comply with:

.1 the damage stability requirements for type 1 ship survival capability and location of cargo spaces in chapter 2 of the IBC Code; or

.2 regardless of the length of the ship, the damage stability requirements in part B-1 of chapter II-1 of the Convention, using the subdivision index R_{INF} as given below:

$$R_{INF} = R + 0.2(1 - R)$$

Chapter 3 – Fire safety measures

3.1 Fire safety measures of a Class INF 1 ship shall be to the satisfaction of the Administration.

3.2 Class INF 2 and 3 ships, regardless of their size, shall be fitted with the following systems and equipment:

.1 a water fire-extinguishing system complying with the requirements of regulation II-2/4 of the Convention;

.2 fixed fire-extinguishing arrangements in machinery spaces of category A, as defined in regulation II-2/3.19 of the Convention, complying with the requirements of regulation I-2/7 of the Convention;

.3 fixed cargo space cooling arrangements, complying with the requirements of regulation II-2/54.2.1.3 of the Convention; and

.4 a fixed fire-detection and fire alarm system, protecting the machinery spaces, accommodation and service spaces, complying with the requirements of regulation II-2/13 of the Convention.

3.3 In a Class INF 3 ship, accommodation spaces, service spaces, control stations and machinery spaces of category A shall be fitted either forward or aft of the cargo spaces, due regard being paid to the overall safety of the ship.

Chapter 4 – Temperature control of cargo spaces

4.1 In Class INF 1, 2 and 3 ships:

.1 adequate ventilation or refrigeration of enclosed cargo spaces shall be provided so that the average ambient temperature within such spaces does not exceed 55°C at any time;

.2 ventilation or refrigeration systems serving cargo spaces intended for the transport of INF cargo shall be independent of those serving other spaces; and

.3 those items essential to operation, such as fans, compressors, heat exchangers, cooling water supply, shall be provided in duplicate for each cargo space and spare parts shall be available, to the satisfaction of the Administration.

Chapter 5 – Structural consideration

The structural strength of deck areas and support arrangements shall be sufficient to withstand the load which is to be sustained.

Chapter 6 – Cargo securing arrangements

6.1   Adequate permanent securing devices shall be provided to prevent movement of the packages within the cargo spaces. In designing permanent devices, due consideration shall be given to the orientation of the packages and the following ship acceleration levels shall be taken into account:

> 1.5*g* longitudinally;*
> 1.5*g* transversely;
> 1.0*g* vertically up;
> 2.0*g* vertically down.

6.2   Alternatively, where packages are carried on the open deck or a vehicle deck, they shall be secured in accordance with the principles of safe stowage and securing of heavy unitized and wheel-based (rolling) cargo approved by the Administration based on the guidelines developed by the Organization.[†]

6.3   Collision chocks, where used, shall be so arranged that they will not interfere or prevent cooling air flow which may be necessary under the provisions of 4.1.

Chapter 7 – Electrical power supplies

7.1   The electrical power supplies in a Class INF 1 ship shall be to the satisfaction of the Administration.

7.2   In Class INF 2 and 3 ships:

  .1   an alternative source of electrical power, complying with the requirements of the international standards acceptable to the Organization,[‡] shall be provided so that damage involving the main supply would not affect the alternative source; and

  .2   the power available from the alternative source shall be sufficient to supply the following services for at least 36 hours:

     .2.1   the equipment provided for the flooding and cooling arrangements referred to in 3.2.3 and 4.1; and

     .2.2   all emergency services required by the Convention.

7.3   In a Class INF 3 ship, the alternative source referred to in 7.2.1 shall be located outside the extent of any damage envisaged under chapter 2.

Chapter 8 – Radiological protection

Depending upon the characteristics of the INF cargo to be carried and upon the design of the ship, additional arrangements or equipment for radiological protection shall, if necessary, be provided to the satisfaction of the Administration.

Chapter 9 – Management and training

Management and training for a ship carrying INF cargo shall be to the satisfaction of the Administration, taking into account developments in the Organization.

Chapter 10 – Shipboard emergency plan

10.1   Every ship carrying INF cargo shall carry on board a shipboard emergency plan.

---

* *g* is the acceleration due to gravity, equal to 9.81 m/s^2.

† Refer to:

  .1   the Code of Safe Practice for Cargo Stowage and Securing, adopted by the Organization by resolution A.714(17);

  .2   the Guidelines for securing arrangements for the transport of road vehicles on ro–ro ships, adopted by the Organization by resolution A.581(14); and

  .3   MSC/Circ.745, on the Guidelines for the preparation of the Cargo Securing Manual.

‡ Refer to the recommendations published by the International Electrotechnical Commission and, in particular, to Publication 92 – Electrical Installations in Ships.

10.2   Such a plan shall be approved by the Administration based on the guidelines developed by the Organization*
and written in a working language or languages understood by the master and officers. As a minimum, the plan
shall consist of:

> .1   the procedure to be followed by the master or other persons having charge of the ship to report an incident
> involving INF cargo, as required by chapter 11 of this Code;

> .2   the list of authorities or persons to be contacted in the event of an incident involving INF cargo;

> .3   a detailed description of the action to be taken immediately by persons on board to prevent, reduce or control
> the release, and mitigate the consequences of the loss, of INF cargo following the incident; and

> .4   the procedures and points of contact on the ship for co-ordinating shipboard action with national and local
> authorities.

10.3   If a ship is required to have a shipboard emergency plan by other international instruments, the various plans may
be combined into a single plan entitled ''Shipboard Marine Emergency Plan''.[†]

Chapter 11 – Notification in the event of an incident involving INF cargo

11.1   The reporting requirements of regulation VII/7-1 of the Convention shall apply both to the loss or likely loss of INF
cargo overboard and to any incident involving a release or probable release of INF cargo, whatever the reason for
such loss or release, including for the purpose of securing the safety of the ship or saving life at sea.

11.2   Such a report shall also be made in the event of damage, failure or breakdown of a ship carrying INF cargo which:

> .1   affects the safety of the ship, including but not limited to, collision, grounding, fire, explosion, structural
> failure, flooding and cargo shifting; or

> .2   results in the impairment of the safety of navigation, including the failure or breakdown of steering gear,
> propulsion system, electrical generating system, and essential shipborne navigational aids.

---

* Refer to the Guidelines for developing shipboard emergency plans for ships carrying materials subject to the INF Code, adopted by the
Organization by resolution A.854(20).
[†] Refer to the Guidelines for a structure of an integrated system of contingency planning for shipboard emergencies, adopted by the
Organization by resolution A.852(20).

APPENDIX

Form of International Certificate of Fitness for the Carriage of INF Cargo[1]

INTERNATIONAL CERTIFICATE OF FITNESS FOR THE CARRIAGE OF INF CARGO

(Official seal)

issued under the provisions of

THE INTERNATIONAL CODE FOR THE SAFE CARRIAGE OF PACKAGED IRRADIATED NUCLEAR FUEL, PLUTONIUM AND HIGH-LEVEL RADIOACTIVE WASTES ON BOARD SHIPS (INF CODE)
(resolution MSC.88(71))

under the authority of the Government of

. . . .

(full official designation of country)

by . . . .

(full designation of the competent person or organization recognized by the Administration)

Particulars of ship[2]

Name of ship . . . .

Distinctive number or letters . . . .

Port of registry . . . .

Gross tonnage . . . .

IMO number . . . .

INF class of ship (1.1.2 of the Code) . . . .

THIS IS TO CERTIFY:

1 that the ship has been surveyed in accordance with the provisions of 1.3.1 of the Code; and

2 that the survey showed that the structure, equipment, fittings, arrangements and material of the ship complied with the applicable provisions of the Code.

This certificate is issued subject to the provisions of 1.3.4 of the Code.

Completion date of the survey on which this certificate is based: . . . .
(dd/mm/yyyy)

Issued at . . . .
(place of issue of Certificate)   *(date)*

The undersigned declares that he is duly authorized by the said Government to issue this Certificate.

. . . .

(signature of official issuing the Certificate and/or seal of issuing authority)

_____

[1] The certificate must be drawn up in the official language of the issuing country. If the language used is neither English, French nor Spanish, the text should include a translation into one of these languages.

[2] Alternatively, the particulars of the ship may be placed horizontally in boxes.

Amendments to chapter 2 were adopted in October 2007 by resolution MSC.241(83).

1   In paragraph 2.2.1, the words "Part B" are replaced by the words "Part B-1".

2   In paragraphs 2.2.2 and 2.3.2, the following new sentence is added at the end of the paragraphs:

"For ships less than 80 m in length, the subdivision index R at 80 m shall be used."

APPENDIX

RESOLUTIONS AND
CIRCULARS
REFERRED TO
IN THE IMDG CODE
AND SUPPLEMENT

Appendix

Contents

Appendix

Appendix

IMO Assembly

Resolution A.489(XII)

Adopted on 19 November 1981

SAFE STOWAGE AND SECURING OF CARGO UNITS AND OTHER ENTITIES IN SHIPS OTHER THAN CELLULAR CONTAINERSHIPS

THE ASSEMBLY,

RECALLING Article 16(i) of the Convention on the Inter-Governmental Maritime Consultative Organization,

RECOGNIZING that there is a need to improve standards of stowage and securing of cargo units and other entities in ships other than cellular containerships,

RECOGNIZING ALSO that special attention should be paid to the stowage of cargo in cargo units and on vehicles,

BELIEVING that the universal application of improved standards would be greatly facilitated if all cargo units, vehicles and other entities for shipment were provided with means for applying portable securing gear,

CONSIDERING that a universal improvement in the standards could best be achieved on an international basis,

1. ADOPTS the Guidelines on the Safe Stowage and Securing of Cargo Units and Other Entities in Ships Other Than Cellular Containerships, the text of which is annexed to the present resolution;

2. RECOMMENDS Governments to issue guidelines for the safe stowage and securing of cargo units and other entities in ships other than cellular containerships in conformity with the annexed Guidelines and, in particular, to require such ships entitled to fly the flag of their State to carry a Cargo Securing Manual as described in the annexed Guidelines.

Annex

GUIDELINES ON THE SAFE STOWAGE AND SECURING OF CARGO UNITS AND OTHER ENTITIES IN SHIPS OTHER THAN CELLULAR CONTAINERSHIPS

1   *Cargo units and other entities* in this context means wheeled cargo, containers, flats, pallets, portable tanks, packaged units, vehicles, etc., and parts of loading equipment which belong to the ship and which are not fixed to the ship.

2   These Guidelines apply to the securing of cargo units or other entities on open or closed decks of ships other than cellular containerships and ships specially designed and fitted for the purpose of carrying containers. Application of the Guidelines should always be at the master's discretion.

3   Applicable parts of the IMDG Code and resolution A.288(VIII) on stowage and securing of containers on deck in ships which are not specially designed and fitted for the purpose of carrying containers* should be observed.

4   Shippers' special advice or guidelines regarding handling and stowage of individual cargo units should be observed.

---

* This resolution has been revoked by A.714(17).

5   When reasonable, cargo units and other entities should be provided with means for safe application of portable securing gear. Such means should be of sufficient strength to withstand the forces which may be encountered on board ships in a seaway.

6   Cargo units and other entities should be stowed in a safe manner and secured as necessary to prevent tipping and sliding. Due regard should be paid to the forces and accelerations to which the cargo units and other entities may be subjected.

7   Ships should be provided with fixed cargo securing arrangements and with portable securing gear. Information regarding technical properties and practical application of the various items of securing equipment on board should be provided.

8   Administrations should ascertain that every ship to which these Guidelines apply is provided with a Cargo Securing Manual appropriate to the characteristics of the ship and its intended service, in particular the ship's main dimensions, its hydrostatic properties, the weather and sea conditions which may be expected in the ship's trading area and also the cargo composition.

9   Where there is reason to suspect that cargo within any unit is packed or stowed in an unsatisfactory way, or that a vehicle is in a bad state of repair, or where the unit itself cannot be safely stowed and secured on the ship, and may therefore be a source of danger to ship or crew, such a unit or vehicle should not be accepted for shipment.

Cargo Securing Manual

10   The information contained in the Cargo Securing Manual should include the following items as appropriate:

.1   details of fixed securing arrangements and their locations (padeyes, eyebolts, elephant feet, etc.);

.2   location and stowage of portable securing gear;

.3   details of portable securing gear including an inventory of items provided and their strengths;

.4   examples of correct application of portable securing gear on various cargo units, vehicles and other entities carried on the ship;

.5   indication of the variation of transverse, longitudinal and vertical accelerations to be expected in various positions on board the ship.

Resolution A.533(13)

Adopted on 17 November 1983

ELEMENTS TO BE TAKEN INTO ACCOUNT WHEN CONSIDERING THE SAFE STOWAGE AND SECURING OF CARGO UNITS AND VEHICLES IN SHIPS

THE ASSEMBLY,

RECALLING Article 16(j) of the Convention on the International Maritime Organization concerning the functions of the Assembly in relation to regulations concerning maritime safety,

RECALLING FURTHER that at its twelfth session it adopted resolution A.489(XII) regarding safe stowage and securing of cargo units and other entities in ships other than cellular containerships,

TAKING ACCOUNT of the IMO/ILO guidelines for training in the packing of cargo in freight containers,

RECOGNIZING that cargo units and vehicles are transported in increasing numbers on seagoing ships,

RECOGNIZING FURTHER that the cargo is stowed on and secured to cargo units and vehicles in most cases at the shipper's premises or at inland terminals and transported by road or rail to ports prior to the seagoing voyage and that the cargo on cargo units and vehicles may not always be adequately stowed or secured for safe sea transport,

REALIZING that adequately stowed and secured cargoes on cargo units and vehicles for road and rail transport in most cases would also be capable of withstanding the forces imposed on them during the sea leg of the transport,

ACKNOWLEDGING that there is a need for cargo units and vehicles presented for transport by sea to be fitted with satisfactory securing arrangements for securing them to the ship, arrangements for the securing of the cargo within the cargo unit or vehicle to facilitate its safe stowage and securing therein and for ships to be fitted with adequate securing points,

BELIEVING that the universal application of improved standards and securing arrangements is best facilitated if the elements to be taken into account when considering such matters are known to, and considered by, all links in the transport chain,

BELIEVING FURTHER that this can best be achieved on an international basis,

HAVING CONSIDERED the recommendation made by the Maritime Safety Committee at its forty-eighth session,

1.   INVITES Governments to issue recommendations to the different links in the transport chain in their countries, responsible for the transport of cargo units and vehicles intended for, and including, sea transport, taking into account the elements set out in the annex to this resolution;

2.   REQUESTS the Secretary-General to bring these elements to the attention of Member Governments and international organizations responsible for the safety of road, rail and sea transport in order that they can be taken into account in the design and construction of cargo units and vehicles and the design and construction of the ships in which they are carried.

Annex

ELEMENTS TO BE TAKEN INTO ACCOUNT WHEN CONSIDERING THE SAFE STOWAGE AND SECURING OF CARGO UNITS* AND VEHICLES IN SHIPS

The elements which should be taken into account relate specifically to the safe shipment of cargo units including vehicles. The aim is to indicate to the various parties involved the principal factors and features which need to be considered when designing and operating the ship or presenting the cargo unit, or vehicle, for such shipment. In addition, it is hoped that the elements will facilitate and promote better understanding of the problems and the needs of the masters of ships so engaged.

---

* *Cargo units* in this context means wheeled or tracked cargo, containers, flats, portable tanks, vehicles and the ship's mobile cargo handling equipment not fixed to the ship.

1   The parties involved

1.1   The elements are intended primarily for the information and guidance of the following parties which, it is considered, are in some way associated with either the design or the operation of the ship or, alternately, with the design, presentation or loading of cargo units including vehicles. They are:

.1   shipbuilders;

.2   shipowners;

.3   shipmasters;

.4   port authorities;

.5   shippers;

.6   forwarding agents;

.7   road hauliers;

.8   stevedores;

.9   cargo unit and vehicle manufacturers;

.10   insurers;

.11   railway operators; and

.12   packers of containers at inland depots.

2   General elements

2.1   It is of the utmost importance to ensure that:

.1   cargo units including vehicles intended for the carriage of cargo in sea transport are in sound structural condition and have an adequate number of securing points of sufficient strength so that they can be satisfactorily secured to the ship. Vehicles should, in addition, be provided with an effective braking system; and

.2   cargo units and vehicles are provided with an adequate number of securing points to enable the cargo to be adequately secured to the cargo unit or vehicle so as to withstand the forces, in particular the transverse forces, which may arise during the sea transport.

3   Elements to be considered by the shipowner and shipbuilder

3.1   The ship should be provided with an adequate number of securing points of sufficient strength, a sufficient number of items of cargo securing gear of sufficient strength and a Cargo Securing Manual. In considering the number and strength of the securing points, items of cargo securing gear and the preparation of the Cargo Securing Manual, the following elements should be taken into account:

.1   duration of the voyage;

.2   geographical area of the voyage;

.3   sea conditions which may be expected;

.4   size, design and characteristics of the ship;

.5   dynamic forces under adverse weather conditions;

.6   types of cargo units and vehicles to be carried;

.7   intended stowage pattern of the cargo units and vehicles; and

.8   weight of cargo units and vehicles

3.2   The Cargo Securing Manual should provide information on the characteristics of cargo securing items and their correct application.

3.3   Ship's mobile cargo handling equipment not fixed to the ship should be provided with adequate securing points.

4   Elements to be considered by the master

4.1   When accepting cargo units or vehicles for shipment and having taken into account the elements listed in paragraph 3.1 above, the master should be satisfied that:

.1   all decks intended for the stowage of cargo units including vehicles are, in so far as is practicable, free from oil and grease;

.2   cargo units including vehicles are in an apparent good order and condition suitable for sea transport, particularly with a view to their being secured;

.3   the ship has on board an adequate supply of cargo securing gear which is maintained in sound working condition;

.4   cargo units including vehicles are adequately stowed and secured to the ship; and

.5   where practicable, cargoes are adequately stowed on and secured to the cargo unit or vehicle.

4.2   In addition, cargo spaces should be regularly inspected to ensure that the cargo, cargo units and vehicles remain safely secured throughout the voyage.

5   Elements to be considered by the shipper, forwarding agents, road hauliers and stevedores (and, where appropriate, by the port authorities)

5.1   Shippers or any other party involved with presenting cargo units including vehicles for shipment should appreciate that such items can be subjected to forces of great magnitude, particularly in the transverse direction and especially in adverse weather conditions. Consequently, it is of importance that they should be constantly aware of this fact and that they ensure that:

.1   cargo units including vehicles are suitable for the intended sea transport;

.2   cargo units including vehicles are provided with adequate securing points for the securing of the cargo unit or vehicle to the ship and the cargo to the cargo unit or vehicle;

.3   the cargo in the cargo unit or vehicle is adequately stowed and secured to withstand the forces which may arise during sea transport; and

.4   in general the cargo unit or vehicle is clearly marked and provided with documentation to indicate its gross weight and any precautions which may have to be observed during sea transport.

Resolution A.581(14)

Adopted on 20 November 1985

GUIDELINES FOR SECURING ARRANGEMENTS FOR THE TRANSPORT OF ROAD VEHICLES ON RO-RO SHIPS

THE ASSEMBLY,

RECALLING Article 15(j) of the Convention on the International Maritime Organization concerning the functions of the Assembly in relation to regulations and guidelines concerning maritime safety,

RECALLING ALSO resolution A.489(XII) on safe stowage and securing of cargo units and other entities in ships other than cellular containerships and MSC/Circ.385 of 8 January 1985* containing the provisions to be included in a Cargo Securing Manual to be carried on board ships,

BEARING IN MIND resolution A.533(13) on elements to be taken into account when considering the safe stowage and securing of cargo units and vehicles in ships,

TAKING ACCOUNT of the revised IMO/ILO Guidelines for the Packing of Cargo in Freight Containers and Vehicles,

RECOGNIZING that the marine transport of road vehicles on ro-ro ships is increasing,

RECOGNIZING ALSO that a number of serious accidents have occurred because of inadequate securing arrangements on ships and road vehicles,

RECOGNIZING FURTHER the need for the Organization to establish guidelines for securing arrangements on board ro-ro ships and on road vehicles,

REALIZING that, given adequately designed ships and properly equipped road vehicles, lashings of sufficient strength will be capable of withstanding the forces imposed on them during the voyage,

REALIZING FURTHER that certain requirements for side guards, particularly those positioned very low on road vehicles, will obstruct the proper securing of the road vehicles on board ro-ro ships and that appropriate measures will have to be taken to satisfy both safety aspects,

BELIEVING that application of the guidelines will enhance safety in the transport of road vehicles on ro-ro ships and that this can be achieved on an international basis,

HAVING CONSIDERED the recommendation made by the Maritime Safety Committee at its fifty-first session,

1.   ADOPTS the Guidelines for Securing Arrangements for the Transport of Road Vehicles on Ro-Ro Ships set out in the annex to the present resolution;

2.   URGES Member Governments to implement these Guidelines at the earliest possible opportunity in respect of new ro-ro ships and new vehicles and, as far as practicable, in respect of existing vehicles which may be transported on ro-ro ships;

3.   REQUESTS the Secretary-General to bring these Guidelines to the attention of Member Governments and relevant international organizations responsible for safety in design and construction of ships and road vehicles for action as appropriate.

Annex[†]

GUIDELINES FOR SECURING ARRANGEMENTS FOR THE TRANSPORT OF ROAD VEHICLES ON RO-RO SHIPS

Preamble

In view of experience in the transport of road vehicles on ro-ro ships, it is recommended that these Guidelines for securing road vehicles on board such ships should be followed. Shipowners and shipyards, when designing and building ro-ro ships to which these Guidelines apply, should take sections 4 and 6 particularly into account. Manufacturers, owners and operators of road vehicles which may be transported on ro-ro ships should take sections 5 and 7 particularly into account.

---

* MSC/Circ. 385 has been replaced by MSC/Circ. 745 of 13 June 1996.

† The text of paragraphs 4.2.3 and 6.1 has been amended by MSC/Circ. 812 of 16 June 1997. Member Governments are invited to bring these amendments to the attention of all parties concerned, with a view to implementing them as soon as possible.

1   Scope

1.1   These Guidelines for securing and lashing road vehicles on board ro–ro ships outline in particular the securing arrangements on the ship and on the vehicles, and the securing methods to be used.

2   Application

2.1   These Guidelines apply to ro–ro ships which regularly carry road vehicles on either long or short international voyages in unsheltered waters. They concern:

    .1   road vehicles as defined in 3.2.1, 3.2.2, 3.2.3 and 3.2.5 with an authorized maximum total mass of vehicles and cargo of between 3.5 and 40 tonnes; and

    .2   articulated road trains as defined in 3.2.4 with a maximum total mass of not more than 45 tonnes, which can be carried on ro–ro ships.

2.2   These Guidelines do not apply to buses.

2.3   For road vehicles having characteristics outside the general parameters for road vehicles (particularly where the normal height of the centre of gravity is exceeded), the location and the number of securing points should be specially considered.

3   Definitions

3.1   *Ro–ro ship* means a ship which has one or more decks either closed or open, not normally subdivided in any way and generally running the entire length of the ship, in which goods (packaged or in bulk, in or on road vehicles (including road tank-vehicles), trailers, containers, pallets, demountable or portable tanks or in or on similar cargo transport units or other receptacles) can be loaded or unloaded, normally in a horizontal direction.

3.2   In these Guidelines the term *road vehicle** includes:

    .1   *Commercial vehicle,* which means a motor vehicle which, on account of its design and appointments, is used mainly for conveying goods. It may also be towing a trailer.

    .2   *Semi-trailer,* which means a trailer which is designed to be coupled to a semi-trailer towing vehicle and to impose a substantial part of its total mass on the towing vehicle.

    .3   *Road train,* which means the combination of a motor vehicle with one or more independent trailers connected by a draw-bar. (For the purpose of section 5 each element of a road train is considered a separate vehicle.)

    .4   *Articulated road train,* which means the combination of a semi-trailer towing vehicle with a semi-trailer.

    .5   *Combination of vehicles,* which means a motor vehicle coupled with one or more towed vehicles. (For the purpose of section 5 each element of a combination of vehicles is considered a separate vehicle.)

4   Securing points on ship's decks

4.1   The ship should carry a Cargo Securing Manual in accordance with resolution A.489(XII), containing the information listed and recommended in paragraph 10 of the annex to that resolution.

4.2   The decks of a ship intended for road vehicles as defined in 3.2 should be provided with securing points. The arrangement of securing points should be left to the discretion of the shipowner provided that for each road vehicle or element of a combination of road vehicles there is the following minimum arrangement of securing points:

    .1   The distance between securing points in the longitudinal direction should in general not exceed 2.5 m. However, there may be a need for the securing points in the forward and after parts of the ship to be more closely spaced than they are amidships.

    .2   The athwartships spacing of securing points should not be less than 2.8 m nor more than 3 m. However, there may be a need for the securing points in the forward and after parts of the ship to be more closely spaced than they are amidships.

    .3   The maximum securing load (MSL) of each securing point should be not less than 100 kN. If the securing point is designed to accommodate more than one lashing (y lashings), the MSL should be not less than $y \times 100$ kN.[†]

---

* Refer to ISO Standard no. 3833.
[†] This is the text of paragraph 4.2.3 as amended by MSC/Circ. 812 of 16 June 1997.

4.3   In ro–ro ships which only occasionally carry road vehicles, the spacing and strength of securing points should be such that the special considerations which may be necessary to stow and secure road vehicles safely are taken into account.

5   Securing points on road vehicles

5.1   Securing points on road vehicles should be designed for securing the road vehicles to the ship and should have an aperture capable of accepting only one lashing. The securing point and aperture should permit varying directions of the lashing to the ship's deck.*

5.2   The same number of securing points (not less than two and not more than six) should be provided on each side of the road vehicle in accordance with the provisions of 5.3.

5.3   Subject to the provisions of notes 1, 2 and 3 hereunder, the minimum number and minimum strength of securing points should be in accordance with the following table:

Gross vehicle mass (GVM) (tonnes)	Minimum number of securing points on each side of the road vehicle	Minimum strength without permanent deformation of each securing point as fitted (kN)
$3.5\,t \leqslant GVM \leqslant 20\,t$	2	$\dfrac{GVM \times 10 \times 1.2}{n}$
$20\,t < GVM \leqslant 30\,t$	3	where n is the total number of securing
$30\,t < GVM \leqslant 40\,t$	4	points on each side of the road vehicle.

Note 1:   For road trains, the table applies to each component, i.e. to the motor vehicle and each trailer, respectively.

Note 2:   Semi-trailer towing vehicles are excluded from the table above. They should be provided with two securing points at the front of the vehicle, the strength of which should be sufficient to prevent lateral movement of the front of the vehicle. A towing coupling at the front may replace the two securing points.

Note 3:   If the towing coupling is used for securing vehicles other than semi-trailer towing vehicles, this should not replace or be substituted for the above-mentioned minimum number and strength of securing points on each side of the vehicle.

5.4   Each securing point on the vehicle should be marked in a clearly visible colour.

5.5   Securing points on vehicles should be so located as to ensure effective restraint of the vehicle by the lashings.

5.6   Securing points should be capable of transferring the forces from the lashings to the chassis of the road vehicle and should never be fitted to bumpers or axles unless these are specially constructed and the forces are transmitted directly to the chassis.

5.7   Securing points should be so located that lashings can be readily and safely attached, particularly where side-guards are fitted to the vehicle.

5.8   The internal free passage of each securing point's aperture should be not less than 80 mm but the aperture need not be circular in shape.

5.9   Equivalent or superior securing arrangements may be considered for vehicles for which the provisions of table 5.3 are unsuitable.

6   Lashings

6.1   The maximum securing load (MSL) of lashings should not be less than 100 kN, and they should be made of material having suitable elongation characteristics.†

6.2   Lashings should be so designed and attached that, provided there is safe access, it is possible to tighten them if they become slack. Where practicable and necessary, the lashings should be examined at regular intervals during the voyage and tightened as necessary.

---

* If more than one aperture is provided at a securing point, each aperture should have the strength for the securing point shown in the table in 5.3.

† This is the text of paragraph 6.1 as amended by MSC/Circ. 812 of 16 June 1997.

6.3   Lashings should be attached to the securing points with hooks or other devices so designed that they cannot disengage from the aperture of the securing point if the lashing slackens during the voyage.

6.4   Only one lashing should be attached to any one aperture of the securing point on the vehicle.

6.5   Lashings should only be attached to the securing points provided for that purpose.

6.6   Lashings should be attached to the securing points on the vehicle in such a way that the angle between the lashing and the horizontal and vertical planes lies preferably between 30° and 60°.

6.7   Bearing in mind the characteristics of the ship and the weather conditions expected on the intended voyage, the master should decide on the number of securing points and lashings to be used for each voyage.

6.8   Where there is doubt that a road vehicle complies with the provisions of table 5.3, the master may, at his discretion, load the vehicle on board, taking into account the apparent condition of the vehicle, the weather and sea conditions expected on the intended voyage and all other circumstances.

7   Stowage

7.1   Depending on the area of operation, the predominant weather conditions and the characteristics of the ship, road vehicles should be stowed so that the chassis are kept as static as possible by not allowing free play in the suspension of the vehicles. This can be done, for example, by compressing the springs by tightly securing the vehicle to the deck, by jacking up the chassis prior to securing the vehicle or by releasing the air pressure on compressed air suspension systems.

7.2   Taking into account the conditions referred to in 7.1 and the fact that compressed air suspension systems may lose air, the air pressure should be released on every vehicle fitted with such a system if the voyage is of more than 24 hours' duration. If practicable, the air pressure should be released also on voyages of a shorter duration. If the air pressure is not released, the vehicle should be jacked up to prevent any slackening of the lashings resulting from any air leakage from the system during the voyage.

7.3   Where jacks are used on a vehicle, the chassis should be strengthened in way of the jacking-up points and the position of the jacking-up points should be clearly marked.

7.4   Special consideration should be given to the securing of road vehicles stowed in positions where they may be exposed to additional forces. Where vehicles are stowed athwartship, special consideration should be given to the forces which may arise from such stowage.

7.5   Wheels should be chocked to provide additional security in adverse conditions.

7.6   Vehicles with diesel engines should not be left in gear during the voyage.

7.7   Vehicles designed to transport loads likely to have an adverse effect on their stability, such as hanging meat, should have integrated in their design a means of neutralizing the suspension system.

7.8   Stowage should be arranged in accordance with the following:

    .1   The parking brakes of each vehicle or of each element of a combination of vehicles should be applied and locked.

    .2   Semi-trailers, by the nature of their design, should not be supported on their landing legs during sea transport unless the landing legs are specially designed for that purpose and so marked. An uncoupled semi-trailer should be supported by a trestle or similar device placed in the immediate area of the drawplate so that the connection of the fifth wheel to the kingpin is not restricted. Semi-trailer designers should consider the space and the reinforcements required and the selected areas should be clearly marked.

Resolution A.852(20)

Adopted on 27 November 1997

GUIDELINES FOR A STRUCTURE OF AN INTEGRATED SYSTEM OF CONTINGENCY PLANNING FOR SHIPBOARD EMERGENCIES

THE ASSEMBLY,

RECALLING Article 15(j) of the Convention on the International Maritime Organization concerning the functions of the Assembly in relation to regulations and guidelines concerning maritime safety and the prevention and control of marine pollution from ships,

RECALLING ALSO that the 1994 International Conference of Contracting Governments to the International Convention for the Safety of Life at Sea (SOLAS), 1974, adopted amendments to that Convention introducing, *inter alia*, a new chapter IX on Management for the Safe Operation of Ships, which makes compliance with the International Management Code for the Safe Operation of Ships and for Pollution Prevention (International Safety Management (ISM) Code) mandatory,

BEING AWARE that shipboard emergency plans addressing different categories of emergencies are required under the provisions of the 1974 SOLAS Convention, as amended, and the International Convention for the Prevention of Pollution from Ships, 1973, as modified by the Protocol of 1978 relating thereto, as amended,

BEING CONCERNED that the presence on board ships of different and non-harmonized emergency plans may be counter-productive in case of an emergency,

RECOGNIZING that many ships already make use of comprehensive and effective emergency plans, such as the Shipboard Oil Pollution Emergency Plan (SOPEP),

CONSCIOUS of the need that human element aspects are borne in mind when rules and recommendations affecting shipboard operations are considered for adoption,

WISHING to assist shipowners, ship operators and other parties concerned in, where this has not yet been done, transposing the provisions regulating emergency plans into a coherent contingency regime,

HAVING CONSIDERED the recommendations made by the Maritime Safety Committee at its sixty-seventh session and by the Marine Environment Protection Committee at its thirty-ninth session,

1.   ADOPTS the Guidelines for a Structure of an Integrated System of Contingency Planning for Shipboard Emergencies, set out in the annex to the present resolution;

2.   INVITES Governments, in the interests of uniformity, to accept the aforementioned structure as being in conformity with the provisions for the development of the shipboard emergency plans required by various instruments adopted by the Organization;

3.   INVITES Governments to refer to these Guidelines when preparing appropriate national legislation;

4.   REQUESTS the Maritime Safety Committee and the Marine Environment Protection Committee to keep the Guidelines under review and amend them as necessary in the light of experience gained.

Annex
GUIDELINES FOR A STRUCTURE OF AN INTEGRATED SYSTEM
OF CONTINGENCY PLANNING FOR SHIPBOARD EMERGENCIES

Contents

Preface

These Guidelines, prepared by the Maritime Safety Committee (MSC) of the International Maritime Organization (IMO), contain guidance to assist in the preparation of an integrated system of contingency planning for shipboard emergencies. It is intended to be used for the preparation and use of a module structure of an integrated system of shipboard emergency plans.

The high number of non-harmonized shipboard contingency plans justifies the development of an integrated system and the harmonization of the structure of contingency plans.

Shipboard emergency preparedness is required under chapter 8 of the ISM Code referred to in chapter IX of the SOLAS Convention, as amended, under chapter III, regulation 24-4 of the SOLAS Convention, as adopted at the SOLAS Conference November 1995, and under MARPOL 73/78, Annex I, regulation 26.

To implement the SOLAS and MARPOL regulations, there must be shipboard procedures and instructions. These Guidelines provide a framework for formulating procedures for the effective response to emergency situations identified by the company and shipboard personnel.

In this context the main objectives of these Guidelines are:

- to assist companies in translating the requirements of the regulations into action by making use of the structure of the integrated system;
- to integrate relevant shipboard emergency situations into such a system;

- to assist in the development of harmonized contingency plans which will enhance their acceptance by shipboard personnel and their proper use in an emergency situation;

- to encourage Governments, in the interests of uniformity, to accept the structure of the integrated system as being in conformity with the provisions for development of shipboard contingency plans as required by various IMO instruments, and to refer to these Guidelines when preparing appropriate national legislation.

1 General remarks

1.1 The ISM Code establishes an international standard for the safe management and operation of ships by defining elements which must be taken into account for the organization of company management in relation to ship safety and pollution prevention. Since emergencies, as well as cargo spillage, cannot be entirely controlled either through design or through normal operational procedures, emergency preparedness and pollution prevention should form part of the company's ship safety management. For this purpose, every company is required by the ISM Code to develop, implement and maintain a Safety Management System (SMS).

1.2 Within this SMS, procedures for describing and responding to potential shipboard emergency situations are required.

1.3 If the preparation of response actions for the many possible varying types of emergency situations which may occur is formulated on the basis of a complete and detailed case-by-case consideration, a great deal of duplication will result.

1.4 To avoid duplication, shipboard contingency plans must differentiate between "initial actions" and the major response effort involving "subsequent response", depending on the emergency situation and the type of ship.

1.5 A two-tier course of action provides the basis for a modular approach, which can avoid unnecessary duplication.

1.6 It is recommended that a uniform and integrated system of shipboard emergency plans should be treated as part of the International Safety Management (ISM) Code, forming a fundamental part of the company's individual Safety Management System (SMS).

1.7 An illustration of how such a structure of a uniform and integrated system of shipboard emergency plans with its different modules can be incorporated into an individual SMS is shown in appendix 1.

2 Integrated system of contingency plans for shipboard emergencies

2.1 *Scope*

2.1.1 The integrated system of shipboard emergency plans (hereinafter referred to as the "system") should provide a framework for the many individual contingency plans (hereinafter referred to as the "plans"), tailored for a variety of potential emergencies, for a uniform and modular designed structure.

2.1.2 Use of a modular designed structure will provide a quickly visible and logically sequenced source of information and priorities, which can reduce error and oversight during emergency situations.

2.2 *Structure of the system*

2.2.1 The structure of the system comprises the following six modules, the titles of which are:

- Module I : Introduction
- Module II : Provisions
- Module III : Planning, preparedness and training
- Module IV: Response actions
- Module V : Reporting procedures
- Module VI: Annex(es).

An example of the arrangement of these modules is shown in appendix 2.

2.2.2 Each module should contain concise information to provide guidance and to ensure that all appropriate and relevant factors and aspects, through the various actions and decisions during an emergency response, are taken into account.

2.3 *Concept of the system*

2.3.1 The system is intended as a tool for integrating the many different plans into a uniform and modular structured frame. The broad spectrum of the many required plans which may be developed by a company will result in the duplication of some elements (e.g. reporting) of these plans. Such duplication can be avoided by using the modular structure of the system referred to in 2.2.1.

2.3.2 Although the initial action taken in any emergency will depend upon the nature and extent of the incident, there are some immediate actions which should always be taken – the so-called "initial actions" (see appendix 4). Therefore, a distinction within the plans between "initial actions" and "subsequent response", which depends on variables like the ship's cargo, type of the ship, etc., will help to assist shipboard personnel in dealing with unexpected emergencies and will ensure that the necessary actions are taken in a priority order.

2.3.3 "Subsequent response" is the implementation of the procedures applicable to the emergency.

3   System modules

3.1   *General principles*

3.1.1 As a starting point for the preparation of the system, appendix 3 provides guidance and a quick overview concerning the kind of information which may be inserted into the individual system modules.

3.1.2 Above all, the system should be developed in a user-friendly way. This will enhance its acceptance by shipboard personnel.

3.1.3 For the system as well as the associated plans to be effective it must be carefully tailored to the individual company and ship. When doing this, differences in ship type, construction, cargo, equipment, manning and route have to be taken into account.

3.2   *Details of the individual modules*

3.2.1   Module I: **Introduction**

3.2.1.1   The system should contain a module entitled "Introduction".

3.2.1.2   The content of this module should provide guidance and an overview of the subject-matter.

3.2.1.3   The following is an example of an introductory text:

INTRODUCTION

1   The system is intended to prepare shipboard personnel for an effective response to an emergency at sea.
2   The prime objective of the system is to provide guidance to shipboard personnel with respect to the steps to be taken when an emergency has occurred or is likely to occur. Of equal benefit is the experience of those involved in developing the plan.
3   The purpose of the system is to integrate contingency plans for shipboard emergency situations and to avoid the development of different, non-harmonized and unstructured plans which would hamper their acceptance by shipboard personnel and their proper use in an emergency situation. Therefore, the system and its integrated plans should be structured and formatted in their layout and content in a consistent manner.
4   The aim of the system is to ensure the most timely and adequate response to emergencies of varied size and nature, and to remove any threat of serious escalation of the situation. Additionally the system provides a structure to prevent critical steps from being overlooked.
5   The system and associated plans should be seen as dynamic, and should be reviewed after implementation and improved through the sharing of experience, ideas and feedback.
6   It should be kept in mind that there could be problems in communication due to differing language or culture of the shipboard personnel. The system, as well as the integrated plans, will be documents used on board by the master, officers and relevant crew members of the ship, and they must be available in the working language of the crew. Any change in these personnel, which results in a change in the crew's working language, requires plans to be issued in the new language. The module should provide information to this effect.
7   The system is to be seen as a tool for implementing the requirements of chapter 8 of the International Safety Management (ISM) Code, or similar regulations in other IMO instruments,* in a practical manner.

* Reference is made to SOLAS 74, chapter III, regulation 24-4, and to MARPOL 73/78, Annex I, regulation 26.

3.2.2   Module II: **Provisions**

3.2.2.1   This module should contain information and explanations on how the system could be developed on the basis of suggestions for improvement made by the individual company and shipboard personnel.

3.2.2.2   The primary objective of shipboard emergency prevention, preparedness and response activities should be to develop and implement an efficient and effective system which will minimize the risks to human life, the marine environment and property, with a continuous effort towards improvement.

3.2.2.3   To achieve this objective, there is a need for co-ordination of, and consistency in, safety procedures between the company and its ships. Therefore, the module should require that company shore-based and shipboard contingency planning and response are consistent and appropriately linked.

3.2.2.4   Safety involves "top-down" and "bottom-up" commitment to active development and application of safety procedures and practices by all persons both ashore and afloat, including management.

3.2.2.5   Free and open communication when evaluating emergency procedures, taking into consideration accidents and near misses when using this system, should be pursued, with the objective of improving accident prevention, preparedness and response aboard ships. The module should take care of this recommendation by providing information for the implementation of an error-reduction strategy with appropriate feedback and procedures for modification of plans.

3.2.2.6   In summary, the module should inform the system user about the most important requirements with which, at a minimum, the plans should comply. The following main elements should be addressed in the module:

- procedures to be followed when reporting an emergency;
- procedures for identifying, describing and responding to potential emergency shipboard situations;
- programmes/activities for the maintenance of the system and associated plans.

3.2.3   Module III: **Planning, preparedness and training**

3.2.3.1   This module should provide for emergency training and education of shipboard personnel with a view to developing general awareness and understanding of actions to be taken in the event of an emergency.

3.2.3.2   The system and plans will be of little value if the personnel who are to use them are not made familiar with them. Module III should therefore provide practical information which enables each key member of the shipboard personnel to know in advance what their duties and responsibilities are and to whom they are to report under the plans.

3.2.3.3   Successful management of an emergency or marine crisis situation depends on the ability of the shipboard personnel, the company, and external emergency co-ordinating authorities to muster sufficient resources in the right positions quickly.

3.2.3.4   An important goal of planning, preparedness and training programmes should be to increase awareness of safety and environmental issues.

3.2.3.5   Training and education should be at regular intervals and, in particular, be provided to shipboard personnel transferred to new assignments.

3.2.3.6   Records of all emergency drills and exercises conducted ashore and on board should be maintained and be available for verification. The drills and exercises should be evaluated as an aid to determining the effectiveness of documented procedures and identifying system improvements.

3.2.3.7   When developing plans for drills and exercises, a distinction should be made between full-scale drills involving all of the parties that may be involved in a major incident and exercises limited to the ship and/or the company.

3.2.3.8   Feedback is essential for refining emergency response plans and emergency preparedness based on the lessons learned from previous exercises or real emergencies, and provides an avenue for continuous improvement. Feedback should ensure that the company, as well as the ship, is prepared to respond to shipboard emergencies (see summarizing flow-diagram in appendix 1).

3.2.3.9   In conclusion, the module should, as a minimum, provide information on the procedures, programmes or activities developed in order to:

- familiarize shipboard personnel with the provisions of the system and plans;
- train and educate shipboard personnel transferred to new assignments about the system and plans;
- schedule regular drills and exercises to prepare shipboard personnel to deal with potential shipboard emergency situations;
- co-ordinate the shipboard personnel and the company's actions effectively, and include and take note of the aid which could be provided by external emergency co-ordinating authorities;
- prepare a workable feedback system.

3.2.4   Module IV: **Response actions**

This module should provide guidance for shipboard personnel in an emergency when the ship is under way, berthed, moored, at anchor, in port or in dry dock.

3.2.4.1   In an emergency, the best course of action to protect the personnel, ship, marine environment and cargo requires careful consideration and prior planning. Standards for shipboard procedures to protect personnel, stabilize conditions, and minimize environmental damage when an incident occurs should therefore be developed.

3.2.4.2   In this context, reference is made to the guidelines already developed by the Organization,* which contain information to provide a starting point and to assist personnel in the preparation of plans for individual ships.

3.2.4.3   The variety of plans to be incorporated into the system should be simple documents which outline procedures different from those used for daily routine operations. With normal operational procedures very difficult problems can be handled, but an emergency situation, whether on the ship at sea or in a port, can extend those involved beyond their normal capabilities.

3.2.4.4   In order to keep the plans held by ship and shore identical, and to reduce possible confusion in an emergency as to who is responsible for which action, plans should make clear whether the action should be taken by shipboard personnel or shoreside personnel.

3.2.4.5   Taking these particulars into consideration, the module "Response actions" should comprise main groupings of emergency shipboard situations.

3.2.4.6   Potential emergency situations should be identified in the plans, including, but not limited to, the following main groups of emergency:

   .1   Fire
   .2   Damage to the ship
   .3   Pollution
   .4   Unlawful acts threatening the safety of the ship and the security of its passengers and crew
   .5   Personnel accidents
   .6   Cargo-related accidents
   .7   Emergency assistance to other ships.

In order to give the company the necessary flexibility for identifying, describing and responding to further shipboard emergency situations, more specific types of emergency should be included in the main groups.

3.2.4.7   The majority of shipboard emergencies can be classified under the above-mentioned main groups. For example, the main group "Damage to ship" can be subdivided to cover other shipboard emergencies, which may require very different responses, such as:

   •   collision
   •   grounding/stranding
   •   heavy weather damage
   •   hull/structural failure, etc.

The detailed response actions should be formulated so as to set in motion the necessary steps to limit the consequence of the emergency and the escalation of damage following, for example, collision or grounding.

3.2.4.8   In all cases, priority should be given to actions which protect life, the marine environment and property, in that order. This means that "initial actions" which are common for all ships, regardless of their type and the cargoes carried, should be fully taken into account when formulating "subsequent response" procedures.

3.2.4.9   The planning of subsequent response actions should include information relating to the individual ship and its cargo, and provide advice and data to assist the shipboard personnel. Examples of such information are listed below:

   .1   Information on:
      •   the number of persons aboard;
      •   the cargo carried (e.g. dangerous goods, etc.);
   .2   Steps to initiate external response:
      •   search and rescue co-ordination;
      •   buoyancy, strength and stability calculations;
      •   engagement of salvors/rescue towage;
      •   lightering capacity;
      •   external clean-up resources;
   .3   Ship drift characteristics
   .4   General information:
      •   co-operation with national and port authorities;
      •   public relations.

---

* Reference is made to Guidelines for the development of Shipboard Oil Pollution Emergency Plans (see resolution MEPC.54(32) as amended by resolution MEPC.86(44)). Reference is also made to Guidelines for the development of Shipboard Marine Pollution Emergency Plans for Oil and/or Noxious Liquid Substances (see resolution MEPC.85(44)).

3.2.4.10   Although shipboard personnel should be familiar with the plan, ease of reference is an important element in compiling and using an effective plan. Allowance must be made for quick and easy access to essential information under stressful conditions.

Appendices 3 and 4 show a detailed picture of the sequence of priorities for "initial actions" in an emergency situation and their link with the "subsequent response".

3.2.4.11   In summary, the module should guide those responsible for developing the system on what should be included in emergency plans, namely:

– co-ordination of response efforts;

– response procedures for the entire spectrum of possible accident scenarios, including methods that protect life, the marine environment and property;

– the person or persons identified by title or name as being in charge of all response activities;

– the communication lines used for ready contact with external response experts;

– information concerning the availability and location of response equipment;

– reporting and communication procedures on board ship.

A seven-step approach flow-chart for emergency plan(s) implementation is presented on page 273.

3.2.5   Module V: **Reporting procedures**

A ship involved in an emergency situation, or in a marine pollution incident, will have to communicate with the appropriate ship interest contacts and coastal State or port contacts. Therefore the system must specify in appropriate detail the procedures for making the initial report to the parties concerned. This module should take care of the following:

3.2.5.1   Every effort should be made to assure that information regarding:

– ship interest contacts;

– coastal State contacts; and

– port contacts

for reporting emergencies are part of the system and are regularly updated.

3.2.5.2   The establishment and maintenance of rapid and reliable 24-hour communication lines between the ship in danger and emergency control centre(s), company's main office and national authorities (RCC, points of contact) is important.

3.2.5.3   Those managing response operations on board and services assisting ashore should keep each other mutually informed of the situation.

3.2.5.4   Details such as telephone, telex and telefax numbers must be routinely updated to take account of personnel changes. Clear guidance should also be provided regarding the preferred means of communication.

3.2.5.5   In this context, reference is made to the Organization's guidelines* and other national specific plans which give sufficient guidance on the following reporting activities necessary:

.1   when to report;

.2   how to report;

.3   whom to contact;

.4   what to report.

3.2.6   Module VI: **Annex(es)**

3.2.6.1   In addition to the information required to respond successfully to an emergency situation, other requirements that will enhance the ability of shipboard personnel to locate and follow up operative part 5 of the plan may be required.

4   Example format for a procedure of a selected emergency situation

An example format of a procedure for a selected emergency situation referred to in 3.2.4 is shown on pages 274 to 278.

---

* Reference is also made to Guidelines for the development of Shipboard Oil Pollution Emergency Plans (see resolution MEPC.54(32) as amended by resolution MEPC.86(44)), and to General principles for ship reporting system and ship reporting requirements, including guidelines for reporting incidents involving dangerous goods, harmful substances and/or marine pollutants (see resolution A.851(20)).

Emergency plan(s) implementation flow-chart

This flow-chart outlines the step-wise approach to carrying out the emergency plan(s) implementation. It indicates steps or objectives to be achieved rather than specific procedures to be followed. Based on experience, a seven-step approach to implementing the plan(s) can be set out which leads to a useful and effective integrated emergency response plan.

STEP 1

Evaluate the risks and hazards which may result in different emergency situations
(Possible events should be identified and their probability of occurrence and consequences must be addressed to set priorities for planning)

↓

STEP 2

Identify the required response tasks
(This step requires a thorough definition of actions which must be taken in an emergency)

↓

STEP 3

Identify the shipboard emergency response participants and establish their roles, resources and communication lines
(There is a limited range of potential participants in emergency response aboard; it is important to identify them early)

↓

STEP 4

Make changes necessary to improve existing plans and integrate them into the system
(Integrating all existing plans into one plan will reveal problems with overlapping activities and complicated interfaces)

↓

STEP 5

Prepare final plan(s) and obtain identity with both the shoreside and shipboard plan(s)
(Once agreement on the integrated plan has been reached, a final plan should be documented out to be kept ready for updating in accordance with the experiences gained under steps 6 and 7)

STEP 6

Educate the emergency response participants about the integrated system and plan(s) and ensure that all emergency responders are trained
(It is important that emergency responders are well trained)

STEP 7

Establish procedures for periodic testing, review and updating of the plan(s)
(Emergency responders should test the plan on a regular basis. Any deficiencies should then be corrected in the plan and the training programme)

MODULE IV

Response actions

Fire	Damage to the ship	Pollution	Unlawful acts threatening .... and crew	Personnel accidents	Cargo-related accidents	Emergency assistance to other ships

▶

Emergency Group: **Fire**

Doc. No.: ....   Page 1 of 4

Issue date: ....   Revision date: ....

1. Purpose and scope

The following procedure defines modes of actions/activities and measures to be taken in case of a **Fire** aboard the vessel. This procedure is a guide but under no circumstances restricts the master's discretion.

2. Responsibilities

The master is responsible for the organizational prerequisites for **Fire** emergency handling and for the availability and immediate use of the fire-fighting systems and safety equipment available but should delegate the various tasks to suitable qualified officers.

3. Measures to be taken

→ **"Initial actions"**

3.1 Measures by the person who observes the fire first

- Activate nearest fire alarm
-
-
-   *[to be developed by the company]*

3.2 Measures by the navigational officer of the watch

- Activate general alarm
- Call master
-
-
-
-   *[to be developed by the company]*

MODULE IV: Response actions

Emergency Group: **Fire**

Doc. No.: ....   Page 2 of 4

Issue date: ....   Revision date: ....

3.3 Measures by the master

- Introduce organized fire-fighting activities
- Keep fire-fighting system(s) – fixed and mobile – ready

[to be developed by the company]

- Make analysis of situation; consider priority of measures - →
- Start/continue fire-fighting measures (activate fire-fighting system(s) available)

- Monitor progress of fire-fighting measures
- Collect additional information - - - - - - - - - - - - - ▼

- Prepare for transmission of distress call/situation report (use prepared standardized format)
- Prepare for record keeping

Follow-up actions

- Prepare for bunker/ballast tank operations (if necessary)
- Call for external response (if necessary)

- Check necessity of abandoning vessel
- Disembark passengers (if necessary)

MODULE VI	
Annex(es)	
• Plans, diagrams	
• Cargo information	
•	
•	

MODULE V
Reporting
Procedures

MODULE IV: Response actions

Emergency Group: **Fire**

Doc. No.: ....
Issue date: ....

Page 3 of 4
Revision date: ....

3.3 **Measures by the master** (continuation)

- Assess (structural) damage to vessel and/or cargo

- Check vessel's seaworthiness, buoyancy, stability, trim, list, etc.
- Observe weather forecasts
- Check measures against cargo-associated or other hazards caused by fire
  (spillage of marine pollutants, released gases, cargo securing, oil spillages, etc.)

MODULE VI
Annex(es)
• Plans, diagrams
• Cargo information
• ....
• ....

MODULE V
Reporting Procedures

Emergency Group Pollution
e.g. **SOPEP**

- Start taking of evidence
- Keep fire watch at fire location
- Restore normal ship routine/operation
- Make used fire-fighting equipment operational
- Transmit final report

END

MODULE IV: Response actions

Emergency Group: **Fire**

Doc. No.: ....

Issue date: ....

Page 4 of 4

Revision date: ....

4. **Additional measures in case of fire aboard in port**

- Inform harbour/shoreside fire brigade → **MODULE V** — Reporting Procedures
- hand over fire control plans to harbour/shoreside fire brigade → **MODULE V** — Reporting Procedures
- inform agency/owner

- Keep international shore connection ready
- Check completeness of crew/passengers/guests, etc. → **MODULE VI** — Annex(es)
- Inform fire brigade about hazardous/dangerous goods

5. **Non-conformity report**

All non-conformities/deficiencies becoming aware by the master, officers and responsible crew members in connection with fire-fighting measures should be collected, recorded and sent to the company/designated person(s) or other nominated person(s) as soon as possible → **MODULE II** — Provisions

MODULE V
Reporting procedures

Emergency Group: **Fire**

1. The master is obliged to report details and to inform all interested parties about the **Fire** emergency and the actions taken so far by means of the fastest telecommunication channels available.

2. In case of a **Fire** the following reporting procedures are recommended:

2.1 **Alert** by radiocommunication ships in the vicinity;

2.2 If the ship stays in or is near port refer to

- coastal State contact list
- port contact list

for assistance;

2.3 **Notify** all relevant ship interest contacts who are to be advised in an emergency (reference is made to ship interest contact list)

Appendix 1

Incorporation of an integrated system of shipboard emergency plans in the Company's individual Safety Management System (SMS) as required by the ISM Code

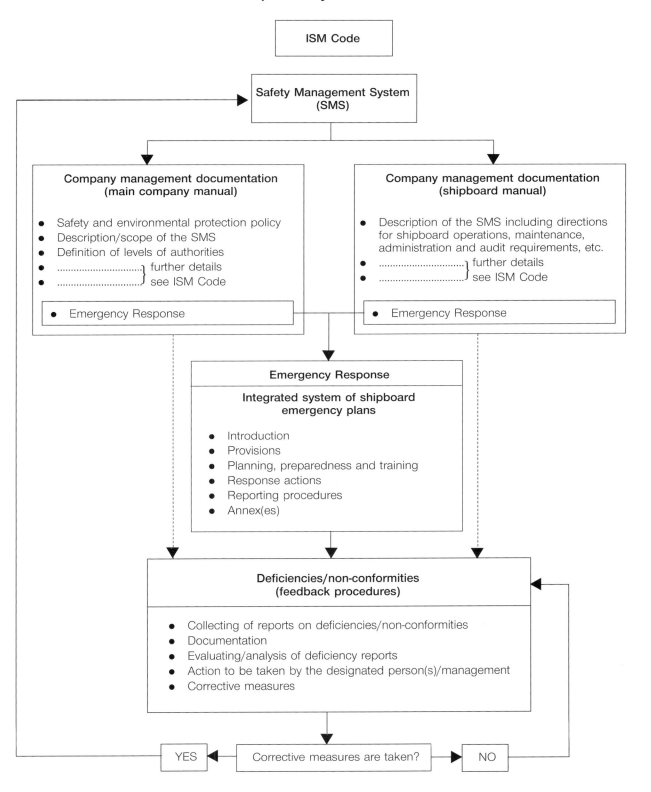

Appendix 2

The module structure of an integrated system for shipboard emergency plans

---

Module I – Introduction
- Introduction text

Module II – Provisions
- Basic information
- Maintenance of the system and associated plans
- Consistency between the system and associated plans/feedback system

---

Module III – Planning, preparedness and training
- Provisions and information for emergency training and education
- Familiarization with the shipboard and shoreside system associated plans
- Responsibilities/communication lines established with all parties involved
- Information of external co-ordinating authorities/provision for regular drills

---

Module IV – Response actions

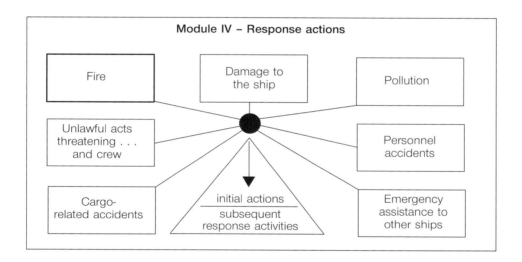

Module V – Reporting procedures
- When to report
- How to report
- Whom to contact
- What to report

Module VI – Annex(es)
- Plans and diagrams concerning details of the ship's general arrangement
- Bunker and ballast information
- Additional documents (e.g. list of contact points)
- Industry guidelines
- Cargo information, etc.

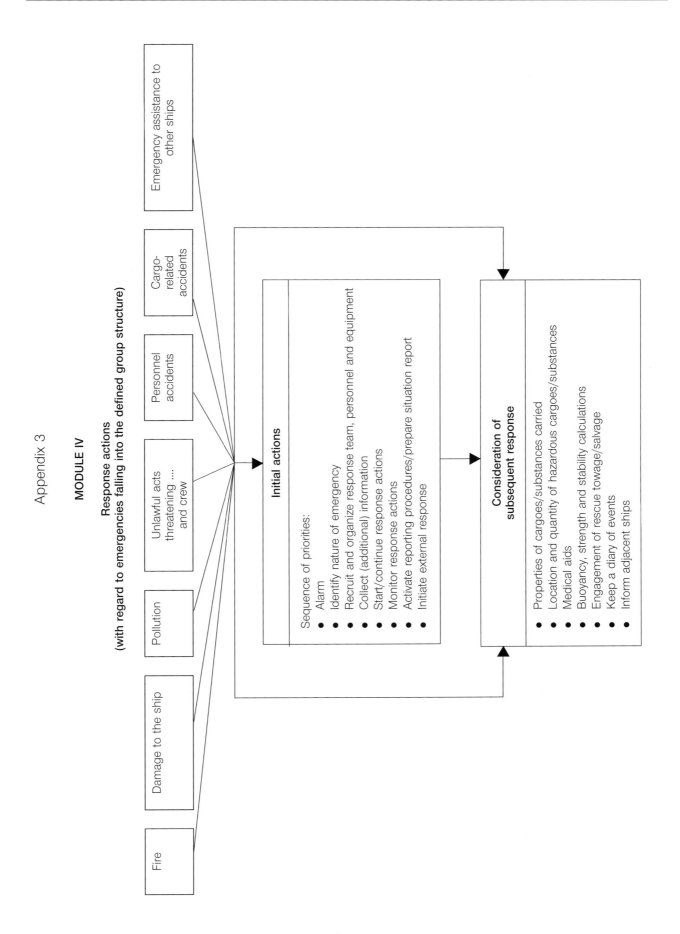

Appendix 3

MODULE IV

Response actions
(with regard to emergencies falling into the defined group structure)

Fire — Damage to the ship — Pollution — Unlawful acts threatening .... and crew — Personnel accidents — Cargo-related accidents — Emergency assistance to other ships

Initial actions

Sequence of priorities:
- Alarm
- Identify nature of emergency
- Recruit and organize response team, personnel and equipment
- Collect (additional) information
- Start/continue response actions
- Monitor response actions
- Activate reporting procedures/prepare situation report
- Initiate external response

Consideration of subsequent response

- Properties of cargoes/substances carried
- Location and quantity of hazardous cargoes/substances
- Medical aids
- Buoyancy, strength and stability calculations
- Engagement of rescue towage/salvage
- Keep a diary of events
- Inform adjacent ships

Appendix 4

MODULE IV: Response actions

Sequence of priorities flow-chart

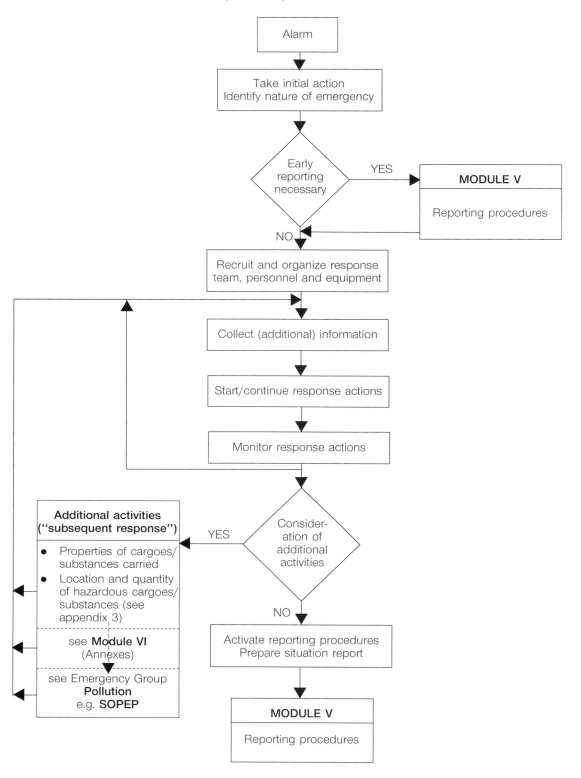

Resolution A.854(20)

Adopted on 27 November 1997

GUIDELINES FOR DEVELOPING SHIPBOARD EMERGENCY PLANS FOR SHIPS CARRYING MATERIALS SUBJECT TO THE INF CODE

THE ASSEMBLY,

RECALLING Article 15(j) of the Convention of the International Maritime Organization concerning the function of this Assembly in relation to regulations and guidelines concerning maritime safety, the prevention and control of marine pollution from ships, and other matters concerning the effect of shipping on the marine environment,

HAVING ADOPTED, by resolution A.853(20), amendments to the INF Code on shipboard emergency plans and notification in the event of an incident involving materials subject to the Code,

RECOGNIZING the need to have a consistent approach to the development of shipboard emergency plans,

HAVING CONSIDERED the recommendations made by the MSC at its sixty-eighth session and by the MEPC at its thirty-ninth session and fortieth session:

1.   ADOPTS the Guidelines for Developing Shipboard Emergency Plans for Ships Carrying Materials subject to the INF Code set out at annex to this resolution; and

2.   URGES Governments, in implementing the provisions referring to this subject in the INF Code, to use the Guidelines set out at annex to this resolution.

Annex

GUIDELINES FOR DEVELOPING SHIPBOARD EMERGENCY PLANS FOR SHIPS CARRYING MATERIALS SUBJECT TO THE INF CODE

Foreword

These Guidelines, prepared by the Marine Environment Protection Committee of the International Maritime Organization (IMO), contain information for the preparation of Shipboard Emergency Plans for Ships Carrying Materials Subject to the IMO Code for the Safe Carriage of Irradiated Nuclear Fuel, Plutonium, and High-Level Radioactive Wastes in Flasks on board Ships (INF Code). These Guidelines were developed as part of the work assigned by the Assembly to the Committees regarding the review and amendment of the INF Code.

The main objectives of these Guidelines are:

–   to assist shipowners in preparing comprehensive shipboard emergency plans for ships carrying INF Code materials; and

–   to assist in responding to shipboard emergencies involving INF Code materials and in providing information in accordance with international law to authorities involved in assisting or handling incidents at sea involving INF Code materials.

In the interest of uniformity, Governments are requested to refer to these Guidelines when preparing appropriate national regulations. While in port or an offshore terminal, the carriage of a shipboard emergency plan for ships carrying materials subject to the INF Code should be subject to inspection by duly authorized officers.

The type of emergency planning and preparedness that is needed for responding to transport incidents involving INF Code materials is, to some extent, similar to that required for responding to transport accidents involving non-radioactive hazardous or noxious substances. Accordingly, emergency response organizations and personnel may apply the concepts

Appendix

used to respond to incidents involving other types of hazardous or noxious substances, employing special knowledge, skills and equipment to deal effectively with the wide range of possible consequences of incidents involving INF Code materials.

In the case where a ship is required to have a shipboard emergency plan by other international instruments, the plan provided for in these Guidelines may be combined with such other plans. In this case, the title of such a combined plan should be "Shipboard Marine Emergency Plan".

1   Introduction

1.1   These Guidelines have been developed to assist in the preparation of Shipboard Emergency Plans for Ships carrying Materials Subject to the INF Code ("Plan(s)"). These Guidelines were developed as part of the work assigned by the Assembly regarding the review and amendment of the INF Code, particularly in view of paragraph 27* of the Code. The Plan (s) should be approved in accordance with the Code.

Definitions for the purpose of these Guidelines

1.2   *Incident* means any occurrence or series of occurrences, including loss of container integrity, having the same origin which results or may result in a release, or probable cargo release of INF Code materials.

1.3   *Shipboard Emergency Plan* or *Plan* means a document that is tailored to a particular ship carrying INF Code materials and contains the procedures to be followed to ensure shipboard preparedness for responding to emergencies.

1.4   *Release* means the escape of INF Code material from its containment system or the loss of an INF Code package.

1.5   The Guidelines are comprised of three sections:

   .1   *Introduction:* This section provides a general overview of the subject matter and introduces the reader to the basic concept of the Guidelines and the Plans that are expected to be developed from them.

   .2   *Essential provisions:* This section provides those elements that should, at a minimum, be included in a Plan.

   .3   *Additional provisions:* This section provides guidance concerning the inclusion of other information in the Plan. Such information may be required by local authorities in ports visited by the ship, or it may be added to provide additional assistance to the ship's master when responding to an emergency situation. The section also provides guidance on updating and training and exercises to test the plan.

Concept of the Guidelines

1.6   The Guidelines are intended to provide a starting point for the preparation of specific Shipboard Emergency Plans for each ship engaged in transporting INF Code materials. Plan writers are cautioned that they should consider in their Plans the many variables that apply to their ships. Some of these variables include: type and size of ship, category of INF Code materials and their physical properties, route, and shore-based management structure. The Guidelines are not intended to be a compilation of menu items from which the Plan writer can select certain sections and produce a workable Plan, but rather a process to ensure preparedness for responding to emergencies. For a Plan to be effective, it should be carefully tailored to the particular ship for which it is intended. Properly used, the Guidelines will ensure that all appropriate issues are considered in developing the Plan.

Concept of the Plan

1.7   The Plan is intended to assist personnel in avoiding the further escalation of an incident and in dealing with an actual or potential release of INF Code materials. Its primary purpose is to set in motion the necessary actions to avoid or minimize a release and to mitigate its effects. Regardless of the magnitude of an incident, effective planning ensures that the necessary actions are taken in a structured, logical, safe, and timely manner.

1.8   The Plan should provide for small or routine emergencies. However, it should also include guidance to assist the master in meeting the demands of a large-scale incident, should the ship become involved in one.

1.9   The need for a predetermined and properly structured Plan is clear when one considers the pressures and multiple tasks facing personnel confronted with an emergency situation. In the heat of the moment, lack of proper planning will often result in confusion, mistakes, and failure to advise key people. Delays will be incurred and time will be wasted, time during which the situation may well worsen. As a consequence, the ship, its personnel, and the public may be exposed to increasing hazards, and greater environmental damage may result.

---

* This corresponds with paragraph 10.2 of the International Code for the Safe Carriage of Packaged Irradiated Nuclear Fuel, Plutonium and High-Level Radioactive Wastes on board Ships.

1.10 Shipboard emergency plans should be realistic, practical, and easy to use. They should be understood by ship management personnel, both on board and ashore, and be evaluated, reviewed, and updated regularly.

1.11 The Plan is envisioned as a simple document. Use of summarizing flow-charts or checklists to guide the master through the various actions and decisions required during an incident response is highly encouraged. These can provide a quickly visible and logically sequenced form of information which can reduce error and oversight during emergency situations. Inclusion of extensive background information on the ship or cargo should be avoided, as this is generally available elsewhere. If such information is relevant, it should be kept in annexes where it will not make it more difficult for ship personnel to locate operative parts of the Plan.

1.12 An example of a summarizing flow-chart referred to in 1.11 is included in appendix I.

1.13 Also, since the Plan is intended to be a document used on board by master and officers of the ship, it is imperative that one copy in the language understood by crew members with responsibilities under the Plan, as well as an English copy, is carried on board. A change in the master and officers which brings about an attendant change in their working languages would require the issuance of the Plan in the new language.

Responsibilities for action

1.14 Responsibilities for preparing and dealing with a marine transport incident involving INF Code materials are generally divided among several entities: Governments, organizations, and persons. The severity, or potential severity, of the incident in terms of its consequences typically would determine the level of response and involvement of these entities.

1.15 The consignor or shipper is responsible for ensuring that, before the transport of INF Code material, carriers are made fully aware of the procedures to be followed, both on board the ship and by shore-based organizations, in the event of an incident involving such materials. It is the responsibility of the consignor or shipper to know and comply with all applicable international, national, State, or local regulations or guidelines pertaining to the shipment of INF Code materials, and how to deal with all the potential difficulties anticipated when shipping by sea. In addition, the consignor should make available to the carrier the appropriate technical information, emergency instructions, and notification information. Generally, the consignor should be prepared to assist in an emergency response to an incident involving any INF Code materials by providing timely and detailed information about shipments and to send immediately emergency response/support assets to an incident site, if required. The planning for such assistance should be complementary to the Plan.

1.16 The carrier also has responsibilities both for safety during transport and in the event of an incident. In general, both the carrier and the consignor should be prepared to respond immediately to an incident involving INF Code materials. The carrier also has the responsibility to know and comply with all applicable regulations pertaining to the carriage of INF Code materials. This may include being informed of the different response procedures in all areas along the route; ensuring that if an incident occurs, it is properly and rapidly assessed by people knowledgeable in responding to incidents involving INF Code material; ensuring that proper emergency instructions are carried on board the ship; facilitating a prompt response by the consignor/shipper and crew in the event of an incident; and ensuring that all required notifications are accomplished in an expeditious manner. Specifically, carrier personnel should ensure that they immediately inform the nearest coastal State, the consignor, and other appropriate authorities and act according to the Plan.

1.17 Distribution of the Plan should be as follows:

- the shipowner and operator should both keep a copy of the Plan and ensure that at least one copy is carried on board.

1.18 The Plan should clearly emphasize the following:

- Without interfering with shipowners' liability, some coastal States consider that it is their responsibility to define techniques and means to be taken against a marine pollution incident and approve such operations which might cause further pollution. States are in general entitled to do so under the International Convention relating to Intervention on the High Seas in Cases of Oil Pollution Casualties, 1969 and the Protocol relating to Intervention on the High Seas in Cases of Pollution by Substances other than Oil, 1973.

1.19 Planning for incidents involving INF Code materials should be approached as part of a process which also includes the emergency response plans of local authorities and organizations. As noted in 1.15 above, the carriers are to be made fully aware of the international, national, State and local regulations pertaining to the shipment of INF Code materials and potential difficulties anticipated when shipping by sea by the consignor or shipper.

1.20 The content of each Plan should be determined by a consideration of the type of ship used for transporting INF Code materials, the packages used for transport, and the potential consequences of related transport incidents. Appendix II provides additional sources of information that may be useful in developing a Plan.

1.21 A shipowner or operator with multiple ships may prepare one plan with a separate ship-specific annex for each ship covered by the Plan and a separate geographic-specific appendix for each coastal State in which the ship(s) operate.

2 Essential provisions of shipboard emergency plan for ships carrying materials subject to the INF Code

2.1   In accordance with paragraph 27* of the Code, the Plan at a minimum should contain:

.1   the procedure to be followed by the master or other persons having charge of the ship in reporting an incident involving INF Code materials, as required by paragraph 29;†

.2   the list of authorities or persons to be contacted in the event of an incident involving INF Code materials;

.3   a detailed description of the action to be taken immediately by persons on board to prevent, reduce or control the release, and mitigate the consequences of the loss, of INF Code materials following the incident; and

.4   the procedures and point of contact on the ship for co-ordinating shipboard action with national and local authorities.

2.2   The Plan should provide specific information regarding the ship, including:

.1   the ship name, country of registry, call sign, and IMO identification number, if applicable;

.2   the name, address, and procedures for contacting the consignor, consignee, shipper, shipowner or operator on a 24-hour basis; and

.3   identification of communication equipment on board.

The coastal State report

2.3   Paragraphs 29 and 30‡ of the INF Code provide that the nearest coastal State should be notified of an actual or probable release. The intent of this provision is to ensure that coastal States are informed without delay of any incident giving rise to pollution, or threat of pollution, of the marine environment, or in the event of damage, failure or breakdown of a ship carrying INF Code materials, so that appropriate action may be taken.

2.4   *When required.* The Plan should provide clear, concise guidance to enable the master to determine when a report to the coastal State is required.

2.5   *Actual release.* A report to the nearest coastal State is required whenever there is any release of INF Code materials. A report should also be made in the event of damage, failure, or breakdown of a ship carrying INF Code materials which affects the safety of the ship, including allision, collision, grounding, fire, explosion, structural failure, flooding, and cargo shifting; and results in the impairment of the safety of navigation, including the failure or breakdown of steering gear, propulsion system, electrical generating system and essential shipborne navigational aids.

2.6   *Probable release.* The Plan should give the master guidance in evaluating a situation which, though not involving an actual release, would present a risk of a release and thus require a report. In judging whether there is such a risk and whether a report should be made, the following factors, as a minimum, should be taken into account:

.1   the nature of the damage, failure or breakdown of the ship, machinery, equipment or the loss of cargo container integrity;

.2   ship location and proximity to land or other navigational hazards;

.3   weather, tide, current, and sea state; and

.4   traffic density.

2.7   It is impracticable to lay down precise definitions of all types of situations involving risks which would warrant an obligation to report. As a general guideline, the master should make a report in cases of:

.1   damage, failure, or breakdown which affects the safety of the ship, such as allision, collision, grounding, fire, explosion, structural failure, flooding, or cargo shifting;

.2   failure or breakdown of machinery or equipment which results in impairment of safety of navigation, such as failure or breakdown of steering gear, propulsion, electrical generating system, and essential shipboard navigational aids; and

.3   loss of cargo container integrity that may involve a release or probable release of INF Code materials.

---

* This corresponds with paragraph 10.2 of the International Code for the Safe Carriage of Packaged Irradiated Nuclear Fuel, Plutonium and High-Level Radioactive Wastes on board Ships.

† This corresponds with paragraph 11.1 of the International Code for the Safe Carriage of Packaged Irradiated Nuclear Fuel, Plutonium and High-Level Radioactive Wastes on board Ships.

‡ These correspond with paragraphs 11.1 and 11.2 of the International Code for the Safe Carriage of Packaged Irradiated Nuclear Fuel, Plutonium and High-Level Radioactive Wastes on board Ships.

2.8   ***Information required****.* The Plan shall specify, in appropriate detail, the procedure for making the initial report to the coastal State. The Organization's Guidelines on Reporting in resolution A.648(16) provide necessary detail for the Plan writer. The Plan should include a prepared message form, an example of which is included in appendix III to these Guidelines. Coastal States are encouraged to take note of the information in this appendix and accept it as sufficient information. Supplementary or follow-up reports should as far as possible use the same format.

2.9   The initial reporting by on-board personnel should include answers to the following questions:

    .1   Are there any injuries on board;

    .2   Is there (or was there) a fire near the INF Code materials;

    .3   What kind of radiological or chemical hazards exist; and

    .4   What are the meteorological conditions, including wind direction?

List of persons, agencies and organizations to be contacted

2.10   The ship involved in an incident involving INF Code material will have to communicate with both coastal State or port contacts and ship interest contacts. The Plan should include descriptions of the primary and secondary communications methods by which notifications will be made.

2.11   When compiling such contact lists, due account should be taken of the need to provide 24-hour contact information and to provide alternatives to the designated contact. These details should be routinely updated to take account of personnel changes and changes to telephone, fax, e-mail and telex numbers. Clear guidance should also be provided regarding the preferred means of communication (telephone, fax, e-mail, telex, etc.).

Coastal State contacts

2.12   In order to expedite response and minimize damage from an incident involving INF Code material, it is essential that the nearest coastal States be notified without delay.

2.13   The Plan should include as an appendix the list of agencies or officials of Administrations responsible for receiving and processing reports of incidents involving INF Code materials. In the absence of a listed focal point, or should any undue delay be experienced in contacting the responsible authority by direct means, the master should be advised to contact the nearest rescue co-ordination centre, coastal radio station, or designated ship movement reporting station by the quickest available means to accomplish the report. See IMO List of National Operational Contact Points.

Port contacts

2.14   For ships in port, notification of local agencies will speed response. Information on regularly visited ports should be included as an appendix to the Plan. Where this is not feasible, the Plan should require the master to obtain details concerning local reporting procedures upon arriving in port.

Ship interest contacts

2.15   The Plan should provide details of all parties with an interest in the ship to be advised in the event of an incident. This information should be compiled in the form of a contact list. When compiling such lists, it should be remembered that, in the event of a serious incident, ship's personnel may be fully engaged in saving life and taking steps to control and minimize the effects of the incident. They should therefore not be hampered by having onerous communications requirements imposed on them.

2.16   Procedures will vary between companies but it is important that the Plan clearly specifies who will be responsible for informing the various interested parties such as cargo owners, insurers and salvage interests. It is also essential that both the ship's Plan and its company's shore-side Plan are co-ordinated to guarantee that all parties having an interest are advised and that duplication of reports is avoided.

2.17   In addition to any radiological expertise of the crew, radiological monitoring and assessment may be delivered by specialized monitoring teams. The Plan should identify points of contact for such teams on a 24-hour basis so that they can be notified expeditiously when their assistance is required.

Shipboard emergency procedures

2.18   Ship personnel will almost always be in the best position to take quick action to prevent, reduce, or control the release of INF Code material from their ship. The Plan should provide the master with clear guidance on how to accomplish such action for a variety of situations. The Plan should identify situations where standard operating procedures or detailed guidance will ensure that the emergency response is prompt, co-ordinated and efficient. The Plan should not only outline action to be taken, but should also identify who on board is responsible as well as the tasks of various crew members, so that confusion during the emergency can be avoided.

2.19   This section of the Plan will vary widely from ship to ship. Differences in ship size, construction, equipment, manning, and even route may result in shifting emphasis being placed on various aspects of this section. As a minimum, the Plan should provide the master with guidance to address emergencies affecting the safe operation of the ship and procedures to counter actual or potential emergencies involving INF Code materials, including:

.1   Procedures for safe removal from the ship of INF Code materials or packages that may have been damaged during loading or unloading.

.2   Various checklists or other means which will ensure that the master considers all appropriate factors when addressing the specific incident. The following are examples of casualties which should be considered:

.2.1   grounding or stranding;

.2.2   fire/explosion;

.2.3   collision;

.2.4   hull failure, serious structural failure, flooding, and/or heavy weather damage, or icing;

.2.5   excessive list;

.2.6   equipment failure (e.g., main propulsion, steering gear, etc.);

.2.7   containment system failure (e.g., release of INF Code cargo, contamination yielding a hazardous condition, or loss of cargo)

.2.8   security threats;

.2.9   submerged or foundered; and

.2.10 wrecked.

Procedures for the crew to prevent, reduce, or control a release of INF Code material

2.20   Loss or damage to the ship may result in the loss of cargo packages. However, for cargo incidents not resulting from a ship incident, a suspected cargo leak which is detected in time and handled properly will not necessarily constitute an imminent threat to the crew or the safe operation of the vessel. However, procedures for dealing with the following incidents should be developed and practised:

.1   abnormal radiation levels detected by remote monitoring instruments;

.2   discovery of abnormal loose contamination on clothing, shoes or in spaces outside of the cargo hold;

.3   flask coolant loss or leak;

.4   movement or shifting of a flask from its transport position;

.5   unexpected temperature rise at the flask surface; and

.6   dropping a flask during loading or unloading.

2.21   In addition to the checklists and personnel duty assignments, the Plan should provide the master with guidance concerning priority actions, stability and stress considerations, and cargo transfer.

Priority actions

2.22   This section outlines some general considerations that apply to a wide range of casualties. The Plan should provide ship-specific guidance to the master concerning these considerations.

.1   In responding to an incident, the master's priority will be to ensure the safety of personnel and the ship and to take action to prevent escalation of the incident. In casualties involving a release of INF Code materials, immediate consideration should be given to measures aimed at preventing contamination of personnel, such as altering course so that the ship is upwind of the released or lost cargo, shutting down non-essential air intakes, using protective clothing, etc. When it is possible to manoeuvre, the master, in conjunction with the appropriate shore authorities, may consider moving the ship to a more suitable location to facilitate emergency repair work, cargo transfer operations, or to reduce the threat posed to any particularly sensitive ocean or shoreline areas. Such manoeuvring should be co-ordinated with the coastal State.

.2   Prior to considering remedial action, the master will need to obtain detailed information on the damage sustained by the ship and INF Code material containers. A visual inspection should be carried out when it is safe to do so. An adequate number of trained crew members should be on board to assess the situation by means of standard equipment and radiological assessment procedures which will enable proper decisions to be made as to what further action is necessary. In certain cases, radiological monitoring and assessment teams may be required to assess properly any consequences of an incident involving the release of INF Code materials. The initial assessment should include consideration of three basic issues:

.2.1   confirming the quantity and type of INF Code materials involved;

.2.2   ascertaining whether the integrity of shipping containers or packages has been breached; and

.2.3   assessing, by monitoring with appropriate instrumentation, the radiological hazards that exist, if any.

.3   On the basis of the results of the initial measurements, the master should assess the need for radiological experts to provide advice. The measurement information should be recorded on a map or sketch of the area of the incident to document the measurement results.

.4   Having assessed the damage sustained, the master will be in a position to decide what action should be taken to prevent or minimize a further or more serious release, and a sufficient number of adequately trained crew members should be on board to assist in such action. Where appropriate, the Plan should provide a list of information required for making damage stability and damaged longitudinal strength assessments.

.5   Ships' crew as well as fire-fighting and radiological monitoring teams may require protective clothing and respiratory protection equipment. Equipment should be pre-selected to protect against radioactive contamination and inhalation of airborne radioactive material.

Cargo transfer

2.23   For those INF Code materials where cargo transfer is practicable, the Plan should provide guidance on the procedures to be followed for ship-to-ship transfer of cargo. Reference may be made in the Plan to existing company guides. A copy of such company procedures for ship-to-ship transfer operations should be kept with the Plan. The Plan should address the need for co-ordinating this activity with the coastal State, as such operation may be subject to its jurisdiction.

Mitigation activities

2.24   When the safety of both the ship and personnel has been addressed, the master can initiate mitigating activities according to the guidance given by the Plan. The Plan should address such as aspects as:

     .1   physical, chemical and radiological properties of the INF Code materials involved;

     .2   containment and other response techniques;

     .3   isolation procedures;

     .4   decontamination of personnel; and

     .5   safe storage of any contaminated materials.

2.25   In order to have the necessary information available to respond to the situations referred to in 2.19 and 2.20, certain plans, drawings, and ship-specific details, such as a layout of a general arrangement plan, should be available on board. The Plan should show where current cargo, bunker, and ballast information – including quantities and specifications – are available.

Security

2.26   Ships may be subject to bomb threats, sabotage, and unauthorized visitors. If not handled properly, these incidents can pose a hazard to the safe operation of the ship. Standard procedures will also prevent over-reaction on the part of the crew which could lead to personnel injury. Procedures should be developed for:

     .1   bomb threats and resulting search;

     .2   search of visitors, luggage, vehicles, and freight during times of heightened threats; and

     .3   gangway procedures, including action in the event of unauthorized boarders.

National and local co-ordination

2.27   Quick, efficient co-ordination between the ship and coastal State or other involved parties becomes vital in mitigating the effects of an incident involving INF Code materials. The Plan should address the need, where appropriate, to contact the coastal State for consultation and/or authorization regarding mitigating actions. See also 1.15 above.

2.28   The identities and roles of various national and local authorities involved vary widely from State to State and from port to port. Approaches to responsibility for release response also vary. Some coastal States have agencies that take charge of response immediately and subsequently bill the owner for the cost. In other coastal States, responsibility for initiating response is placed on the shipowner.

3   Additional provisions

3.1   In addition to the provisions identified as core provisions, additional guidance may be provided in the Plan. The topics of such guidance include provision of diagrams and drawings; ship-carried response equipment, including radiological monitoring equipment; public affairs; record-keeping; product response information; and reference materials.

Plans and diagrams

3.2   In addition to the plans required by 2.25 above, other details concerning the ship's design and construction may be appended to the Plan or their location identified.

Response equipment

3.3   Ships may carry on board equipment to assist in response. The type and quantity of this equipment may vary depending on the type of INF Code materials carried. The Plan should indicate an inventory of such equipment. It should also provide directions for safe use and guidelines to assist the master in determining when such use is warranted. Care should be exercised to ensure that the use of such equipment by the crew is practical and consistent with safety considerations. The Plan should establish personnel responsibilities for the deployment of the equipment, its oversight, and maintenance. In order to ensure its safe and effective use, the Plan should also provide for crew training in the use of it.

Shore-side response co-ordinator or qualified individual

3.4   The Plan should provide guidance, if applicable, for the master for requesting and co-ordinating initial response actions with the person responsible for mobilizing shore-side response personnel and equipment.

Planning standards

3.5   To facilitate consideration of the amount of response resources which should be requested, possible scenarios should be analysed and accordingly planned for.

Public information

3.6   The shipowners may want to include in the Plan guidance for the master in dealing with the distribution of information to the news media. Such guidance should be fashioned to reduce the burden on ship's personnel already busy with the emergency at hand.

Record-keeping

3.7   As with any other incident that may eventually involve liability, compensation, and reimbursement issues, the owner may want to include in the Plan guidance for the keeping of appropriate records of the INF Code material incident. Apart from detailing all actions taken on board, records might include communications with outside authorities, owners, and other parties, and decisions and information passed and received. Details on the radiological monitoring undertaken should also be recorded.

Plan review

3.8   Regular review of the Plan by the owner, operator, or master is recommended to ensure that the specific information contained therein is current. A feedback system should be employed which will allow quick capture of changing information and incorporation of it into the Plan. This feedback system should incorporate the following two means:

   .1   Periodic review: the Plan should be reviewed by the owner or operator at least yearly to capture changes in local law or policy, contact names and numbers, ship characteristics, or company policy; and

   .2   Event review: after any use of the Plan in response to an incident, its effectiveness should be evaluated by the owner or operator and modifications made accordingly.

Plan exercises

3.9   The Plan will be of little value if it is not made familiar to the personnel who use it. Training and regular exercises will ensure that the Plan functions as expected and that the contacts and communications specified are accurate. Such training and exercises may be held in conjunction with other shipboard training and exercises and appropriately logged. Where ships carry response equipment, hands-on experience with it by crew members will greatly enhance safety and effectiveness in an emergency situation. After the performance of such exercises, the Plan may need to be modified.

Training procedures

3.10 The Plan may address the training procedures and programmes of the shipowner or operator to assure an acceptable level of knowledge and professionalism in the crew. The consignors and carriers involved in the transport of INF Code materials should provide training related to their emergency instructions and the potential hazards of the types of materials involved. Training programmes should be geared to the roles that personnel should play in responding to an incident. Provisions should be made for periodic brief refresher training in order to maintain the proficiency of all personnel in the emergency response organization and to review incident experience and practical problems. Guidance on the use of radiological monitoring equipment carried on board should also be provided.

3.11 The purpose of training is to provide basic information to the ship's crew. The training should cover in brief the subjects clearly applicable to such incidents. The information should include the fundamentals of first aid, radiological hazards, protective measures, and transport regulations (especially those aspects concerning transport documents, markings, labels and placards and fire control). Basic principles to protect people from radiation exposure and radioactive contamination and to control the spread of contamination should be included in the training. The preparation of standard training material is recommended to facilitate the success of such a training project.

Technical training

3.12 A more extensive training programme is necessary to maintain the skills of the master and ship's officers. Training for these persons should include, at a minimum, incident assessment techniques using radiological monitoring instruments, implementation of protective measures, use of protective clothing and equipment, basic meteorology, and further detailed instructions on the transport regulations and on the packaging of radioactive materials.

Exercise and drill procedures

3.13 The Plan may also address the exercise and drill programme to be carried out by the vessel owner or operator to maintain an appropriate level of preparedness. Exercise scenarios could be developed and used to test the response capabilities and skills of the master and the crew. Exercises could be based upon realistic accident exercise scenarios designed to test all major aspects of the plans. Exercises should aim at testing the effectiveness of communication links, the mobilization of emergency resources and specialized teams, and of the co-operation between agencies and services involved. Another objective of the exercises is to strengthen the confidence of the personnel that they can adequately handle an incident. Equipment and instruments specified in the emergency plans could be used in exercises. Exercises should be clearly identified as such in communications or messages related thereto.

3.14 Drills, which are more limited in scope than exercises, are designed to develop, test and maintain special skills of individuals. For example, a communications and notification drill might test the proficiency of personnel in giving notification of an incident, alerting various organizations, and in operating communications equipment. A fire-fighting drill could be limited to the operation of fire-fighting equipment. Thus, drills can be considered as subsets of exercises, i.e., many drills conducted at the same time, in a co-ordinated fashion, constitute an exercise.

3.15 Provision may be made for the critique of drills and exercises by qualified observers. The results of drills and exercises should be used as a basis for improving the emergency plans, as appropriate. Recording of communications and videotaping the exercises are valuable aids for learning by the participants. Reports and critiques of actual emergencies should also be used as training aids.

3.16 Provision should be made for testing radiological instruments, communications and other equipment. The condition of equipment should be checked periodically, in conjunction with drills or exercises, and at other times, as warranted. A record of all drills and exercises should be maintained on board the ship showing date and results of the event. Additionally, any faults or deficiencies identified should be documented and corrected quickly.

Salvage

3.17 The Plan should contain information on the crew's responsibilities in an incident where a ship is partially or fully disabled, and what constitutes dangerous conditions. A decision process should be outlined in the Plan that will aid the master in determining when salvage assistance should be obtained. The decision process should include, but not be limited to, the following:

    .1   Nearest land or hazard to navigation;

    .2   Ship's set and drift;

    .3   Location and time of impact with hazard based on ship's set and drift;

    .4   Estimated time of incident repair; and

    .5   Determination of nearest capable assistance and response time (i.e., for tug assistance, the time it will take to get on scene and secure the tow). When an incident occurs to a ship under way that reduces its manoeuvrability, the master needs to determine the window of opportunity considering the response time of assistance, regardless of estimated time of repair. It would not be prudent to hesitate in calling for assistance when the time needed to repair something goes beyond the window of opportunity.

3.18 Plans should contain lists and means of contacting and securing salvage assistance.

Appendix I

Shipboard Marine Pollution Emergency Plan for INF Code materials

Example summary flow-chart

This flow diagram is an outline of the course of action that shipboard personnel should follow in responding to an incident involving INF Code materials based on the Guidelines published by the Organization. This diagram is not exhaustive and should not be used as a sole reference in response. Consideration should be given for inclusion of specific references to the Plan. The steps are designed to assist ship personnel in actions to prevent or control the release or loss of INF Code materials. These steps fall into two main categories – reporting and action.

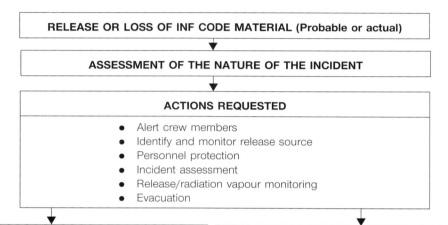

RELEASE OR LOSS OF INF CODE MATERIAL (Probable or actual)

↓

ASSESSMENT OF THE NATURE OF THE INCIDENT

↓

ACTIONS REQUESTED

- Alert crew members
- Identify and monitor release source
- Personnel protection
- Incident assessment
- Release/radiation vapour monitoring
- Evacuation

REPORTING

By master and/or designated crew member

When to report

- All probable and actual release or loss.
- In event of damage, failure or breakdown of ship.

How to report

- Rescue co-ordination centre (at sea).
- By quickest means to coastal radio station *or* Designated ship movement reporting station *or* By quickest available means to local authorities.

Whom to contact

- Nearest coastal State.
- Harbour and terminal operators (in port).
- Head charterer; cargo owner, ship owner.
- Refer to contact lists.

What to report

- Initial report (Res. A.648(16)).
- Follow-up reports.
- Characteristics of involved INF Code materials.
- Weather and sea conditions.
- Assistance required
  - Salvage
  - Lightening capacity
  - Response equipment

ACTION TO CONTROL RELEASE

Measures to respond to the release/loss of INF Code material posing threat to the marine environment

Navigational measures	Seamanship measures
<ul><li>Alter course/position and/or speed</li><li>Change of list and/or trim</li><li>Anchoring</li><li>Initiate towage</li><li>Assess safe haven requirements</li><li>Weather/tide/swell forecasting</li><li>Record of events and communications taken</li><li>Setting aground</li></ul>	<ul><li>Safety assessment and precaution on priority</li><li>Advice on priority countermeasures/ preventive measures</li><li>Damage stability and stress considerations</li><li>Set up shipboard response for: – Leak sealing – Overpacks – Fire fighting – Handling of shipboard response equipment – Control of contaminated equipment – Radiation monitoring</li></ul>

↓

STEPS TO INITIATE EXTERNAL RESPONSE

- Refer to coastal port State listings for local assistance.
- Refer to ship interest contact list.
- External clean-up resources required.
- Continued monitoring of activities.

Appendix II

Additional references for the development of emergency plans for ships transporting material subject to the INF Code

American National Standard (ANSI) for Highway Route Controlled Quantities of Radioactive Materials – Domestic Barge Transport, ANSI N14.24 (1985) (available in English, French, Russian and Spanish).

Code for the Safe Carriage of Irradiated Nuclear Fuel, Plutonium and High-Level Radioactive Wastes in Flasks on board Ships, International Maritime Organization (IMO), (Res. A.748(18)) (available in English, French and Spanish).

Convention on Assistance in the Case of a Nuclear Accident or Radiological Emergency, International Atomic Energy Agency (IAEA) (1986).

Convention on Early Notification of a Nuclear Accident, IAEA, INFCIRC/335 (1986).

Convention on the Physical Protection of Nuclear Material, IAEA, INFCIRC/274/Rev.1 (1979).

Emergency Response Planning and Preparedness for Transport Accidents Involving Radioactive Material, IAEA, Safety Series No. 87 (1988) (ISBN 92-0-123088-5) (available in English).

International Basic Safety Standards for Protection against Ionizing Radiation and the Safety of Radiation Sources, IAEA, Safety Series Number 115 (1996).

International Convention on Oil Pollution Preparedness, Response and Co-operation, IMO (1990) (ISBN 92-801-1267-8) (available in English, French and Spanish).

International Maritime Dangerous Goods (IMDG) Code, IMO (available in English, French and Spanish).

Manual on Oil Pollution, Section II, Contingency Planning, IMO (1995) (ISBN 92-801-1330-5) (available in English, French and Spanish).

Regulations for the Safe Transport of Radioactive Material 1985, IAEA, Safety Series No. ST-1 (as amended, 1996) (ISBN 92-0-104996-X) (available in English, French, Russian and Spanish).

Appendix III

SHIPBOARD EMERGENCY PLAN FOR VESSELS CARRYING INF CODE MATERIALS SAMPLE FORMAT FOR INITIAL NOTIFICATION

AA (SHIP NAME, CALL SIGN, FLAG)

BB (DATE AND TIME OF EVENT, UTC)

D D H H M M

CC (POSITION, LAT, LONG)   OR DD (BEARING, DISTANCE FROM LANDMARK)

N S
d d m m

d d d   n miles

E W
d d d m m

EE (COURSE)   FF (SPEED, KNOTS)

d d d   kn kn 1/10

LL (INTENDED TRACK)

MM (RADIO STATION(S) GUARDED)

NN (DATE AND TIME OF NEXT REPORT, UTC)

D D H H M M

PP (TYPE AND QUANTITY OF CARGO ON BOARD)

QQ (BRIEF DETAILS OF DEFECTS/DEFICIENCIES/DAMAGE)

RR (BRIEF DETAILS OF POLLUTION, RADIOLOGICAL OR CHEMICAL HAZARDS THAT EXIST)

SS (BRIEF DETAILS OF WEATHER AND SEA CONDITIONS)

— direction   — direction

— speed   (Beaufort)   — height   (m)

TT (CONTACT DETAILS OF SHIP'S OWNER/OPERATOR/AGENT)

UU (SHIP SIZE AND TYPE)
LENGTH: (m) BREADTH: (m) DRAUGHT: (m) TYPE:

XX (ADDITIONAL INFORMATION)

Footnote: The alphabetical reference letters in the above format are from "General principles for ship reporting systems and ship reporting requirements, including guidelines for reporting incidents involving dangerous goods, harmful substances and/or marine pollutants" adopted by the International Maritime Organization by resolution A.851(20). The letters do not follow the complete alphabetical sequence as certain letters are used to designate information required for other standard reporting formats, e.g., those used to transmit route information.

Appendix

Resolution A.984(24)

Adopted on 1 December 2005

FACILITATION OF THE CARRIAGE OF IMDG CODE CLASS 7 RADIOACTIVE MATERIALS INCLUDING THOSE IN PACKAGED FORM USED IN MEDICAL OR PUBLIC HEALTH APPLICATIONS

THE ASSEMBLY,

RECALLING Article 15(j) of the Convention on the International Maritime Organization concerning the functions of the Assembly in relation to regulations and guidelines concerning maritime safety and the prevention and control of marine pollution from ships,

HAVING CONSIDERED the general purpose of the Convention on Facilitation of International Maritime Traffic, 1965, as amended, in particular article III,

REAFFIRMING that chapter VII of the International Convention for the Safety of Life at Sea, 1974, as amended (1974 SOLAS Convention) and the International Maritime Dangerous Goods (IMDG) Code contain sufficient and adequate provisions for the safe carriage of dangerous goods in packaged form including IMDG Code class 7 radioactive materials,

BEING AWARE of difficulties encountered in the carriage of certain IMDG Code class 7 radioactive materials including those used for medical or public health applications,

BEING CONCERNED about the potential adverse consequences that denial of carriage of IMDG Code class 7 radioactive materials used in medical applications, for example cobalt-60 and those radioisotopes used in radiotherapy and nuclear medicine, might have on public health,

NOTING the efforts of the Facilitation Committee, at its thirty-first and thirty-second sessions, to address and resolve the issue, and in particular the approval of FAL.6/Circ.12 on ''Difficulties encountered in the shipment of the IMDG Code class 7 radioactive materials and, in particular, cobalt-60'',

NOTING ALSO the work done by the International Atomic Energy Agency (IAEA) in an effort to assist in the alleviation of the difficulties encountered in the carriage of IMDG Code class 7 radioactive materials,

NOTING FURTHER the progress made by the IAEA in conjunction with the International Federation of Air Line Pilots' Associations on the problems related to refusals of air shipments of radioactive materials, in particular those used for medical applications, and the establishment, by the General Conference of the IAEA, through resolution GC(49)/RES/9, of a steering committee to oversee the resolution of the problem, as recommended by the IAEA Transport Safety Standards Committee,

ALSO NOTING that cessation of the transport of radioactive materials, except those used in medical or public health applications, through the regions of small island developing States is an ultimate desired goal of small island developing States and some other countries, and recognizing the right of freedom of navigation in accordance with international law,

RECOGNIZING the diverse and important uses of radioactive material, including cobalt-60, and the need to ensure the effective and efficient carriage of this medical isotope for the benefit of public health,

1.   INVITES Member Governments to note that carriage of IMDG Code class 7 radioactive materials, when carried out in compliance with the relevant provisions of chapter VII of the 1974 SOLAS Convention, the IMDG Code and the recommendations contained in MSC/Circ.675 on ''Recommendations on the safe transport of dangerous cargoes and related activities in port areas'', meets the necessary safety requirements and should be facilitated;

2.   ALSO INVITES Member Governments to recognize the beneficial uses of IMDG Code class 7 radioactive materials in packaged form used in medical or public health applications and to facilitate their expeditious transportation;

3.   FURTHER INVITES Member Governments to work with relevant national authorities and industry associations to raise the required level of awareness and to help alleviate the difficulties encountered in the carriage of IMDG Code class 7 radioactive materials including those in packaged form used in medical or public health applications;

4.   URGES Member Governments and non-governmental organizations with consultative status to bring to the attention of the Facilitation Committee any instances, together with the associated reasons, where the carriage of IMDG Code class 7 radioactive materials, including those in packaged form used in medical or public health applications, encounter difficulties or are refused carriage aboard ship or in or through ports, so as to enable the Facilitation Committee to consider the matter further; to determine the actions required, and to report to the twenty-fifth regular session of the Assembly on the progress made towards resolving these issues;

5.   REQUESTS the Facilitation Committee, in co-operation with other bodies of the Organization, to continue to work with a view to resolving difficulties encountered in the carriage of all IMDG Code class 7 radioactive materials, including those used in medical or public health applications, and to continue to co-operate with the IAEA in this respect;

6.   AGREES that resolution of the difficulties encountered in the carriage of IMDG Code class 7 radioactive materials requires continued co-operation between the Organization and the IAEA and with any bodies the latter may set up to deal with the issue;

7.   REQUESTS ALSO the Secretary-General to explore the possibility of establishing an *ad hoc* mechanism within the Organization to co-ordinate efforts to speedily resolve difficulties in the carriage of IMDG Code class 7 radioactive materials, in close co-operation with the IAEA.

Maritime Safety Committee and Marine Environment Protection Committee

Resolution MSC.122(75)
(adopted on 24 May 2002)

ADOPTION OF THE INTERNATIONAL MARITIME DANGEROUS GOODS (IMDG) CODE

THE MARITIME SAFETY COMMITTEE,

RECALLING Article 28(b) of the Convention on the International Maritime Organization concerning the functions of the Committee,

NOTING the adoption by the Assembly of resolution A.716(17) on the International Maritime Dangerous Goods (IMDG) Code,

RECOGNIZING the need to provide a mandatory application of the agreed international standards for the carriage of dangerous goods by sea,

NOTING ALSO resolution MSC.123(75) by which it adopted amendments to chapter VII of the International Convention for the Safety of Life at Sea (SOLAS), 1974, as amended (hereinafter referred to as "the Convention"), to make the provisions of the IMDG Code mandatory under the Convention,

HAVING CONSIDERED, at its seventy-fifth session, the text of the proposed IMDG Code,

1.   ADOPTS the International Maritime Dangerous Goods (IMDG) Code, the text of which is set out in the annex* to the present resolution;

2.   NOTES that, under the aforementioned amendments to chapter VII of the Convention, future amendments to the IMDG Code shall be adopted, brought into force and shall take effect in accordance with the provisions of article VIII of the Convention concerning the amendment procedures applicable to the Annex to the Convention other than chapter I thereof;

3.   INVITES Contracting Governments to the Convention to note that the IMDG Code will take effect on 1 January 2004 upon entry into force of the amendments to chapter VII of the Convention;

4.   AGREES that Contracting Governments to the Convention may apply the IMDG Code in whole or in part on a voluntary basis as from 1 January 2003;

5.   REQUESTS the Secretary-General to transmit certified copies of this resolution and its annex to all Contracting Governments to the Convention;

6.   FURTHER REQUESTS the Secretary-General to transmit copies of this resolution and its annex to all Members of the Organization which are not Contracting Governments to the Convention;

7.   NOTES that the annexed IMDG Code supersedes the existing Code adopted by resolution A.716(17).

---

* The annex to this resolution has not been reproduced here.

Resolution MSC.123(75)
(adopted on 24 May 2002)

ADOPTION OF AMENDMENTS TO THE INTERNATIONAL CONVENTION FOR THE SAFETY OF LIFE AT SEA, 1974, AS AMENDED

THE MARITIME SAFETY COMMITTEE,

RECALLING Article 28(b) of the Convention on the International Maritime Organization concerning the functions of the Committee,

RECALLING FURTHER article VIII(b) of the International Convention for the Safety of Life at Sea (SOLAS), 1974 (hereinafter referred to as "the Convention"), concerning the amendment procedure applicable to the Annex to the Convention, other than to the provisions of chapter I thereof,

HAVING CONSIDERED, at its seventy-fifth session, amendments to the Convention, proposed and circulated in accordance with article VIII(b)(i) thereof,

1.   ADOPTS, in accordance with article VIII(b)(iv) of the Convention, amendments to the Convention, the text of which is set out in the annex to the present resolution;

2.   DETERMINES, in accordance with article VIII(b)(vi)(2)(bb) of the Convention, that the said amendments shall be deemed to have been accepted on 1 July 2003, unless, prior to that date, more than one third of the Contracting Governments to the Convention or Contracting Governments the combined merchant fleets of which constitute not less than 50% of the gross tonnage of the world's merchant fleet, have notified their objections to the amendments;

3.   INVITES SOLAS Contracting Governments to note that, in accordance with article VIII(b)(vii)(2) of the Convention, the amendments shall enter into force on 1 January 2004 upon their acceptance in accordance with paragraph 2 above;

4.   REQUESTS the Secretary-General, in conformity with article VIII(b)(v) of the Convention, to transmit certified copies of the present resolution and the text of the amendments contained in the annex to all Contracting Governments to the Convention;

5.   FURTHER REQUESTS the Secretary-General to transmit copies of this resolution and its annex to Members of the Organization, which are not Contracting Governments to the Convention.

Annex

AMENDMENTS TO THE INTERNATIONAL CONVENTION FOR THE SAFETY OF LIFE AT SEA, 1974, AS AMENDED*

CHAPTER VI
Carriage of cargoes

Regulation 2
Cargo information

14   *In existing paragraph 2.3, the words "regulation VII/2" are replaced by the words* "the IMDG Code, as defined in regulation VII/1.1".

---

* Amendments to chapters IV (Radiocommunications), V (Safety of Navigation) and Certificates, which are not directly relevant to the IMDG Code, have been omitted from this text.

Regulation 5
Stowage and securing

15   *In existing paragraph 1, the words* "Cargo and cargo units" *are replaced by the words* "Cargo, cargo units and cargo transport units".

16   *In existing paragraph 2, the words* "cargo carried in cargo unit" *are replaced by the words* "cargo, cargo units and cargo transport units".

17   *In existing paragraph 4, the words* "cargo units" *are replaced by the words* "cargo units and cargo transport units" *(in two places).*

18   *In existing paragraph 5, the word* "Containers" *is replaced by the words* "Freight containers" *and in the last line, after* "(CSC)", *at the end of the sentence, the words* ", as amended" *are added.*

19   *Existing paragraph 6 is replaced by the following:*

"All cargoes, other than solid and liquid bulk cargoes, cargo units and cargo transport units shall be loaded, stowed and secured throughout the voyage in accordance with the Cargo Securing Manual approved by the Administration. In ships with ro-ro spaces, as defined in regulation II-2/3.41, all securing of such cargoes, cargo units and cargo transport units, in accordance with the Cargo Securing Manual, shall be completed before the ship leaves the berth. The Cargo Securing Manual shall be drawn up to a standard at least equivalent to relevant guidelines developed by the Organization."

Regulation 6
Acceptability for shipment

20   *In existing paragraph 3, the words* "regulation VII/2" *are replaced by the words* "the IMDG Code, as defined in regulation VII/1.1".

CHAPTER VII
Carriage of dangerous goods

21   *Existing part A is replaced by the following new part A and part A-1:*

"PART A
CARRIAGE OF DANGEROUS GOODS IN PACKAGED FORM

Regulation 1
Definitions

For the purpose of this chapter, unless expressly provided otherwise:

1   *IMDG Code* means the International Maritime Dangerous Goods (IMDG) Code adopted by the Maritime Safety Committee of the Organization by resolution MSC.122(75), as may be amended by the Organization, provided that such amendments are adopted, brought into force and take effect in accordance with the provisions of article VIII of the present Convention concerning the amendment procedures applicable to the annex other than chapter I.

2   *Dangerous goods* mean the substances, materials and articles covered by the IMDG Code.

3   *Packaged form* means the form of containment specified in the IMDG Code.

Regulation 2
Application

1   Unless expressly provided otherwise, this part applies to the carriage of dangerous goods in packaged form in all ships to which the present regulations apply and in cargo ships of less than 500 gross tonnage.

2   The provisions of this part do not apply to ships' stores and equipment.

3   The carriage of dangerous goods in packaged form is prohibited except in accordance with the provisions of this chapter.

4   To supplement the provisions of this part, each Contracting Government shall issue, or cause to be issued, detailed instructions on emergency response and medical first aid relevant to incidents involving dangerous goods in packaged form, taking into account the guidelines developed by the Organization.

Regulation 3
Requirements for the carriage of dangerous goods

The carriage of dangerous goods in packaged form shall be in compliance with the relevant provisions of the IMDG Code.

Regulation 4
Documents

1   In all documents relating to the carriage of dangerous goods in packaged form by sea, the proper shipping name of the goods shall be used (trade names alone shall not be used) and the correct description given in accordance with the classification set out in the IMDG Code.

2   The transport documents prepared by the shipper shall include, or be accompanied by, a signed certificate or a declaration that the consignment, as offered for carriage, is properly packaged, marked, labelled or placarded, as appropriate, and in proper condition for carriage.

3   The person(s) responsible for the packing/loading of dangerous goods in a cargo transport unit shall provide a signed container/vehicle packing certificate stating that the cargo in the unit has been properly packed and secured and that all applicable transport requirements have been met. Such a certificate may be combined with the document referred to in paragraph 2.

4   Where there is due cause to suspect that a cargo transport unit in which dangerous goods are packed is not in compliance with the requirements of paragraph 2 or 3, or where a container/vehicle packing certificate is not available, the cargo transport unit shall not be accepted for carriage.

5   Each ship carrying dangerous goods in packaged form shall have a special list or manifest setting forth, in accordance with the classification set out in the IMDG Code, the dangerous goods on board and the location thereof. A detailed stowage plan, which identifies by class and sets out the location of all dangerous goods on board, may be used in place of such a special list or manifest. A copy of one of these documents shall be made available before departure to the person or organization designated by the port State authority.

Regulation 5
Cargo Securing Manual

Cargo, cargo units and cargo transport units, shall be loaded, stowed and secured throughout the voyage in accordance with the Cargo Securing Manual approved by the Administration. The Cargo Securing Manual shall be drawn up to a standard at least equivalent to the guidelines developed by the Organization.

Regulation 6
Reporting of incidents involving dangerous goods

1   When an incident takes place involving the loss or likely loss overboard of dangerous goods in packaged form into the sea, the master, or other person having charge of the ship, shall report the particulars of such an incident without delay and to the fullest extent possible to the nearest coastal State. The report shall be drawn up based on general principles and guidelines developed by the Organization.

2   In the event of the ship referred to in paragraph 1 being abandoned, or in the event of a report from such a ship being incomplete or unobtainable, the company, as defined in regulation IX/1.2, shall, to the fullest extent possible, assume the obligations placed upon the master by this regulation.

PART A-1
CARRIAGE OF DANGEROUS GOODS IN SOLID FORM IN BULK

Regulation 7
Definitions

Dangerous goods in solid form in bulk means any material, other than liquid or gas, consisting of a combination of particles, granules or any larger pieces of material, generally uniform in composition, which is covered by the IMDG Code and is loaded directly into the cargo spaces of a ship without any intermediate form of containment, and includes such materials loaded in a barge on a barge-carrying ship.

Regulation 7-1
Application

1   Unless expressly provided otherwise, this part applies to the carriage of dangerous goods in solid form in bulk in all ships, to which the present regulations apply and in cargo ships of less than 500 gross tonnage.

2   The carriage of dangerous goods in solid form in bulk is prohibited except in accordance with the provisions of this part.

3   To supplement the provisions of this part, each Contracting Government shall issue, or cause to be issued, detailed instructions on the safe carriage of dangerous goods in solid form in bulk which shall include instructions on emergency response and medical first aid relevant to incidents involving dangerous goods in solid form in bulk, taking into account the guidelines developed by the Organization.

Regulation 7-2
Documents

1   In all documents relating to the carriage of dangerous goods in solid form in bulk by sea, the bulk cargo shipping name of the goods shall be used (trade names alone shall not be used).

2   Each ship carrying dangerous goods in solid form in bulk shall have a special list or manifest setting forth the dangerous goods on board and the location thereof. A detailed stowage plan, which identifies by class and sets out the location of all dangerous goods on board, may be used in place of such a special list or manifest. A copy of one of these documents shall be made available before departure to the person or organization designated by the port State authority.

Regulation 7-3
Stowage and segregation requirements

1   Dangerous goods in solid form in bulk shall be loaded and stowed safely and appropriately in accordance with the nature of the goods. Incompatible goods shall be segregated from one another.

2   Dangerous goods in solid form in bulk, which are liable to spontaneous heating or combustion, shall not be carried unless adequate precautions have been taken to minimize the likelihood of the outbreak of fire.

3   Dangerous goods in solid form in bulk, which give off dangerous vapours, shall be stowed in a well ventilated cargo space.

Regulation 7-4
Reporting of incidents involving dangerous goods

1   When an incident takes place involving the loss or likely loss overboard of dangerous goods in solid form in bulk into the sea, the master, or other person having charge of the ship, shall report the particulars of such an incident without delay and to the fullest extent possible to the nearest coastal State. The report shall be drawn up based on general principles and guidelines developed by the Organization.

2   In the event of the ship referred to in paragraph 1 being abandoned, or in the event of a report from such a ship being incomplete or unobtainable, the company, as defined in regulation IX/1.2, shall, to the fullest extent possible, assume the obligations placed upon the master by this regulation."

PART D
SPECIAL REQUIREMENTS FOR THE CARRIAGE OF PACKAGED IRRADIATED
NUCLEAR FUEL, PLUTONIUM AND HIGH-LEVEL RADIOACTIVE WASTES
ON BOARD SHIPS

Regulation 14
Definitions

22   *Existing paragraph 2 is replaced by the following:*

"*INF cargo* means packaged irradiated nuclear fuel, plutonium and high-level radioactive wastes carried as cargo in accordance with class 7 of the IMDG Code."

23   *Existing paragraph 6 is deleted.*

Appendix

Resolution MSC.157(78)
(adopted on 20 May 2004)

ADOPTION OF AMENDMENTS TO
THE INTERNATIONAL MARITIME DANGEROUS GOODS (IMDG) CODE

THE MARITIME SAFETY COMMITTEE,

RECALLING Article 28(b) of the Convention on the International Maritime Organization concerning the functions of the Committee,

NOTING resolution MSC.122(75) by which it adopted the International Maritime Dangerous Goods Code (hereinafter referred to as "the IMDG Code"), which has become mandatory under chapter VII of the International Convention for the Safety of Life at Sea (SOLAS), 1974, as amended (hereinafter referred to as "the Convention") on 1 January 2004,

NOTING ALSO article VIII(b) and regulation VII/1.1 of the Convention concerning the amendment procedure for amending the IMDG Code,

HAVING CONSIDERED, at its seventy-eighth session, amendments to the IMDG Code, proposed and circulated in accordance with article VIII(b)(i) of the Convention,

1.   ADOPTS, in accordance with article VIII(b)(iv) of the Convention, amendments to the IMDG Code, the text of which is set out in the annex* to the present resolution;

2.   DETERMINES, in accordance with article VIII(b)(vi)(2)(bb) of the Convention, that the said amendments shall be deemed to have been accepted on 1 July 2005, unless, prior to that date, more than one third of the Contracting Governments to the Convention or Contracting Governments the combined merchant fleets of which constitute not less than 50% of the gross tonnage of the world's merchant fleet, have notified their objections to the amendments;

3.   INVITES Contracting Governments to the Convention to note that, in accordance with article VIII(b)(vii)(2) of the Convention, the amendments shall enter into force on 1 January 2006 upon their acceptance in accordance with paragraph 2 above;

4.   BEING COGNIZANT that amendments to other modal instruments dealing with the carriage of dangerous goods come into force on 1 January 2005;

5.   ENCOURAGES Contracting Governments to the Convention to apply the aforementioned amendments in whole or in part on a voluntary basis as from 1 January 2005;

6.   REQUESTS the Secretary-General, in conformity with article VIII(b)(v) of the Convention, to transmit certified copies of the present resolution and the text of the amendments contained in the annex to all Contracting Governments to the Convention;

7.   FURTHER REQUESTS the Secretary-General to transmit copies of this resolution and its annex to Members of the Organization which are not Contracting Governments to the Convention.

---

* The annex to this resolution has not been reproduced here.

Resolution MSC.205(81)
(adopted on 18 May 2006)

ADOPTION OF AMENDMENTS
TO THE INTERNATIONAL MARITIME DANGEROUS GOODS (IMDG) CODE

THE MARITIME SAFETY COMMITTEE,

RECALLING Article 28(b) of the Convention on the International Maritime Organization concerning the functions of the Committee,

NOTING resolution MSC.122(75) by which it adopted the International Maritime Dangerous Goods Code (hereinafter referred to as "the IMDG Code"), which has become mandatory under chapter VII of the International Convention for the Safety of Life at Sea, 1974, as amended (hereinafter referred to as "the Convention"),

NOTING ALSO article VIII(b) and regulation VII/1.1 of the Convention concerning the amendment procedure for amending the IMDG Code,

HAVING CONSIDERED, at its eighty-first session, amendments to the IMDG Code, proposed and circulated in accordance with article VIII(b)(i) of the Convention,

1.   ADOPTS, in accordance with article VIII(b)(iv) of the Convention, amendments to the IMDG Code, the text of which is set out in the annex* to the present resolution;

2.   DETERMINES, in accordance with article VIII(b)(vi)(2)(bb) of the Convention, that the said amendments shall be deemed to have been accepted on 1 July 2007, unless, prior to that date, more than one third of the Contracting Governments to the Convention or Contracting Governments the combined merchant fleets of which constitute not less than 50% of the gross tonnage of the world's merchant fleet, have notified their objections to the amendments;

3.   INVITES Contracting Governments to the Convention to note that, in accordance with article VIII(b)(vii)(2) of the Convention, the amendments shall enter into force on 1 January 2008 upon their acceptance in accordance with paragraph 2 above;

4.   AGREES that Contracting Governments to the Convention may apply the aforementioned amendments in whole or in part on a voluntary basis as from 1 January 2007;

5.   REQUESTS the Secretary-General, in conformity with article VIII(b)(v) of the Convention, to transmit certified copies of the present resolution and the text of the amendments contained in the annex to all Contracting Governments to the Convention;

6.   FURTHER REQUESTS the Secretary-General to transmit copies of this resolution and its annex to Members of the Organization which are not Contracting Governments to the Convention.

---

* The annex to this resolution has not been reproduced here.

Appendix

Resolution MSC.262(84)
(adopted on 16 May 2008)

ADOPTION OF AMENDMENTS TO
THE INTERNATIONAL MARITIME DANGEROUS GOODS (IMDG) CODE

THE MARITIME SAFETY COMMITTEE,

RECALLING Article 28(b) of the Convention on the International Maritime Organization concerning the functions of the Committee,

NOTING resolution MSC.122(75) by which it adopted the International Maritime Dangerous Goods Code (hereinafter referred to as "the IMDG Code"), which has become mandatory under chapter VII of the International Convention for the Safety of Life at Sea (SOLAS), 1974, as amended (hereinafter referred to as "the Convention"),

NOTING ALSO article VIII(b) and regulation VII/1.1 of the Convention concerning amendment procedure for amending the IMDG Code,

HAVING CONSIDERED, at its eighty-fourth session, amendments to the IMDG Code, proposed and circulated in accordance with article VIII(b)(i) of the Convention,

1. ADOPTS, in accordance with article VIII(b)(iv) of the Convention, amendments to the IMDG Code, the text of which is set out in the annex* to the present resolution;

2. DETERMINES, in accordance with article VIII(b)(2)(bb) of the Convention, that the said amendments shall be deemed to have been accepted on 1 July 2009, unless, prior to that date, more than one third of the Contracting Governments to the Convention, or Contracting Governments the combined merchant fleets of which constitute not less than 50% of the gross tonnage of the world's merchant fleet, have notified their objections to the amendments;

3. INVITES Contracting Governments to the Convention to note that, in accordance with article VIII(b)(vii)(2) of the Convention, the amendments shall enter into force on 1 January 2010 upon their acceptance in accordance with paragraph 2 above;

4. AGREES that Contracting Governments to the Convention may apply the aforementioned amendments in whole or in part on a voluntary basis as from 1 January 2009;

5. REQUESTS the Secretary-General, in conformity with article VIII(b)(v) of the Convention, to transmit certified copies of the present resolution and the text of the amendments contained in the annex to all Contracting Governments to the Convention;

6. FURTHER REQUESTS the Secretary-General to transmit copies of this resolution and its annex to Members of the Organization which are not Contracting Governments to the Convention.

---

* The annex to this resolution has not been reproduced here.

MSC/Circ. 506/Rev. 1 of 10 January 1990

CONTAINER PACKING CERTIFICATES/VEHICLE PACKING DECLARATIONS

1   The regulations governing the carriage of dangerous goods by sea are contained in chapter VII of the 1974 SOLAS Convention, as amended. Part A of chapter VII regulates the carriage of dangerous goods both in packaged form and in solid form in bulk. Regulation VII/1.3 prohibits the carriage of such cargoes in ships engaged on international voyages except when carried in accordance with the requirements of part A of chapter VII.

2   Regulation VII/1.4 requires that each Contracting Government issue, or cause to be issued, detailed instructions on safe packing and stowage of dangerous goods which include the precautions necessary in relation to other cargo.

3   The provisions of part A of chapter VII are supplemented by the IMDG Code, adopted by the Organization by resolution A.81(IV), and the relevant sections and related parts of appendix B of the Code of Safe Practice for Solid Bulk Cargoes (BC Code), adopted by the Organization by resolution A.434(XI), as have been or may be amended by the Organization's Maritime Safety Committee.

4   Information on the status of adoption and implementation of the IMDG Code is regularly disseminated through an MSC.2 circular.*

5   Regulation 5 of part A of SOLAS chapter VII regulates documentation. The shipping documents to be prepared by the shipper shall include, or be accompanied by, a signed certificate or declaration that the shipment offered for transport is properly packaged and marked, labelled or placarded, as appropriate, and in proper condition for transport.

6   The requirements for shipping documents are explained in the IMDG Code. Subsections 12.3 and 17.7 of the General Introduction to the Code recommend that, when dangerous goods are packed or loaded into a freight container or vehicle, the persons responsible for packing or loading the goods into the container or vehicle should provide a container packing certificate/vehicle packing declaration, the details of which are described in the Code. In addition, the container/vehicle/unit identification number(s) should be indicated.

7   The Maritime Safety Committee has been informed that members of the International Chamber of Shipping (ICS) had reported that, in a number of ports, some of which are located in countries which had advised the Organization that they had implemented the IMDG Code, it is difficult and often impossible to obtain container packing certificates. This creates great difficulties for ship operators and, where the flag State regulations require strict compliance with the IMDG Code, the cargo has to be refused if the certificate cannot be obtained. However, the most serious threat facing all ship operators is the risk that dangerous goods may be packed or loaded into a container which, because no packing certificate has been issued, may not be placarded to indicate the danger of its contents. Experience has shown that such a container can remain undetected during transport and may therefore be incorrectly stowed, thus creating a potential danger to the ship. Such a container also poses a serious threat to the safety of inland transport, container terminals and ports.

8   The Organization has also been informed that in a number of accidents involving containers packed or loaded with dangerous goods no information on their contents had been available.

9   Where there is reason to suspect that a unit into which dangerous goods have been packed or loaded is not in compliance with the provisions of the IMDG Code, or where a container packing certificate/vehicle packing declaration is not available, the unit should not be accepted for shipment.

10   The Maritime Safety Committee has agreed that an amendment to regulation VII/5 of SOLAS should be developed by the Sub-Committee on the Carriage of Dangerous Goods to include the provision of container packing certificates/vehicle packing declarations.

11   The Maritime Safety Committee has also decided that, in the interim, Governments should be urged to review their national legislation and take such measures as they consider necessary to require container packing certificates and vehicle packing declarations to be provided by the packer of the unit.

12   To assist Governments in the introduction, at national level, of appropriate legal requirements that such certificates and declarations are provided, the relevant extracts from the General Introduction of the IMDG Code are annexed.†

---

* Refer also to chapter 7.9 of the IMDG Code.

† The amended texts of subsections 12.3 and 17.7 of the General Introduction to the IMDG Code are not reproduced here.

MSC/Circ. 745 of 13 June 1996

GUIDELINES FOR THE PREPARATION OF THE CARGO SECURING MANUAL

1   In accordance with regulations VI/5 and VII/6 of SOLAS 1974, as amended, cargo units and cargo transport units shall be loaded, stowed and secured throughout the voyage in accordance with the Cargo Securing Manual approved by the Administration, which shall be drawn up to a standard at least equivalent to the guidelines developed by the Organization.

2   The Maritime Safety Committee, at its sixty-sixth session (28 May to 6 June 1996), considered the draft guidelines for the preparation of the Cargo Securing Manual prepared by the Sub-Committee on Dangerous Goods, Solid Cargoes and Containers (DSC) at its first session (5 to 9 February 1996), and approved the Guidelines as amended and set out in the annex to this circular.

3   These Guidelines are based on the provisions contained in the annex to MSC/Circ.385 but have been expanded to include the applications explicit to ships which are equipped or adapted for the carriage of freight containers, taking into account the provisions of the Code of Safe Practice for Cargo Stowage and Securing (CSS Code), as amended. They are of a general nature and intended to provide guidance on the preparation of such Cargo Securing Manuals, which are required on all types of ships engaged in the carriage of cargoes other than solid and liquid bulk cargoes.

4   Member Governments are invited to bring these Guidelines to the attention of all parties concerned, with the aim of having Cargo Securing Manuals carried on board ships prepared appropriately and in a consistent manner, and to implement them as soon as possible and, in any case, not later than 31 December 1997.

5   This Circular replaces MSC/Circ. 385 dated 8 January 1985.

Annex

Guidelines for the preparation of the Cargo Securing Manual

PREAMBLE

In accordance with the International Convention for the Safety of Life at Sea, 1974 (SOLAS), chapters VI and VII, and the Code of Safe Practice for Cargo Stowage and Securing, cargo units including containers shall be stowed and secured throughout the voyage in accordance with a Cargo Securing Manual, approved by the Administration.

The Cargo Securing Manual is required on all types of ships engaged in the carriage of all cargoes other than solid and liquid bulk cargoes.

The purpose of these Guidelines is to ensure that Cargo Securing Manuals cover all relevant aspects of cargo stowage and securing and to provide a uniform approach to the preparation of Cargo Securing Manuals, their layout and content. Administrations may continue accepting Cargo Securing Manuals drafted in accordance with MSC/Circ.385 provided that they satisfy the requirements of these Guidelines. If necessary, those Manuals should be revised explicitly when the ship is intended to carry containers in a standardized system.

It is important that securing devices meet acceptable functional and strength criteria applicable to the ship and its cargo. It is also important that the officers on board are aware of the magnitude and direction of the forces involved and the correct application and limitations of the cargo-securing devices. The crew and other persons employed for the securing of cargoes should be instructed in the correct application and use of the cargo-securing devices on board the ship.

Chapter 1 – General

1.1   Definitions

Cargo-securing devices are all fixed and portable devices used to secure and support cargo units.

Maximum securing load (MSL) is a term used to define the allowable load capacity for a device used to secure cargo to a ship. *Safe working load (SWL)* may be substituted for MSL for securing purposes, provided this is equal to or exceeds the strength defined by MSL.

Standardized cargo means cargo for which the ship is provided with an approved securing system based upon cargo units of specific types.

Semi-standardized cargo means cargo for which the ship is provided with a securing system capable of accommodating a limited variety of cargo units, such as vehicles, trailers, etc.

Non-standardized cargo means cargo which requires individual stowage and securing arrangements.

1.2 General information

This chapter should contain the following general statements:

.1 "The guidance given herein should by no means rule out the principles of good seamanship, neither can it replace experience in stowage and securing practice."

.2 "The information and requirements set forth in this Manual are consistent with the requirements of the vessel's trim and stability booklet, International Load Line Certificate (1966), the hull strength loading manual (if provided) and with the requirements of the International Maritime Dangerous Goods (IMDG) Code (if applicable)."

.3 "This Cargo Securing Manual specifies arrangements and cargo-securing devices provided on board the ship for the correct application to and the securing of cargo units, containers, vehicles and other entities, based on transverse, longitudinal and vertical forces which may arise during adverse weather and sea conditions."

.4 "It is imperative to the safety of the ship and the protection of the cargo and personnel that the securing of the cargo is carried out properly and that only appropriate securing points or fittings should be used for cargo securing."

.5 "The cargo-securing devices mentioned in this Manual should be applied so as to be suitable and adapted to the quantity, type of packaging, and physical properties of the cargo to be carried. When new or alternative types of cargo-securing devices are introduced, the Cargo Securing Manual should be revised accordingly. Alternative cargo-securing devices introduced should not have less strength than the devices being replaced."

.6 "There should be a sufficient quantity of reserve cargo-securing devices on board the ship."

.7 "Information on the strength and instructions for the use and maintenance of each specific type of cargo-securing device, where applicable, is provided in this manual. The cargo-securing devices should be maintained in a satisfactory condition. Items worn or damaged to such an extent that their quality is impaired should be replaced."

Chapter 2 – Securing devices and arrangements

2.1 Specification for fixed cargo-securing devices

This sub-chapter should indicate and where necessary illustrate the number, locations, type and MSL of the fixed devices used to secure cargo and should as a minimum contain the following information:

.1 a list and/or plan of the fixed cargo-securing devices, which should be supplemented with appropriate documentation for each type of device as far as practicable. The appropriate documentation should include information as applicable regarding:

- name of manufacturer
- type designation of item with simple sketch for ease of identification
- material(s)
- identification marking
- strength test result or ultimate tensile strength test result
- result of non-destructive testing
- MSL;

.2 fixed securing devices on bulkheads, web frames, stanchions, etc. and their types (e.g. padeyes, eyebolts, etc.), where provided, including their MSL;

.3 fixed securing devices on decks and their types (e.g. elephant-feet fittings, container fittings, apertures, etc.) where provided, including their MSL;

.4 fixed securing devices on deckheads, where provided, listing their types and MSL; and

.5 for existing ships with non-standardized fixed securing devices, the information on MSL and location of securing points is deemed sufficient.

2.2   Specification for portable cargo-securing devices

This sub-chapter should describe the number of and the functional and design characteristics of the portable cargo-securing devices carried on board the ship, and should be supplemented by suitable drawings or sketches if deemed necessary. It should contain the following information as applicable:

.1   a list of the portable securing devices, which should be supplemented with appropriate documentation for each type of device as far as practicable. The appropriate documentation should include information as applicable regarding:

- name of manufacturer
- type designation of item with simple sketch for ease of identification
- material(s), including minimum safe operational temperature
- identification marking
- strength test result or ultimate tensile strength test result.
- result of non-destructive testing
- MSL;

.2   container stacking fittings, container deck securing fittings, fittings for interlocking of containers, bridge-fittings, etc., their MSL and use;

.3   chains, wire lashings, rods, etc., their MSL and use;

.4   tensioners (e.g. turnbuckles, chain tensioners, etc.), their MSL and use;

.5   securing gear for cars, if appropriate, and other vehicles, their MSL and use;

.6   trestles and jacks, etc., for vehicles (trailers) where provided, including their MSL and use; and

.7   anti-skid material (e.g. soft boards) for use with cargo units having low frictional characteristics.

2.3   Inspection and maintenance schemes

This sub-chapter should describe inspection and maintenance schemes of the cargo-securing devices on board the ship.

2.3.1 Regular inspections and maintenance should be carried out under the responsibility of the master. Cargo-securing device inspections as a minimum should include:

.1   routine visual examinations of components being utilized; and

.2   periodic examinations/retesting as required by the Administration. When required, the cargo-securing devices concerned should be subjected to inspections by the Administration.

2.3.2 This sub-chapter should document actions to inspect and maintain the ship's cargo-securing devices. Entries should be made in a record book, which should be kept with the Cargo Securing Manual. This record book should contain the following information:

.1   procedures for accepting, maintaining and repairing or rejecting cargo-securing devices; and

.2   record of inspections.

2.3.3 This sub-chapter should contain information for the master regarding inspections and adjustment of securing arrangements during the voyage.

2.3.4 Computerized maintenance procedures may be referred to in this sub-chapter.

Chapter 3 – Stowage and securing of non-standardized and semi-standardized cargo

3.1   Handling and safety instructions

This sub-chapter should contain:

.1   instructions on the proper handling of the securing devices; and

.2   safety instructions related to handling of securing devices and to securing and unsecuring of units by ship or shore personnel.

3.2   Evaluation of forces acting on cargo units

This sub-chapter should contain the following information:

.1   tables or diagrams giving a broad outline of the accelerations which can be expected in various positions on board the ship in adverse sea conditions and with a range of applicable metacentric height (GM) values;

.2   examples of the forces acting on typical cargo units when subjected to the accelerations referred to in paragraph 3.2.1 and angles of roll and metacentric height (GM) values above which the forces acting on the cargo units exceed the permissible limit for the specified securing arrangements as far as practicable;

.3   examples of how to calculate number and strength of portable securing devices required to counteract the forces referred to in 3.2.2 as well as safety factors to be used for different types of portable cargo-securing devices. Calculations may be carried out according to annex 13 to the Code of Safe Practice for Cargo Stowage and Securing (CSS Code)* or methods accepted by the Administration;

.4   it is recommended that the designer of a Cargo Securing Manual converts the calculation method used into a form suiting the particular ship, its securing devices and the cargo carried. This form may consist of applicable diagrams, tables or calculated examples; and

.5   other operational arrangements such as electronic data processing (EDP) or use of a loading computer may be accepted as alternatives to the requirements of the above paragraphs 3.2.1 to 3.2.4, providing that this system contains the same information.

3.3   Application of portable securing devices on various cargo units, vehicles and stowage blocks

3.3.1 This sub-chapter should draw the master's attention to the correct application of portable securing devices, taking into account the following factors:

.1   duration of the voyage;

.2   geographical area of the voyage with particular regard to the minimum safe operational temperature of the portable securing devices;

.3   sea conditions which may be expected;

.4   dimensions, design and characteristics of the ship;

.5   expected static and dynamic forces during the voyage;

.6   type and packaging of cargo units including vehicles;

.7   intended stowage pattern of the cargo units including vehicles; and

.8   mass and dimensions of the cargo units and vehicles.

3.3.2 This sub-chapter should describe the application of portable cargo-securing devices as to number of lashings and allowable lashing angles. Where necessary, the text should be supplemented by suitable drawings or sketches to facilitate the correct understanding and proper application of the securing devices to various types of cargo and cargo units. It should be pointed out that for certain cargo units and other entities with low friction resistance, it is advisable to place soft boards or other anti-skid material under the cargo to increase friction between the deck and the cargo.

3.3.3 This sub-chapter should contain guidance as to the recommended location and method of stowing and securing of containers, trailers and other cargo-carrying vehicles, palletized cargoes, unit loads and single cargo items (e.g. woodpulp, paper rolls, etc.), heavyweight cargoes, cars and other vehicles.

3.4   Supplementary requirements for ro–ro ships

3.4.1 The Manual should contain sketches showing the layout of the fixed securing devices with identification of strength (MSL) as well as longitudinal and transverse distances between securing points. In preparing this sub-chapter further guidance should be utilized from IMO Assembly resolutions A.533(13) and A.581(14) as appropriate.

3.4.2 In designing securing arrangements for cargo units, including vehicles and containers, on ro–ro passenger ships and specifying minimum strength requirements for securing devices used, forces due to the motion of the ship, angle of heel after damage or flooding and other considerations relevant to the effectiveness of the cargo-securing arrangement should be taken into account.

3.5   Bulk carriers

If bulk carriers carry cargo units falling within the scope of chapter VI/5 or chapter VII/5 of the SOLAS Convention, this cargo shall be stowed and secured in accordance with a Cargo Securing Manual, approved by the Administration.

---

* See IMO sales publication IA292E.

Chapter 4 – Stowage and securing of containers and other standardized cargo

4.1   Handling and safety instructions

This sub-chapter should contain:

- .1   instructions on the proper handling of the securing devices; and

- .2   safety instructions related to handling of securing devices and to securing and unsecuring of containers or other standardized cargo by ship or shore personnel.

4.2   Stowage and securing instructions

This sub-chapter is applicable to any stowage and securing system (i.e. stowage within or without cellguides) for containers and other standardized cargo. On existing ships the relevant documents regarding safe stowage and securing may be integrated into the material used for the preparation of this chapter.

4.2.1   *Stowage and securing plan*

This sub-chapter should consist of a comprehensive and understandable plan or set of plans providing the necessary overview on:

- .1   longitudinal and athwartship views of under-deck and on-deck stowage locations of containers as appropriate;

- .2   alternative stowage patterns for containers of different dimensions;

- .3   maximum stack masses;

- .4   permissible vertical sequences of masses in stacks;

- .5   maximum stack heights with respect to approved sight lines; and

- .6   application of securing devices using suitable symbols with due regard to stowage position, stack mass, sequence of masses in stack and stack height. The symbols used should be consistent throughout the Cargo Securing Manual.

4.2.2   *Stowage and securing principle on deck and under deck*

This sub-chapter should support the interpretation of the stowage and securing plan with regard to container stowage, highlighting:

- .1   the use of the specified devices; and

- .2   any guiding or limiting parameters such as dimension of containers, maximum stack masses, sequence of masses in stacks, stacks affected by wind load, height of stacks.

It should contain specific warnings of possible consequences from misuse of securing devices or misinterpretation of instructions given.

4.3   Other allowable stowage patterns

This sub-chapter should provide the necessary information for the master to deal with cargo stowage situations deviating from the general instructions addressed under sub-chapter 4.2, including appropriate warnings of possible consequences from misuse of securing devices or misinterpretation of instructions given.

Information should be provided with regard to, *inter alia:*

- .1   alternative vertical sequences of masses in stacks;

- .2   stacks affected by wind load in the absence of outer stacks;

- .3   alternative stowage of containers with various dimensions; and

- .4   permissible reduction of securing effort with regard to lower stack masses, lesser stack heights or other reasons.

4.4   Forces acting on cargo units

This sub-chapter should present the distribution of accelerations on which the stowage and securing system is based, and specify the underlying condition of stability. Information on forces induced by wind and sea on deck cargo should be provided.

It should further contain information on the nominal increase of forces or accelerations with an increase of initial stability. Recommendations should be given for reducing the risk of cargo losses from deck stowage by restrictions to stack masses or stack heights, where high initial stability cannot be avoided.

MSC/Circ. 860 of 22 May 1998

GUIDELINES FOR THE APPROVAL
OF OFFSHORE CONTAINERS HANDLED IN OPEN SEAS

1   The Maritime Safety Committee, at its sixty-ninth session (11 to 20 May 1998), considered and approved draft revised Guidelines for the approval of offshore containers handled in open seas, as set out in the annex to this circular.

2   These Guidelines are based on the provisions contained in the annex to MSC/Circ.613, which have been updated to reflect more clearly the relevant provisions in the Recommendation on Harmonized Interpretation and Implementation of the International Convention for Safe Containers (CSC), 1972, as amended (CSC/Circ.100) and the IMDG Code and recent practice in the design of offshore containers.

3   Member Governments are invited to bring these Guidelines to the attention of all parties concerned with the approval, manufacture, inspection and operation of offshore containers.

4   This Circular replaces MSC/Circ.613 dated 18 June 1993.

Annex

Guidelines for the approval of offshore containers handled in open seas

1   The Maritime Safety Committee, at its sixty-second session, approved amendments to the Recommendation on Harmonized Interpretation and Implementation of the International Convention for Safe Containers, 1972 (CSC). The revised Recommendation was circulated as CSC/Circ.100 dated 30 June 1993 and has been included as a supplement in the 1996 edition of the CSC.

2   Paragraph 3.3 of the revised Recommendation on Harmonized Interpretation and Implementation of the CSC states that the Convention does not apply to offshore containers that are handled in open seas. There are several reasons for applying special design and testing parameters to offshore containers:

.1   the tests set out in Annex II to the CSC are designed to cover the forces on containers encountered in general marine transport, loading and unloading in ports and in inland transport. However, offshore containers are used to supply offshore installations and are typically shipped on the open deck of purpose-built supply vessels and are lifted onto and off the offshore installation by cranes on the installations. Such operations may often take place in very unfavourable weather and sea conditions;

.2   spreader beams, as used for lifting ordinary containers, cannot be used when lifting offshore containers; and

.3   the types of offshore containers used are often purpose-built and include closed and open dry cargo containers, dry bulk cargo containers and portable tanks. Offshore containers, unlike ISO containers, are not standardized with regard to sizes or gross mass; many have a smaller base area than the 7 m^2 in the lower limiting definition of a container in the CSC.

3   Sections 12 and 13 of the General Introduction to the International Maritime Dangerous Goods (IMDG) Code recognize the special nature of offshore containers and portable tanks. These sections state that the design and testing of offshore containers and offshore tank-containers should take into account the dynamic lifting and impact forces that may occur when a container or tank is handled in open seas in adverse weather and sea conditions and that the requirements for such containers and tanks should be determined by the approving competent authority.

4   For the purposes of these guidelines, "offshore containers" should be taken to mean portable units specially designed for repeated use in the transport of goods or equipment to, from or between fixed and/or floating offshore installations and ships. Such units include containers and portable tanks for dangerous goods as defined in sections 12 and 13 of the General Introduction to the IMDG Code.

5   These guidelines are intended to assist approving competent authorities in developing detailed requirements for offshore containers. For the purposes of these guidelines, the "approving competent authority" includes organizations duly authorized by the Administration.

Approval

6   Approving competent authorities should base their approval of offshore containers both on calculations and on testing, taking into account the dynamic lifting and impact forces that may occur when handling in open seas.

Design

7   Offshore containers should be fitted with special pad eyes, suitable for the attachment of purpose-built slings connected with shackles. Where ISO corner fittings are mounted in conjunction with pad eyes, these corner fittings are not intended for lifting offshore.

8   In order to facilitate handling in open seas, offshore containers should be pre-slung. Such slings should be permanently attached to the container and considered to be part of the container. The dynamic forces which occur when handling containers in open seas will be higher than those encountered during normal quayside handling. This should be taken into account when determining the requirements for slings on offshore containers by multiplying the normal safety factor for slings by an additional factor. The fact that light containers will be subject to relatively higher dynamic forces than heavier containers should also be taken into account. Minimum material requirements for impact toughness should be specified when high-strength steel is used in, e.g., chains, links and shackles.

9   Since offshore containers may not always be secured on supply vessels, such containers should be designed so as to withstand 30° tilting in any direction when fully loaded. Cargo may normally be assumed to be evenly distributed with the centre of gravity at the half height of the container, but on containers for dedicated transport (e.g. special bottle rack containers for gas bottles in fixed positions) the actual centre of gravity should be used.

10   Protruding parts on an offshore container that may catch on other containers or structures should be avoided. Doors and hatches should be secured against opening during transport and lifting. Hinges and locking devices should be protected against damage from impact loads.

11   Strength calculations should include lifting with the attached lifting sling and any other applicable means of handling (e.g., lifting with fork-lift trucks). Impact loads on the sides and bottom of containers should also be considered in these calculations and impact properties should be included in the requirements for structural steel materials. However, calculations, including static equivalency of point loads, in combination with the tests as set out in paragraph 13 should normally be considered sufficient.

12   Containers are sometimes temporarily used on floating or fixed offshore installations as storage space, laboratories, accommodation or control stations, etc. When used this way, the container will also be subject to the regulations applicable for the offshore installation in addition to transport-related requirements based on these guidelines.

Testing

13   At least one offshore container of each design type should be subjected to the following tests:

.1   *4-point lifting test*

Internal load: a uniformly distributed load such that the total mass of the container and test load is equal to 2.5R, where R is the maximum allowable combined mass of the container and its cargo. The container should be lifted with a lifting sling attached to each of its four pad eyes with an angle to the vertical equal to the design angle.

.2   *2-point lifting test*

Internal load: a uniformly distributed load such that the total mass of the container and test load is equal to 1.5R. A container fitted with four pad eyes should be lifted from only two pad eyes situated diagonally opposite each other.

.3   *Vertical impact test*

Internal load: a uniformly distributed load such that the total mass of the container and test load is equal to R. The container should be suspended at an inclined angle with the lowest corner at least 50 mm above a rigid floor. The container should then be quickly released so that it will have a speed of at least 1 m/s on initial impact.

.4   *Other tests*

Other tests, designed to demonstrate the ability of a container type to withstand other handling or transport forces, such as those described in relevant standards or the CSC, may also be required by the approving competent authority.

14   The tested offshore container should suffer no permanent damage or deformation in any of the tests which would render it incapable of being used for its designed purpose.

15   In order to ensure that offshore containers of the same design type are manufactured to the approved design, the approving competent authority should examine and test as many units as it considers necessary.

16   Offshore containers that have been designed, manufactured, tested and approved according to these guidelines should be clearly marked "Offshore Container" on an approval plate in accordance with the appendix. The details shown in the appendix represent minimum requirements.

Inspection

17   Offshore containers should be inspected at least annually, as deemed appropriate, by the approving competent authority. The date of inspection and the mark of the inspector should be marked on the container, preferably on a plate fitted for this purpose. The inspection plate may be combined with the approval plate (paragraph 16) and any other official approval or data plates on a single base plate. It should be noted that the inspection plates on offshore containers commonly show the date of the last inspection, unlike Safety Approval Plates on containers subject to the CSC which are marked with the date when the first periodic examination is due and in the case of containers covered by a periodic examination scheme (PES), with the date by which the next examination is due.

Standards and rules

18   The following standards and rules on offshore containers, not all of which cover all aspects of the design and testing in these guidelines, are known to exist or be under preparation and should be consulted as appropriate:

–   BS 7072: British Standard Code of Practice for Inspection and Repair of Offshore Containers;

–   Det Norske Veritas (DNV): Certification Note 2.7-1, Offshore Containers;

–   Det Norske Veritas (DNV): Certification Note 2.7-2, Offshore Service Containers; and

–   pr EN 12079: Offshore Containers – Design, construction, testing, inspection and marking (under preparation by the European Committee for Standardization (CEN)).

Appendix

OFFSHORE CONTAINER		
Name of manufacturer:		
Month/year of manufacture:		
Identification No:		
Maximum gross mass:	kg	lb
Tare-mass:	kg	lb
Payload:	kg	lb
Approval No:		

Approval plate

MSC/Circ. 1027 of 6 June 2002

CARRIAGE OF DANGEROUS GOODS

Documents of compliance with the special requirements for ships carrying dangerous goods under the provisions of regulation II-2/19* of SOLAS 74, as amended

1   The Maritime Safety Committee, at its sixty-third session (16 to 25 May 1994), considered and approved a standard format for the document of compliance required by regulation II-2/54.3 of SOLAS 1974, as amended.

2   The Committee, at that session, agreed that the period of validity of the document of compliance should not exceed 5 years and should not be extended beyond the expiry date of the valid Cargo Ship Safety Construction Certificate issued to the ship concerned under the provisions of SOLAS regulation I/12.

3   The Maritime Safety Committee, at its seventy-fifth session (15 to 24 May 2002), in view of the amendments to SOLAS chapter II-2, adopted by resolution MSC.99(73), considered and approved a revised standard format for the document of compliance required by regulation II-2/19.4* of SOLAS 1974, as amended, which should apply from 1 July 2002.

4   The revised standard format of the document of compliance recommended for use and acceptance by Member Governments and Contracting Governments to the SOLAS Convention is annexed hereto.

5   This Circular supersedes MSC/Circ. 642 dated 6 June 1994.

---

* See also MSC/Circ.1148.

Annex

Standard format of the document of compliance

Special Requirements for Ships carrying Dangerous Goods

Issued in pursuance of the requirement of regulation II-2/19.4
of the International Convention for the Safety of Life at Sea, 1974,
as amended, under the authority of
the Government of . . . .

Name of ship: . . . .

Distinctive number or letters: . . . .

Port of registry: . . . .

Ship type: . . . .

IMO Number (if applicable): . . . .

THIS IS TO CERTIFY:

.1 that the construction and equipment of the above mentioned ship was found to comply with the provisions of regulation II-2/19 of the International Convention for the Safety of Life at Sea, 1974, as amended; and

.2 that the ship is suitable for the carriage of those classes of dangerous goods as specified in the appendix hereto, subject to any provisions in the International Maritime Dangerous Goods (IMDG) Code and the Code of Safe Practice for Solid Bulk Cargoes (BC Code) for individual substances, materials or articles also being complied with.

This document is valid until . . . .

Issued at . . . . 20. . . . .
(Signature of authorized official issuing the certificate)

Note: There are no special requirements in the above-mentioned regulation II-2/19 for the carriage of dangerous goods of classes 6.2 and 7, and for the carriage of dangerous goods in limited quantities, as required in chapter 3.4 of the IMDG Code.

Appendix

Appendix

Spaces to be indicated in the plans with numbers
corresponding with the table below

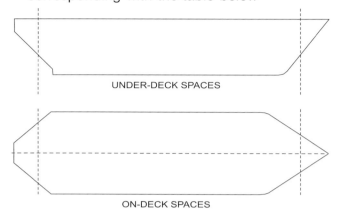

UNDER-DECK SPACES

ON-DECK SPACES

Class \ Hold	1	2	3	.	.	.	.	.	.
1.1–1.6									
1.4S									
2.1									
2.2									
2.3									
3 FP < 23°C c.c.									
3 FP ⩾ 23°C – ⩽ 61°C c.c.									
4.1									
4.2									
4.3									
5.1									
5.2									
6.1 liquids									
6.1 liquids FP < 23°C c.c.									
6.1 liquids FP ⩾ 23°C – ⩽ 61°C c.c.									
6.1 solids									
8 liquids									
8 liquids FP < 23°C c.c.									
8 liquids FP ⩾ 23°C – ⩽ 61°C c.c.									
8 solids									
9									

P Indicates PACKAGED GOODS PERMITTED

A Indicates PACKAGED AND BULK GOODS ALLOWED

X NOT ALLOWED

Remarks related to the information in the table above as applicable:

. . . .

Note: Cargoes in bulk may be listed individually by name and class.

MSC/Circ. 1087 of 18 June 2003

GUIDELINES FOR PARTIALLY WEATHERTIGHT HATCHWAY COVERS ON BOARD CONTAINERSHIPS

1   The Maritime Safety Committee, at its seventy-seventh session (28 May to 6 June 2003), recognizing the need to standardize the conditions for the fitting of partially weathertight hatchway covers on containerships and to develop recommendations on installation of such covers on containerships, and having considered proposals by the forty-fifth session of the Sub-Committee on Stability and Load Lines and on Fishing Vessels Safety (SLF), the seventh session of the Sub-Committee on Dangerous Goods, Solid Cargoes and Containers (DSC) and the forty-seventh session of the Sub-Committee on Fire Protection (FP), approved the Guidelines for partially weathertight hatchway covers on board containerships, as set out in the annex.

2   Member Governments are invited to bring the annexed Guidelines to all the parties concerned for their application, as appropriate, urging them, in particular, to apply the measures for construction and equipment contained in sections 1 and 2 of the Guidelines to ships constructed on or after 1 January 2004 and to implement the operational measures contained in section 3 of the Guidelines as soon as possible for all ships.

Annex

Guidelines for partially weathertight hatchway covers on board containerships

1   Location of hatchways, height of coamings and weathertightness of hatchway covers

1.1   Introduction

Requirements relating to the height of coamings and to the weathertightness of hatchway covers located above the superstructure deck are left to the discretion of the Administration, pursuant to regulation 14(2) of the International Convention on Load Lines (LL), 1966. This section of the Guidelines is intended to serve as a guide when decisions are made on whether to accept partially weathertight hatchway covers on board containerships, in accordance with regulation 14(2) of the 1966 LL Convention.

1.2   Design considerations and criteria

1.2.1   Coamings and hatchway covers to exposed hatchways situated above the second superstructure tier or its equivalent, or above the third tier or its equivalent, in the forward quarter of the ship's length, may be regarded as being situated above the superstructure deck, for the purpose of giving effect to regulation 14(2) of the 1966 LL Convention. Partially weathertight hatch covers fitted to hatchways situated in such locations may be accepted subject to the following conditions.

1.2.2   Coamings and hatchway covers may be fitted to hatchways located on exposed decks situated at least two standard superstructure heights above the actual freeboard deck or an assumed freeboard deck, on the basis of which a calculation of the freeboard may be made corresponding to the draught, which should be not less than that which would correspond to the freeboard actually assigned to the ship. If any part of the hatchway is forward of a point located a quarter of a ship's length (0.25L) from the forward perpendicular, this hatchway should be located on an exposed deck which is situated at least three standard superstructure heights above the actual or assumed freeboard. It should be noted that use is made of a notional freeboard deck solely for the purpose of measuring the height of the deck on which hatchways are located; it may consist of an imaginary or a virtual deck which, under such circumstances, is not used for the actual assignment of the freeboard. The freeboard of the ship should be assigned on the basis of an actual deck, referred to as the *freeboard deck*, which should be determined in accordance with the provisions of the 1966 LL Convention and of IACS Unified Interpretation LL39, as contained in LL.3/Circ.77.

1.2.3   The height of the hatchway coamings should not be less than 600 mm.

1.2.4   Non-weathertight gaps between the hatchway covers should be regarded as unprotected openings with respect to the requirements relating to intact stability and damage stability calculations. The gaps should also be as small as possible and proportional to the capacity of the bilge pumping system and the estimated amount of water penetration, as well as to the capacity and the operational efficiency of the fire-extinguishing system, and in any case should be not more than 50 mm.

1.2.5   Labyrinths, gutters or other equivalent means should be fitted close to the edges of each hatch cover at right angles with the openings in order to reduce to a minimum the quantity of water that might penetrate into the hold from the upper surface of each cover. Figures 1.2.5-1 and 1.2.5-2 are examples of labyrinth and gutter arrangements.

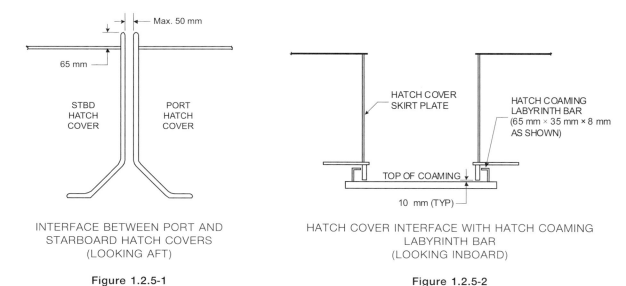

INTERFACE BETWEEN PORT AND
STARBOARD HATCH COVERS
(LOOKING AFT)

Figure 1.2.5-1

HATCH COVER INTERFACE WITH HATCH COAMING
LABYRINTH BAR
(LOOKING INBOARD)

Figure 1.2.5-2

1.2.6   Scantlings for hatchway covers and the components of clamping devices used to secure the covers to the structure supporting them and the coamings should be at the very least equivalent to those applying to weathertight hatchway covers and be in accordance with the relevant provisions of a recognized organization* or with the appropriate national standards established by the Administration and which provide for an equivalent level of safety.

2   Increase of carbon dioxide fire-extinguishing media for fixed gas fire-extinguishing systems

2.1   Introduction

This section of the Guidelines is intended to serve as a guide when decisions are made on whether to accept partially weathertight hatchway covers on board containerships in accordance with SOLAS regulations II-2/10.7.1.1 and II-2/20.6.1.1, and the relevant provisions of the Fire Safety Systems Code (chapter 5, paragraph 2.2.1.1), taking into account the leakage of carbon dioxide fire-extinguishing media through clear gaps between hatchway covers.

2.2   Increase of carbon dioxide fire-extinguishing media

If a container cargo hold fitted with partially weathertight hatchway covers is protected by a fixed carbon dioxide fire-extinguishing system, the amount of carbon dioxide for the cargo space should be increased in accordance with one of the following formulae, as appropriate:

$$CO_2^{INC}{}_{30\%} = 60 \cdot A_T \cdot \sqrt{\frac{B}{2}} \qquad (2.2\text{-}1)$$

$$CO_2^{INC}{}_{45\%} = 4 \cdot A_T \cdot \sqrt{\frac{B}{2}} \qquad (2.2\text{-}2)$$

where:

$CO_2^{INC}{}_{30\%}$: increase of carbon dioxide for cargo spaces not intended for carriage of motor vehicles with fuel in their tanks for their own propulsion (kg);

---

* *Recognized organization* means an organization that has been recognized in accordance with SOLAS regulation XI/1.

$CO_2{}^{INC}{}_{45\%}$: increase of carbon dioxide for cargo spaces intended for carriage of motor vehicles with fuel in their tanks for their own propulsion (kg);

A_T: total maximum area of clear gaps (m^2); and

B: breadth of cargo space protected by the carbon dioxide fire-extinguishing systems (m).

3 Stowage and segregation of cargo transport units containing dangerous goods

3.1 Introduction

This section of the Guidelines is intended to serve as a guide when decisions are made on the stowage and segregation of cargo transport units (CTUs) containing dangerous goods on containerships fitted with partially weathertight hatchway covers. For the purpose of the stowage and segregation of CTUs containing dangerous goods on containerships fitted with partially weathertight hatchway covers, the effect of clear gaps, as defined below, should be taken into consideration. The effects of other structures such as labyrinths are not considered, as no clear path exists into the hold.

3.2 Definitions

For the purpose of the application of this section of the Guidelines:

.1 *clear gap* means a clear unobstructed passage between hatchway covers that provides a path for dangerous goods to enter the cargo hold;

.2 *effective gutterbar* means a gutterbar the height of which is not less than 50 mm and also includes labyrinth bar; and

.3 *sensitive vertical line* means a vertical line under deck within one container space from a clear gap in athwartships direction(s) as specified by "C" in figures 3.2.3-1 and 3.2.3-2 below or equivalent.

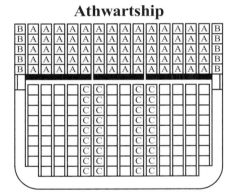

Athwartship   **Athwartship**

Figure 3.2.3-1 – Illustration of vertical lines   Figure 3.2.3-2 – Illustration of vertical lines

Note: Vertical row positions "on-deck", not directly above clear gaps between hatchway covers, are specified by "A". Vertical row positions with less than 50% footing on the hatch are specified by "B". Where containers are placed in the outermost vertical row, positions with more than 50% footing on the hatch cover are deemed to qualify as position(s) "A".

3.3 Partially weathertight hatchway covers fitted with effective gutterbars

Partially weathertight hatchway covers fitted with effective gutterbars can be regarded as "resistant to fire and liquid" for the purposes of stowage and segregation of CTUs containing dangerous goods on containerships fitted with such hatchway covers. Therefore, no special provision, other than those set out in paragraph 3.4, applies to the stowage and segregation of CTUs containing dangerous goods on or under the hatchway covers fitted with effective gutterbars. Gutterbars showing any visible structural damage, which would reduce their effectiveness, do not meet the definition in paragraph 3.2.2.

3.4 Special requirement for "on-deck" stowage

3.4.1 *Prohibition of stowage directly above clear gaps*

CTUs containing dangerous goods should not be stowed in the vertical lines specified by "X" in figure 3.4.1, above cargo holds fitted with partially weathertight hatchway covers having a clear gap, unless the cargo hold complies with the relevant requirements for the class and flashpoint of the dangerous goods in SOLAS regulation II-2/19. When "not in the same vertical line unless separated by a deck" is required in the IMDG Code and CTUs containing dangerous goods are stowed in position "X", as shown in figure 3.4.1 below, CTUs containing incompatible dangerous goods should not be stowed under deck in vertical lines indicated by "C" in figures 3.2.3-1 or 3.2.3-2.

Athwartship

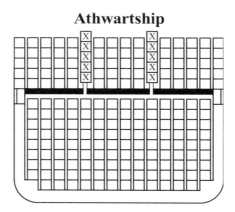

Figure 3.4.1 – Illustration of prohibited stowage of dangerous goods

3.4.2 Special requirement for on-deck stowage of CTUs above hatchway covers without effective gutterbars

Where hatchway covers are not fitted with effective gutterbars, CTUs containing dangerous goods should not be stowed in the vertical lines specified by "A" in figures 3.2.3-1 and 3.2.3-2, above cargo holds fitted with partially weathertight hatchway covers, unless the cargo hold complies with the relevant requirements for the class and flashpoint of the dangerous goods in SOLAS regulation II-2/19.

3.4.3 On-deck stowage of CTUs above cargo hold with effective gutterbars

Where hatchway covers are fitted with effective gutterbars, CTUs containing dangerous goods can be stowed in all vertical lines specified by "A" and "B" in figures 3.2.3-1 and 3.2.3-2 except as provided in paragraph 3.4.1, above cargo holds fitted with partially weathertight hatchway covers, regardless of whether the cargo hold under the hatchway cover complies with the relevant requirements in SOLAS regulation II-2/19.

3.5 Special requirement for segregation

3.5.1 Special requirement for segregation and stowage of CTUs on partially weathertight hatchway covers without effective gutterbars

Where "not in the same vertical line unless separated by a deck" is required in the IMDG Code, the following applies:

.1   when the reference CTU is stowed on deck in positions specified by "A" in figures 3.2.3-1 and 3.2.3-2, CTUs containing incompatible dangerous goods should not be stowed within the relevant sensitive vertical lines under deck. Examples are illustrated in figures 3.5.1-1 and 3.5.1-2; and

.2   when the reference CTU is stowed under deck in positions as specified by "C" in figures 3.2.3-1 and 3.2.3-2, CTUs containing incompatible dangerous goods should not be stowed on the hatches above the hold. Example is illustrated in figure 3.5.1-3.

3.5.2 Segregation of CTUs related to hatchway covers with effective gutterbars

Where hatchway covers are fitted with effective gutterbars, segregation of CTUs containing dangerous goods on board containerships should be in accordance with the segregation requirements in paragraph 7.2.3.2 of the IMDG Code for containerships.

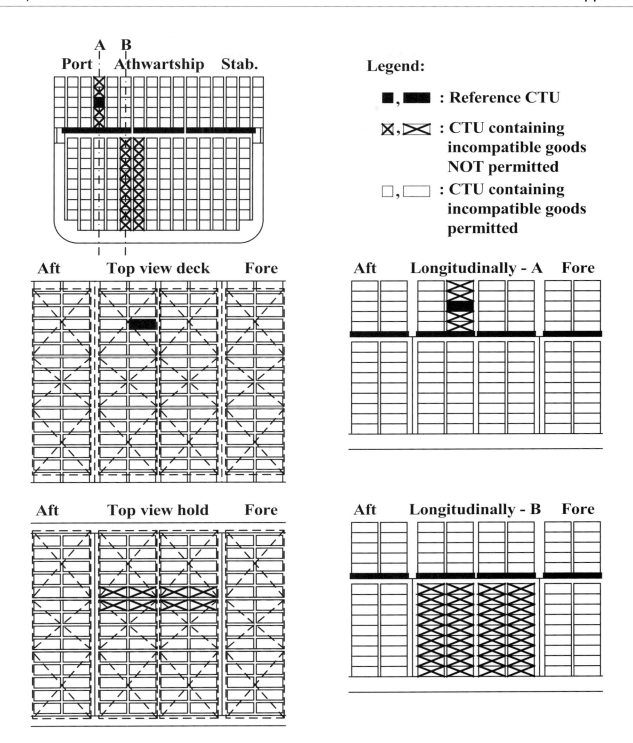

Figure 3.5.1-1 – *Example of segregation within sensitive vertical lines
(reference CTU is above left hatchway cover)*

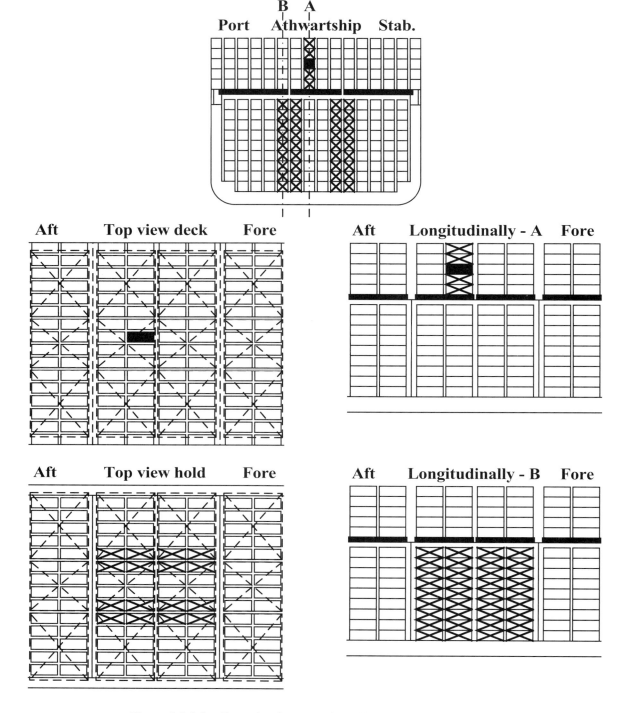

Figure 3.5.1-2 – *Example of segregation within sensitive vertical lines (reference CTU is above centre hatchway covers)*

Appendix

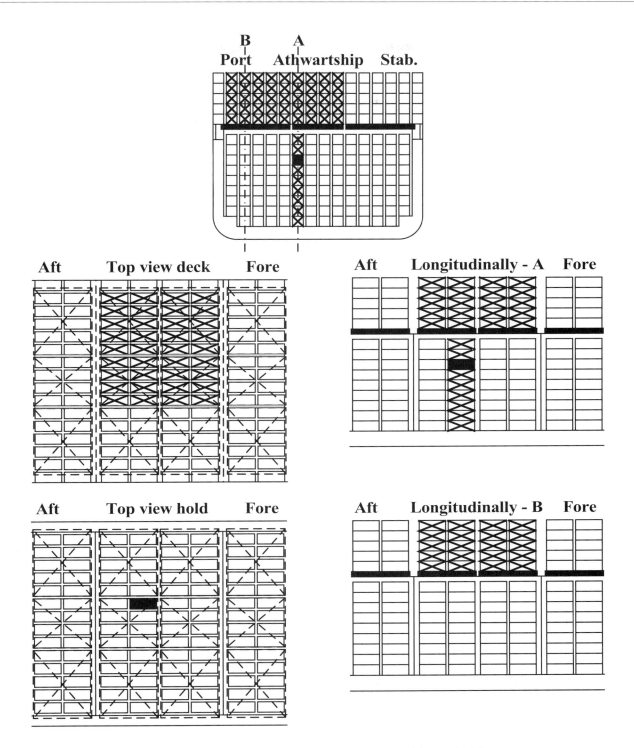

Figure 3.5.1-3 – *Example of segregation within sensitive vertical lines*
(reference CTU is in sensitive vertical line under deck)

Appendix

MSC/Circ.1147 of 15 December 2004

QUESTIONNAIRE ON INSPECTIONS OF CONTAINERS/VEHICLES CARRYING PACKAGED DANGEROUS GOODS

1   The Sub-Committee on Dangerous Goods, Solid Cargoes and Containers (DSC), at its ninth session (27 September to 1 October 2004), in recalling the provisions of MSC/Circ.859, whereby Member Governments are invited to submit reports to the Organization on the results of inspection on the compliance with the International Maritime Dangerous Goods (IMDG) Code of cargo transport units carrying dangerous goods, supported proposals that, in order to obtain an accurate reflection of the degree of such inspections taking place, it would be appropriate to carry out a survey to ascertain the full extent of such inspections.

2   The Maritime Safety Committee, at its seventy-ninth session (1 to 10 December 2004), concurred with the approach taken by the Sub-Committee and instructed the Secretariat to collate the information received, in response to the questionnaire, and to report the results to DSC 10.

3   Member Governments are requested to provide the information requested in the questionnaire set out in the annex and to forward completed questionnaires to the Secretariat by 1 June 2005.

Annex

IMO Survey – inspections of containers/vehicles carrying packaged dangerous goods

1   What specific arrangements do you have in place to accord with MSC/Circ.859 to carry out inspections of freight containers/vehicles carrying packaged dangerous goods in relation to compliance with the IMDG Code?

2   How frequently are the above arrangements carried out?

3   If no arrangements are in place, do you propose to institute inspections and when will they be instituted?

4   When did you last send in a report of the findings of inspections to the IMO?

5   What did your last report of inspections indicate as a level of compliance?

6   What initiatives to raise awareness of the requirements of the IMDG Code do you have in place?

7   What enforcement actions have been taken in the past 12 months as a result of your inspections?

8   The IMDG Code is mandatory. What activities in relation to the shipment of packaged dangerous goods are envisaged by your organization because of its mandatory nature?

Please complete the above questionnaire as fully as possible and return this form by 1 June 2005.

Co-ordinates of responding Member Government to include complete address, telephone and facsimile numbers and, if possible, an e-mail address.

MSC/Circ.1148 of 15 December 2004

CARRIAGE OF DANGEROUS GOODS

Issuing and renewal of document of compliance with the special requirements applicable to ships carrying dangerous goods

1   At its seventy-fifth session (15 to 24 May 2002), the Maritime Safety Committee considered and approved a standard format for the document of compliance required by regulation II-2/19.4 of the 1974 SOLAS Convention, as amended, applicable as from 1 July 2002. This format is reproduced in circular MSC/Circ.1027.

2   Recognizing the need to take into account the amendments to table 19.3 of SOLAS regulation II-2/19 which the Committee had adopted by resolution MSC.134(76), the Maritime Safety Committee, at its seventy-ninth session (1 to 10 December 2004), decided that it was necessary to highlight the prohibition on stowage of class 5.2 dangerous goods under deck or in enclosed ro–ro spaces in documents of compliance required by regulation II-2/19 of the SOLAS Convention, as amended, for any ship built on or after 1 July 2004 when issuing or renewing the said documents.

3   Recognizing also that this prohibition on stowage under the IMDG Code is also applicable to all ships built before 1 July 2004 and subject to regulation II-2/19 (or II-2/54) of the SOLAS Convention, as amended, the Committee also decided that the prohibition on stowage would have to be taken into account when renewing documents of compliance for:

    .1   any passenger ship built on or after 1 September 1984 and before 1 July 2004;

    .2   any cargo ship of 500 gross tonnage and above built on or after 1 September 1984 and before 1 July 2004; and

    .3   any cargo ship of less than 500 gross tonnage built on or after 1 February 1992 and before 1 July 2004.

4   In addition, at the same session, the Committee recalled that the standard document of compliance format set out in circular MSC/Circ.1027 should be used when renewing documents of ships subject to SOLAS regulation II-2/54 applicable before 1 July 2002, and that in such cases the references to regulations II-2/19 and II-2/19.4 appearing in the standard format should be replaced by references to regulations II-2/54 and II-2/54.3, respectively.

5   Member Governments are invited to draw this circular to the attention of authorities responsible for issuing and renewing documents of compliance, bodies acting on behalf of these governments, and shipowners, ship operators and masters, with a view to harmonizing the practices of the various administrations.

6   Member Governments are also invited to draw this circular to the attention of authorities tasked by the port State with carrying out inspections of ships, and to recommend them to take the above into account when discharging their responsibilities.

MSC.1/Circ.1202 of 14 June 2006

INSPECTION PROGRAMMES FOR CARGO TRANSPORT UNITS (CTUs) CARRYING DANGEROUS GOODS

1   The Maritime Safety Committee, at its sixty-ninth session (11 to 20 May 1998), noted with concern that Member Government reports on inspection programmes carried out on cargo transport units carrying dangerous goods have shown that there is still a lack of general compliance with applicable IMO standards.

2   Noting, however, that, in those countries where regular inspection programmes have been implemented, a considerable improvement has been experienced in the general compliance with those standards, the Committee decided to urge Governments, especially those who have not yet done so, to implement such inspection programmes on a regular basis, using the relevant IMO codes and guidelines as standards.

3   To avoid the diverting of dangerous goods to ports where inspections are not carried out, a regional approach should be taken.

4   The following items should, as a minimum, be covered by the inspection programme referred to above:

    .1   placarding and marking;

    .2   labelling (of packages);

    .3   documentation;

    .4   packaging (inappropriate or damaged);

    .5   portable tank or road tank vehicles (inappropriate or damaged);

    .6   stowage/securing inside the freight containers, vehicles and other CTUs;

    .7   segregation of cargo;

    .8   Container Safety Convention (CSC) Safety Approval Plate;

    .9   serious structural deficiencies*; and

    .10   tie-down attachments of road tank vehicles.

5   To aid the Organization in evaluating the reports received, Governments are invited to submit them in a structured manner, preferably using the standard format given in the annex, containing at least the following information:

    .1   number of freight containers, vehicles and other CTUs examined;

    .2   number of freight containers, vehicles and other CTUs with deficiencies; and

    .3   number of deficiencies relating to each inspection item as referred to in paragraph 4.

6   This circular replaces MSC/Circ.859 dated 22 May 1998.

---

* On this issue only, the inspection programme should be extended to cover all CSC containers. For the determination of specific deficiencies, the guidance on serious structural deficiencies in containers given in CSC/Circ.134 should be applied. In addition, the provisions of 7.4.6.4.2 in the IMDG Code apply to CSC containers carrying class 1 dangerous goods.

Annex

Results of inspection programmes

Country _____

Item	Number	Percentage
Inspected units (5.1)		
Units with deficiencies (5.2): – total – stuffed inside the country – stuffed outside the country		
Deficiencies (5.3): Documentation (4.3): – Dangerous Goods Declaration – Container/Vehicle Packing Certificate		
Placarding and marking (4.1)		
CSC Convention Safety Approval Plate (4.8)		
Serious structural deficiencies (4.9)		
Tie-down attachments of road tank vehicles (4.10)		
Portable tank or road tank vehicles (inappropriate or damaged) (4.5)		
Labelling (of packages) (4.2)		
Packaging (inappropriate or damaged) (4.4)		
Segregation of cargo (4.7)		
Stowage/securing inside the unit (4.6)		

''Unit'' means ''freight containers, vehicles and other CTUs''.

MSC-MEPC.2/Circ.1 of 18 July 2006

DISPOSAL OF FUMIGANT MATERIAL

1   The Marine Environment Protection Committee, at its fifty-third session (18 to 22 July 2005), and the Maritime Safety Committee, at its eighty-first session (10 to 19 May 2006), considered a report, concerning the discharge of active packages of the cargo fumigant Magnesium Phosphide into New Zealand's marine waters.

2   The Committees' attention was drawn to the fact that, while there appeared to be no prohibition on the discharge of such material pursuant to the existing marine pollution prevention conventions, the discharge of active packages, producing phosphine gas, represented a significant risk to the public who may encounter them at sea.

3   The attention of Member Governments is, therefore, drawn to the following observations.

4   The most recent version of the IMO Recommendations on the safe use of pesticides in ships, incorporated into the Supplement to the IMDG Code (hereafter referred to as IMO Recommendations) recommends, *inter alia*, that:

   .1   fumigation of this nature should only be undertaken by a suitably qualified and trained person;

   .2   a "fumigator-in-charge" should be designated by the fumigation company, government agency or appropriate authority. He should be able to provide documentation to the master confirming his competence and authorization;

   .3   the master should be provided with written instructions by the fumigator-in-charge on the type of fumigant used, the hazards involved, the threshold limit values (TLV) and the precautions to be taken, and in view of the highly toxic nature of all commonly used fumigants these should be followed carefully;

   .4   clear written instructions should be given to the master of the ship, to the receiver of the cargo and to the authorities at the discharging port as to how any powdery residues are to be disposed of. Furthermore, with regard to fumigation to be continued in transit, the ship should carry instructions on the disposal of residual material; and

   .5   annex 4 of the IMO Recommendations also provides a Model Checklist for in-transit fumigation with phosphine, which should be completed and signed by both the fumigator-in-charge and the master.

5   It is, therefore, recommended that Member Governments issue regulations to oblige ships that carry solid cargoes requiring fumigation to ensure that all waste and residues are disposed of in appropriate manner, either by incineration or by disposal on shore, as recommended by the manufacturer.

6   Member Governments are invited to bring the above information to the attention of shipowners, ship operators, companies, shipmasters, fumigation companies and all other parties concerned, requesting that appropriate action be taken in accordance with the provisions of the relevant IMO instruments.

Facilitation Committee

FAL.2/Circ.51/Rev.1 of 14 February 2002

Convention on Facilitation of International Maritime Traffic, 1965

Shipping Documentation

IMO FAL Form 7 – Dangerous Goods Manifest

1   The Facilitation Committee, at its twenty-sixth session (7 to 11 September 1998), approved the draft FAL Form 8 set out in the annex to FAL.2/Circ. 49, as amended, for inclusion in the Annex to the FAL Convention and circulation, after endorsement of the editorial changes by the Editorial and Technical Group (E & T Group) of the DSC Sub-Committee, encouraged the use of FAL Form 8 (Dangerous Goods Manifest) and invited comments thereon to FAL 27, if any. The DSC Sub-Committee, at its fourth session (22 to 26 February 1999), endorsed the FAL Form 8, as editorially amended by the E & T Group and set out as annex to FAL.2/Circ.51.

2   The Committee, at its twenty-eighth session (30 October to 3 November 2000), agreed to delete the reference to the Multimodal Dangerous Goods Declaration as FAL Form 7 (FAL.2/Circ.48) in Appendix 1 to the FAL Convention, as this document was only relevant to commercial entities, and that the Dangerous Goods Manifest should be referred to in the Annex to the Convention as FAL Form 7. Information on this change of FAL Form numbers has been circulated by FAL.2/Circ.65.

3   The Committee, at its twenty-ninth session (7 to 11 January 2002), amended the existing format of the Dangerous Goods Manifest (FAL.2/Circ.51, annex), as set out in the annex to this circular, and urged Member Governments who have not responded to the request for information on the status of implementation of the FAL Forms (FAL 29/8 – Secretariat), including the new FAL Form 7 (Dangerous Goods Manifest), to do so at their earliest convenience.

4   Member Governments and international organizations are invited to bring the attached revised format of the Dangerous Goods Manifest (FAL Form 7) to the attention of all parties concerned with the transport of dangerous goods by sea.

Annex

DANGEROUS GOODS MANIFEST

(As required by SOLAS 74, chapter VII, regulation 5.5, MARPOL 73/78, annex III, regulation 4(3) and chapter 5.4, paragraph 5.4.3.1 of the IMDG Code)

PAGE NUMBER (e.g., 5 of 7)

NAME OF SHIP

IMO NUMBER

NATIONALITY OF SHIP

MASTER'S NAME

VOYAGE REFERENCE

PORT OF LOADING

PORT OF DISCHARGE

SHIPPING AGENT

BOOKING/ REFERENCE NUMBER	MARKS & NUMBERS CONTAINER ID. NO(s). VEHICLE REG. NO(s).	NUMBER AND KIND OF PACKAGES	PROPER SHIPPING NAME	CLASS	UN NUMBER	PACKING GROUP	SUBSIDIARY RISK(S)	FLASHPOINT (IN °C, c.c.)	MARINE POLLUTANT	MASS (kg) GROSS/NET	EmS	STOWAGE POSITION ON BOARD

AGENT'S SIGNATURE _____

MASTER'S SIGNATURE _____

PLACE AND DATE _____

PLACE AND DATE _____

IMO FAL FORM 7

FAL.6/Circ.12 of 11 July 2005

DIFFICULTIES ENCOUNTERED IN THE SHIPMENT OF
IMDG CODE CLASS 7 RADIOACTIVE MATERIAL AND, IN PARTICULAR, COBALT-60

1   The Facilitation Committee, at its thirty-first (19 to 23 July 2004) and thirty-second (4 to 8 July 2005) sessions, considered the increasing difficulties encountered in the worldwide shipment of cobalt-60, an IMDG Code class 7 radioactive material with UN 2916.*

2   The Committee, at its thirty-second session (4 to 8 July 2005), bearing in mind the conclusions and recommendations of the Sub-Committee on Dangerous Goods, Solid Cargoes and Containers, which considered the matter from the technical point of view at its ninth session (27 September to 1 October 2004), and the results of the consideration of the issue by the International Atomic Energy Agency, in an effort to foster the alleviation of the difficulties encountered, adopted the Advice on the shipment of IMDG Code class 7 radioactive material and, in particular, cobalt-60, which is set out in the annex.

3   Member Governments are urged to bring this circular and the annexed Advice to the attention of their Public Authorities, of owners, operators and masters of ships entitled to fly their flag and of owners and operators of ports located within the area under their jurisdiction.

4   The Committee remains, in particular, concerned about the potential adverse consequences the denial of shipment of IMDG Code class 7 radioactive materials used in medical applications, for example cobalt-60 and those radioisotopes used in radiotherapy and nuclear medicine in general, might have on public health.

5   Member Governments and non-governmental organizations with consultative status are urged to bring to the attention of the Committee any instances, together with the associated reasons, where the shipment of IMDG class 7 radioactive materials and, in particular those which have medical or public health applications, encounter difficulties or are refused aboard ship or in or through ports, so as to enable the Committee to consider the matter further and to determine the actions required.

Annex

Advice on the shipment of IMDG Code class 7 radioactive material
and in particular cobalt-60

General

1   Shipping and handling of IMDG Code class 7 radioactive materials, when carried out in compliance with the relevant provisions of SOLAS chapter VII, the IMDG Code and the recommendations contained in MSC/Circ.675 on Recommendations on the safe transport of dangerous cargoes and related activities in port areas, should be considered as meeting the necessary safety requirements and should be facilitated.

Specific advice related to transport of cobalt-60

2   Cobalt-60, a non-fissile IMDG Code class 7 radioactive material with UN 2916, is used to sterilize approximately 45% of all single-use medical supplies used worldwide, such as syringes, surgeons' gloves, bandages, and a wide variety of other products. Cobalt-60 is also relied upon to sterilize a vast array of consumer products and is used to make the food supply safer by eliminating food pathogens and to reduce the incidence of disease-carrying insects. Finally, cobalt-60 is one of the radioisotopes used in the treatment of cancer.

---

* The Committee was advised, at its thirty-first session, that difficulties were also encountered with the shipment of tantalite, an iron manganese tantalum niobium oxide, which is an inert ore shipped in bulk and which is classified as IMDG Code class 7 radioactive material.

3   Cobalt-60 emits high-energy gamma rays that are used to eliminate harmful micro-organisms, bacteria and pathogens from a variety of products, including single-use surgical and medical supplies, lab ware, packing materials, pharmaceutical products, cosmetics, raw materials, spices, fruits, seafood, poultry and red meat. The gamma rays kill micro-organisms, bacteria and pathogens, without damaging the product, thus preventing the spread of diseases and infections. The radiation treatment process does not induce radioactivity in the product. After the completion of the radiation process the product is available for immediate use.

4   The transport of cobalt-60 has a humanitarian dimension and is critical to the interest of public health and is thus for the benefit of society at large. The use of sterile disposable medical products in clinics and hospitals worldwide is linked directly to a reasonable and safe system for international supply and delivery of cobalt-60. The rising number of incidents of denial of shipments of cobalt-60 are seriously jeopardizing this supply and as a result this trend is having a negative impact on global health care.

Efforts of the IAEA

5   The International Atomic Energy Agency (IAEA) in an effort to assist in the alleviation of the difficulties encountered in the shipment of IMDG Code class 7 radioactive materials has, inter alia, developed:

   .1   a half-day Training programme for cargo handlers. This programme can be dovetailed to the existing training programmes on handling dangerous goods;

   .2   a half-day Training programme for Public Authorities. This programme familiarizes Public Authorities with the safety standards so that IMDG Code class 7 radioactive material is moved safely and smoothly; and

   .3   a Radiation protection programme specifically for Public Authorities which is to be included in a Safety Guide which is under preparation.

6   Further details in relation to the aforesaid programmes may be obtained from the IAEA.*

Recommended actions

7   Member Governments and those concerned should facilitate the efficient, cost-effective and expeditious handling and shipment of cobalt-60 aboard ships and in and through ports, provided it is shipped in accordance with the provisions in paragraph 1, because, ultimately, national populations rely on this material and, therefore, Governments have a vested interest in facilitating its transport.

8   Member Governments should work with relevant national authorities and industry associations to raise awareness of these matters as a means to help alleviate the difficulties encountered in the shipment of IMDG Code class 7 radioactive materials and in particular cobalt-60.

---

* Mr. M.E. Wangler
  Head, Safety of Transport of Radioactive Material Unit
  NSRW
  IAEA
  Wagramerstrasse 5
  A-1400 Vienna
  Austria
  E-mail: M.E.Wangler@iaea.org

Appendix

FAL.6/Circ.15 of 12 July 2006

DIFFICULTIES ENCOUNTERED IN THE SHIPMENT OF DANGEROUS CARGOES AND, IN PARTICULAR, SPORTING AMMUNITION AND RELATED COMPONENTS (IMDG CODE DIVISION 1.4S)

1   The Facilitation Committee, at its thirty-third session (3 to 7 July 2006), considered the difficulties encountered in the worldwide shipment of dangerous cargoes and in particular sporting ammunition (cartridges with inert projectile) and related components UN 0012, classified as IMDG Code division 1.4S.

2   The Committee, in an effort to foster the alleviation of the difficulties encountered, adopted the Advice on the shipment of sporting ammunition and related components (IMDG Code division 1.4S), which is set out in the annex.

3   The Committee remains concerned about the potential adverse effects the denial of shipment of dangerous cargoes might have on international trade and expeditious handling and shipment of such cargoes.

4   Member Governments and international organizations are urged to bring to the attention of the Committee any instances, together with the associated reasons, where the shipment of dangerous cargoes encounter difficulties or are refused aboard ship or in or through ports, so as to enable the Committee to consider the matter further and to determine the actions required.

5   Member Governments are urged to bring this Circular and the annexed Advice to the attention of their Public Authorities, of owners, operators and masters of ships entitled to fly their flag and of owners and operators of ports located within the area under their jurisdiction.

Annex

Advice on the shipment of dangerous cargoes and, in particular, sporting ammunition and related components (IMDG Code division 1.4S)

General

1   Shipping and handling of dangerous cargoes, including IMDG Code division 1.4S materials, when carried out in compliance with the relevant provisions of SOLAS chapter VII, the IMDG Code and the recommendations contained in Recommendations on the safe transport of dangerous cargoes and related activities in port areas (MSC/Circ.675, as amended), should be considered as meeting the necessary safety requirements and should be facilitated.

Specific advice

2   Materials of IMDG Code division 1.4S are recognized worldwide as being among the safest products of IMDG Code class 1, with an excellent safety record. These materials are so packed and designed that any hazardous effects arising from accidental functioning are confined within the packages unless the package has been degraded by fire, in which case all blast or projection effects are limited to the extent that they do not scientifically hinder fire-fighting or other emergency response efforts in the immediate vicinity of the package.

3   In the IMDG Code, part 3, dangerous goods list, all prescriptions for the shipment are established on the basic concept that class 1.4S products are extremely safe for transport. In fact these goods belong to stowage category 5 (IMDG Code, 7.1.7.2 to 7.1.7.5.5) for which is prescribed the same stowage system both for cargo or passenger ships. Products in division 1.4S may be transported in any amount on passenger ships (IMDG Code, 7.1.5.2). They can be stowed in the outermost row (IMDG Code, 7.1.7.4.1.2), without stowage level containment prescription (IMDG Code, 7.7.1.4) and are exempt from stowage provisions related to securement (IMDG Code, 7.1.7.4.4) and separation from living quarters and machinery spaces (IMDG Code, 7.1.7.4.6) for class 1 (IMDG Code, 7.1.7.3).

Recommended actions

4   Member Governments and those concerned should facilitate the efficient, cost-effective and expeditious handling and shipment of dangerous cargoes including IMDG Code division 1.4S materials aboard ships and in and through ports, provided that these cargoes are shipped in accordance with the provisions in paragraph 1.

5   Member Governments should work with relevant national authorities and industry associations to raise awareness of the provisions of SOLAS chapter VII, the IMDG Code and the recommendations contained in Recommendations on the safe transport of dangerous cargoes and related activities in port areas (MSC/Circ.675, as amended), in order to help alleviate the difficulties encountered in the shipment of dangerous cargoes.

Sub-Committee on Dangerous Goods, Solid Cargoes and Containers

DSC/Circ.4 of 4 April 1997

REPORTS ON INCIDENTS INVOLVING DANGEROUS GOODS OR MARINE POLLUTANTS IN PACKAGED FORM ON BOARD SHIPS OR IN PORT AREAS

1   The Sub-Committee on Dangerous Goods, Solid Cargoes and Containers (DSC), at its second session (24 to 28 February 1997), considered four incident reports which had been submitted by Member Governments in accordance with MSC/Circ.559, "Development of Guidelines to ensure the reporting to the Organization of incidents involving dangerous goods or marine pollutants in packaged form on board ships or in port areas" (see attached annexes).

2   Recognizing the importance of alerting Administrations and other parties concerned to the dangers involved in handling dangerous goods and highlighting the consequences of non-compliance with the requirements of the IMDG and BC Codes, the Sub-Committee agreed to disseminate the collated information on incidents involving dangerous goods or marine pollutants by means of a DSC circular.

3   Member Governments are invited to bring this circular to the attention of shipowners, ship operators, seafarers, shippers, terminal operators and other parties concerned.

Annex 1

Chemical incident involving POLYMERIC BEADS, EXPANDABLE (Hong Kong)

1   On 29 July 1996, whilst in Hong Kong waters, a 793 GT single-hold vessel sustained an explosion and flash fire in the cargo hold, resulting in the hospitalization of seven crewmen. Two were so seriously burned that they were not released until October 1996, and are still in need of medical treatment.

2   At the time of the explosion, the vessel had on board 18 containers loaded with "Expandable Polystyrene" and 14 containers loaded with "Polyester Yarn".

3   The seat of the explosion was found to be in three of the containers loaded with "Expandable Polystyrene". The source of ignition has not been established nor why only three containers were affected.

4   A subsequent investigation showed:

.1   the cargo was Class 9 UN No. 2211 POLYMERIC BEADS, expandable evolving flammable vapour;

.2   there was no declaration by the shipper that the goods were dangerous goods within the meaning of the IMDG Code;

.3   the goods were packed in paper bags. Paper bags are not acceptable as appropriate packing for UN No. 2211; and

.4   the cargo was stowed under deck without any mechanical ventilation.

5   As a result of the non declaration by the shipper, all parties involved in the transport chain were not aware of the dangers. There was no dangerous goods declaration nor packing certificates in respect of the cargo.

6   Finally, the force of the explosion shifted the remainder of the cargo, causing the vessel to list five degrees. On this occasion, this was not critical as the vessel was in smooth waters. No cell guides could be found inside the cargo hold – the containers being secured by the combined use of chains, hooks, turnbuckles and steel wires. A more adequate securing system may have prevented the cargo from shifting.

Annex 2

Chemical incident involving THIOUREA DIOXIDE (Hong Kong)

1 Shortly before noon on 6 October 1996, a 20 foot freight container in a Hong Kong container terminal port began to emit dense white fumes containing ammonia, carbon dioxide and hydrogen sulphide.

2 It took the Hong Kong Fire Services three hours to control the situation. During this period over 400 workers were evacuated from the container terminal port. Eight persons were taken to hospital suffering from the effects of inhaling the vapour; six were released and two were detained overnight.

3 A subsequent investigation showed that the container had 320 fibre drums of Thiourea Dioxide and more than 80% of them were leaking. The weight of the shipment was said to be 16,000 kilograms.

4 The container originated from Xingang, China and was in the container terminal port for 6 days prior to being exported to Jakarta, Indonesia.

5 The ambient temperature was 29°C with a relative humidity of 77%. In the preceding twenty four hours there had been 4.1 millimetres of precipitation. Isolated and violent showers had occurred that morning at a location 2 kilometres from the container yard.

Annex 3

Self-heating and fire in a bulk cargo of Direct Reduced Iron (United States)

1 On 29 February 1996, the M/V B. ONAL anchored in Delaware Bay reported that it was experiencing a fire in its Number five cargo hold. Responding to this report, the U.S. Coast Guard discovered that the cargo in this hold, identified as "Passivated Direct Reduced Iron" was self-heating and emitting flammable gases. The cargo hatch had been lifted by pressure build-up, and the paint on the engine-room side of the bulkhead separating the engine-room from the hold was blistered. The temperature on the exterior (engine-room) side of this bulkhead reached 149°C (300°F). The situation was stabilized by injecting nitrogen into the cargo hold to create an inert atmosphere. This proved effective and the temperature of the cargo decreased drastically within 24 hours. The vessel remained in this condition for eight weeks while the cargo's owners sought a shore facility willing to provide a suitable area for unloading the affected cargo. On 27 April the cargo was finally offloaded and quenched with fresh water. There was no significant structural damage to the vessel that could be attributed to this incident.

2 It is suspected that water may have entered the cargo hold during the voyage through an ill-fitting cargo hatch. This would lead to the oxidation of the Direct Reduced Iron, resulting in the condition described above.

3 When transported on the territorial waters of United States, Direct Reduced Iron is subject to United States Federal Regulations and may only be transported under the terms of a Special Permit issued by the U.S. Coast Guard. The terms of such Special Permits are consistent with the provisions of the BC Code.

Annex 4

Fire in Charcoal, non activated (The Netherlands)

1 During the course of 1996, the port authorities of the Port of Rotterdam were confronted with four almost identical cases of fire on board ships due to self-heating of charcoal.

2 It concerned charcoal, non-activated, shipped under UN No. 1361, class 4.2. The charcoal was packaged in small (UN-approved) bags, which were packed for handling purposes in large bags and loaded into containers. The majority of the containers was loaded under deck.

3   Due to the fire, some of the containers had collapsed and the bottom had fallen out, whereby the charcoal was released into the hold. As the result thereof, the bilge-system became clogged with charcoal and the water used for fire fighting accumulated in the hold. Fortunately, no personal injuries were reported and the fire did not spread to other cargoes.

4   When in the Port of Rotterdam, the local fire-fighting was asked for assistance, using deep-well pumps to drain the water. Unloading of the remainder of the cargo was complicated as the bottom of the containers had been burnt away. In some cases the waste cargo was removed by using barges. It is needless to say that high removal costs were involved.

5   These incidents show that charcoal, non-activated is indeed dangerous material and that it is essential for safety on board that all the requirements as mentioned in the IMDG Code are complied with. It is therefore extremely important that the material is sufficiently heat-treated and cooled down before packing. Also, the self-heating test for carbon as required on the schedule should be passed successfully.

DSC/Circ. 8 of 24 July 2001

INCIDENT REPORTS INVOLVING DANGEROUS CARGOES

1   The Sub-Committee on Dangerous Goods, Solid Cargoes and Containers (DSC), at its sixth session (16 to 20 July 2001), considered a number of reports on casualties and incidents involving dangerous cargoes submitted by Governments and international organizations concerned.

2   The Sub-Committee's attention was particularly drawn to:

   .1   an incident (DSC 5/7/6) on board a ship concerning an explosion involving cargo declared on the Bill of Lading as "Iron Oxide Fines" comprising 40% of the shipment, the remaining 60% being Direct Reduced Iron (DRI) fines. The requirements of the BC Code with respect to the transport of the cargoes concerned should be duly observed and complied with.

   .2   a recent inspection of Cargo Transport Units (CTUs) unloaded in ports (DSC 5/7) indicated that some were under fumigation, but not actually declared as such and in some cases, these aerated CTUs arrive with "Degas Certificates" stating that the fumigant has been removed and when opened, still have a high level of fumigant inside. The requirements of the IMDG Code with respect to the transport of CTUs under fumigation should be duly observed and complied with as improper procedures of fumigation and misdeclaration of CTUs under fumigation could have serious consequences, especially at final destinations where the container first gets opened.

   .3   an incident (DSC 5/7/3) of a charcoal fire on board a ro-ro passenger ship. The lorry and its trailer were not reported to carry any dangerous goods. The crew found charcoal packed in paper bags and matches. MATCHES, SAFETY (UN1944) belong to class 4.1. CHARCOAL is sometimes dangerous, sometimes not. The provisions of the IMDG Code do not apply to a consignment of charcoal which passes the test for self-heating as reflected in the United Nations Recommendations on the Transport of Dangerous Goods, Manual of Tests and Criteria and is accompanied by an appropriate certificate from a laboratory accredited by the competent authority. No such a certificate was found and the consignment of charcoal was not reported to be dangerous goods. Self-ignition of the charcoal is believed to have caused the fire.

3   Member Governments are invited to bring the above information to the attention of shipowners, ship operators, companies, shipmasters, shippers and all other parties concerned requesting that appropriate action be taken in accordance with the provisions of the relevant IMO instruments.

DSC/Circ. 10 of 10 March 2003

INCIDENT REPORTS INVOLVING DANGEROUS CARGOES

Zinc Skimmings
(see Zinc Ashes UN 1435)

1   The Sub-Committee on Dangerous Goods, Solid Cargoes and Containers (DSC), at its seventh session (23 to 27 September 2002), considered a number of reports on casualties and incidents involving dangerous cargoes submitted by Member Governments and international organizations concerned.

2   The Sub-Committee's attention was particularly drawn to a report on the foundering of the cargo vessel 'Thor Emilie' (DSC 7/INF.4), loaded with Zinc Skimmings which were erroneously described as Oxyde Zinc Ore. After the founder, it became clear that the ship's cargo was not Oxyde Zinc Ore but Zinc Skimmings, which is covered by the Code of Safe Practice for Solid Bulk Cargoes (BC Code) as a product able to evolve hydrogen and toxic gases when in contact with moisture or water, and for its carriage special permission and special equipment is required on board.

3   Although SOLAS VI-2 states that "the shipper shall provide the master or his representative with appropriate information on the cargo sufficiently in advance of loading to enable the precautions which may be necessary for proper stowage and safe carriage of the cargo to be put into effect", it was evident during the investigation that this provision was not taken into account during the carriage of the cargo.

4   The Sub-Committee noted the following conclusions drawn by the investigating team:

    .1   the foundering occurred extremely fast due to a heavy explosion/detonation in the cargo hold of the ship;

    .2   the master, with the knowledge about the characteristic of the cargo as understood by him, could not anticipate that during the voyage an explosive atmosphere could generate in the cargo hold;

    .3   the master, after the explosion, did not have any possibility of initiating effective measures for search and rescue of other crew members;

    .4   the brokering firm did not receive information about the correct description of the cargo and its UN number from the shipper neither before nor during the chartering negotiations with the owner's chartering manager;

    .5   the master, when he did not notice the description of the cargo as Zinc Skimmings on the statement before and on the final cargo documents, which he signed before departure, prevented himself from discontinuing the loading and have the ship discharged;

    .6   the ship with respect to her equipment and crew and the stowing of the cargo was fully seaworthy if the cargo had been harmless; however, for such a dangerous cargo, the ship did not meet the requirements for carriage, neither in construction nor in equipment;

    .7   the negotiations between the broker and the owner's chartering manager could have discontinued if the owner's chartering manager had insisted upon receipt of proper documentation to the effect that the cargo was non-dangerous;

    .8   the owner's chartering manager, when he did not notice the description of the cargo as Zinc Skimmings in the final cargo documents, which he received about two hours after the departure of the ship, did not advise the master from breaking off the actual voyage; and

    .9   for safe carriage of dangerous goods it is a precondition that these goods are documented and properly described by using the proper shipping name and the associated UN number. A high degree of trust is placed on the shipper in meeting this requirement.

5   The investigation recommends that the owner establish a procedure in the ISM system to the effect that it is made certain, when entering into a charter party, that the owner's charterers receive proper documentation of the cargo for which the charterers bid, including an exact notification of whether the cargo is listed under an UN number, and if so which UN number. The investigation further recommends to the owner that the charterers go through a certified dangerous goods course.

6   Member Governments are invited to bring the above information to the attention of shipowners, ship operators, companies, shipmasters, shippers and all other parties concerned, requesting that appropriate action be taken in accordance with the provisions of the relevant IMO instruments.

DSC/Circ. 11 of 30 April 2003

SHIPS CARRYING FUMIGATED BULK CARGOES

1   The Sub-Committee on Dangerous Goods, Solid Cargoes and Containers (DSC), at its seventh session (23 to 27 September 2002), considered a number of reports on casualties and incidents involving dangerous cargoes submitted by Governments and international organizations concerned.

2   The Sub-Committee's attention was drawn to the risks associated with ships carrying solid bulk cargoes (DSC 7/6/2), which have been treated with toxic gases (fumigated) and might negatively affect the safety and health of personnel. These include:

   .1   the assumption that the concentration of the toxic fumigant is sufficiently low when the ship arrives in the port of discharge, as to avoid safety and health risks to ship and shore personnel or enforcement officers. Unfortunately, this is not always the case and there are reported incidents where employees have been exposed to the fumigant, usually phosphine, causing health problems;

   .2   unlike cargo transport units (CTU's), ships containing bulk cargo under fumigation are not required to be labelled as such. So they are not visibly recognized as a potential safety and health risk; and

   .3   though some ports require a notification to the Harbour Master, and/or appropriate authorities, from the Master of a ship containing fumigated bulk cargo, wishing to enter the port, that action has been taken to make the ship's holds and the cargo gas-free, such notification does not always take place, resulting in potential health risks for the ship's crew, terminal personnel and others when the ship is being unloaded.

The attention of Member Governments is drawn to the following observations:

   .4   the International Convention for the Safety of Life at Sea (SOLAS) regulation VI/4, obliges that appropriate precautions shall be taken in the use of pesticides in ships, in particular for the purposes of fumigation. *The Recommendations on the Safe Use of Pesticides in Ships*, recommended to governments in pursuance of their obligations under chapter VI of the SOLAS Convention, as amended, are intended as a guide to competent authorities, mariners, fumigators, fumigant and pesticide manufacturers, and others concerned; and

   .5   for bulk carriers SOLAS requires a Safety Management System that should contain safety procedures for fumigated cargoes. For ships other than bulk carriers that transport fumigated bulk cargoes, the Safety Management System became mandatory on 1 July 2002.

3   It is therefore recommended that Member Governments issue regulations to oblige ships that carry solid bulk cargoes under fumigation to notify accordingly the Harbour Master, as well as any other appropriate authorities, prior to arrival in port and to ensure that the ship's hold and its cargo are gas-free upon berthing the ship.

4   Member Governments are invited to bring the above information to the attention of shipowners, ship operators, companies, shipmasters, shippers and all other parties concerned, requesting that appropriate action be taken in accordance with the provisions of the relevant IMO instruments.

DSC/Circ. 12 of 11 November 2003, corrected by Corr. 1 and Corr. 2

GUIDANCE ON THE CONTINUED USE OF EXISTING IMO TYPE PORTABLE TANKS AND ROAD TANK VEHICLES FOR THE TRANSPORT OF DANGEROUS GOODS

1   The Sub-Committee on Dangerous Goods, Solid Cargoes and Containers (DSC), at its eighth session (22 to 26 September 2003), recalled that the Maritime Safety Committee, at its seventy-second session (17 to 26 May 2000), had adopted amendment 30-00 to the IMDG Code, which had been prepared in the revised, reformatted and harmonized form of the IMDG Code; and had agreed to an entry into force date of 1 January 2001 with a twelve-month transitional period until 31 December 2001. The reformatted Code included new provisions for the construction and use of multimodal UN portable tanks.

2   During the reformatting process, the Sub-Committee agreed that existing IMO type portable tanks and road tank vehicles may continue to be used for the lifetime of the tank, provided they also comply with the provisions set out in 3.2.1 (column 12) and in 4.2.0 of the IMDG Code. However, the detailed provisions for such tanks, which were contained in section 13 of the IMDG Code, amendment 29-98, were not included in the IMDG Code, amendment 30-00, and its subsequent edition.

3   The Sub-Committee, noting that IMDG Code amendment 31-02 would attain mandatory status from 1 January 2004, developed the annexed Guidance explaining the provisions of 3.2.1 (column 12) and 4.2.0 of the IMDG Code and reproducing the construction provisions applicable to such tanks.

4   Member Governments are invited to bring the attached Guidance to the attention of shipowners, ship operators, companies, seafarers and, in particular, tank owners and operators, inspecting and certifying authorities, consignors and shippers, and all other parties concerned with the transport of dangerous goods in packaged form by sea.

Annex

Guidance on the continued use of existing IMO type portable tanks and road tank vehicles for the transport of dangerous goods

Note: Any reference to the Code refers to the IMDG Code, as amended. All other references refer to paragraphs within this circular.

Contents:

Section 1   Introduction
Section 2   Use of IMO type portable tanks and road tank vehicles
Section 3   Provisions for the design, construction, inspection and testing of IMO type portable tanks and road tank vehicles.

Section 1   Introduction

1.1   The purpose of this circular is to enable tank manufacturers and operators, certifying and inspection authorities, consignors and others engaged in the transport of dangerous goods in IMO type portable tanks and road tank vehicles designed, constructed and approved before 1 January 2003 to meet their duties.

The main objective is to clarify the use of such tanks taking into account their construction provisions which are given in section 3 of this circular.

The provisions of this circular apply to IMO type 1, 2, 5 and 7 portable tanks and IMO type 4, 6 and 8 road tank vehicles.

However, this circular does not apply to IMO type 4, 6 and 8 road tank vehicles that have been designed, constructed and approved in accordance with chapter 6.8 of the Code.

Definitions of the IMO tank types can be found in the **Note** to paragraph 4.2.0 of the Code.

Portable tanks designed, constructed, and approved in accordance with chapters 4.2 and 6.7 of the Code are referred to as "UN portable tanks" in this circular.

1.2   Transitional provisions

When the provisions for the construction and use of UN portable tanks were included in the Code, transitional provisions related to IMO type portable tanks and road tank vehicles were also included in order to:

- promote the construction and use of new UN portable tanks and
- take into account the existing IMO type tanks and the goods they were authorized to transport.

These transitional provisions are in paragraph 4.2.0 and in paragraph 3.2.1 (column 12) of the Code and are summarized below:

.1   The design, construction and approval of IMO type portable tanks and road tank vehicles in accordance with the provisions of section 13 of Amendment 29-98 to the Code were permitted until 1 January 2003 (see 4.2.0 of the Code)

.2   The use of all IMO type portable tanks and road tank vehicles is permitted for the transport of dangerous goods in accordance with the Code until the end of their life provided that such tanks are inspected and tested in accordance with chapter 6.7 of the Code. If evidence of any unsafe condition is found, the tank shall not be returned to service until the deficiency is corrected.

.3   Until 1 January 2010, the portable tank instruction that shall be used for each substance permitted in an IMO type portable tank or road tank vehicle is assigned in column (12) of the Dangerous Goods List in chapter 3.2 of the Code. If no T code is indicated in column (12), the T code in column (13) shall be used.

.4   Until 1 January 2010, the tank special provisions (TP note) applicable to dangerous goods authorized to be transported in IMO type portable tanks are indicated in column (12) and column (14) of the Dangerous Goods List. If no TP note is indicated in column (12) of the Dangerous Goods List, TP notes indicated in column (14) apply to the appropriate substance.

.5   From 1 January 2010, the transport of dangerous goods in IMO type portable tanks and road tank vehicles will be permitted in accordance with columns (13) and (14) only.

There is no requirement to re-certify IMO type portable tanks as UN portable tanks.

Examples:

Example No.	UN No. (1)	Proper Shipping Name (PSN) (2)	Packing Group (5)	Tank Instructions		
				IMO (12)	UN (13)	Provisions (14)
1	1760	CORROSIVE LIQUID, N.O.S.	I	–	T14	TP2 TP9 TP27
1	1760	CORROSIVE LIQUID, N.O.S.	II	–	T11	TP2 TP27
2	1760	CORROSIVE LIQUID, N.O.S.	III	T4	T7	TP1 TP28
3	1802	PERCHLORIC ACID	II	TP28	T7	TP2

Example 1   The IMO type portable tank used for UN 1760 (Packing Group I and II) shall comply with the provisions of columns (13) and (14).

Example 2   Until 1 January 2010, the IMO type portable tank complying with the provisions of columns (12) and (14) may be used for UN 1760 PG III. However, from 1 January 2010 the IMO type portable tank used for UN 1760 PG III shall comply with the provisions of columns (13) and (14) only.

Example 3   Until 1 January 2010, the IMO type portable tank complying with the provisions of columns (12), (13) and (14) may be used for UN 1802. However, from 1 January 2010 the IMO type portable tank used for UN 1802 shall comply with the provisions of columns (13) and (14) only.

Section 2   Use of IMO type portable tanks and road tank vehicles

Note: Chapter 4.2 of the Code applies to IMO type portable tanks and road tank vehicles. However, IMO portable tanks and road tank vehicles need not conform to the design and construction provisions detailed in 6.7.2 to 6.7.4 of the Code. The purpose of this section is to clarify the application of the T code and the TP notes to IMO portable tanks and road tank vehicles with respect to their design and construction provisions set out in section 3.

Portable tank instructions and special provisions

2.1   General

2.1.1 This section includes the portable tank instructions and special provisions applicable to dangerous goods authorized to be transported in IMO type portable tanks and road tank vehicles. Each portable tank instruction is identified by an alphanumeric designation (T1 to T75). The Dangerous Goods List in chapter 3.2 of the Code indicates the portable tank instruction that shall be used for each substance permitted for transport in an IMO type portable tank or road tank vehicle. When no portable tank instruction appears in the Dangerous Goods List, transport of the substance in portable tanks or road tank vehicles is not permitted unless a competent authority approval is granted as set out in 6.7.1.3 of the Code. Portable tank special provisions are assigned to specific dangerous goods in the Dangerous Goods List in chapter 3.2 of the Code. Each portable tank special provision is identified by an alphanumeric designation (such as TP1). A listing of the portable tank special provisions is provided in 2.5.

2.2   Portable tank instructions

2.2.1 Portable tank instructions apply to dangerous goods of classes 1 to 9. Portable tank instructions provide specific information relevant to portable tanks provisions applicable to specific substances. These provisions shall be met in addition to the general provisions of section 3.

2.2.2 For substances of classes 3 to 9, the portable tank instructions indicate the applicable minimum test pressure, the minimum shell thickness (in mild steel), bottom opening provisions and pressure relief provisions.

2.2.3 Non-refrigerated liquefied gases are assigned to portable tank instruction T50 of this circular which provides the maximum allowable working pressures, bottom opening provisions, pressure relief provisions and maximum filling density for non-refrigerated liquefied gases permitted for transport in portable tanks or road tank vehicles.

2.2.4 Refrigerated liquefied gases are assigned to portable tank instruction T75.

2.3   Determination of the appropriate portable tank instructions

When a specific portable tank instruction is specified in the Dangerous Goods List, additional portable tanks which possess higher test pressures, greater shell thicknesses, more stringent bottom opening and pressure relief device arrangements may be used. The following guidelines apply to determining the appropriate portable tanks or road tank vehicles which may be used for transport of particular substances:

Portable tank instruction specified	*Portable tank instructions also permitted*
T1	T2, T3, T4, T5, T6, T7, T8, T9, T10, T11, T12, T13, T14, T15, T16, T17, T18, T19, T20, T21, T22
T2	T4, T5, T7, T8, T9, T10, T11, T12, T13, T14, T15, T16, T17, T18, T19, T20, T21, T22
T3	T4, T5, T6, T7, T8, T9, T10, T11, T12, T13, T14, T15, T16, T17, T18, T19, T20, T21, T22
T4	T5, T7, T8, T9, T10, T11, T12, T13, T14, T15, T16, T17, T18, T19, T20, T21, T22
T5	T10, T14, T19, T20, T22
T6	T7, T8, T9, T10, T11, T12, T13, T14, T15, T16, T17, T18, T19, T20, T21, T22
T7	T8,T9, T10, T11, T12, T13, T14, T15, T16, T17, T18, T19, T20, T21, T22
T8	T9, T10, T13, T14, T19, T20, T21, T22
T9	T10, T13, T14, T19, T20, T21, T22
T10	T14, T19, T20, T22
T11	T12, T13, T14, T15, T16, T17, T18, T19, T20, T21, T22
T12	T14, T16, T18, T19, T20, T22
T13	T14, T19, T20, T21, T22
T14	T19, T20, T22
T15	T16, T17, T18, T19, T20, T21, T22
T16	T18, T19, T20, T22
T17	T18, T19, T20, T21, T22
T18	T19, T20, T22
T19	T20, T22
T20	T22
T21	T22
T22	None
T23	None

Appendix

2.4   Portable tank instructions

T1–T22	PORTABLE TANK INSTRUCTIONS			T1–T22
These portable tank instructions apply to liquid and solid substances of classes 1 and 3 to 9. The general provisions of section 3 shall be met.				
Portable tank instruction	Minimum test pressure (bar)	Minimum shell thickness (in mm – mild steel) (see 3.5)	Pressure relief provisions (see 3.9)	Bottom opening provisions (see 3.7)
T1	1.5	see 3.5.2	see 3.9.1	see 3.7.2
T2	1.5	see 3.5.2	see 3.9.1	see 3.7.3
T3	2.65	see 3.5.2	see 3.9.1	see 3.7.2
T4	2.65	see 3.5.2	see 3.9.1	see 3.7.3
T5	2.65	see 3.5.2	see 3.9.3	Not allowed
T6	4	see 3.5.2	see 3.9.1	see 3.7.2
T7	4	see 3.5.2	see 3.9.1	see 3.7.3
T8	4	see 3.5.2	see 3.9.1	Not allowed
T9	4	6	see 3.9.1	Not allowed
T10	4	6	see 3.9.3	Not allowed
T11	6	see 3.5.2	see 3.9.1	see 3.7.3
T12	6	see 3.5.2	see 3.9.3	see 3.7.3
T13	6	6	see 3.9.1	Not allowed
T14	6	6	see 3.9.3	Not allowed
T15	10	see 3.5.2	see 3.9.1	see 3.7.3
T16	10	see 3.5.2	see 3.9.3	see 3.7.3
T17	10	6	see 3.9.1	see 3.7.3
T18	10	6	see 3.9.3	see 3.7.3
T19	10	6	see 3.9.3	Not allowed
T20	10	8	see 3.9.3	Not allowed
T21	10	10	see 3.9.1	Not allowed
T22	10	10	see 3.9.3	Not allowed

T50	PORTABLE TANK INSTRUCTION				T50
This portable tank instruction applies to non-refrigerated liquefied gases. The general provisions of 4.2.2 of the Code and section 3 shall be met.					
UN No.	Non-refrigerated liquefied gases	Max. allowable working pressure (bar) Small; Bare; Sunshield; Insulated	Openings below liquid level	Pressure relief provisions (see 3.42)	Maximum filling density (kg/l)
1005	Ammonia, anhydrous	29.0 25.7 22.0 19.7	Allowed	see 3.42.3	0.53
1009	Bromotrifluoromethane (Refrigerant gas R 13B1)	38.0 34.0 30.0 27.5	Allowed	Normal	1.13
1010	Butadienes, stabilized	7.5 7.0 7.0 7.0	Allowed	Normal	0.55
1011	Butane	7.0 7.0 7.0 7.0	Allowed	Normal	0.51
1012	Butylene	8.0 7.0 7.0 7.0	Allowed	Normal	0.53
1017	Chlorine	19.0 17.0 15.0 13.5	Not allowed	see 3.42.3	1.25
1018	Chlorodifluoromethane (Refrigerant gas R 22)	26.0 24.0 21.0 19.0	Allowed	Normal	1.03
1020	Chloropentafluoroethane (Refrigerant gas R 115)	23.0 20.0 18.0 16.0	Allowed	Normal	1.06
1021	1-Chloro-1,2,2,2-tetrafluoroethane (Refrigerant gas R 124)	10.3 9.8 7.9 7.0	Allowed	Normal	1.20
1027	Cyclopropane	18.0 16.0 14.5 13.0	Allowed	Normal	0.53
1028	Dichlorodifluoromethane (Refrigerant gas R 12)	16.0 15.0 13.0 11.5	Allowed	Normal	1.15
1029	Dichlorofluoromethane (Refrigerant gas R 21)	7.0 7.0 7.0 7.0	Allowed	Normal	1.23
1030	1,1-Difluoroethane (Refrigerant gas R 152a)	16.0 14.0 12.4 11.0	Allowed	Normal	0.79
1032	Dimethylamine, anhydrous	7.0 7.0 7.0 7.0	Allowed	Normal	0.59

Appendix

T50	PORTABLE TANK INSTRUCTION *(continued)*				*T50*

This portable tank instruction applies to non-refrigerated liquefied gases. The general provisions of 4.2.2 of the Code and section 3 shall be met.

UN No.	Non-refrigerated liquefied gases	Max. allowable working pressure (bar) Small; Bare; Sunshield; Insulated	Openings below liquid level	Pressure relief provisions (see 3.42)	Maximum filling density (kg/l)
1033	Dimethyl ether	15.5 13.8 12.0 10.6	Allowed	Normal	0.58
1036	Ethylamine	7.0 7.0 7.0 7.0	Allowed	Normal	0.61
1037	Ethyl chloride	7.0 7.0 7.0 7.0	Allowed	Normal	0.80
1040	Ethylene oxide with nitrogen up to a total pressure of 1 MPa (10 bar) at 50°C	– – – 10.0	Not allowed	see 3.42.3	0.78
1041	Ethylene oxide and carbon dioxide mixture with more than 9% but not more than 87% ethylene oxide	see MAWP definition in 3.38.6	Allowed	Normal	see 4.2.2.7
1055	Isobutylene	8.1 7.0 7.0 7.0	Allowed	Normal	0.52
1060	Methylacetylene and propadiene mixture, stabilized	28.0 24.5 22.0 20.0	Allowed	Normal	0.43
1061	Methylamine, anhydrous	10.8 9.6 7.8 7.0	Allowed	Normal	0.58
1062	Methyl bromide with not more than 2% chloropicrin	7.0 7.0 7.0 7.0	Not allowed	see 3.42.3	1.51
1063	Methyl chloride (Refrigerant gas R40)	14.5 12.7 11.3 10.0	Allowed	Normal	0.81
1064	Methyl mercaptan	7.0 7.0 7.0 7.0	Not allowed	see 3.42.3	0.78
1067	Dinitrogen tetroxide	7.0 7.0 7.0 7.0	Not allowed	see 3.42.3	1.30
1075	Petroleum gas, liquefied	see MAWP definition in 3.38.6	Allowed	Normal	see 4.2.2.7
1077	Propylene	28.0 24.5 22.0 20.0	Allowed	Normal	0.43
1078	Refrigerant gas, N.O.S.	see MAWP definition in 3.38.6	Allowed	Normal	see 4.2.2.7

T50	PORTABLE TANK INSTRUCTION *(continued)*				T50

This portable tank instruction applies to non-refrigerated liquefied gases. The general provisions of 4.2.2 of the Code and section 3 shall be met.

UN No.	Non-refrigerated liquefied gases	Max. allowable working pressure (bar) Small; Bare; Sunshield; Insulated	Openings below liquid level	Pressure relief provisions (see 3.42)	Maximum filling density (kg/l)
1079	Sulphur dioxide	11.6 / 10.3 / 8.5 / 7.6	Not allowed	see 3.42.3	1.23
1082	Trifluorochloroethylene, stabilized (Refrigerant gas R 1113)	17.0 / 15.0 / 13.1 / 11.6	Not allowed	see 3.42.3	1.13
1083	Trimethylamine, anhydrous	7.0 / 7.0 / 7.0 / 7.0	Allowed	Normal	0.56
1085	Vinyl bromide, stabilized	7.0 / 7.0 / 7.0 / 7.0	Allowed	Normal	1.37
1086	Vinyl chloride, stabilized	10.6 / 9.3 / 8.0 / 7.0	Allowed	Normal	0.81
1087	Vinyl methyl ether, stabilized	7.0 / 7.0 / 7.0 / 7.0	Allowed	Normal	0.67
1581	Chloropicrin and methyl bromide mixture with more than 2% chloropicrin	7.0 / 7.0 / 7.0 / 7.0	Not allowed	see 3.42.3	1.51
1582	Chloropicrin and methyl chloride mixture	19.2 / 16.9 / 15.1 / 13.1	Not allowed	see 3.42.3	0.81
1858	Hexafluoropropylene (Refrigerant gas R 1216)	19.2 / 16.9 / 15.1 / 13.1	Allowed	Normal	1.11
1912	Methyl chloride and methylene chloride mixture	15.2 / 13.0 / 11.6 / 10.1	Allowed	Normal	0.81
1958	1,2-Dichloro-1,1,2,2-tetrafluoroethane (Refrigerant gas R 114)	7.0 / 7.0 / 7.0 / 7.0	Allowed	Normal	1.30
1965	Hydrocarbon gas, mixture liquefied, N.O.S.	see MAWP definition in 3.38.6	Allowed	Normal	see 4.2.2.7
1969	Isobutane	8.5 / 7.5 / 7.0 / 7.0	Allowed	Normal	0.49
1973	Chlorodifluoromethane and chloropentafluoroethane mixture with fixed boiling point, with approximately 49% chlorodifluoromethane (Refrigerant gas R 502)	28.3 / 25.3 / 22.8 / 20.3	Allowed	Normal	1.05

T50	PORTABLE TANK INSTRUCTION *(continued)*				*T50*
This portable tank instruction applies to non-refrigerated liquefied gases. The general provisions of 4.2.2 of the Code and section 3 shall be met.					
UN No.	Non-refrigerated liquefied gases	Max. allowable working pressure (bar) Small; Bare; Sunshield; Insulated	Openings below liquid level	Pressure relief provisions (see 3.42)	Maximum filling density (kg/l)
1974	Chlorodifluorobromomethane (Refrigerant gas R 12B1)	7.4 7.0 7.0 7.0	Allowed	Normal	1.61
1976	Octafluorocyclobutane (Refrigerant gas RC 318)	8.8 7.8 7.0 7.0	Allowed	Normal	1.34
1978	Propane	22.5 20.4 18.0 16.5	Allowed	Normal	0.42
1983	1-Chloro-2,2,2-trifluoroethane (Refrigerant gas R 133a)	7.0 7.0 7.0 7.0	Allowed	Normal	1.18
2035	1,1,1-Trifluoroethane (Refrigerant gas R 143a)	31.0 27.5 24.2 21.8	Allowed	Normal	0.76
2424	Octafluoropropane (Refrigerant gas R 218)	23.1 20.8 18.6 16.6	Allowed	Normal	1.07
2517	1-Chloro-1,1-difluoroethane (Refrigerant gas R 142b)	8.9 7.8 7.0 7.0	Allowed	Normal	0.99
2602	Dichlorodifluoromethane and difluoroethane azeotropic mixture with approximately 74% dichlorodifluoromethane (Refrigerant gas R 500)	20.0 18.0 16.0 14.5	Allowed	Normal	1.01
3057	Trifluoroacetyl chloride	14.6 12.9 11.3 9.9	Not allowed	see 3.42.3	1.17
3070	Ethylene oxide and dichlorodifluoromethane mixture, with not more than 12.5% ethylene oxide	14.0 12.0 11.0 9.0	Allowed	see 3.42.3	1.09
3153	Perfluoro(methyl vinyl ether)	14.3 13.4 11.2 10.2	Allowed	Normal	1.14
3159	1,1,1,2-Tetrafluoroethane (Refrigerant gas R 134a)	17.7 15.7 13.8 12.1	Allowed	Normal	1.04
3161	Liquefied gas, flammable, N.O.S.	see MAWP definition in 3.38.6	Allowed	Normal	see 4.2.2.7
3163	Liquefied gas, N.O.S.	see MAWP definition in 3.38.6	Allowed	Normal	see 4.2.2.7

T50		PORTABLE TANK INSTRUCTION *(continued)*			*T50*
This portable tank instruction applies to non-refrigerated liquefied gases. The general provisions of 4.2.2 of the Code and section 3 shall be met.					
UN No.	Non-refrigerated liquefied gases	Max. allowable working pressure (bar) Small; Bare; Sunshield; Insulated	Openings below liquid level	Pressure relief provisions (see 3.42)	Maximum filling density (kg/l)
3220	Pentafluoroethane (Refrigerant gas R 125)	34.4 30.8 27.5 24.5	Allowed	Normal	0.95
3252	Difluoromethane (Refrigerant gas R 32)	43.0 39.0 34.4 30.5	Allowed	Normal	0.78
3296	Heptafluoropropane (Refrigerant gas R 227)	16.0 14.0 12.5 11.0	Allowed	Normal	1.20
3297	Ethylene oxide and chlorotetrafluoroethane mixture, with not more than 8.8% ethylene oxide	8.1 7.0 7.0 7.0	Allowed	Normal	1.16
3298	Ethylene oxide and pentafluoroethane mixture, with not more than 7.9% ethylene oxide	25.9 23.4 20.9 18.6	Allowed	Normal	1.02
3299	Ethylene oxide and tetrafluoroethane mixture, with not more than 5.6% ethylene oxide	16.7 14.7 12.9 11.2	Allowed	Normal	1.03
3318	Ammonia solution, relative density less than 0.880 at 15°C in water, with more than 50% ammonia	see MAWP definition in 3.38.6	Allowed	see 3.42.3	see 4.2.2.7
3337	Refrigerant gas R 404A	31.6 28.3 25.3 22.5	Allowed	Normal	0.82
3338	Refrigerant gas R 407A	31.3 28.1 25.1 22.4	Allowed	Normal	0.94
3339	Refrigerant gas R 407B	33.0 29.6 26.5 23.6	Allowed	Normal	0.93
3340	Refrigerant gas R 407C	29.9 26.8 23.9 21.3	Allowed	Normal	0.95

T75	PORTABLE TANK INSTRUCTION	T75
This portable tank instruction applies to refrigerated liquefied gases. The general provisions of 4.2.3 of the Code and section 3 shall be met.		

Appendix

2.5   Portable tank special provisions

Portable tank special provisions are assigned to certain substances to indicate provisions which are in addition to or in lieu of those provided by the portable tank instructions or the provisions in section 3. Portable tank special provisions are identified by an alpha-numeric designation beginning with the letters "TP" (tank provision) and are assigned to specific substances in columns 12 and 14 of the Dangerous Goods List in chapter 3.2 of the Code. The following is a list of the portable tank special provisions:

TP1 – The degree of filling prescribed in 4.2.1.9.2 of the Code shall not be exceeded.

TP2 – The degree of filling prescribed in 4.2.1.9.3 of the Code shall not be exceeded.

TP3 – For substances transported above 50°C, the degree of filling prescribed in 4.2.1.9.5.1 of the Code shall not be exceeded.

TP4 – The degree of filling shall not exceed 90% or, alternatively, any other value approved by the competent authority (see 4.2.1.15.2 of the Code).

TP5 – The degree of filling prescribed in 4.2.3.6 of the Code shall not be exceeded.

TP6 – To prevent the tank bursting in any event, including fire engulfment, it shall be provided with pressure relief devices which are adequate in relation to the capacity of the tank and to the nature of the substance transported. The device shall also be compatible with the substance.

TP7 – Air shall be eliminated from the vapour space by nitrogen or other means.

TP8 – The test pressure for the portable tank may be reduced to 1.5 bar when the flashpoint of the substances transported is greater than 0°C.

TP9 – A substance under this description shall only be transported in a portable tank under an approval granted by the competent authority.

TP10 – A lead lining, not less than 5 mm thick, which shall be tested annually, or another suitable lining material approved by the competent authority is required.

TP11 – [Reserved]

TP12 – This substance is highly corrosive to steel.

TP13 – Self-contained breathing apparatus shall be provided when this substance is transported.

TP14 – [Reserved]

TP15 – [Reserved]

TP16 – The tank shall be fitted with a special device to prevent under-pressure and excess pressure during normal transport conditions. This device shall be approved by the competent authority. Pressure relief provisions are as indicated in 3.9.3 to prevent crystallization of the product in the pressure relief valve.

TP17 – Only inorganic non-combustible materials shall be used for thermal insulation of the tank.

TP18 – Temperature shall be maintained between 18°C and 40°C. Portable tanks containing solidified methacrylic acid shall not be reheated during transport.

TP19 – The calculated shell thickness shall be increased by 3 mm. Shell thickness shall be verified ultrasonically at intervals midway between periodic hydraulic tests.

TP20 – This substance shall only be transported in insulated tanks under a nitrogen blanket.

TP21 – The shell thickness shall be not less than 8 mm. Tanks shall be hydraulically tested and internally inspected at intervals not exceeding 2.5 years.

TP22 – Lubricant for joints or other devices shall be oxygen-compatible.

TP23 – Transport permitted under special conditions prescribed by the competent authorities.

TP24 – The portable tank may be fitted with a device located, under maximum filling conditions, in the vapour space of the shell to prevent the build-up of excess pressure due to the slow decomposition of the substance transported. This device shall also prevent an unacceptable amount of leakage of liquid in the case of overturning or entry of foreign matter into the tank. This device shall be approved by the competent authority or its authorized body.

TP25 – Sulphur trioxide 99.95% pure and above may be transported in tanks without an inhibitor provided that it is maintained at a temperature equal to or above 32.5°C.

TP26 – When transported under heated conditions, the heating device shall be fitted outside the shell. For UN 3176, this provision only applies when the substance reacts dangerously with water.

TP27 – A portable tank having a minimum test pressure of 4 bar may be used if it is shown that a test pressure of 4 bar or less is acceptable according to the test pressure definition in 3.2.7.

TP28 – A portable tank having a minimum test pressure of 2.65 bar may be used if it is shown that a test pressure of 2.65 bar or less is acceptable according to the test pressure definition in 3.2.7.

TP29 – A portable tank having a minimum test pressure of 1.5 bar may be used if it is shown that a test pressure of 1.5 bar or less is acceptable according to the test pressure definition in 3.2.7.

TP30 – This substance shall be transported in insulated tanks.

TP31 – This substance shall be transported in tanks in solid state.

2.6   Use of IMO type 4, 6 and 8 tanks

2.6.1 IMO type 4, 6 and 8 tanks may be used according to the provisions of section 3. This provision shall only be used for short international voyages.

2.6.2 IMO type 4 tanks shall be attached to the chassis when transported on board ships.

Section 3   Provisions for the design, construction, inspection and testing of IMO type portable tanks and road tank vehicles

Sub-section A   GENERAL PROVISIONS FOR PORTABLE TANKS AND ROAD TANK VEHICLES FOR DANGEROUS SUBSTANCES OTHER THAN CLASS 2

3.1   Preamble

3.1.1 Elements of this sub-section apply to portable tanks and road tank vehicles intended for the transport of dangerous substances, except for those of class 2, by sea. In addition to these provisions, or unless otherwise specified, the applicable requirements of the International Convention for Safe Containers (CSC) 1972, as amended, should be fulfilled by any tank which meets the definition of a "container" within the terms of that Convention. The International Convention for Safe Containers does not apply to offshore tank-containers that are handled in open seas. The design and testing of offshore tank-containers should take into account the dynamic lifting and impact forces that may occur when a tank is handled in open seas in adverse weather and sea conditions. The requirements for such tanks should be determined by the approving competent authority (see also MSC/Circ. 613 as amended). Such containers should be based on MSC/Circ. 860 "Guidelines for the approval of offshore containers handled in open seas" (as amended).

3.1.2 Attention is drawn to the fact that no provisions have been included in respect of any additional fire-fighting equipment which may be necessary on ships transporting these tanks.

3.1.3 In order to take into account progress in science and technology, the use of alternative arrangements may have been considered where these offer at least an equivalent level of safety in use in respect of compatibility with the properties of the substances transported and equivalent or superior resistance to impact, loading and fire.

3.1.4 These provisions do not apply to rail tank-wagons (except for materials of class 7), non-metallic tanks, tanks intended for the transport of liquids having a capacity of 450 litres or less and tanks for substances of class 2.

3.2   Definitions

3.2.1 For the purposes of these provisions:

3.2.2 *IMO type portable tank* means a tank having a capacity of more than 450 litres whose shell is fitted with items of service equipment and structural equipment necessary for the transport of dangerous substances whose vapour pressure is not more than 3 bar (absolute) at a temperature of 50°C. It is a tank that has stabilizing members external to the shell and is not permanently secured on board the ship. Its contents should not be loaded or discharged while the tank remains on board. It should be capable of being loaded and discharged without the need of removal of its structural equipment and be capable of being lifted on and off the ship when loaded. Road tank-vehicles, rail tank-wagons, non-metallic tanks and intermediate bulk containers (IBCs) are not considered to fall within the definition for portable tanks.

3.2.3 *Shell* means the tank proper, including openings and their closures, but does not include service equipment (see 3.2.4).

3.2.4 *Service equipment of a shell* means filling and discharge, venting, safety, heating and heat-insulating devices and measuring instruments.

3.2.5 *Structural equipment* means the reinforcing, fastening, protective or stabilizing members of the shell.

3.2.6 *Maximum allowable working pressure* means a pressure that is not less than the higher of the following two pressures, measured at the top of the tank while in operating position:

    .1   the highest effective pressure allowed in the shell during filling or discharge; or

    .2   the maximum effective gauge pressure to which tanks for liquids should be designed, which is the sum of the following partial pressures minus 1 bar:

    .2.1   the vapour pressure (in bar) at 65°C; and

    .2.2   the partial pressure (in bar) of air or other gases in the ullage space being determined by a maximum ullage temperature of 65°C and a liquid expansion due to the increase of the bulk mean temperature of $t_r - t_f$ (t_f = filling temperature, usually 15°C; t_r = 50°C; the maximum mean bulk temperature).

3.2.7 *Test pressure* means the maximum gauge pressure at the top of a tank during a hydraulic test.

3.2.8 *Design pressure* means the pressure used, according to a recognized pressure vessel code, as indicated in 3.3.11 for the design of every element of the tank.

The design pressure should never be less than the highest of the following three pressures:

    .1   the working pressure as given in 3.2.6.1; or

    .2   the sum of the pressure as given in 3.2.6.2 and the dynamic head pressure, determined on the basis of the dynamic forces due to inertia specified in 3.4.1 minus 1.0 bar; such a dynamic head pressure should never be taken to be less than 0.35 bar; or

    .3   the required test pressure divided by 1.5.

3.2.9 *Discharge pressure* means the highest pressure actually built up in the shell when it is being discharged by pressure.

3.2.10 *Leakage test* means a test which consists of subjecting the shell to an effective internal pressure equivalent to the maximum allowable working pressure, but not less than 0.2 bar (gauge).

3.2.11 *Total mass* means the mass of the shell, its service equipment and structural equipment, and the heaviest load authorized to be transported.

3.2.12 *Start-to-discharge pressure* means the value of increasing static pressure below which no bubbling occurs when a pressure relief valve is tested by means of air under water seal at the outlet.

3.2.13 *Type 1 portable tank* means a portable tank fitted with pressure relief devices, having a maximum allowable working pressure of 1.75 bar or above.

3.2.14 *Type 2 portable tank* means a portable tank fitted with pressure relief devices, having a maximum allowable working pressure equal to or above 1.0 bar but below 1.75 bar, intended for the transport of certain dangerous liquids of low hazard.

3.2.15 *Type 4 tank* is a road tank vehicle with a permanently attached tank or a tank attached to a chassis, with at least four twist locks that take account of ISO standards, having a capacity of more than 450 litres and fitted with pressure relief devices. Such a road tank should comply with the requirements of the competent authority. It need not comply fully with the relevant provisions for type 1 or 2 portable tanks. Special provisions for type 4 tanks are given in 3.24.5. Type 4 tanks should only be used on short international voyages.

3.2.16 *Road tank vehicle* is a vehicle fitted with a tank complying with the relevant provisions for type 1 or 2 portable tanks or is a type 4 tank, intended for the transport of dangerous liquids by both road and sea modes of transport, the tank of which is permanently or rigidly attached to the vehicle during all normal operations of loading, discharging and transport and is neither filled nor discharged on board and is driven on board on its own wheels.

3.2.17 *No bottom openings* means that the shell of the tank is not pierced below the liquid level in the tank. When existing openings are blanked off, this should be by means of suitable blank flanges welded to the shell internally and externally.

3.2.18 For the purposes of this sub-section, *tank* means a portable tank or a road tank vehicle.

3.3   General provisions for the design, construction, and operation of tanks

3.3.1 Shells should be manufactured of ductile metallic materials suitable for shaping. For welded shells, only a material whose weldability has been fully demonstrated should be used. Welds should be skilfully made and afford complete safety. Tank materials should be suitable for the marine environment.

3.3.2 Tanks, fittings and pipework should be manufactured of material which is either:

    .1   substantially immune to attack by the substance being transported; or

    .2   properly passivated or neutralized by chemical reaction with that substance; or

    .3   lined with other corrosion-resistant material directly bonded to the material of the shell or attached by equivalent means.

3.3.3 Gaskets, where used, should be made of materials not subject to attack by the contents of the tank.

3.3.4 If lining is applied, the lining of the tank and its fittings and pipings should be continuous, and should extend around the face of any flanges. Where external fittings are welded to the tank, the lining should be continuous through the fittings and around the face of external flanges.

3.3.5 Lining material should be substantially immune to attack by the substance transported, homogeneous, non-porous, and should have thermal-expansion and elasticity characteristics that are compatible with the material of the shell and pipings.

3.3.6 Care should be taken to avoid damage by galvanic action due to the juxtaposition of dissimilar metals.

3.3.7 The materials of the tank, including any devices, gaskets and accessories, should not adversely affect the contents of the tank.

3.3.8 Tanks should be designed and manufactured with supports to provide a secure base during transport and with suitable lifting and tie-down attachments. Road tank vehicles should be fitted with tie-down attachments and secured on board in such a way that the suspension is not left in free play.*

3.3.9 Tanks intended for the transport of flammable liquids having a flashpoint of not more than 61°C c.c. should be capable of being electrically earthed, e.g. should have installed a grounding stud or other suitable device with a minimum cross-sectional area of 0.5 cm^2. Measures should be taken to prevent a dangerous electrostatic discharge, for instance, in lined tanks or in tanks with plastic components, which are not electrically conductive. The aim of these measures is to assure electrical continuity.

3.3.10   Shells, their attachments and their service and structural equipment should be designed to withstand, without loss of contents, at least the internal pressure due to the contents and the static and dynamic stresses in normal handling and transport. For tanks that are intended for use as offshore tank-containers, the dynamic stresses imposed by handling in open seas should be taken into account.

3.3.11   Tanks should be designed, manufactured and tested in accordance with a recognized pressure vessel code, taking into account the design pressure as defined in 3.2.8.

3.3.12   Tanks should be of a design capable of being stress-analysed mathematically or experimentally by resistance strain gauges, or by any other acceptable method.

3.3.13   Tanks should be designed and manufactured to withstand a test pressure equal to at least 1.5 times the maximum allowable working pressure. However, the test pressure should never be lower than 1.5 bar. Specific provisions are laid down for various substances authorized to be carried in tanks in the Dangerous Goods List of the Code. Attention is also drawn to the minimum shell thickness provisions, specified in 3.5.1 to 3.5.8.

3.3.14   Tanks without vacuum-relief valves should be designed to withstand an external pressure at least 0.4 bar above the internal pressure. Tanks equipped with vacuum-relief valves should be designed to withstand an external overpressure of 0.21 bar or greater and should have their vacuum-relief valve set to relieve at minus (–) 0.21 bar, except that a greater negative setting may be utilized provided the external design pressure is not exceeded. All vacuum-relief valves used on tanks for the transport of liquids with flashpoints below 61°C (c.c.) should be equipped with a flame trap.

3.3.15   Tanks intended to contain certain dangerous substances should be provided with additional protection, which may take the form of additional thickness of the shell or a higher test pressure, the additional thickness or higher test pressure being determined in the light of the dangers inherent in the substances concerned. The provisions for each substance are given in the Dangerous Goods List of the Code.

---

* Attention is drawn to the Guidelines for securing arrangements for the transport of road vehicles on ro–ro ships (resolution A.581(14)).

3.4   Design criteria

3.4.1 Tanks and their fastenings should, under the maximum permissible load, be capable of absorbing the following dynamic forces:

- .1 *in the direction of travel:* twice the total mass;

- .2 *horizontally at right angles to the direction of travel:* the total mass (where the direction of travel is not clearly determined, the maximum permissible load should be equal to twice the total mass);

- .3 *vertically upwards:* the total mass; and

- .4 *vertically downwards:* twice the total mass (total loading including the effect of gravity).

3.4.2 Under each of these loads, the safety factors to be observed for the primary combined stress should be as follows:

- .1 for metals having a clearly defined yield point, a safety factor of 1.5 in relation to the determined yield stress; or

- .2 for metals with no clearly defined yield point, a safety factor of 1.5 in relation to the guaranteed 0.2% (1.0% for austenitic steels) proof stress.

Note: The above loads do not give rise to an increase in the pressure in the vapour space.

3.4.3 At the test pressure the membrane stress in the shell should conform to the material-dependent limitations prescribed below:

- .1 for metals and alloys exhibiting a clearly defined yield point or characterized by a guaranteed conventional yield stress R_e (generally 0.2% proof stress; for austenitic steels 1.0% proof stress), the membrane stress should not exceed $0.75R_e$ or $0.50R_m$, whichever is lower.

- .2 In the case of steel, the elongation at fracture, in per cent, should not be less than $10,000/R_m$ where R_m is in N/mm^2, with an absolute minimum of 20% based on a standard gauge length of 50 mm. In the case of aluminium, the elongation at fracture, in per cent, should not be less than $10,000/6R_m$, where R_m is in N/mm^2, with an absolute minimum of 12%.

3.4.4 The specimens used to determine the elongation at fracture should be taken transversely to the direction of rolling and be so secured that:

$$L_o = 5d,$$

or

$$L_o = 5.65 \sqrt{A}$$

where:

L_o = gauge length of the specimen before the test;

d = diameter; and

A = cross-sectional area of the test specimen.

3.5   Minimum shell thickness

3.5.1 The minimum shell thickness referred to in this sub-section may be used only if design criteria calculations do not indicate that a greater thickness is required.

3.5.2 The cylindrical portions and ends of tanks should have a thickness of not less than that determined by the following formula:*

$$e = \frac{C}{\sqrt[3]{(R_m \times A)}}$$

where:

e = minimum required thickness of the metal to be used, in mm;

R_m = guaranteed minimum tensile strength of the metal to be used, in N/mm^2;

A = guaranteed minimum elongation (as a percentage) of the metal to be used on fracture under tensile stress; see 3.4.3;

C = 107 (equivalent to 5 mm mild steel) for tanks intended for the transport of powdery or granular solid substances and for tanks of not more than 1.80 m in diameter intended for the transport of liquids

or

C = 128 (equivalent to 6 mm mild steel) for tanks of more than 1.80 m in diameter.

* The constant C is derived from the following formula: $e \times \sqrt[3]{(R_m \times A)} = e_o \times \sqrt[3]{(R_{mo} \times A_o)}$, where the sub-index 'o' refers to mild steel and the part of the equation without sub-index 'o' refers to the metal used. The relationship with mild steel as employed by the Code is attached to the constant C, where $C = e_o \times \sqrt[3]{(R_{mo} \times A_o)}$.

3.5.3 Where additional thickness of the shell is required for certain dangerous substances, this is given by the T code assigned to those substances. See the minimum shell thickness specified in the table in subsection 2.4.

For calculation purposes the required constant C to be taken is given in the table below:

Where the table in subsection 2.4 specifies:	C to be used for calculation is:
6 mm	128
8 mm	171
10 mm	213
12 mm	256

3.5.4 Except as provided in 3.5.5, the cylindrical portions and ends of all tanks should have a thickness of at least 3 mm regardless of the material of construction. For type 4 tanks the provisions of 3.24.5 may be applied.

3.5.5 Where additional protection of the tanks against damage is provided, the competent authority may, for a tank having a test pressure below 2.65 bar (i.e. type 2 portable tank), authorize a reduction in the minimum thickness in proportion to the protection provided.

For such protected tanks the thickness should not be less than that determined in accordance with 3.5.2, where:

$C = 64$ (equivalent to 3 mm mild steel) for tanks of not more than 1.80 m in diameter; and

$C = 85$ (equivalent to 4 mm mild steel) for tanks of more than 1.80 m in diameter.

3.5.6 The additional protection referred to in 3.5.5 may be provided by overall external structure protection such as a suitable "sandwich" construction with the outer shielding secured to the shell, double-wall construction or the shell supported in a complete framework with longitudinal and transverse structural members.

3.5.7 There should be no sudden change in plate thickness at the attachment of the head to the cylindrical portion of the shell, and after forming the head the plate thickness at the knuckle should not be less than the minimum thickness required by this sub-section.

3.5.8 In no case should the wall thickness of any portion of the shell be less than that prescribed in this sub-section.

3.6   Service equipment

3.6.1 Service equipment (valves, fittings, safety devices, gauging devices and the like) should be so arranged as to be protected against the risk of being wrenched off or damaged during transport and handling. If the connection between the frame and the shell allows relative movement as between the sub-assemblies, the equipment should be so fastened as to permit such movement without risk of damage to working parts. Equipment protection should offer a degree of safety comparable to that of the shell. For offshore tank-containers, where positioning of service equipment and the design and strength of protection for such equipment is concerned, the increased danger of impact damage when handling such tanks in open seas should be taken into account.

3.6.2 All shell openings other than openings for pressure relief devices and inspection openings should be provided with manually operated stop valves situated as near to the shell as is practicable.

3.6.3 A tank or each of its compartments should be provided with an opening large enough to enable the tank or compartment to be inspected.

3.6.4 Whenever possible, external fittings should be grouped together.

3.6.5 All tank connections should be clearly marked to indicate the function of each.

3.6.6 Stop valves with screwed spindles should close by clockwise rotation. Each valve should be designed and constructed for a rated pressure not less than the maximum allowable working pressure of the tank at the temperatures expected to be encountered.

3.6.7 All piping should be of suitable material. Welded pipe joints should be used wherever possible. Where copper tubing is permitted, joints should be brazed or have an equally strong metal union. The melting point of brazing material should be no lower than 525°C. Such joints should, in any event, be such as not to decrease the strength of the tubing, as may happen by cutting of threads. Ductile metals should be used in the construction of valves or accessories. The bursting strength of all piping and pipe fittings should be at least four times the strength at the maximum allowable working pressure of the tank and at least four times the strength at the pressure to which it may be subjected in service by the action of a pump or other device (except pressure relief valves) the action of which may subject portions of the piping to pressures greater than the tank maximum allowable working pressure. Suitable provisions should be made in every case to prevent damage to piping due to thermal expansion and contraction, jarring and vibration.

3.7 Bottom openings

3.7.1 Certain substances listed in the Dangerous Goods List of the Code should not be transported in tanks with bottom openings (bottom-discharge tanks). As an exception, for type 4 tanks, existing openings and hand inspection holes may be closed by bolted flanges mounted both internally and externally, fitted with product-compatible gaskets. Such arrangement should be approved by the competent authority.

3.7.2 Except as may otherwise be provided in the case of tanks intended for the transport of certain crystallizable, highly viscous or extremely hazardous substances, every bottom-discharge tank should be equipped with two serially mounted and mutually independent shutoff devices as follows:

.1 an internal stop valve; that is a stop valve within the tank or within a welded flange or its companion flange, or within a coupling which is an integral part of the tank, such that:

.1.1 the control devices are so designed as to prevent any unintended opening through impact or other inadvertent act;

.1.2 the valve may be operable from above or below; and

.1.3 if possible, the setting of the valve (open or closed) can be verified from the ground.

.2 At the end of each discharge pipe:

.2.1 a sluice valve; or

.2.2 a bolted blank flange; or

.2.3 a suitable screw cap or other liquid-tight closure.

3.7.3 For certain substances, as indicated by a reference to this paragraph in a table in subsection 2.4, bottom-discharge tanks should be equipped with three serially mounted and mutually independent shutoff devices as follows:

.1 an internal stop valve as provided in 3.7.2 except that it should be possible to close the valve from an accessible position of the tank that is remote from the valve itself;

.2 an external valve; and

.3 at the end of the discharge pipe:

.3.1 a bolted blank flange; or

.3.2 a suitable screw cap or other liquid-tight closure.

3.7.4 The internal shutoff device should continue to be effective in the event of damage to the external control device.

3.7.5 In order to avoid any loss of contents in the event of damage to external discharge fittings, e.g. pipe sockets, lateral shutoff devices, the internal stop valve and its seating should be protected against the danger of being wrenched off by external stresses or should be so designed as to resist them. The filling and discharge devices, including flanges or threaded plugs and protective caps, if any, should be capable of being secured against any unintended opening.

3.8 Safety relief

3.8.1 All tanks should be closed and fitted with a pressure relief device. All pressure relief devices should be to the satisfaction of the competent authority.

3.9 Pressure relief devices

3.9.1 Every tank of 1,900 litres or more, or every independent compartment of a tank of similar capacity, should be provided with one or more pressure relief valves of the spring-loaded type and may in addition have a frangible disc or fusible element in parallel with the spring-loaded valves, except when precluded by a reference to 3.9.3 in a table in subsection 2.4.

3.9.2 Pressure relief devices should be designed to prevent the entry of foreign matter, the leakage of liquid and the development of any dangerous excess pressure.

3.9.3 Tanks intended for the transport of certain highly toxic substances, which are assigned to a T Code where this paragraph is indicated, should have a pressure relief arrangement approved by the competent authority. The arrangement should comprise a spring-loaded pressure relief valve preceded by a frangible disc except that a tank in dedicated service may be fitted with an approved relief system offering an equivalent hermetic seal. The space between the frangible disc and the valve should be provided with a pressure gauge or suitable tell-tale indicator. This arrangement permits the detection of disc rupture, pinholing or leakage which could cause a malfunction of the spring-loaded valve. The frangible disc in this instance should rupture at a nominal pressure that is 10% above the start-to-discharge pressure of the valve.

3.9.4 Every tank with a capacity of less than 1,900 litres should be fitted with a pressure relief device which may be a frangible disc. If no spring-loaded pressure relief valve is used, the frangible disc should be set to rupture at a nominal pressure equal to the test pressure.

3.9.5 If the tank is fitted with arrangements for air-pressure or inert-gas-pressure discharge, the inlet line should be provided with a suitable pressure relief device set to operate at a pressure not higher than the maximum allowable working pressure of the tank. A stop valve should be provided at the entry to the tank.

3.10   Setting of pressure relief devices

3.10.1   It should be noted that the devices should operate only in conditions of excessive rise in temperature, as the tank will not during transport be subject to undue fluctuations of pressure due to operating procedures (see, however, 3.13.2).

3.10.2   The required pressure relief valve should be set to start to discharge at a nominal pressure of five-sixths of the test pressure in the case of tanks having a test pressure up to and including 4.5 bar and 110% of two-thirds of the test pressure in the case of tanks having a test pressure of more than 4.5 bar. The valve should, after discharge, close at a pressure not lower than 10% below the pressure at which discharge starts, and should remain closed at all lower pressures provided that this provision not be so construed as to prevent the use of vacuum-relief or combination pressure-relief and vacuum-relief valves.

3.11   Fusible elements

3.11.1   Fusible elements, if allowed in the Dangerous Goods List of the Code, should function at a temperature between 110°C and 149°C provided that the developed pressure in the tank at the fusing temperature of the element does not exceed the test pressure of the tank. They should be placed at the top of the tank in the vapour space and in no case should they be shielded from external heat.

3.12   Frangible discs

3.12.1   Except as provided in 3.9.3, frangible discs, if used, should rupture at a nominal pressure equal to the test pressure. Particular attention should be given to the provisions of 3.6.1 if frangible discs are used.

3.13   Capacity of relief devices

3.13.1   The spring-loaded relief valve required by 3.9.1 should have a minimum diameter of 31.75 mm. Vacuum-relief valves, if used, should have a minimum through area of 2.84 cm^2.

3.13.2   The combined delivery capacity of the relief devices in condition of complete engulfment of the tank in fire should be sufficient to limit the pressure in the tank to 20% above the start-to-discharge pressure of the relief device. Emergency pressure relief devices may be used to achieve the full relief capacity prescribed. Emergency pressure relief devices may be of the spring-loaded, frangible or fusible type.

To determine the total certified capacity of the relief devices, which may be regarded as being the sum of the individual capacities of the several devices, the following formula may be used:

$$Q = 12.4 \frac{FA^{0.82}}{LC} \sqrt{\frac{ZT}{M}}$$

where:

the accumulating condition is 20% above the start-to-discharge pressure of the relief device;

Q is the minimum required rate of discharge in cubic metres of air per second at standard conditions: 1 bar and 0°C (273 K);

F is a coefficient with the following value:

.1   for uninsulated tanks $F = 1$

.2   for insulated tanks $F = U(649 - t)/13.6$ but in no case is less than 0.25

where:

U = thermal conductance of the insulation, in kW/(m^2 K), at 38°C

t = actual temperature of the substance at loading (°C); if this temperature is unknown, let $t = 15$°C;

The value of F given in .2 above may be taken provided that:

– the insulation is jacketed with a material having a melting point not less than 649°C; and

– the insulation system will remain effective at all temperatures up to 649°C;

A is the total external surface area of tank in square metres;

Z is the gas compressibility factor in the accumulating condition (if this factor is unknown, let Z equal 1.0);

T is the absolute temperature in kelvin (°C + 273) above the pressure relief devices and in the accumulating condition;

L is the latent heat of vaporization of the liquid, in kJ/kg, in the accumulating condition;

M is the molecular mass of the discharged gas;

C is the constant which is derived from equation (2) as a function of the ratio k of specific heats:

$$k = \frac{C_p}{C_v} \qquad (1)$$

where:

C_p is the specific heat at constant pressure and

C_v is the specific heat at constant volume;

when $k > 1$, in this case C may be taken from the table that follows

$$\left.\begin{array}{l} C = \sqrt{k\left(\frac{2}{k+1}\right)^{\frac{k+1}{k-1}}} \\[2mm] \text{when } k = 1 \text{ or } k \text{ is unknown} \\[2mm] C = \frac{1}{\sqrt{e}} = 0.607 \end{array}\right\} \qquad (2)$$

where: e is the mathematical constant 2.7183

VALUES FOR THE CONSTANT C WHEN k >1

k	C	k	C	k	C
1.00	0.607	1.26	0.660	1.52	0.704
1.02	0.611	1.28	0.664	1.54	0.707
1.04	0.615	1.30	0.667	1.56	0.710
1.06	0.620	1.32	0.671	1.58	0.713
1.08	0.624	1.34	0.674	1.60	0.716
1.10	0.628	1.36	0.678	1.62	0.719
1.12	0.633	1.38	0.681	1.64	0.722
1.14	0.637	1.40	0.685	1.66	0.725
1.16	0.641	1.42	0.688	1.68	0.728
1.18	0.645	1.44	0.691	1.70	0.731
1.20	0.649	1.46	0.695	2.00	0.770
1.22	0.652	1.48	0.698	2.20	0.793
1.24	0.656	1.50	0.701		

3.13.3   Alternatively to using the formula above, tanks designed for the transport of liquids may have their relief devices sized in accordance with the following table. This table assumes an insulation value of $F = 1$ and should be adjusted accordingly if the tank is insulated. Other values used in determining this table are:

$M = 86.7 \quad T = 394 \text{ K} \quad L = 334.94 \text{ kJ/kg} \quad C = 0.607 \quad Z = 1$

MINIMUM EMERGENCY VENT CAPACITY Q IN CUBIC METRES OF AIR PER SECOND AT 1 bar AND 0°C (273 K)

A Exposed area (square metres)	Q (Cubic metres of air per second)	A Exposed area (square metres)	Q (Cubic metres of air per second)
2	0.230	37.5	2.539
3	0.320	40	2.677
4	0.405	42.5	2.814
5	0.487	45	2.949
6	0.565	47.5	3.082
7	0.641	50	3.215
8	0.715	52.5	3.346
9	0.788	55	3.476
10	0.859	57.5	3.605
12	0.998	60	3.733
14	1.132	62.5	3.860
16	1.263	65	3.987
18	1.391	67.5	4.112
20	1.517	70	4.236
22.5	1.670	75	4.483
25	1.821	80	4.726
27.5	1.969	85	4.967
30	2.115	90	5.206
32.5	2.258	95	5.442
35	2.400	100	5.676

3.14   Marking of pressure relief devices

3.14.1   Every pressure relief device should be plainly and permanently marked with the pressure or temperature at which it is set to discharge and the rated free-air delivery of the device. Where practicable, the following particulars should also be shown:

> .1   the manufacturer's name and the relevant catalogue number; and

> .2   allowable tolerances at start-to-discharge pressure (frangible disc) and allowable temperature tolerances (fusible elements).

3.15   Connections to pressure relief devices

3.15.1   Connections to pressure relief devices should be of sufficient size to enable the required discharge to pass unrestricted to the safety device. No stop valve should be installed between the shell and the pressure relief devices except where duplicate devices are provided for maintenance or other reasons and the stop valves serving the devices actually in use are locked open or the stop valves are interlocked so that at least one of the devices is always in use. Vents from the pressure relief devices, where used, should deliver the relieved vapour or liquid to the atmosphere in conditions of minimum back-pressure on the relieving device.

3.16   Siting of pressure relief devices

3.16.1   Pressure relief device inlets should be sited on top of the tank in a position as near the longitudinal and transverse centre of the tank as possible. All pressure relief device inlets should be situated in the vapour space of the tank and the devices so arranged as to ensure that the escaping vapour is discharged unrestrictedly and in such a manner that it cannot impinge upon the shell. Protective devices which deflect the flow of vapour are permissible provided the required relief-device capacity is not reduced.

3.16.2   Arrangements should be made to prevent access to the devices by unauthorized persons and to protect the devices from damage caused by the tank overturning.

3.17   Gauging devices

3.17.1   Glass level-gauges, or gauges made of other easily destructible material, which are in direct communication with the contents of the tank should not be used.

3.18   Tank support, frameworks, lifting and tie-down attachments[*]

3.18.1   Tanks should be designed and manufactured with a support structure to provide a secure base during transport. Skids, frameworks, cradles or other similar devices are acceptable. The loadings specified in 3.4.1 should also be considered in this aspect of design.

3.18.2   The design of tank mountings (e.g., cradles and frameworks) and tank lifting and tie-down attachments should not cause undue concentration of stress in any portion of the tank. Permanent lifting and tie-down attachments should be fitted to all tanks. They should preferably be fitted to the tank supports. Otherwise, these attachments should be secured to reinforcing plates located on the shell at the points of support.

3.18.3   In the design of supports and frameworks, due regard should be paid to the effects of environmental corrosion, and in calculations for all structural members not constructed of corrosion-resistant materials a minimum corrosion allowance, determined by the competent authority, should be provided.

3.18.4   Tank frameworks intended to be lifted or secured by their corner castings should be subjected to internationally accepted tests, such as those set forth in the CSC Convention. The use of such frameworks within an integrated system is generally encouraged. In addition, for road tank vehicles, tie-down attachments should be located on the tank support or vehicle structure in such a manner that the springing system is not left in free play. Offshore tank-containers should be subjected to tests that take into account the dynamic lifting and impact forces that may occur when a tank is handled on open seas.

3.18.5[†]   Fork-lift pockets of tanks should be capable of being closed off. The means of closing fork-lift pockets should be a permanent part of the framework or permanently attached to the framework.

3.18.5.1 Single-compartment tanks with a nominal length of less than 3.65 m (12 feet) need not comply with 3.18.5 provided that:

> .1   the tank shell and all fittings are well protected from being hit by the fork's blades; and

> .2   the distance between the centres of the fork-lift pockets is at least $\frac{1}{2}$ of the maximum length of the portable tank unit.

---

[*] Attention is drawn to the Guidelines for securing arrangements for the transport of road vehicles on ro–ro ships (resolution A.581(14)).

[†] Existing tanks should have complied with this provision from 1 January 1996.

Appendix

3.18.6   Tanks should be carried only on vehicles whose fastenings are capable, in conditions of maximum permissible loading of the tanks, of absorbing the forces specified in 3.4.1.

3.19   Approval, testing and marking of tanks

3.19.1   The competent approval authority or a body authorized by that authority should have issued, in respect of every new design of a tank, a certificate attesting that the tank and its attachments surveyed by that authority or that body are suitable for the purpose for which they are intended and meet the construction and equipment provisions of this sub-section and, where appropriate, the special provisions of 2.2.6. The prototype test results and an approval number should have been specified in a test report. If the tanks are manufactured without change in structural design, this approval should have been deemed to be design approval. The approval number should consist of the distinguishing sign or mark of the State in whose territory the approval was granted and a registration number.

3.19.2   Design approval should have been given in respect of at least one tank of each design and each size, it being, however, understood that a set of tests made on a tank of one size may have served for the approval of smaller tanks made of a material of the same kind and thickness by the same fabrication technique and with identical supports and equivalent closures and other appurtenances.

3.19.3   The shell and items of equipment of each tank should be inspected and tested, either together or separately, first before being put into service (initial inspection and test) and thereafter at no more than five-year intervals (periodic inspection and test). The initial inspection and test should have included a check of the design characteristics, an internal and external examination and a hydraulic pressure test. If the shell and equipment have been pressure-tested separately, they should together be subjected after assembly to a leakage test. The periodic inspections and tests should include an internal and external examination and, as a general rule, a pressure test.

   .1   Sheathing, thermal insulation and the like should be removed only to the extent required for reliable appraisal of the tank's condition. The initial and periodic pressure tests should be carried out, by the competent authority, at the test pressure indicated on the data plate of the tank, except in cases where periodic tests at lower test pressures are authorized.

   .2   The tank should be inspected for corroded areas, dents or other conditions which indicate weakness that might render the tank unsafe in transport and, while under pressure, for leakage. If any evidence of such unsafe condition is discovered, the tank should not be placed in or returned to service until it has been repaired and the test, repeated, has been passed.

3.19.4   Before tanks were put into service, and thereafter at intervals midway between the five-yearly inspection and tests specified in 3.19.3, the following tests and inspections were performed:

   .1   a leakage test, where required;

   .2   a test of satisfactory operation of all service equipment; and

   .3   an internal and external inspection of the tanks and their fittings with due regard to the substances transported.

3.19.5   The 2.5-year (midway) inspection and test may be carried out within 3 months before or after the specified date. The date of the 2.5-year inspection should be durably marked on, or as near as possible to, the metal identification plate required in 3.20.1. When marking is not done on the plate, the characters should be at least 32 mm in height and of a contrasting colour to the tank.

3.19.6   The 2.5-year internal inspections may be waived or substituted for by other test methods by the competent authority in the case of tanks intended for dedicated transport. A portable tank may not be filled and offered for transport after the date of expiry of the last 5-year or 2.5-year periodic inspection and test as required by 3.19.3 and 3.19.4. However, a portable tank filled prior to the date of expiry of the last periodic inspection and test may be transported for a period not to exceed three months beyond the date of expiry of the last periodic test or inspection. In addition, a portable tank may be transported after the date of expiry of the last periodic test and inspection:

   .1   After emptying but before cleaning, for purposes of performing the next required test and inspection prior to refilling; and

   .2   Unless otherwise approved by the competent authority, for a period not to exceed six months beyond the date of expiry of the last periodic test and inspection, in order to allow the return of dangerous goods for proper disposal or recycling. Reference to this authorization should be entered in the dangerous goods shipping document.

3.19.7   When the tank is damaged, it should be so repaired as to comply with the provisions of this circular.

3.19.8   In all cases where cutting, burning or welding operations on the shell of the tank have been effected, that work should be to the approval of the competent authority and a hydrostatic test to at least the original test pressure should be carried out.

3.19.9   The certificate and the test report required under 3.19.1 and the certificate showing the results of the initial hydrostatic test for each tank issued by the competent authority or its approved inspecting agency should be retained by the authority or agency and the owners during the time the tank is in service. As a minimum, the certificate issued under 3.19.1 should provide the information required in 3.20.1.

3.20 Marking

3.20.1 Every tank should be fitted with a corrosion-resistant metal plate permanently attached in a place readily accessible for inspection. At least the following particulars should be marked on the plate in characters at least 3 mm in height by stamping, engraving, embossing or any similar method. If, for reasons of tank arrangements, the plate cannot be permanently attached to the shell, the shell should be marked with at least those particulars required by a recognized pressure vessel code in a manner prescribed by that code.

The plate should be kept free of paint to ensure that the markings will be legible at all times.

Country of manufacture . . . .

IMO tank   Approval   Approval

type no. . . . .   country . . . .   number . . . .

Manufacturer's name or mark . . . .

Registration number . . . .

Year of manufacture . . . .

Test pressure . . . . (bar)/(MPa)*

Maximum allowable working pressure . . . . (bar)/(MPa)*

Water capacity at 20°C . . . . (litres)
(The water capacity should be established to within 1% by practical test rather than by calculation.)

Maximum gross mass . . . .(kg)

Original hydrostatic test date and witness identification . . . .

Code to which tank is designed . . . .

Metallurgic design temperature (only if above +50°C or below –20°C) . . . .

Maximum allowable working pressure for coils (where coils used) . . . . (bar)/(MPa)*

Tank material . . . .

Equivalent thickness in mild steel . . . . (mm)

Lining material (if any) . . . .

Capacity of each compartment (in compartmented tanks) . . . . litres

Month, year and test pressure of most recent periodic test:

. . . . month . . . . year . . . . (bar)/(MPa)*

Stamp of expert who carried out most recent test . . . .

   * The unit used should be marked.

3.20.2 Special-purpose tanks should be marked on the identification plate to indicate the substance they are permitted to transport.

3.20.3 If a tank is designed and approved for handling in open seas, the words OFFSHORE CONTAINER should be marked on the identification plate.

3.21 Transport provisions

3.21.1 The shells and service equipment of tanks should be manufactured so as to withstand impact or overturning or, alternatively, they should, during transport, be adequately protected against lateral and longitudinal impact and against overturning.

Examples of protection of shells against collision:

   .1 protection against lateral impact may consist, for example, of longitudinal bars protecting the shell on both sides at the level of the median line;

.2 protection of tanks against overturning may consist, for example, of reinforcement rings or bars fixed across the frame;

.3 protection against rear impact may consist of a bumper or frame; or

.4 external fittings should be designed or protected so as to preclude the release of contents upon impact or overturning of the tank upon the fittings.

3.21.2 Certain substances are chemically unstable. They are to be accepted for transport only if the necessary steps have been taken to prevent their dangerous decomposition, transformation, or polymerization during transport. To this end, care should in particular be taken to ensure that tanks do not contain any substances liable to promote these reactions.

3.22 [Reserved]

3.23 Handling provisions

3.23.1 Fork-lift pockets of tanks should be closed off when the tank is filled. This provision does not apply to tanks which, according to 3.18.5.1, need not be provided with means for closing off the fork-lift pockets.

3.24 Road tank vehicles

3.24.1 A road tank vehicle for long international voyages should be fitted with a tank complying with the provisions for type 1 or 2 portable tanks and should comply with the relative provisions for tank supports, frameworks, lifting and tie-down attachments in 3.18.1 to 3.18.4, and in addition comply with the provisions in 3.24.3 and 3.24.4.

3.24.2 A road tank vehicle for short international voyages should either:

.1 comply with the provisions of 3.24.1; or

.2 be constructed as a type 4 tank, as defined in 3.2.15, complying with the provisions of 3.24.3, 3.24.4 and 3.24.5.

3.24.3 The tank supports and tie-down arrangements* of road tank vehicles should be included in the visual external inspection provided for in 3.19.4.

3.24.4 The vehicle of a road tank vehicle should be tested and inspected in accordance with the road transport provisions of the competent authority of the country in which the vehicle is operated.

3.24.5 *Type 4 tanks*

3.24.5.1 Type 4 tanks should only be authorized for short international voyages. They should comply with the provisions of 3.3, 13.1.4, 3.5 and 3.18 or, if they do not comply fully with these provisions, they should be certified by the competent authority for road transport of the substances to be transported by road and should at least comply with the following minimum provisions:

.1 they should have been subjected during construction to a minimum hydraulic test pressure equal to that specified for the relevant T code (see 2.4);

.2 the thickness of cylindrical portions and ends in mild steel should be:

.2.1 not more than 2 mm thinner than the thickness specified in column 9 of the above-indicated list of substances;

.2.2 subject to an absolute minimum thickness of 4 mm of mild steel; and

.2.3 for other materials, subject to an absolute minimum thickness of 3 mm;

.3 the maximum effective gauge pressure developed by the substances to be transported should not exceed the maximum allowable working pressure of the tank; and

.4 the primary combined stresses in supports, tie-down attachments* and tank structures in way of them due to static forces and to dynamic forces as defined in 3.4.1 should not exceed $0.8R_e$, where R_e is explained in 3.4.3. The said stresses may be calculated or measured.

3.24.5.2 The materials of construction of type 4 tanks, if they do not comply with the provisions of 3.3.1 to 3.3.7, should at least comply with the requirements of the competent authority for the transport by road of the substances to be transported by road.

3.24.5.3 Tank supports on permanently attached type 4 tanks, if they do not comply with the provisions of 3.18, should at least comply with the requirements of the competent authority for the transport by road of the substances to be transported by road.

3.24.5.4 Type 4 tanks should, as a minimum, be tested and inspected in accordance with the requirements of the competent authority for the transport by road of the substances to be transported by road.

---

* See also IMO Assembly resolution A.581(14) of 20 November 1985, Guidelines for securing arrangements for the transport of road vehicles on ro–ro ships.

3.24.5.5 The protection of valves and accessories of type 4 tanks should at least comply with the requirements of the competent authority for the transport by road of the substances to be transported by road.

3.24.5.6 The joints in shells of type 4 tanks should at least be made by fusion welding and comply with the requirements of the competent authority for the transport by road of the substances to be transported by road.

3.24.5.7 Type 4 tanks should at least be provided with manholes or other openings in the tank which comply with the requirements of the competent authority for the transport by road of the substances to be transported by road.

3.24.5.8 Tank nozzles and external fittings on type 4 tanks should at least comply with the requirements of the competent authority for the transport by road of the substances to be transported by road, except that, irrespective of road requirements, tanks with bottom openings should not be used for substances for which bottom openings would not be permitted for transport by sea in other types of tanks, unless exempted in accordance with 3.7.1.

3.24.5.9 All type 4 tanks should be closed tanks and, if they do not comply with the provisions of 3.8 to 3.16, they should at least be fitted with pressure relief devices of the type required in the relevant T code (see 2.4). The devices should be acceptable to the competent authority for the transport by road of the substances to be transported. The start-to-discharge pressure of such devices should in no case be less than the maximum allowable working pressure, nor greater than 25% above that pressure.

3.24.5.10   Type 4 tanks should be attached to the chassis when transported on board ship. Type 4 tanks which are not permanently attached to the chassis should be marked "IMO type 4" in letters at least 32 mm high.

3.25   [Reserved]

3.26   [Reserved]

**3.27   Special provisions relating to tanks for the transport of dangerous substances
            at elevated temperatures in liquid, molten or resolidified form**

3.27.1   The following general provisions relate particularly to tanks for the transport of dangerous substances at elevated temperatures in either liquid or molten form and of molten dangerous substances in resolidified form.

3.27.2   The design of the tank, the choice of materials, insulation, fittings and service equipment should take into account the highest temperature reached during filling, discharge and transport and should be compatible with the substances to be transported.

3.27.3   The highest temperature reached during filling, discharge and transport, if it is in excess of 65°C, should be used when calculating the maximum allowable working pressure as defined in 3.2.6. The minimum test pressure should never be less than the pressure indicated for the relevant T code.

3.27.4   [Reserved]

3.27.5   When tanks are used for the transport of liquids at a temperature above the flashpoint, they should be capable of being electrically earthed, e.g., they should have installed a grounding stud or other suitable device with a minimum cross-sectional area of 0.5 cm². Measures should be taken to prevent a dangerous electrostatic discharge, for instance, in lined tanks or in tanks with plastic components which are not electrically conductive. The aim of these measures is to assure electrical continuity.

3.27.6   The temperature of the outer surface of the shell or of the thermal insulation should not exceed 70°C during transport.

3.27.7   An additional hazard during transport can be expected from flammable vapours emanating from contaminated insulation by spillage of the product during loading or unloading.

3.27.8   [Reserved]

3.27.9   *Heating systems*

3.27.9.1   The heating system should not allow a substance to reach a temperature at which the pressure in the tank exceeds its design pressure or causes other hazards (e.g. thermal decomposition or increased corrosivity).

3.27.9.2   For some substances the heating system should be fitted outside the inner shell. However, a pipe used for discharging the substance may be equipped with a heating jacket. These substances are assigned to TP26.

3.27.9.3 *Protection against explosion*

    .1   In no case should the temperature at the surface of the heating element for internal heating equipment or the temperature at the tank shell for external heating equipment exceed 80% of the autoignition temperature of the substance carried. Power for internal heating elements should not be available unless the heating elements are completely submerged.

.2   If the electrical heating system is installed inside the tank, an earth leakage circuit breaker should be installed with a releasing current of <100 mA.

.3   Electrical switch cabinets mounted to tanks should not have a direct connection to the tank interior and should provide protection of at least the equivalent of type IP 56 according to IEC 144 or IEC 529.

3.27.9.4 The heating system should be subject to inspection and tests, including pressure tests on heating coils or ducts as appropriate, together with the other equipment indicated in 3.19.

3.27.10 Bottom openings should be in accordance with 3.7. However, all shutoff devices may be external.

3.28   Special provisions relating to tanks for the transport of solid dangerous substances (e.g. powdery or granulated materials)

3.28.1   [Reserved]

3.28.2   [Reserved]

3.28.3   [Reserved]

3.28.4   *Special provisions for tanks dedicated to the transport of solid substances which do not liquefy during transport*

.1   [Reserved]

.2   Every bottom-discharge tank should be equipped with at least two serially mounted and mutually independent shutoff devices. An internal stop valve is not required.

.3   The design of the tank and the choice of materials, fittings and service equipment should be suitable for, and compatible with, the substances to be transported.

3.29   Special provisions relating to tanks for the transport of flammable liquids (class 3)

3.29.1   All tanks intended for the transport of flammable liquids should be closed tanks and be fitted with pressure relief devices in accordance with 3.9 to 3.16.

3.29.2   [Reserved]

3.30   [Reserved]

3.31   [Reserved]

3.32   [Reserved]

3.33   [Reserved]

3.34   [Reserved]

3.35   [Reserved]

3.36   [Reserved]

Sub-section B   GENERAL PROVISIONS FOR PORTABLE TANKS AND ROAD TANK VEHICLES FOR NON-REFRIGERATED LIQUEFIED GASES OF CLASS 2

3.37   Preamble

3.37.1   The provisions of this sub-section apply to portable tanks (type 5 tanks) and road tank vehicles (type 6 tanks) intended for the transport of non-refrigerated liquefied gases of class 2. In addition to these provisions and unless otherwise specified, the applicable requirements of the International Convention for Safe Containers (CSC), 1972, as amended, should be fulfilled by any portable tank which meets the definition of a "container" within the terms of that Convention. The International Convention for Safe Containers does not apply to offshore tank-containers that are handled in open seas. The design and testing of offshore tank-containers should take into account the dynamic lifting and impact forces that may occur when a tank is handled in open seas in adverse weather and sea conditions. The requirements for such tanks should be determined by the approving competent authority (see MSC/Circ. 613 as amended). Such requirements should be based on MSC/Circ. 860, Guidelines for the approval of offshore containers handled in open seas.

3.37.2   In order to take into account progress in science and technology, the use of alternative arrangements which offer at least equivalent safety in use in respect of compatibility with the properties of the gases transported and equivalent or superior resistance to impact, loading and fire may have been considered by the national competent authority.

3.37.3   [Reserved]

3.37.4   [Reserved]

3.37.5   The provisions of this sub-section do not apply to rail tank-wagons, non-metallic tanks or tanks having a capacity of 1,000 litres or less.

3.37.6   [Reserved]

3.38   Definitions

3.38.1   For the purposes of these provisions:

3.38.2   For the purposes of this sub-section, *tank* means a portable tank or the carrying tank of a road tank vehicle the shell of which is fitted with items of service equipment and structural equipment necessary for the transport of gases. A tank should be capable of being transported, loaded and discharged without the need of removal of its structural equipment.

3.38.3   *Shell* means the pressure vessel proper, including openings and their closures.

3.38.4   *Service equipment of a shell* means filling and discharge, venting, safety, heating and heat-insulating devices and measuring instruments.

3.38.5   *Structural equipment* means the reinforcing, fastening, protective and stabilizing members external to the shell and for a road tank vehicle includes fastenings to running gear or chassis.

3.38.6   *Maximum allowable working pressure* (MAWP) means the maximum gauge pressure permissible at the top of the tank in its operating position. It may be no less than the vapour pressure at the design reference temperature less one bar of any product which can be loaded and carried, and any pressure which might be used during loading or unloading. In no case should the MAWP be less than 7 bar.

3.38.7   *Test pressure* means the highest pressure which arises in the shell during the hydraulic pressure test.

3.38.8   *Discharge pressure* means the highest pressure actually built up in the shell when it is being discharged by pressure.

3.38.9   *Leakage test* is the test which submits the shell, complete with those items of service equipment necessary for filling, discharge, safety and measuring, to an effective internal pressure equivalent to the MAWP. The procedure to be adopted should be approved by the competent authority.

3.38.10   *Total mass* means the mass of the portable tank or road tank vehicle with the heaviest load authorized for transport.

3.38.11   *Design reference temperature* means the temperature at which the vapour pressure of the tank contents is determined for the purpose of calculating the MAWP. The design reference temperature should be less than the critical temperature of the gas to be transported to ensure that the gas at all times is liquefied.

For portable tanks the temperature to be taken is as follows:

.1   for a tank with a diameter of 1.5 metres or less: 65°C;

.2   for a tank with a diameter of more than 1.5 metres:

.2.1   without insulation or sun shield: 60°C;

.2.2   with sun shield: 55°C; and

.2.3   with insulation: 50°C.*

For a road tank vehicle the temperature to be taken is to be agreed by the competent authorities.

3.38.12   *Mild steel* means steel with a guaranteed minimum tensile strength of 360 N/mm^2 and a guaranteed minimum percentage elongation of 27.

3.38.13   *Filling ratio* means the average mass of gas in kilograms per litre of tank capacity (kg/ℓ).

---

* This reference temperature is envisaged but dependent on the quality of the insulation system.

3.38.14   *Type 5 tank* means a portable tank as defined in 3.38.2 fitted with pressure relief devices. It should be capable of being lifted when full and its contents should not be loaded or discharged whilst the tank remains on board ship.

3.38.15   *Type 6 tank* means a road tank vehicle and includes a semi-trailer with a permanently attached tank as defined in 3.38.2 fitted with pressure relief devices. It should be fitted with permanent attachments such that it can be secured on board ship; however, its contents should not be loaded or discharged whilst the vehicle remains on board. A road tank vehicle should be carried only on short international voyages.

3.38.16   *Competent authorities* means, in respect of those provisions solely applicable to road tank vehicles, the authority concerned with approval for transport by sea and also the authority concerned with approval for international transport by road. Where the latter authority does not exist, the relevant national authority should be substituted.

3.39   General provisions for the construction and operation of tanks for non-refrigerated liquefied gases

3.39.1   Shells should be made of steel suitable for shaping. For welded shells only a material whose weldability has been fully demonstrated should be used. If the manufacture-procedure or the materials make it necessary, the tanks should be heat-treated with a suitable heat treatment both after welding operations and after forming. Welds should be skilfully made and afford complete safety. Tank materials should be suitable for the external environment in which they may be carried, e.g. the marine environment. The use of aluminium as a material of construction should be specifically authorized for use in the marine mode in the Dangerous Goods List of the Code. In those cases where aluminium is authorized, it should be insulated to prevent significant loss of physical properties when it is subjected to a heat load of 2.60 gcal/cm^2·s for a period of 30 minutes. The insulation system should remain effective at all temperatures of up to 650°C and should be jacketed with a material with a melting point of not less than 650°C. The insulation system should be approved by the competent authority. Steel should be resistant to brittle fracture and to fissuring corrosion under stress. For portable tanks the temperature range to be taken into account should be between –30°C and the design reference temperature unless more stringent conditions are specified by the competent authority. For road tank vehicles the temperature range is to be agreed by the competent authorities.

3.39.2   Tanks, fittings, and pipework should be constructed of material which is either:

   .1   substantially immune to attack by the gas transported; or

   .2   properly passivated or neutralized by chemical reaction with that gas.

3.39.3   Gaskets, where used, should be made of materials not subject to attack by the contents of the tank.

3.39.4   Care should be taken to avoid damage by galvanic action due to the juxtapositon of dissimilar metals.

3.39.5   The tanks, including any devices, appendages, coverings or fittings that can be expected to come into contact with the contents, should be constructed of materials that cannot be damaged by or enter into dangerous reactions with the contents.

3.39.6   Portable tanks should be designed and fabricated with supports to provide a secure base during transport and with suitable lifting and tie-down attachments. Road tank vehicles should be fitted with tie-down attachments and secured on board in such a way that the suspension is not left in free play.*

3.39.7   Shells, their attachments and their service and structural equipment should be designed to withstand, without loss of contents, at least the internal pressure due to the contents, plus the most severe combination of the static and dynamic stresses in normal handling and transport. For tanks that are intended for use as offshore tank-containers the dynamic stresses imposed by handling in open seas should be taken into account.

3.39.8   Tanks should be manufactured to a technical code recognized by the competent authority. Shells should be designed, manufactured and tested in accordance with a recognized pressure vessel code, taking into account corrosion, mass of contents, MAWP and, if applicable, the effect of superimposed stresses due to dynamic forces in accordance with 3.39.10.

3.39.9   Tanks should be designed to withstand an external pressure of at least 0.4 bar gauge above the internal pressure without permanent deformation. When the tank is to be subjected to a significant vacuum before loading or during discharge, it should be designed to withstand an external pressure of at least 0.9 bar gauge and should be proven to that pressure.

---

* Attention is drawn to the Guidelines for securing arrangements for the transport of road vehicles on ro–ro ships (resolution A.581(14)).

3.39.10 The minimum dynamic loads to be withstood should be based on:

   .1 *in the direction of travel:* twice the total mass;

   .2 *horizontally at right angles to the direction of travel:* the total mass (where the direction of travel is not clearly determined the maximum permissible load should be equal to twice the total mass);

   .3 *vertically upwards:* the total mass; and

   .4 *vertically downwards:* twice the total mass (total loading, including the effect of gravity).

The said loads should be considered separately.

3.39.11 Where portable tanks are transported on vehicles, the fastenings of tank and vehicle should be capable of absorbing the forces specified in 3.39.10.

3.39.12 Tanks intended to contain certain gases, listed in the Dangerous Goods List of the Code, should be provided with additional protection, which may take the form of additional thickness of the shell or a higher test pressure, the additional thickness or higher test pressure being determined in the light of the dangers inherent in the substances concerned; or of a protective device approved by the competent authority.

3.39.13 Thermal insulation systems should satisfy the following provisions:

   .1 If the shells of tanks intended for the transport of gases are equipped with thermal insulation, such insulation should either:

   .1.1 consist of a shield covering not less than the upper third but not more than the upper half of the tank's surface and separated from the shell by an air space about 4 cm across; or

   .1.2 consist of a complete cladding of adequate thickness of insulating materials protected so as to prevent the ingress of moisture and damage under normal transport conditions. If the protected covering is so closed as to be gastight, a device should be provided to prevent any dangerous pressure from developing in the insulation layer in the event of inadequate gastightness of the shell or of its items of equipment.

   .2 The thermal insulation should be so designed as not to hinder access to the fittings and discharge devices.

3.40   Cross-sectional design

3.40.1 Tanks should be of a circular cross-section.

3.40.2 Tanks should be designed and constructed to withstand a test pressure equal to at least 1.3 times the MAWP. Specific provisions are laid down for various gases in tank instruction T50 of this circular. Attention is also drawn to the minimum shell thickness provisions specified in 3.41.1 to 3.41.2.

3.40.3 Having regard to the risk of brittle fracture, the maximum and minimum filling and tank working temperatures should be taken into account when choosing materials and determining wall thickness. Material properties should be to the satisfaction of the competent authority.

3.40.4 At the test pressure the primary membrane stress in the shell should conform to the material-dependent limitations prescribed below:

   .1 for metals and alloys exhibiting a clearly defined yield point or characterized by a guaranteed conventional yield stress R_e (generally 0.2% residual elongation; for austenitic steels, 1% residual elongation), the stress should not exceed $0.75R_e$ or $0.50R_m$, whichever is lower;

   .2 the elongation at fracture of steel, in per cent, should not be less than $10,000/R_m$, with an absolute minimum of 20%; the elongation at fracture of aluminium, in per cent, should not be less than $10,000/6R_m$, with an absolute minimum of 12%;

   .3 R_m is the guaranteed minimum tensile strength, given in N/mm^2; and

   .4 when fine-grain steel is used for road tank vehicles, the minimum elongation at fracture of material used is to be agreed between the competent authorities but should not be less than 16%.

3.40.5 It should be noted that the specimens used to determine the elongation at fracture should be taken transversely to the direction of rolling and be so secured that:

$$L_o = 5d,$$

or

$$L_o = 5.65 \sqrt{A}$$

where:

   L_o = gauge length of the specimen before the test;

   d = diameter; and

   A = cross-sectional area of the test specimen.

3.41   Minimum shell thickness

3.41.1   The cylindrical portions and ends of all tanks should have a thickness not less than that determined by the following formula:*

$$e = \frac{C}{\sqrt[3]{(R_m \times A)}}$$

where:

    e = minimum required thickness of the metal to be used, in mm;

    R_m= guaranteed minimum tensile strength of the metal to be used, in N/mm^2;

    A = guaranteed minimum elongation (as a percentage) of the metal to be used on fracture under tensile stress; see 3.40.4;

    C = 107 (equivalent to 5 mm mild steel) for tanks of not more than 1.80 m in diameter; and

    C = 128 (equivalent to 6 mm mild steel) for tanks of more than 1.80 m in diameter.

    * The constant C is derived from the following formula: $e \times \sqrt[3]{(R_m \times A)} = e_o \times \sqrt[3]{(R_{mo} \times A_o)}$, where the sub-index 'o' refers to mild steel and the part of the equation without sub-index 'o' refers to the metal used. The relationship with mild steel as employed by the Code is attached to the constant C, where $C = e_o \times \sqrt[3]{(R_{mo} \times A_o)}$.

3.41.2   The cylindrical portions and ends of all tanks should have a thickness of at least 4 mm regardless of the materials of construction.

3.41.3   There should be no sudden change in plate thickness at the attachment of the head to the cylindrical portion of the shell, and after forming the head the plate thickness at the knuckle should not be less than the minimum thickness required by this sub-section.

3.41.4   In no case should the wall thickness of any portion of the shell be less than that prescribed in this sub-section.

3.42   Service equipment

3.42.1   Service equipment (valves, fittings, safety devices, gauging devices and the like) should be arranged so as to be protected against the risk of being wrenched off or damaged during transport and handling. If the connection between any tank and framework or any tank and running gear or chassis allows relative movement as between the sub-assemblies, the equipment should be so fastened as to permit such movement without risk of damage to working parts. Equipment protection should offer a degree of safety comparable to that of the tank shell. For offshore tank-containers, where positioning of service equipment and the design and strength of protection for such equipment is concerned, the increased danger of impact damage when handling such tanks in open seas should be taken into account.

3.42.2   All orifices in the shell more than 1.5 mm in diameter except those for safety valves, inspection openings or closed bleed holes should be provided with three mutually independent shutoff devices in series, the first being an internal stop valve, flow-restricting valve or equivalent device, the second being an external stop valve and the third being a blank flange or equivalent device.

3.42.2.1   A flow-restricting valve should be so fitted that its seating is inside the shell or inside a welded flange or if fitted externally its mountings should be designed so that in the event of impact its effectiveness should be maintained.

3.42.2.2   Flow-restricting valves should be selected and fitted so as to close automatically when the rated flow specified by the manufacturer is reached. Connections and accessories leading to or from such a valve should have the capacity for a flow greater than the rated flow of the flow-restricting valve.

3.42.3   For filling and discharge openings the first shutoff device should be an internal stop valve and the second should be a stop valve placed in an accessible position on each discharge or filling pipe.

3.42.4   For filling and discharge openings of tanks intended for the transport of flammable or toxic gases, the internal stop valve should be an instant-closing safety device which closes automatically in the event of unintended movement of the tank or fire engulfment. It should also be possible to operate this device by remote control.

3.42.5   The shells of tanks may be equipped, in addition to filling, discharge and gas-pressure-equalizing orifices, with openings in which gauges, thermometers and manometers can be fitted. Connections for such instruments must be made by suitably welded nozzles or pockets and not be screwed connections through the shell.

3.42.6   A tank should be provided with an opening large enough for the tank to be inspected internally.

3.42.7   For portable tanks, external fittings should be grouped together.

3.42.8   All tank connections should be clearly marked to indicate the function of each.

3.42.9   Stop valves with screwed spindles should close by clockwise rotation.

3.42.10   All piping should be of suitable material. Welded pipe joints should be used. Non-malleable metals should not be used in the construction of valves or accessories. The bursting strength of all piping and pipe fittings should be at least four times the strength at the MAWP of the tank and at least four times the strength at the pressure to which the tank may be subjected in service by the action of a pump or other device (except pressure relief valves), the action of which may subject portions of the piping to pressures greater than the tank MAWP. Suitable provisions should be made in every case to prevent damage to piping due to thermal expansion and contraction, jarring and vibration.

3.42.11   Tanks intended for the transport of flammable gases should be capable of being electrically earthed.

3.43   Bottom openings

3.43.1   For certain gases listed in tank instruction T50 of this circular, shell openings in portable tanks below the liquid level are not allowed for any purpose.

3.4.3.2   Openings in the shell of a road tank vehicle should be subject to the agreement of the competent authorities.

3.44   Pressure relief devices

3.44.1   Tanks should be provided with one or more spring-loaded pressure relief devices of a type that will resist dynamic forces, including surge. Frangible discs not in series with a spring-loaded pressure relief device are not permitted.

For portable tanks the devices should open at a pressure not less than 1.0 times the MAWP and be fully open at a pressure of 1.1 times the MAWP.

For road tank vehicles the devices should open at a pressure not less than 1.0 times the MAWP and be fully open at a pressure not exceeding the test pressure.

The devices should, after discharge, close at a pressure not lower than 10% below the pressure at which discharge starts and should remain closed at all lower pressures.

3.44.2   Pressure relief devices should be designed to prevent the entry of foreign matter, the leakage of gas and the development of any dangerous excess pressure.

3.44.3   Tanks for the transport of certain gases listed in tank instruction T50 of this circular should have a pressure relief device approved by the competent authority. The pressure relief device arrangement should comprise a spring-loaded pressure relief valve preceded by a frangible disc, except that a tank in dedicated service may be fitted with an approved relief system offering an equivalent hermetic seal. The space between the frangible disc and the valve should be provided with a pressure gauge or a suitable tell-tale indicator. This arrangement permits the detection of disc rupture, pinholing or leakage which could cause a malfunction of the device. The frangible disc, in this instance, should rupture at the start-to-discharge pressure of the relief valve.

3.44.4   It should be noted that the safety device should operate only in conditions of excessive rise in temperature, as the tank will not, during transport, be subject to undue fluctuations of pressure due to operating procedures (see, however, 3.45.1).

3.45   Capacity of pressure relief devices

3.45.1   For portable tanks the combined delivery capacity of the devices should be such that, in the event of total fire engulfment, the pressure (including accumulation) inside the shell does not exceed 1.1 times the MAWP. Spring-loaded pressure relief devices should be used to achieve the full relief capacity prescribed.

3.45.1.1   To determine the total required capacity of the devices, which may be regarded as being the sum of the individual capacities of the several devices, the following formula may be used:

$$Q = 12.4 \frac{FA^{0.82}}{LC} \sqrt{\frac{ZT}{M}}$$

> This formula applies only to liquefied gases which have critical temperatures well above the temperature at the accumulating condition. For gases which have critical temperatures near or below the temperature at the accumulating condition, the calculation of the pressure relief device delivery capacity should consider further thermodynamic properties of the gas.

where:

> the accumulating condition is 20% above the start-to-discharge pressure of the relief device;
>
> Q is the minimum required rate of discharge in cubic metres of air per second at standard conditions: 1 bar and 0°C (273 K);
>
> F is a coefficient with the following value:
>
> > .1   for uninsulated tanks $F = 1$
> >
> > .2   for insulated tanks $F = U(649 - t)/13.6$ but in no case is less than 0.25

where:

U = thermal conductance of the insulation, in kW/(m²·K), at 38°C

t = actual temperature of the substance at loading (°C); if this temperature is unknown, let $t = 15°C$;

The value of F given in .2 above may be taken provided that:

- the insulation is jacketed with a material having a melting point not less than 649°C; and

- the insulation system will remain effective at all temperatures up to 649°C;

A is the total external surface area of tank in square metres;

Z is the gas compressibility factor in the accumulating condition (if this factor is unknown, let Z equal 1.0);

T is the absolute temperature in kelvin (°C + 273) above the pressure relief devices and in the accumulating condition;

L is the latent heat of vaporization of the liquid, in kJ/kg, in the accumulating condition;

M is the molecular mass of the discharged gas;

C is the constant which is derived from equation (2) as a function of the ratio k of specific heats:

$$k = C_p/C_v \qquad (1)$$

where:

C_p is the specific heat at constant pressure and

C_v is the specific heat at constant volume;

when $k > 1$, in this case C may be taken from the table that follows

$$\left.\begin{array}{l} C = \sqrt{k\left(\frac{2}{k+1}\right)^{\frac{k+1}{k-1}}} \\ \text{when } k = 1 \text{ or } k \text{ is unknown} \\ C = \frac{1}{\sqrt{e}} = 0.607 \end{array}\right\} \quad (2)$$

where: e is the mathematical constant 2.7183

VALUES FOR THE CONSTANT C WHEN k >1

k	C	k	C	k	C
1.00	0.607	1.26	0.660	1.52	0.704
1.02	0.611	1.28	0.664	1.54	0.707
1.04	0.615	1.30	0.667	1.56	0.710
1.06	0.620	1.32	0.671	1.58	0.713
1.08	0.624	1.34	0.674	1.60	0.716
1.10	0.628	1.36	0.678	1.62	0.719
1.12	0.633	1.38	0.681	1.64	0.722
1.14	0.637	1.40	0.685	1.66	0.725
1.16	0.641	1.42	0.688	1.68	0.728
1.18	0.645	1.44	0.691	1.70	0.731
1.20	0.649	1.46	0.695	2.00	0.770
1.22	0.652	1.48	0.698	2.20	0.793
1.24	0.656	1.50	0.701		

3.45.2   For road tank vehicles the delivery capacity of the pressure relief devices should be subject to the agreement of the competent authorities.

3.46   Marking of pressure relief devices

3.46.1   Every pressure relief device of a portable tank should be plainly and permanently marked with the pressure at which it is set to discharge and the rated free-air delivery of the device at 15°C and one bar. Capacity marked on devices should be as rated at a pressure not greater than 110% of the set pressure.

3.47   Connections to pressure relief devices

3.47.1   Connections to pressure relief devices should be of sufficient size to enable the required discharge to pass unrestricted to the device. No stop valve should be installed between the tank shell and the pressure relief devices except where duplicate equivalent devices are provided for maintenance and the stop valves serving the devices actually in use are locked open or the stop valves are interlocked so that at least one of the duplicate devices is always in use. Vents from the pressure relief devices, where used, should deliver the relieved vapour or liquid to the atmosphere in conditions of minimum back-pressure on the device.

3.48   Siting of pressure relief devices

3.48.1   Pressure relief device inlets should be sited on top of any portable tank in a position as near the longitudinal and transverse centre of the tank as possible. All pressure relief device inlets should be situated in the vapour space of the tanks and the devices so arranged as to ensure that the escaping vapour is discharged unrestricted and in such a manner that it cannot impinge upon the tank shell. Protective devices which deflect the flow of vapour are permissible provided the required valve capacity is not reduced.

3.48.2   Arrangements should be made to prevent access to the devices by unauthorized persons and to protect the devices from damage caused by the tank overturning.

3.49   Gauging devices

3.49.1   Glass level-gauges, or gauges made of other easily destructible material, which are in direct communication with the contents of the tank should not be used.

3.50   Tank support, frameworks, lifting and tie-down attachments*

3.50.1   Tanks should be designed and fabricated with a support structure to provide a secure base during transport. Skids, frameworks, cradles or other similar devices are acceptable. Cradles or other devices attaching a tank to the chassis or running gear of a road tank vehicle are acceptable. The loads specified in 3.39.10 should be taken into account in this aspect of design.

3.50.1.1   Under each of these loads for portable tanks, the safety factors to be observed should be as follows:

   .1   for metals having a clearly defined yield point, a safety factor of 1.5 in relation to the determined yield stress; or

   .2   for metals with no clearly defined yield point, a safety factor of 1.5 in relation to the guaranteed 0.2% proof stress.

3.50.2   For road tank vehicles, the stress levels due to each load should not exceed those permitted in 3.40.4.1.

3.50.3   If the landing legs of a road tank vehicle are to be used as support structure, the loads specified in 3.39.10 should be taken into account in their design and method of attachment. Any bending stress induced in the shell as a result of this manner of support should also be included in the design calculations.

3.50.4   The combined stresses caused by tank mountings (e.g., cradles, frameworks, etc.) and tank lifting and tie-down attachments should not cause excessive stress in any portion of the tank shell.

3.50.4.1   Permanent lifting and permanent tie-down attachments should be fitted to all portable tanks. Permanent tie-down attachments should be fitted to all road tank vehicles. Lifting and tie-down attachments should preferably be fitted to the tank support structure but they may be secured to the reinforcing plates located on the shell at the points of support, bearing in mind the provisions of 3.51.7.

3.50.5   Securing arrangements (tie-down attachments) should be fitted to the tank support structure and the towing vehicle of a road tank vehicle. Semi-trailers unaccompanied by a towing vehicle should be accepted for shipment only if the trailer supports and the securing arrangements and the position of stowage are agreed with the competent authority.

3.50.6   In the design of supports and frameworks, due regard should be paid to the effects of environmental corrosion, and in calculations for all structural members not constructed of corrosion-resistant materials a minimum corrosion allowance, determined by the competent authority, should be provided.

3.50.7   Portable tank frameworks intended to be lifted or secured by their corner castings should be subjected to internationally accepted special tests, for example the ISO system. The use of such frameworks within an integrated system is generally encouraged. Offshore tank-containers should be subjected to tests that take into account the dynamic lifting and impact forces that may occur when a tank is handled in open seas.

3.50.8   Fork-lift pockets of portable tanks should be capable of being closed off.

3.51   Approval, testing and marking of type 5 tanks

3.51.1   The competent approval authority or a body authorized by that authority should have issued, in respect of every new design of a tank, a certificate attesting that the tank and its attachments surveyed by that authority or that body are suitable for the purpose for which they are intended and meet the construction and equipment provisions of this sub-section and, where appropriate, the particular provisions for the gases in tank instruction T50 of this circular. Such certificate should show the gases or group of gases allowed to be transported in the tank. The prototype test results, the gases for whose transport the tank is approved and an approval number should have been specified in a test report. If a series of tanks are manufactured without

---

* Attention is drawn to the Guidelines for securing arrangements for the transport of road vehicles on ro–ro ships (resolution A.581(14)).

change in structural design, this approval should have been deemed to be a design approval. The approval number should consist of the distinguishing sign or mark of the State in whose territory the approval was granted, i.e. the distinguishing sign for use in international traffic, as prescribed by the Convention on Road Traffic, Vienna, 1968, and a registration number.

3.51.2   Design approval should have been given in respect of at least one tank of each design and each size, it being, however, understood that a set of tests made on a tank of one size may serve for the approval of smaller tanks made of a material of the same kind and thickness by the same fabrication technique and with identical supports and equivalent closures and other appurtenances.

3.51.3   The shell and items of equipment of each tank should be inspected and tested, either together or separately, first before being put into service (initial inspection and test) and thereafter at not more than five-year intervals (periodic inspection and test).

3.51.3.1   The initial inspection and test should have included a check of the design characteristics, and internal and external examination and a hydraulic pressure test. If the shell and equipment have been pressure-tested separately, they should together be subjected after assembly to a leakage test. All welds in the shell should have been tested in the initial inspection by radiographic, ultrasonic or another suitable non-destructive method. This does not apply to the metal sheathing of an insulation.

3.51.3.2   The periodic inspections and tests should include an internal and external examination and, as a general rule, a pressure test.

3.51.3.2.1   Sheathing thermal insulation and the like should be removed only to the extent required for reliable appraisal of the tank's condition.

3.51.3.3   The initial and periodic pressure tests should be carried out by an expert approved by the competent authority, at the test pressure indicated on the data plate of the tank except in cases where periodic tests at lower test pressures are authorized.

3.51.3.4   While under pressure, the tank should be inspected for leakage or other conditions which indicate weaknesses that might render the tank unsafe in transport, and if any evidence of such unsafe condition is discovered, the tank should not be placed in or returned to service until it has been repaired and the test, repeated, has been passed.

3.51.4   Before tanks were put into service, and thereafter at intervals midway between the inspections and tests specified in 3.51.3, the following tests and inspections should be performed:

.1   a leakage test, where required;

.2   a test of satisfactory operation of all service equipment; and

.3   an internal and external inspection of the tanks and their fittings with due regard to the gases transported.

3.51.5   The 2.5-year (midway) inspection and test may be carried out within 3 months of the specified date. The date of the 2.5-year inspection should be durably marked on or as near as possible to the metal identification plate required in 3.55.1. When marking is not done on the plate, the characters should be at least 32 mm in height and of a contrasting colour to the tank.

3.51.6   The 2.5-year internal inspections may be waived or substituted by other test methods by the competent authority in the case of tanks intended for the transport of one substance. A portable tank may not be filled and offered for transport after the date of expiry of the last 5-year or 2.5-year periodic inspection and test as required by 3.51.3 and 3.51.4. However, a portable tank filled prior to the date of expiry of the last periodic inspection and test may be transported for a period not to exceed three months beyond the date of expiry of the last periodic test or inspection. In addition, a portable tank may be transported after the date of expiry of the last periodic test and inspection:

.1   After emptying but before cleaning, for purposes of performing the next required test and inspection prior to refilling; and

.2   Unless otherwise approved by the competent authority, for a period not to exceed six months beyond the date of expiry of the last periodic test and inspection, in order to allow the return of dangerous goods for proper disposal or recycling. Reference to this authorization should be entered in the dangerous goods shipping document.

3.51.7   When a tank, other than its shell, is damaged it should not be allowed for use unless it has been repaired, so as to comply with these provisions. When the shell is damaged, it should be repaired and retested in conformity with 3.51.8.

3.51.8   In all cases where cutting, burning or welding operations on the shell of a tank have been effected, that work should be to the approval of the competent authority and a hydrostatic test to at least the original test pressure should be carried out.

3.51.9   A certificate from the competent authority or its approved inspecting agency affirming that the tank complies with the provisions of the IMDG Code should be issued and should be retained by the authority and the owners during the time the tank is in service. All information required in 3.55.2 and 3.55.3 should also be included in this certificate.

3.52   [Reserved]

3.53   [Reserved]

3.54   Approval, testing and marking of type 6 tanks

3.54.1   Road tank vehicles are to be authorized for short international voyages only.

3.54.2   For any road tank vehicles intended for transport of a substance listed in tank instruction T50 of this circular, there should be in existence a valid certificate issued by or on behalf of the competent authority for road transport authorizing transport of that substance by road.

3.54.3   The competent authority for sea transport or a body authorized by that authority should have issued additionally in respect of a road tank vehicle a certificate attesting compliance with the relevant design, construction and equipment provisions of this sub-section and, where appropriate, the special provisions for the gases listed in T50 of this circular. The certificate should list the gases allowed to be transported.

3.54.4   A road tank vehicle should be periodically tested and inspected in accordance with the requirements of the competent authority for road transport.

3.54.5   Road tank vehicles should be marked in accordance with 3.55. However, where the marking required by the competent authority for road transport is substantially in agreement with that of 3.55.1, it will be sufficient to endorse the plate attached to the road tank vehicle with "IMO type 6".

3.55   Marking

3.55.1   Every tank should be fitted with a corrosion-resistant metal plate permanently attached in a place readily accessible for inspection. At least the following particulars should be marked on the plate in characters at least 3 mm in height by stamping, engraving, embossing or any similar method. If, for reasons of tank arrangements, the plate cannot be permanently attached to the shell, the shell should be marked with at least those particulars required by a recognized pressure vessel code in a manner prescribed by that code.

3.55.2   The plate should be kept free of any paint to ensure that the markings will be legible at all times.

Country of manufacture . . . .

IMO tank   Approval   Approval
type no. . . . .   country . . . .   number . . . .

Manufacturer's name or mark . . . .

Registration number . . . .

Year of manufacture . . . .

Test pressure . . . . (bar)/(MPa) gauge*

Maximum allowable working pressure . . . . (bar)/(MPa) gauge*

Water capacity at 20°C . . . . (litres)
(The water capacity should be established to within 1% by practical test rather than by calculation.)

Original hydrostatic test date and witness identification . . . .

Code to which tank is designed . . . .

Design reference temperature . . . .(°C)

Metallurgic design temperature (only if below −30°C) . . . .

Tank material . . . .

Equivalent thickness in mild steel . . . . (mm)

Month, year and test pressure of most recent periodic test:

. . . . month . . . . year . . . . (bar)/(MPa) gauge*

    * The unit used should be marked.

3.55.3   The following particulars should be marked either on the tank itself or on a metal plate firmly secured to the tank.

Names of owner and operator . . . .

Name of gas being carried (and maximum mean bulk temperature if other than 50°C) . . . .

Date of the last inspection . . . .

Maximum permissible gross mass . . . . (kg)

Unladen (tare) mass . . . . (kg)

3.55.4   If a tank is designed and approved for handling in open seas, the words OFFSHORE CONTAINER should be marked on the identification plate.

3.55.5   [Reserved]

3.55.6   Unless the name of the gas being transported appears on the metal plate specified in 3.55.3, a copy of the certificate specified in 3.51.1 should be made available upon request of a competent authority and readily provided by the consignor, consignee or agent, as appropriate.

3.56   Transport provisions

3.56.1   Tanks should not be offered for transport:

.1   in an ullage condition liable to produce an unacceptable hydraulic force due to surge within the tank;

.2   when leaking;

.3   when damaged to such an extent that the integrity of the tank or its lifting or securing arrangements may be affected; and

.4   unless the service equipment has been examined and found to be in good working order.

3.56.2   Empty tanks not cleaned and not gas-free should comply with the same provisions as tanks filled with the substance previously carried.

3.56.3   During transport, portable tanks should be adequately protected against lateral and longitudinal impact and against overturning. If the shells and the service equipment are so constructed as to withstand impact or overturning they need not be protected in this way.

Examples of protection of shells against collision:

.1   protection against lateral impact may consist, for example, of longitudinal bars protecting the shell on both sides at the level of the median line;

.2   protection of tanks against overturning may consist, for example, of reinforcement rings or bars fixed across the frame;

.3   protection against rear impact may consist of a bumper or frame;

.4   external fittings should be designed or protected so as to preclude the release of contents upon impact or overturning of the tank upon the fittings.

3.56.4   Certain gases are chemically unstable. They are to be accepted for transport only if the necessary steps have been taken to prevent their dangerous decomposition, transformation or polymerization during transport. To this end, care should in particular be taken to ensure that tanks do not contain any substances liable to promote these reactions.

Sub-section C   GENERAL PROVISIONS FOR PORTABLE TANKS AND ROAD TANK VEHICLES FOR REFRIGERATED LIQUEFIED GASES OF CLASS 2

3.57   Preamble

3.57.1   The provisions of this sub-section apply to portable tanks (type 7 tanks) and road tank vehicles (type 8 tanks) intended for the transport of refrigerated liquefied gases of class 2. In addition to the provisions of this sub-section and unless otherwise specified, the applicable requirements of the International Convention for Safe Containers (CSC), 1972, as amended, should be fulfilled by any portable tank which meets the definition of a "container" within the terms of that Convention. The International Convention for Safe Containers does not apply to offshore tank-containers that are handled in open seas. The design and testing of offshore tank-containers should take into account the dynamic lifting and impact forces that may occur when a tank is handled in open seas in adverse weather and sea conditions. The requirements for such tanks should be determined by the approving competent authority (see also MSC/Circ. 613 as amended). Such requirements should be based on MSC/Circ. 860, Guidelines for the approval of offshore containers handled in open seas.

3.57.2   In order to take into account progress in science and technology, the use of alternative arrangements which offer at least equivalent safety in use in respect of compatibility with the properties of the substances transported and equivalent or superior resistance to impact, loading and fire may be considered by the national competent authority.

3.57.3   [Reserved]

3.57.4   [Reserved]

3.57.5   Construction, equipment, testing, marking and operation of portable tanks and road tank vehicles should be subject to acceptance by the competent authority of the country in which they are approved.

3.57.6   These provisions do not apply to rail tank-wagons, non-metallic tanks or tanks having a capacity of 1,000 litres or less.

3.58   Definitions

3.58.1   For the purposes of these provisions:

3.58.2   *Type 7 tank* means a thermally insulated portable tank fitted with items of service and structural equipment necessary for the transport of refrigerated liquefied gases. The portable tank should be capable of being transported, loaded and discharged without the need of removal of its structural equipment, and should be capable of being lifted when full. It should not be permanently secured on board the ship. Its contents should not be loaded or discharged while the portable tank remains on board.

3.58.3   *Type 8 tank* means a road tank vehicle and includes a semi-trailer with a permanently attached thermally insulated tank fitted with items of service equipment and structural equipment necessary for the transport of refrigerated liquefied gases. It should be fitted with permanent attachments such that it can be secured on board ship. However, its contents should not be loaded or discharged whilst the vehicle remains on board. A road tank vehicle should only be carried on short international voyages.

3.58.4   *Tank* means a construction, which normally consists of:

   .1   a jacket and one or more inner shells where the space between the shell or shells and the jacket incorporates thermal insulation and is exhausted of air (vacuum insulation); or

   .2   a jacket and an inner shell with an intermediate layer of solid thermally insulating material (e.g., solid foam); or

   .3   an outer shell with an inner layer of solid thermally insulating material.

3.58.5   *Shell* means a pressure vessel proper, including openings and their closures.

3.58.6   *Service equipment of a tank* means filling and discharge, venting, safety, thermal-insulating devices and measuring instruments.

3.58.7   *Structural equipment* means the reinforcing, fastening, protective and stabilizing members external to a tank and includes, for a road tank vehicle, fastenings to running gear or chassis.

3.58.8   *Maximum allowable working pressure* (MAWP) means the maximum effective gauge pressure permissible at the top of the shell of a loaded tank in its operating position.

3.58.9   *Test pressure* means the maximum gauge pressure which arises in the shell during the pressure test.

3.58.10   *Leakage test* means a test which consists of subjecting the shell, complete with its service equipment, to an effective internal pressure equivalent to the MAWP. The procedure to be adopted should be approved by the competent authority.

3.58.11   *Total mass* means the mass of the portable tank or road tank vehicle with the heaviest load authorized for transport.

3.58.12   *Holding time* means the time that will elapse from the moment the liquid starts boiling at atmospheric pressure up to the moment the pressure of the tank contents reaches the MAWP under equilibrium conditions.

3.58.13   *Minimum design temperature* means the lowest contents temperature at which the tank can be used.

3.58.14   *Competent authorities* means, in respect of those provisions solely applicable to road tank vehicles, the authority concerned with approval for transport by sea and also the authority concerned with approval for international transport by road. Where the latter does not exist, the relevant national authority should be substituted.

3.59   General provisions for the design, construction and operation of tanks for refrigerated liquefied gases

3.59.1   Shells should be made of steel, aluminium or aluminium alloys, suitable for shaping and of adequate ductility and toughness at the minimum design temperature, having regard to the risk of brittle fracture. Only materials whose weldability has been fully demonstrated should be used. Welds should be skilfully made and afford complete safety and, if the manufacturing procedure of the material so requires, the shell should be suitably heat-treated to guarantee adequate toughness in the weld and in the heat-affected zones.

3.59.1.1   Jackets should be made of steel. Jackets of aluminium may be used for road tank vehicles with the approval of the competent authority. Any part of a portable tank, including fittings and pipe-work, that is exposed to the environment should be compatible with the marine environment.

3.59.2   Any part of a tank, including fittings and pipe-work, which can be expected normally to come into contact with the substance transported should be compatible with that substance.

3.59.3   Care should be taken to avoid damage by galvanic action due to the juxtaposition of dissimilar metals.

3.59.4   The thermal insulation should include complete covering of the shell or shells externally or internally with effective insulating materials. External insulation should be protected so as to prevent the ingress of moisture and other damage under normal transport conditions, either by a jacket or other suitable cladding.

3.59.5   If the jacket is so closed as to be gastight, a device should be provided to prevent any dangerous pressure from developing in the insulation space in the event of inadequate gastightness of the shell or of its items of equipment.

3.59.6   Tanks intended for the transport of refrigerated liquefied gases having a boiling point below −182°C at atmospheric pressure should not include material in the thermal insulation which may react with oxygen in a dangerous manner. Compact means of attachment between a shell and jacket may contain plastics materials, provided their material properties at their service temperature are proved to be sufficient.

3.59.7   Insulating materials should not deteriorate unduly in service.

3.59.8   A holding time should be calculated at the design stage and take into account:

   .1   effectiveness of the insulation system provided;

   .2   MAWP;

   .3   degree of filling;

   .4   assumed ambient temperature of 50°C;

   .5   physical properties of the individual substance to be transported.

3.59.9   The jacket of a vacuum-insulated double-wall tank should have either an external design pressure of at least 100 kPa (1 bar) gauge pressure calculated in accordance with a recognized code, or a calculated collapsing pressure of at least 200 kPa (2 bar) gauge pressure. Internal and external reinforcement devices may be included in calculating the ability of the jacket to resist the external pressure.

3.59.10   Portable tanks should be designed and manufactured with supports to provide a secure base during transport and with suitable lifting and tie-down attachments. Road tank vehicles should be fitted with tie-down attachments and secured on board in such a way that the suspension is not left in free play.

3.59.11   Shells of portable tanks, their attachments and their service and structural equipment should be constructed to withstand, without loss of contents, at least the internal pressure and thermal loads due to the contents, taking into account the most severe combination of the static and dynamic loads under normal handling and transport conditions. For tanks that are intended for use as offshore tank-containers, the dynamic stresses imposed by handling in open seas should be taken into account.

3.59.12   Portable tanks and their fastenings should be capable of withstanding separately applied forces, based on:

   .1   twice the total mass acting in the direction of travel of the tank simultaneous with the weight of the tank;

   .2   the total mass acting horizontally at right angles to the direction of travel of the tank (where the direction of travel is not clearly determined, the total mass should be used) simultaneous with the weight of the tank;

   .3   the total mass acting vertically upwards;

   .4   twice the total mass acting vertically downwards.

3.59.13   Under each of these loads, for portable tanks, the safety factors to be observed should be:

   .1   for metals having a clearly defined yield point, a safety factor of 1.5 in relation to the determined yield stress; or

   .2   for metals with no clearly defined yield point, a safety factor of 1.5 in relation to the guaranteed 0.2% proof stress (1.0% proof stress for austenitic steels).

3.59.14   The tank of a road tank vehicle and its fastenings should be capable of withstanding such separately applied static and dynamic loads as may be agreed between the competent authorities. Under the condition of each load, the stress level should not exceed that permitted in 3.59.19.1.

3.59.15   Shells should be designed and manufactured to withstand a test pressure equal to at least 1.3 times the MAWP.

3.59.16   For shells with vacuum insulation, the test pressure should not be less than 1.3 times the sum of the MAWP and 100 kPa (1 bar).

3.59.17   In no case should the test pressure be less than 300 kPa (3 bar) gauge pressure.

3.59.18   Attention is also drawn to the minimum shell thickness provisions specified in 3.60.2 and 3.60.3.

3.59.19   At the test pressure, the primary membrane stress in the shell should conform to the material-dependent limitations prescribed below:

.1   for metals and alloys exhibiting a clearly defined yield point or characterized by a guaranteed conventional yield stress R_e (generally 0.2% proof stress; for austenitic steels 1.0% proof stress), the membrane stress should not exceed $0.75R_e$ or $0.50R_m$, whichever is lower, where R_m in N/mm^2 is the guaranteed minimum tensile strength;

.2   in the case of steel, the elongation at fracture, in per cent, should not be less than $10,000/R_m$, where R_m is in N/mm^2, with an absolute minimum of 17%. In the case of aluminium, the elongation at fracture, in per cent, should not be less than $10,000/R_m$, where R_m is in N/mm^2, with an absolute minimum of 12%.

3.59.20   The specimens used to determine the elongation at fracture should be taken transversely to the direction of rolling and be so secured that:

$$L_o = 5d,$$

or

$$L_o = 5.65 \sqrt{A}$$

where:

L_o = gauge length of the specimen before the test;

d = diameter; and

A = cross-sectional area of the test specimen.

3.59.21   Shells should be of a circular cross-section.

3.59.22   Tanks should be manufactured to a technical code recognized by the competent authority. Shells should be designed, manufactured and tested in accordance with a recognized pressure vessel code, taking into account corrosion, mass of contents, MAWP and the effect of superimposed stresses due to dynamic forces in accordance with 3.59.12.

3.60   Minimum shell thickness

3.60.1   The shells should have a thickness of not less than that determined by the following formula*:

$$e = \frac{C}{\sqrt[3]{(R_m \times A)}}$$

where:

e = minimum required thickness of the metal to be used, in mm;

R_m = guaranteed minimum tensile strength of the metal to be used, in N/mm^2;

A = guaranteed minimum elongation (as a percentage) of the metal to be used on fracture under tensile stress; see 3.59.15;

C = 107 (equivalent to 5 mm mild steel) for tanks of not more than 1.80 m in diameter; and

C = 128 (equivalent to 6 mm mild steel) for tanks of more than 1.80 m in diameter.

C = 64 for shells of vacuum-insulated tanks of not more than 1.80 m in diameter; and

C = 85 for shells of vacuum-insulated tanks of more than 1.80 m in diameter.

   * The constant C is derived from the following formula: $e \times \sqrt[3]{(R_m \times A)} = e_o \times \sqrt[3]{(R_{mo} \times A_o)}$, where the sub-index 'o' refers to mild steel and the part of the equation without sub-index 'o' refers to the metal used. The relationship with mild steel as employed by the Code is attached to the constant C, where $C = e_o \times \sqrt[3]{(R_{mo} \times A_o)}$.

3.60.2   Portable tanks should have a shell thickness of at least 3 mm regardless of the material of construction. Road tank vehicles may have a lesser thickness, subject to the agreement of the competent authorities.

3.60.3   There should be no sudden change in plate thickness at the attachment of the head to the cylindrical portion of the shell, and, after forming the head, the plate thickness at the knuckle should be not less than that determined by a recognized pressure vessel code or as required by 3.60.1 to 3.60.2, as applicable.

3.61   Service equipment

3.61.1   Service equipment (valves, fittings, safety devices, gauging devices and the like) should be so arranged as to be protected against the risk of being wrenched off or damaged during handling and transport. If the connection between a frame and a tank, a jacket and a shell, or a tank and a chassis or running gear allows relative movement, the equipment should be fastened so as to permit such movement without risk of damage to working parts. Equipment protection should offer a degree of safety comparable to that of the tank shell. For offshore tank-containers, where positioning of service equipment and the design and strength of protection for such equipment is concerned, the increased danger of impact damage when handling such tanks in open seas should be taken into account.

3.61.2   Each filling opening and each discharge opening in tanks used for the transport of flammable gases should be fitted with three independent shutoff devices in series, the first being a stop valve situated as close as possible to the jacket, the second being a stop valve and the third being a blank flange or equivalent device. Each filling opening and each discharge opening in tanks used for the transport of non-flammable gases should be provided with at least two independent shutoff devices in series, the first being a stop valve situated as close as possible to the outer jacket and the second being a blank flange or equivalent device.

3.61.3   For sections of piping which can be closed at both ends and where liquid product can be trapped, a method of automatic pressure relief, to prevent excess pressure, should be provided.

3.61.4   Vacuum-insulated tanks need not have an opening for inspection.

3.61.5   External fittings should preferably be grouped together.

3.61.6   All tank connections should be clearly marked to indicate the function of each.

3.61.7   Stop valves with screwed spindles should close by clockwise rotation.

3.61.8   All piping should be of a suitable material. Where tanks are subject to the fire engulfment provision of 3.63.3, only steel piping and welded joints should be used between the shell and the connection to the first closure of any outlet. The method of attaching the closure to this connection should be to the satisfaction of the competent authority. Elsewhere pipe-joints should be welded wherever necessary.

3.61.9   Joints of copper tubing should be brazed or have an equally strong metal union. These joints should, in any event, not be such as to decrease the strength of the tubing as may happen by cutting of threads. The melting point of brazing materials should be no lower than 525°C.

3.61.10   Only metals which are ductile at the lowest operating temperatures should be used in the construction of valves and accessories.

3.61.11   The bursting strength of all piping and pipe fittings should be at least four times the strength at the MAWP of the tank and at least four times the strength at the pressure to which it may be subjected in service by the action of a pump or other device (except pressure relief valves).

3.61.12   Suitable provisions should be made in every case to prevent damage to piping due to thermal expansion and contraction, jarring and vibration.

3.61.13   Tanks for the transport of flammable gases should be capable of being electrically earthed.

3.62   Pressure relief devices

3.62.1   Every shell should be provided with at least two independent pressure relief valves of the spring-loaded type except that, in the case of a road tank vehicle used for non-flammable refrigerated gases, one of the valves may be replaced by a frangible disc.

3.62.2   Shells for non-flammable refrigerated liquefied gases may, in addition, have frangible discs in parallel with the spring-loaded valves as specified in 3.63.2 and 3.63.3.

3.62.3   Pressure relief devices should be designed to prevent:

   .1   accumulation of moisture and the entry of foreign matter; and

   .2   the leakage of gas and the development of any dangerous excess pressure.

3.62.4   Pressure relief devices should be approved by the competent authority.

3.63   Capacity and setting of pressure relief devices

3.63.1   The capacity of each spring-loaded pressure relief valve should be sufficient to limit the pressure to 110% of the MAWP due to normal pressure rise. These valves should be set to start to discharge at the nominal pressure equal to the MAWP and should, after discharge, close at a pressure not lower than 90% of the MAWP and remain closed at all lower pressures.

3.63.2   In the case of loss of vacuum of a vacuum-insulated tank, or loss of 20% of the insulation of a tank insulated with solid materials, the combined capacity of all valves installed should be sufficient to limit the pressure to 110% of the MAWP. For helium, this capacity may be achieved by the use of frangible discs in combination with the required safety relief valves. These discs should rupture at a nominal pressure equal to the test pressure.

3.63.3   For portable tanks, the provisions of 3.63.2 should be considered together with complete engulfment in fire, under which circumstances the combined capacity of all pressure relief devices installed should be sufficient to limit the pressure to the test pressure. Frangible discs, if used, should rupture at a nominal pressure equal to the test pressure.

3.63.4   With respect to complete fire engulfment, the competent authority should examine the heat input to the tank in the fire exposure condition. Having established the heat input, the required capacity of the relief devices should be calculated in accordance with a well-established technical code.

3.63.5   For a road tank vehicle, where a frangible disc is used for the purposes of 3.62.1, it should rupture at a nominal pressure equal to the test pressure.

3.64   Markings on pressure relief devices

3.64.1   Every pressure relief device of a portable tank should be plainly and permanently marked with the pressure at which it is set to discharge and the rated free-air delivery of the device at 15°C and one bar. Capacity marked on devices should be as rated at a pressure not greater than 110% of the set pressure.

3.65   Connections to pressure relief devices

3.65.1   Connections to pressure relief devices should be of sufficient size to enable the required discharge to pass unrestricted to the safety devices. No stop valve should be installed between the shell and the pressure relief devices except where additional devices are provided for maintenance or other reasons and the stop valves serving the devices actually in use are locked open or the stop valves are interlocked so that the provisions of 3.63 are always fulfilled. Vents from the pressure relief devices, where used, should deliver the relieved vapour or liquid to the atmosphere in conditions of minimum back-pressure on the relieving device.

3.66   Siting of pressure relief devices

3.66.1   All pressure relief device inlets should be situated in the vapour space of the shells and the devices so arranged as to ensure that the escaping vapour is discharged unrestrictedly and in such a manner that it cannot impinge upon the portable tank. Protective devices which deflect the flow of vapour are permissible, provided the required capacity is not reduced.

3.66.2   Arrangements should be made to prevent access to the devices by unauthorized persons and to protect the devices from damage caused by the tank overturning.

3.67   Gauging devices

3.67.1   Glass level-gauges, or gauges made of other easily destructible material, which are in direct communication with the contents of the shell should not be used.

3.67.2   A connection for a vacuum gauge should be provided in the jacket of a vacuum-insulated portable tank.

3.68   Tank support framework, lifting, and tie-down attachments*

3.68.1   Tanks should be designed and manufactured with a support structure to provide a secure base during transport. Skids, frameworks, cradles, or other similar devices are acceptable. The cradles or other devices attaching a tank to the chassis or running gear of a road tank vehicle are considered acceptable.

3.68.1.1   For portable tanks, the loads specified in 3.59.12 and safety factors in 3.59.13 should be taken into account in this aspect of design, whilst for road tank vehicles the design calculations should include loads and factors agreed as in 3.59.14.

3.68.1.2   If the landing legs of a road tank vehicle are to be used as support structure, the loads agreed as in 3.59.14 should be taken into account in their design and method of attachment. Bending stress induced in the shell as a result of this manner of support should be included in design calculations.

3.68.2   Permanent lifting and permanent tie-down attachments should be fitted to all portable tanks. Permanent tie-down attachments should be fitted to all road tank vehicles. Lifting and tie-down attachments should preferably be fitted to the tank support structure but they may be secured to the reinforcing plates located on the tank at the points of support.

3.68.2.1   Securing arrangements (tie-down attachments) should be fitted to the tank support structure and the towing vehicle of a road tank vehicle. Semi-trailers unaccompanied by a towing vehicle should be accepted for shipment only if the trailer supports and the securing arrangements and the position of stowage are agreed with the competent authority.

3.68.2.2   The combined stresses caused by tank mountings (e.g. cradles, frameworks, etc.) and tank lifting and tie-down attachments should not cause excessive stress in any portion of the tank.

---

* Attention is drawn to the Guidelines for securing arrangements for the transport of road vehicles on ro–ro ships (resolution A.581(14)).

3.68.3   In the design of supports and frameworks, due regard should be paid to the effects of environmental corrosion; in calculations for all structural members not constructed of corrosion-resistant materials, a minimum corrosion allowance determined by the competent authority should be provided.

3.68.4   Portable tank frameworks intended to be lifted or secured by their corner castings should be subjected to internationally accepted special tests, for example the ISO system. The use of such frameworks within an integrated system is generally encouraged. Offshore tank-containers should be subjected to tests that take into account the dynamic lifting and impact forces that may occur when a tank is handled in open seas.

3.69   Approval, testing and marking of type 7 tanks

3.69.1   The competent approval authority or a body authorized by that authority should have issued, in respect of every new design of a portable tank, a certificate attesting that the portable tank and its attachments surveyed by that authority or that body are suitable for the purpose for which they are intended and meet the construction and equipment provisions of this sub-section. Such a certificate should include the gases or group of gases allowed to be transported in the portable tank. The results of the prototype test, the gases for whose transport the portable tank is approved and an approval number should be specified in a test report. If a series of portable tanks are manufactured without change in structural design, this approval should have been deemed to be a design approval. The approval number should consist of the distinguishing sign or mark of the State in whose territory the approval was granted, i.e. the distinguishing sign for use in international traffic, as prescribed by the Convention on Road Traffic, Vienna, 1968, and a registration number.

3.69.2   Design approval should have been given in respect of at least one portable tank of each design and each size, it being, however, understood that a set of tests made on a portable tank of one size may have served for the approval of smaller portable tanks made of a material of the same kind and thickness by the same fabrication technique and with equivalent support, closures and other appurtenances.

3.69.3   The shell and items of equipment of each tank should be inspected and tested, either together or separately, before being put into service (initial inspection and test) and thereafter at not more than five-year intervals (periodic inspection and test).

3.69.3.1   The initial inspection and test should have included a check of the design characteristics and internal and external examination and a hydraulic pressure test. In special cases, and with the agreement of a competent authority, the hydraulic pressure test may be replaced by a pressure test using another liquid or gas. If the shell and equipment have been pressure-tested separately, they should together be subjected, after assembly, to a leakage test. All welds in the shell should be tested in the initial test by radiographic, ultrasonic or another suitable non-destructive method. This does not apply to the jacket.

3.69.3.2   The periodic inspections and tests should consist of an external examination of the portable tank and a leakage test. In the case of non-vacuum-insulated tanks, the jacket and thermal insulation and the like should be removed only to the extent required for a reliable appraisal of the portable tank's condition. In the case of a vacuum-insulated tank there should be a vacuum reading.

3.69.3.3   The initial and periodic tests should be carried out as required by the competent authority.

3.69.3.4   While under pressure, the tank should be inspected for leakage or other conditions which indicate weaknesses that might render the tank unsafe in transport; if any evidence of such unsafe condition is discovered, the portable tank should not be placed in or returned to service until it has been repaired and the test, repeated, has been passed.

3.69.4   Before a portable tank is put into service, and thereafter at intervals midway between the inspections and tests provided in 3.69.3, the following tests and inspections should be performed:

    .1   a leakage test, where required;

    .2   a test of satisfactory operation of all service equipment;

    .3   an external inspection of the portable tank and its fittings with due regard to the gases transported; and

    .4   a vacuum reading, where applicable.

3.69.5   The 2.5-year (midway) inspection and test may be carried out within 3 months before or after the specified date. The date of the 2.5-year inspection should be durably marked on or as near as possible to the metal identification plate required in 3.71.1. When marking is not done on the plate, the characters should be at least 32 mm in height and of a contrasting colour to the tank. A portable tank may not be filled and offered for transport after the date of expiry of the last 5-year or 2.5-year periodic inspection and test as required by 3.69.3 and 3.69.4. However, a portable tank filled prior to the date of expiry of the last periodic inspection and test may be transported for a period not to exceed three months beyond the date of expiry of the last periodic test or inspection. In addition, a portable tank may be transported after the date of expiry of the last periodic test and inspection:

    .1   after emptying but before cleaning, for purposes of performing the next required test and inspection prior to refilling; and

.2   unless otherwise approved by the competent authority, for a period not to exceed six months beyond the date of expiry of the last periodic test and inspection, in order to allow the return of dangerous goods for proper disposal or recycling. Reference to this authorization should be entered in the dangerous goods shipping document.

3.69.6   When a portable tank is damaged it should not be allowed to be used until it has been repaired so as to comply with these provisions. When the shell is damaged, it should be repaired and retested in conformity with 3.69.7.

3.69.7   In all cases where cutting, burning or welding operations on the shell of a portable tank have been carried out, that work should be to the satisfaction of the competent authority and a pressure test to at least the original test pressure should be carried out.

3.69.8   Certificates showing the results of the test should be issued by the competent authority. All information required in 3.71.2 and 3.71.3 should also be included in this certificate.

3.70   Approval, testing and marking of type 8 tanks

3.70.1   Road tank vehicles are to be authorized for short international voyages only.

3.70.2   For any road tank vehicle intended for transport of a refrigerated liquefied gas there should be in existence a valid certificate issued by or on behalf of the competent authority for road transport authorizing transport of that substance by road.

3.70.3   The competent authority for sea transport or a body authorized by that authority should issue additionally in respect of a road tank vehicle a certificate attesting compliance with the relevant design, construction and equipment provisions of this sub-section. The certificate should list the gases allowed to be transported.

3.70.4   A road tank vehicle should be tested and inspected in accordance with the requirements of the competent authority for road transport.

3.70.5   Road tank vehicles should be marked in accordance with 3.71. However, where the marking required by the competent authority for road transport is substantially in agreement with that of 3.71.1, it will be sufficient to endorse the metal plate attached to the road tank vehicle with "IMO type 8"; the reference to holding time may be omitted.

3.71   Marking

3.71.1   Every tank should be fitted with a corrosion-resistant metal plate permanently attached in a place readily accessible for inspection. At least the following particulars should be marked on the plate in characters at least 3 mm in height by stamping, engraving, embossing or any similar method.

3.71.2   If, for reasons of tank arrangements, the plate cannot be permanently attached to the shell, the shell should be marked with at least those particulars required by a recognized pressure vessel code in a manner prescribed by that code.

3.71.3   The plate should be kept free of any paint to ensure that the markings will be legible at all times.

Country of manufacture . . . .

IMO tank   Approval   Approval
type no. . . . .   country . . . .   number . . . .

Manufacturer's name or mark . . . .

Registration number . . . .

Year of manufacture . . . .

Test pressure . . . . (bar)/(MPa) gauge*

Maximum allowable working pressure . . . . (bar)/(MPa) gauge*

Water capacity at 20°C of each compartment . . . . (litres)
(The water capacity should be established to within 1% by practical test rather than by calculation.)

Original pressure test date and witness identification . . . .

Code to which the shell is designed . . . .

Minimum design temperature . . . .(°C)

Maximum total mass . . . .(kg)

Unladen (tare) mass . . . .(kg)

Shell material . . . .

Month, year and test pressure of most recent periodic test:

. . . . month . . . . year . . . . (bar)/(MPa) gauge*

Stamp of expert who carried out most recent test . . . .

The names, in full, of the gases for whose transport the tank is approved . . . .

. . . .

Either "thermally insulated" or "vacuum-insulated" . . . .

   * The unit used should be indicated.

3.71.4   The following particulars should be durably marked either on the tank itself or on a metal plate firmly secured to the portable tank.

Names of owner and operator . . . .

Name of gas being transported (and minimum mean bulk temperature) . . . .

Date of the last inspection . . . .

Total mass . . . . (kg)

Holding time . . . . (days)

3.71.5   If a tank is designed and approved for handling in open seas, the words OFFSHORE CONTAINER should be marked on the identification plate.

3.71.6   [Reserved]

3.71.7   Unless the name of the gas being transported appears on the metal plate specified in 3.71.1, a copy of the certificate specified in 3.69.1 should be made available if requested by a competent authority and be provided readily by the consignor, consignee or agent, as appropriate.

3.72   Transport provisions

3.72.1   [Reserved]

3.72.2   [Reserved]

3.72.3   During transport, tanks should be adequately protected against lateral and longitudinal impact and against overturning. If the tanks and the service equipment are so constructed as to withstand impact or overturning, they need not be protected in this way.

3.72.4   Examples of protection of shells against collision:

   .1   protection against lateral impact may consist, for example, of longitudinal bars protecting the tank on both sides at the level of the median line;

   .2   protection of portable tanks against overturning may consist, for example, of reinforcement rings or bars fixed across the frame;

   .3   protection against rear impact may consist of a bumper or frame;

   .4   external fittings should be designed or protected so as to preclude the release of contents upon impact or overturning of the tank upon the fittings.

3.72.5   Portable tanks should not normally be offered for sea transport of longer duration than the holding time. Due consideration should also be given to any delays which might be encountered.

3.72.6   Road tank vehicles should not be offered for carriage by sea in a condition that would lead to venting during the voyage under normal conditions.

DSC/Circ.13 of 14 October 2003

INCIDENT INVOLVING TRANSPORT OF ILMENITE CLAY

1   The Sub-Committee on Dangerous Goods, Solid Cargoes and Containers (DSC), at its eighth session (22 to 26 September 2003), considered an investigation report submitted by Finland on M.V. MARIA VG which developed a list of 20° at sea due to liquefaction of a cargo believed to be ilmenite sand.

Following investigation, the cargo was revealed to be Ilmenite Clay and also that the master had not followed the procedures as laid out in SOLAS chapter VI.

2   The Sub-Committee's attention was drawn to the conclusion of the investigation that:

   .1   the cargo was too wet, almost saturated (pore space filled with water) and the measured moisture contents varied between 39–46%. This clearly exceeded the assumed average moisture status of about 28%. The estimate was based on post production reviews and it did not include the moisture increase caused by rain in the open storage field;

   .2   the water content of the cargo clearly exceeded the Transportable Moisture Limit (TML) value of 22.7%, determined for this investigation. The TML value had never been determined from the part of the shipper, although one transport had been aborted due to excess moisture. The practice in the shipping did not correspond to the normal practices of the Code of Safe Practice for Solid Bulk Cargoes (BC Code) issued by IMO;

   .3   the Master of the ship did not for his part request a report of the actual moisture content of the cargo or the TML value for the cargo;

   .4   the cargo condensed during the loading and transportation – the water in the pores was pushed upward in the cargo – causing liquefying of the top part of the cargo into a mass fully saturated with water – which may have been affected further by the pore pressure caused by the water pushing upwards;

   .5   the density of the waste concentrate contributed to the condensation process; and

   .6   the liquefied pressurized slurry could shift in the hold almost like a liquid.

3   It is therefore recommended that in transporting such cargoes, particular attention should be paid to the following:

   .1   the manufacturer/shipper of a new product transported in bulk should provide additional information in the form of a certificate on the moisture content of the cargo and its TML, as required by SOLAS VI/2.2 of SOLAS;

   .2   the cargo shall fulfil the assessment of accessibility of consignments for safe shipment as outlined in section 4 of the BC Code; furthermore, cargoes which may liquefy should be tested prior to loading in accordance with section 8 of the BC Code;

   .3   a certificate of the moisture content of the transported cargo and of the acceptable TML value shall accompany the cargo;

   .4   the Master of the ship is responsible for ensuring that he receives cargo fit for maritime transportation, i.e. he shall require a certificate of the moisture content of the cargo and of the fact that the TML value has been determined and that it is correct; and

   .5   liquefying cargoes should be stored and transported under conditions that prevent more water from seeping into the cargo as a result of rain or during the transportation.

4   Member Governments are invited to bring the above information to the attention of shipowners, ship operators, companies, shipmasters, shippers and all other parties concerned, requesting that appropriate action be taken in accordance with the provisions of the relevant IMO instruments when transporting such cargoes.

DSC/Circ.23 of 23 January 2004

INCIDENT REPORTS INVOLVING LIGHTERS OR LIGHTER REFILLS

1   The Sub-Committee on Dangerous Goods, Solid Cargoes and Containers (DSC), at its eighth session (22 to 26 September 2003), considered a report submitted by Germany (DSC 8/INF.3), whereby specific checks of imported containers loaded with UN 1057, LIGHTERS or LIGHTER REFILLS carried out at the ports in Germany in the form of gas measurements had shown that in an increasing number of containers there were explosive gas concentrations caused by leaking lighters or lighter refills and, following discussion of dangers involved in handling such cargoes, decided that this information should be disseminated to Member Governments so that Administrations and other parties concerned are alerted about these dangers.

2   In pursuance of this decision, the attention of Member Governments is drawn to the following measures required in German ports when checks are performed on the containers containing lighters or lighter refills or in the case of damage to such containers, to ensure safety of personnel and to avoid other risks:

.1   no smoking in the vicinity of such containers;

.2   all sources of ignition should be avoided (i.e., engine should be stopped, any devices that are not explosion-proof, such as radio sets, flashlights or mobile phones, should not be used);

.3   the danger area should be left and sealed off; and

.4   the Police and the fire service should be called.

3   In addition, when handling containers containing disposable lighters the following recommended safety measures should be taken:

.1   the container should be vented for at least 30 minutes in the open air prior to unloading (the doors on the windward side should be opened) and all sources of ignition within a radius of 2 m should be avoided. There should be no sinks or other inlets on the ground within a radius of 5 m;

.2   the load should be checked for damage or other irregularities (e.g., unusual smell). If there is suspicion that a consignment contains defective lighters or lighter refills or they are releasing excessive gas, unloading and handling may begin only after an expert (e.g., a chemist) has decided on how to proceed;

.3   sufficient venting of the store-room (natural or mechanical venting) should be ensured;

.4   particular fire protection measures should be laid down and co-ordinated with the fire service, if necessary. In rooms designated for smoking, open fire or open light, waste disposal (e.g. packaging waste, cleaning rags) should be prohibited;

.5   staff instructions should be displayed at appropriate places; and

.6   safety information boards should be displayed at all entrances to the storage area.

4   Member Governments are invited to bring the above information to the attention of shipowners, ship operators, companies, shipmasters, shippers and all other parties concerned.

DSC/Circ.26 of 7 October 2004

INCIDENTS INVOLVING TRANSPORT OF ZINC INGOTS

1   The Sub-Committee on Dangerous Goods, Solid Cargoes and Containers (DSC), at its ninth session (27 September to 1 October 2004), considered an investigation report submitted by Italy on three different ships carrying zinc ingots. Inside the holds of the above ships arsine was accumulated in high concentrations. Four crew members felt ill after entering into cargo holds and one of the crew members died in the local hospital.

Following investigations, the cargo present on board of the above ships was revealed to be Zinc Ingots 98.5% pure or less GOB (good ordinary brand).

2   The Italian Maritime Administration has issued a safety guideline which requires a special atmosphere's test in all cargo holds on board ships loaded with zinc ingots. These tests are carried out before opening cargo hatches, by a competent chemist, in order to guarantee that the atmosphere inside the holds is safe for entry/work during opening and unloading operations, taking into account the presence of toxic or flammable gases or other hazards.

3   The Sub-Committee's attention was drawn to the conclusions of the investigation that:

     .1   the first test on board of the first ship revealed a concentration of arsine of 10 ppm. Such tests had been carried out around a week after the accident and after the holds of the ship had been left open for some time. This supposes that the concentration of arsine in the atmosphere of the closed holds at the time of entry of the crew members was much higher than the 10 ppm stated above;

     .2   afterwards official sanitary reports confirmed that the arsine (arsenic hydride: AsH_3), evidently present in the holds of the first and second ships in higher concentration in comparison to the threshold's limit, was responsible for the death of a sailor and the hospitalization of other crew members;

     .3   the tests on board the third ship revealed a concentration of arsine of 3 ppm in the holds. Precautionary tests of the port chemist avoided an incident on board this ship because the level of concentration of arsine was also, in this case, dangerous to the human health;

     .4   the above report shows two common characteristics: the presence of arsine and fresh water;

     .5   the development of arsine was possibly due to the presence of zinc ash not completely removed from the surface of ingots;

     .6   tests carried out on board other ships carrying only zinc ingots of 99.995% purity or more SHG (special high grade) had not revealed any detectable concentration of arsine inside the cargo holds.

4   It is therefore recommended that, in transporting zinc ingots 98.5% pure or less GOB (good ordinary brand), particular attention should be paid to the following:

     .1   wet cargo should not be loaded and weathertightness of hatches should be ensured;

     .2   the cargo should be kept dry and not be handled during precipitation;

     .3   suitable gas detectors for the measurements of hydrogen and arsine and, at least, two sets of self-contained breathing apparatus, additional to those required by regulation II-2/10.10 of the 1974 SOLAS Convention, as amended, should be provided;

     .4   continuous mechanical ventilation is required. Ventilation should be such that any escaping gases cannot reach living quarters on or under deck;

     .5   entry into the holds without wearing the self-contained breathing apparatus must not be permitted until ventilation of the holds has been carried out and after tests reveal no detectable concentration of arsine/flammable gases inside the holds;

     .6   tests must be carried out before opening cargo hatches, by a competent person, in order to guarantee that the atmosphere inside the holds is safe for entry/work during opening and unloading operations, taking into account the presence of toxic or flammable gases or other hazards;

     .7   possible ignition sources as well as hotwork, burning, smoking, electrical sparking should be eliminated during handling and transport.

5   Member Governments are invited to bring the above information to the attention of shipowners, ship operators, companies, shipmasters, shippers and all other parties concerned, requesting that appropriate action be taken when transporting such cargoes.

DSC/Circ.27 of 7 October 2004

EXPLOSION IN A CARGO HOLD LOADED WITH RECYCLED ALUMINIUM

1   The Sub-Committee on Dangerous Goods, Solid Cargoes and Containers (DSC), at its ninth session (27 September to 1 October 2004), considered the casualty report of the explosion in a cargo hold of a ship which occurred on 2 December 2002, resulting in injuries to crew members and the subsequent loss of the ship.

2   At the time of the accident, the ship was carrying an aluminium oxide cargo originating from the processing of recycled aluminium (brand-named "Serox" or "Oxiton") which is used for cement production. This cargo had been carried as non-dangerous goods since its introduction as "Serox" or "Oxiton".

3   The accident was reported to have been caused by the fact that the cargo came into contact with water, resulting in generation of flammable gas at a speed which resulted in the formation of an explosive air/gas mixture in a closed and poorly ventilated hold. Through the investigation of the casualty, this cargo was classified as a class 4.3 product under UN. 3170 "ALUMINIUM SMELTING BY-PRODUCTS", but it was not documented as such by the shipper.

4   Similar accidents have occurred in the past and to prevent such accidents when carrying these cargoes, all requirements for the carriage of dangerous goods should be strictly observed, in particular:

   .1   requirements of documentation for cargo as required by regulation VII/7-2 of the SOLAS Convention;

   .2   the general requirements of the BC Code; and

   .3   requirements of the entry for ALUMINIUM SMELTING BY-PRODUCTS UN 3170 in the Code of Safe Practice for Solid Bulk Cargoes (BC Code), including continuous mechanical ventilation.

5   The "Hazard" section of the BC Code schedule for UN 3170 indicates possible formation of gas such as hydrogen, ammonia and acetylene. It should be noted that in this incident and others of a similar nature the smell of ammonia, a gas, was noticed during cargo operations. The presence of ammonia would generally indicate the presence of additional gases which may be flammable. It is therefore advisable that if ammonia is found present, suitable preventive measures are taken as further outlined.

6   Member Governments are invited to bring the above information to the attention of shipowners, ship operators, companies, shipmasters, shippers and all other parties concerned, requesting that appropriate action be taken when transporting such cargoes.

DSC.1/Circ.36 of 6 October 2005

ACCIDENTS INVOLVING TRANSPORT OF DIRECT REDUCED IRON FINES

1   The Sub-Committee on Dangerous Goods, Solid Cargoes and Containers, at its tenth session (26 to 30 September 2005), considered a preliminary report of an explosion during the transport of Direct Reduced Iron Fines, where six crew members were killed and the ship was a total loss. In considering the report, the Sub-Committee was advised of another accident involving a similar cargo, which may self-heat and/or evolve hydrogen in contact with water.

2   The Sub-Committee commenced developments of a schedule for this cargo to be inserted in the BC Code without reaching a decision on the suitability of this cargo to be carried in bulk. Although most of the schedule was agreed, it was not possible to reach an agreement on the following points:

      .1   possible limitations regarding the cargo condition at the time of shipment;

      .2   ventilation or inerting of the cargo hold during the transport; and

      .3   possible effects on the cargo of any changes during the voyage.

3   Member Governments are invited to bring the above information to the attention of shippers, terminal operators, shipowners, ship operators, companies, charterers, shipmasters and all other parties concerned, requesting that extreme care and appropriate action be taken, taking into account the provisions of relevant IMO instruments when handling and transporting this type of cargo in bulk.

4   The Sub-Committee urges Member Governments and the industry to submit to the Organization relevant information regarding safe handling and transportation of this cargo at their earliest convenience.

DSC.1/Circ.55 of 18 October 2007

CARRIAGE OF DANGEROUS GOODS

**Guidance on the application of chapter 2.10 (Marine Pollutants)
of the International Maritime Dangerous Goods (IMDG) Code (amendment 33-06)**

1   The Sub-Committee on Dangerous Goods, Solid Cargoes and Containers at its twelfth session (17–21 September 2007), noting that the hazard evaluation procedure of the Globally Harmonized System for Classification and Labelling of Chemicals (GHS) is not, as yet, applicable to the criteria used for the classification of packaged dangerous goods as marine pollutants in the current version of the IMDG Code (amendment 33-06) and that the GESAMP/EHS Working Group, in its capacity as an advisory body when disagreements arise under the self-classification system has no longer a role to play, has agreed to the guidance on the application of chapter 2.10 (Marine Pollutants) of the International Maritime Dangerous Goods (IMDG) Code (amendment 33-06) as detailed in the ensuing paragraphs.

2   In reference to paragraph 2.10.2.6 of the IMDG Code (amendment 33-06), when a substance, material or article is suspected to possess properties that may meet the criteria of a marine pollutant or a severe marine pollutant according to the criteria in 2.10.4 of the IMDG Code (amendment 33-06) but is not identified in the IMDG Code, such substance, material or article may be transported as a marine pollutant or a severe marine pollutant in accordance with the provisions of the IMDG Code and, in that context, it should be noted that the responsibility for correct declaration of substance, material or article, including its declaration as marine pollutant or severe marine pollutant, rests with the shipper. In that case, relevant data to GESAMP need not be submitted.

3   In reference to paragraph 2.10.2.7 of the IMDG Code (amendment 33-06), with the approval of the competent authority, substances, materials or articles that are identified as a marine pollutant or a severe marine pollutant in the IMDG Code but which, in accordance with BLG/Circ.13 on Hazard evaluation of substances transported by ships or in accordance with data provided by the shipper, no longer meet the criteria for designation as a marine pollutant or a severe marine pollutant need not be transported in accordance with the provisions of the IMDG Code.

4   Member Governments and international organizations are invited to bring the above guidance to the attention of all concerned.

5   This circular shall be invalid upon entry into force of amendment 34-08 of the IMDG Code.

Notes

Notes

Notes

Notes